ADVANCED DIGITAL TECHNOLOGIES IN FINANCIAL AND BUSINESS MANAGEMENT

Unleashing the Power of Artificial Intelligence, Machine Learning, Blockchain, and the Internet of Things

ADVANCED DIGITAL TECHNOLOGIES IN FINANCIAL AND BUSINESS MANAGEMENT

Unleashing the Power of Artificial Intelligence, Machine Learning, Blockchain, and the Internet of Things

Jyoti Batra Arora, PhD

Nitish Pathak, PhD

Neelam Sharma, PhD

Editors

APPLE ACADEMIC PRESS

First edition published 2025

Apple Academic Press Inc.
1265 Goldenrod Circle, NE,
Palm Bay, FL 32905 USA

760 Laurentian Drive, Unit 19,
Burlington, ON L7N 0A4, Canada

CRC Press
2385 NW Executive Center Drive,
Suite 320, Boca Raton FL 33431

4 Park Square, Milton Park,
Abingdon, Oxon, OX14 4RN UK

Library and Archives Canada Cataloguing in Publication

CIP data on file with Canada Library and Archives

Library of Congress Cataloging-in-Publication Data

CIP data on file with US Library of Congress

ISBN: 978-1-77491-768-8 (hbk)
ISBN: 978-1-77491-769-5 (pbk)
ISBN: 978-1-00355-827-9 (ebk)

About the Editors

Jyoti Batra Arora, PhD

Jyoti Batra Arora, PhD, is an academician and philanthropist. She is affiliated with the Institute of Chartered Accountants of India. Keen on research and academics, she has 14 years of enriched experience in teaching. She has a patent published to her credit. She has authored books with many renowned publishers and is also assisting many international journals as an editorial board member. Her areas of interest are mobile communication, cybersecurity, networking, the Internet of Things, software engineering, computer technology trends, etc. She received a Best Researcher Award in 2019 and has also been nominated as session chair and advisory committee member for several international and national conferences. As a resource person, she has delivered many sessions on her research area in faculty development programs, management development programs, and training programs. She was awarded her PhD in Computer Science from Banasthali Vidyapeeth University, India.

Nitish Pathak, PhD

Nitish Pathak, PhD, is working as an Associate Professor in the Department of CSE at Bhagwan Parshuram Institute of Technology, Guru Gobind Singh Indraprastha University (GGSIPU), Delhi, India. He earned his Ph.D. (CSE) from Uttarakhand Technical University, Dehradun. He completed his M.Tech (CSE) in 2010. He has more than 19 years of experience in the fields of Engineering Education, Corporate, Research, and Administration. He has worked for almost a decade in various capacities at Bharati Vidyapeeth and GGSIPU, Delhi. He has also worked for HCL Technologies, Noida.

His research interests include Trusted Operating Systems, Empirical Software Engineering, Artificial Intelligence, and Machine Learning Applications. He has more than one hundred and forty (140) international journals and conference publications, patents, books, and book chapter publications. He has authored/edited 10 books with national/international level publishers (Wiley, Apple Academic Press, IIP, Namya).

He has received various awards and certificates of appreciation for his academic, research, and administration activities. He is the recipient of the prestigious Directorate Award (2008 and 2009) for best teaching performance. He received the best research paper publication award (2018, 2019, and 2020) from Bharati Vidyapeeth, GGSIPU, Delhi. He received the INDIACom Outstanding Contribution Award (2018, 2019) and the CSI Outstanding Contribution Award (2015) from Bharati Vidyapeeth, GGSIPU, Delhi.

He is a Guest Editor, Lead Guest Editor, and Associate Editor for various SCI and other reputed journals like CMC-Computers, Materials & Continua, USA, Wireless Communications and Mobile Computing, United Kingdom, International Journal of Computer Trends and Technology (IJCTT), Malaysia, and many more SCI journals from Elsevier, Springer, Wiley, and MDPI, etc.

He has been associated with various conferences as a Technical Program Committee Member, Session Chair, Reviewer, Conference Advisory Committee Member, etc.

He has been proactively involved with professional associations and is a Life Member of the Computer Society of India (CSI), Indian Society for Technical Education (ISTE), and the International Association of Engineers (IAENG).

Neelam Sharma, PhD

Neelam Sharma, PhD, is an Assistant Professor (Senior Scale) at Maharaja Agrasen Institute of Technology (MAIT), New Delhi, affiliated with Guru Gobind Singh Indraprastha University (GGSIPU), Government of NCT of Delhi. She completed her Ph.D. in Computer Science and Engineering from Uttarakhand Technical University, Dehradun. She received her M.Tech. in Information Technology from the University School of Information, Communication and Technology (USICT), GGSIPU, New Delhi. She completed her B.Tech. in IT from GGSIPU, New Delhi. She has more than 19 years of extensive teaching experience at the graduate level. She is the recipient of the Best Research Paper Publication Award in 2017, 2019, 2020, and the Best Research Paper Publication Award in 2021 on Teacher's Day from Maharaja Agrasen Institute of Technology, GGSIPU, New Delhi. She has attended and conducted various seminars, conferences, workshops, and faculty development programs, etc. Original results have been published in more than 95 papers in international journals, proceedings of international conferences, patents, and book chapters, etc. She has been proactively involved with professional associations and is a life member of CSI and ISTE. She is a reviewer for various international journals. Her major interests include Wireless Sensor Networks, Wireless Body Area Networks, Mobile Communications, AI & IoT, Information Security, Computer Graphics and Multimedia Technology, and Database Management Systems, etc.

Contents

Contributors

A. Abirami
Assistant Professor, Department of Computer Science and Engineering, Easwari Engineering College, Chennai, Tamil Nadu, India

Jyoti Batra Arora
Faculty – IT, Institute of Chartered Accountants of India, Noida, India

Ashima Bhatnagar Bhatia
Dean Research, Vivekananda Institute of Professional Studies – TC, New Delhi, India

S. Bhuvaneswari
Assistant Professor, Department of Computer Science and Engineering, Easwari Engineering College, Chennai, Tamil Nadu, India

Brijmohan Daga
Department of Computer Engineering, Fr. Conceicao Rodrigues College of Engineering (FRCRCE), Mumbai, Maharashtra, India

R. Deepakraj
Student, Department of Computer Science and Engineering, Easwari Engineering College, Chennai, Tamil Nadu, India

Jayden Jude Dsouza
Department of Computer Engineering, Fr. Conceicao Rodrigues College of Engineering (FRCRCE), Mumbai, Maharashtra, India

Austin Bernard Fernandes
Department of Computer Engineering, Fr. Conceicao Rodrigues College of Engineering (FRCRCE), Mumbai, Maharashtra, India

Priyanka Garg
Assistant Professor, Department of Skill Faculty of Management Studies and Research, Shri Vishwakarma Skill University, Gurugram, Haryana, India

Samiksha Garg
Department of Computer Applications, Maharaja Surajmal Institute, Delhi, India

R. D. Gomathi
Department of English, Kongu Engineering College, Perundurai, Tamil Nadu, India

Abdo H. Guroob
Department of Business Information Technology, Zanzibar University, Zanzibar, Tanzania

Rachana Jaiswal
Assistant Professor, Department of Business Management, HNB Garhwal (A Central) University, Srinagar, Uttarakhand, India

Neha A. Kantikar
Department of Electronics and Communication Engineering, M.S. Ramaiah Institute of Technology (Affiliated to VTU), Bangalore, Karnataka, India

Prabhpreet Kaur
Faculty, Department of Computer Engineering and Technology, Guru Nanak Dev University, Amritsar, Punjab, India

Shama Kouser
Lecturer, Department of Computer Science Jazan University, Saudi Arabia

Arvind Kumar
Associate Professor, Faculty of Computer Applications, MRIIRS, Aravalli Hills, Faridabad, Haryana, India

Priyanka Mahajan
Research Scholar, Department of Computer Engineering and Technology, Guru Nanak Dev University, Amritsar, Punjab, India

Radhika Mahajan
Dean Research, Vivekananda Institute of Professional Studies – TC, New Delhi, India

S. Maheswaran
Department of Electronics and Communication Engineering, Kongu Engineering College, Perundurai, Tamil Nadu, India

D. H. Manjaiah
Department of Post Graduate Studies and Research in Computer Science, Mangalore, Karnataka, India

Kiran Menghani
Assistant Professor, School of Business, Woxsen University, Hyderabad, India

Masooda Modak
Department of Computer Engineering, SIES Graduate School of Technology, Nerul, Navi Mumbai, Maharashtra, India

Rahul Reddy Nadikattu
Senior IEEE Member, University of Cumbersome, USA

P. Nandish
Department of Electronics and Communication Engineering, M.S. Ramaiah Institute of Technology (Affiliated to VTU), Bangalore, Karnataka, India

S. Nandita
Department of Electronics and Communication Engineering, Kongu Engineering College, Perundurai, Tamil Nadu, India

Kalyani Pampattiwar
Department of Computer Engineering, SIES Graduate School of Technology, Nerul, Navi Mumbai, Maharashtra, India

Namrata Patel
Department of Computer Engineering, SIES Graduate School of Technology, Nerul, Navi Mumbai, Maharashtra, India

Nitish Pathak
Bhagwan Parshuram Institute of Technology (BPIT), GGSIPU, New Delhi, India

P. Rithika
Department of Electronics and Communication Engineering, Kongu Engineering College, Perundurai, Tamil Nadu, India

S. Sathesh
Department of Electronics and Communication Engineering, Kongu Engineering College, Perundurai, Tamil Nadu, India

Shallu Sehgal
Associate Professor, Department of Business Management, Shoolini Institute of Life Sciences and Business Management, Solan, Himachal Pradesh, India

I. Mohammed Shafiq
Department of Electronics and Communication Engineering, Kongu Engineering College, Perundurai, Tamil Nadu, India

Srushti Suraj Shah
Department of Computer Engineering, Fr. Conceicao Rodrigues College of Engineering (FRCRCE), Mumbai, Maharashtra, India

Dhiraj Sharma
Assistant Professor, School of Management Studies, Punjabi University, Patiala, Punjab, India

Neelam Sharma
Maharaja Agrasen Institute of Technology, GGSIPU, New Delhi, India

Seema Shokeen
Department of Business Administration, Maharaja Surajmal Institute, Delhi, India

Pooja Singh
Department of Computer Applications, Maharaja Surajmal Institute, Delhi, India

Y. Syamala
Department of IoT, Seshadri Rao Gudlavalleru Engineering College, JNTUK, Kakinada, Andhra Pradesh, India

Gayatri Pramod Varma
Department of Computer Engineering, Fr. Conceicao Rodrigues College of Engineering (FRCRCE), Mumbai, Maharashtra, India

K. Kaarthic Varun
Student, Department of Computer Science and Engineering, Easwari Engineering College, Chennai, Tamil Nadu, India

Richa Vijay
Assistant Professor, Faculty of Computer Applications, MRIIRS, Aravalli Hills, Faridabad, Haryana, India

Pawan Whig
Dean Research, Vivekananda Institute of Professional Studies – TC, New Delhi, India

Haile Anteneh Yihunie
Lecturer, Debre Tabor University, Ethiopia; PhD Scholar, School of Management Studies, Punjabi University, Patiala, Punjabi, India

Abbreviations

6G	6th generation
ACF	autocorrelation function
AGI	artificial general intelligence
AI	artificial intelligence
AIC	Akaike information criterion
AIoT	artificial intelligence of things
AIS	accounting information system
ANN	artificial neural network
AR	augmented reality
AR	auto-regressive
ARIMA	autoregressive integrated moving average
ARIMA-LSTM	ARIMA-with long short-term memory
BDA	big data analytics
BI	business intelligence
BIA	business intelligence and analytics
BIC	Bayesian information criterion
BiLSTM	bidirectional long short-term memory
BP	back propagation
BTC	Bitcoin
CAGR	compound annual growth rate
CBI	contemporary business intelligence
CC	cloud computing
CCPA	California Consumer Privacy Act
CNN	convolution neural network
CNN-BiLSTM	convolution neural network-bidirectional LSTM
Cobots	collaborative robots
CRM	customer relationship management
CRN	cognitive radio network
DAI	decentralized autonomous insurer
DARPA	Defense's Advanced Research Projects Agency
DJIA	Dow Jones Industrial Average
DLT	distributed ledger technology
DOB	date of birth
EDW	enterprise data warehouse
EHRs	electronic health records
ERP	enterprise resource planning
ETH	Ethereum

Ewma	exponential weighted moving average
EWT	empirical wavelet transform
GAN	generative adversarial network
GDP	gross domestic product
GPU	graphical processing unit
GRANN	grey relational artificial neural network
GUIs	graphical user interfaces
GW	gateway
HCI	human-computer interaction
HMI	human-machine interaction
HML	human-machine learning
HMT	human-machine teaming
HRC	human-robot collaboration
ICT	information and communication technologies
ID Card	identity card
IDE	integrated development environment
IFAC	international federation of accountants
IIoT	industrial Internet of things
IoT	Internet of things
IPA	intelligent process automation
IPFS	inter-planetary file system
IT	information technology
KPIs	key performance indicators
KYC	know-your-customer
LDA	latent Dirichlet allocation
LR	linear regression
LSA	latent semantic analysis
LSTM	long short-term memory
LTC	Litecoin
MA	moving average
MAE	mean absolute error
MAPE	mean absolute percentage error
ML	machine learning
MLP	multi-layer perceptron
NLP	natural language processing
NLTK	natural language toolkit
NRTBI	near-real-time business intelligence
NSE	National Stock Exchange
NYSE	New York Stock Exchange
OCR	optical character recognition
OHLC	open-high-low-close
OLTP	online transaction processing servers
OPA	optimal partition algorithm

ORELM	outlier robust extreme learning machine
P2P	peer-to-peer
PACF	partial autocorrelation function
PBE-DA	pseudonym-based encryption with different authorities
PCA	principal component analysis
PKG	private key generation
RBF	radial basis function
RMSE	root-mean-square error
RNN	recurrent neural network
RPA	robotic process automation
RW	random walk
SARIMA	seasonal ARIMA
SARIMAX	seasonal auto-regressive integrated moving average with exogenous factors
SBI	situational business intelligence
SBI	State Bank of India
SMP	stock market prediction
SoFi	social finance
SSBI	self-service business intelligence
SVM	support vector machine
Vas	virtual assistants
WIMP	window, icon, menus, pointer
ZKPs	zero-knowledge proofs

Preface

The success of the information technology industry is contingent on many advanced technologies and techniques. On a day-to-day basis, the industry is growing and developing new technologies. The technological implementation of these technologies in each and every sector has given a new platform to each and every business sector. A few technologies, namely artificial intelligence, machine learning, blockchain, and the Internet of Things, are implanted in the deep roots of business and financial services. This book, *Advanced Digital Technologies in Financial and Business Management: Unleashing the Power of Artificial Intelligence, Machine Learning, Blockchain, and the Internet of Things,* explains the theoretical information along with the technical implementation of these technologies in finance and business services.

This book represents a pathway of these emerging technologies for the development of various business sectors and to strengthen economic growth. The amalgamation of these techniques and trends in the financial and business sectors develops and enhances the understanding, skills, and competence for planning and performing various types of assignments in these sectors.

The main aim of this book is to connect the different sectors with IoT, AI, Blockchain, ML, and other emerging technologies to create innovative business and finance management applications.

The many academic areas covered in this book include IoT, AI, blockchain, ML, and the recent development of these emerging technologies in the financial and accounting business sectors. This book is ideally designed for computer professionals, researchers, academicians, student fraternities, etc., seeking knowledge and skills on AI, ML, blockchain, and IoT in financial and business management. This book comprises 14 chapters describing the details of aforesaid technologies in various business sectors.

Chapter 1: "Amalgamation of Artificial Intelligence (AI) and Data Science in Taxation" demonstrates the significance of combining AI and data science in taxation. This chapter also explains AI, the use of AI in tax administration, the expansion of tax collection, etc.

Chapter 2: "A Retrospection of Business Intelligence in the Era of Big Data Analytics and Artificial Intelligence for Fintech" presents and investigates the importance of employing big data analytics (BDA), data mining, and AI while establishing and refining existing business intelligence in order to handle the problem that has been identified. In addition, the opportunities and challenges related to the development of value from data via the implementation of modern business intelligence techniques in the context of Fintech are also discussed.

Chapter 3: "From Data to Insights: How AI and IoT are Reshaping Financial Services" focuses on the amalgamation of AI and IoT in the financial industry, discussing its evolution, use cases, and benefits, along with a little briefing about the contribution of AI and IoT as individual emerging technologies.

Chapter 4: "Blockchain for Insurance Claims Management" discusses how consensus methods, smart contracts, and machine learning algorithms can be used to simplify the claims process, protect claim transactions, and prevent fraud. Furthermore, this chapter also discusses the blockchain-based IoT approach in the insurance domain, along with recent advances in blockchain.

Chapter 5: "Industrial Automation: 6G with Artificial Intelligence," highlights artificial intelligence with 6G in industries. This chapter shows how these technologies are applied in autonomous vehicle networks, cybersecurity, scientific discovery, healthcare applications, industrial security, and event identification by avoiding damage to both human beings and machines.

Chapter 6: "A New Deep Learning Approach for Stock Price Prediction Using CNN-BiLSTM and ARIMA-LSTM" demonstrates the algorithms and experimental results, ground-breaking techniques for stock price forecasting, hybrid methods, time series models, and comparison of BiLSTM, CNN, and ARIMA-LSTM with prediction accuracy.

Chapter 7: "Unleashing the Power of AI in Business, Finance, Industry 4.0, and Banking 4.0," gives details about AI, cognitive technology, data analysis, AI algorithms, consumer preference prediction, and sales maximization. This chapter highlights the importance of AI in various sectors like business, finance, banking, retail, insurance, and Banking 4.0, etc.

Chapter 8, "Applications of Quantum Machine Learning in Financial Services," highlights the quantum machine learning approaches for financial services, such as fraud detection, prediction, credit scoring, and stock market forecasting.

Chapter 9: "Human Machine Collaboration in Business Processes" offers content comprehension as an application of human machine collaboration in business processes. The chapter has made a point of emphasizing how important it is to design interfaces while taking into account the cognitive and physical limitations of people. In order to achieve a higher score of human-device interaction, the prosperous utilization of human-computer interaction is discussed.

Chapter 10, "Amalgamation of AI and Blockchain in Auditing," analyzes the potential effects of blockchain technology on accounting in general and AI-enabled auditing in particular. Along with this, this chapter also encourages stakeholders like consultants to collaborate on scheming blockchain ecologies that are appropriate for secretarial and audit as those who alter cloud-based accounting.

Chapter 11: "Prominent Portrayal of AI Accompanying Transpiring Technologies in Business and Finance" elaborates on the present scenario of AI in financial and business managerial services. This chapter amalgamates the productive relationship between AI and other emanating technologies with respect to business and finance management.

Chapter 12: "The Collaboration Between Humans and Machines," highlights automation and human-machine collaboration and concludes that it can greatly improve efficiency, accuracy, and productivity in various industries and tasks.

Chapter 13: "Application of Data Science and Artificial Intelligence in Retail Sector," presents the application of data science, big data, and the use of AI in the retail sector, store management, one-click ordering, anticipatory shipping, and customer service.

Chapter 14: "AI and Data Science in Business Services: Enhancing Efficiency and Driving Innovation" provides a comprehensive overview of AI and data science in business services, predictive analytics, customer sentiment analysis, and advanced data visualization techniques and examines the various applications of these technologies and their impact on the industry.

As an editor, it is my moral duty to acknowledge and represent gratitude to the esteemed authors for their valuable contribution and to the publisher for their support. We are also thankful to the authors whose chapters are not placed in this book, probably because of their minor shortcomings, but they put in their efforts.

—Editor

Jyoti Batra Arora, PhD

CHAPTER 1

Amalgamation of Artificial Intelligence (AI) and Data Science in Taxation

DHIRAJ SHARMA,[1] HAILE ANTENEH YIHUNIE,[2,3] and NITISH PATHAK[4]

[1]*School of Management Studies, Punjabi University, Patiala, Punjab, India*

[2]*Debre Tabor University, Ethiopia*

[3]*School of Management Studies, Punjabi University, Patiala, Punjabi, India*

[4]*Bhagwan Parshuram Institute of Technology (BPIT), GGSIPU, New Delhi, India*

ABSTRACT

Now more than ever, technology is advancing, and the tax system is within everyone's reach. Experts in academia and the corporate world agree that Artificial Intelligence (AI) has vastly enhanced tax administration thanks to its myriad of real-world applications. This paper aims to demonstrate the significance of combining AI and data science in taxation. Specifically, the article explains the theoretical and empirical literature on the use of Artificial Intelligence (AI) by tax administrations, the significance of AI in tax administration, the risks of implementing AI in taxation, the prerequisites for implementing AI in taxation, the use of AI in tax administration, and the primary classification of AI in the tax system. In the end, the research found that applying AI to taxation aids the tax administration in providing better services.

Advanced Digital Technologies in Financial and Business Management: Unleashing the Power of Artificial Intelligence, Machine Learning, Blockchain, and the Internet of Things. Jyoti Batra Arora, Nitish Pathak, and Neelam Sharma (Eds.)

1.1 INTRODUCTION

Brautigam et al. (2008) said that constructing a sound tax system is comparable to constructing a solid nation. In fact, both activities are likely to advance more quickly and soundly if they are undertaken together. Technology advancement is more apparent now than ever, and the tax system cannot be out of reach. Information technology saves time and costs for taxpayers and the tax administration. That is why Barnay et al. (2018) said that tax authorities worldwide differ in the maturity of their innovation in four areas: digitized interactions, advanced analytics, process automation, and talent management.

We previously thought that Artificial Intelligence was exclusively employed in science fiction, but it is currently being applied to a broader range of real activities than we once believed. Artificial intelligence directly impacts how nations and organizations accomplish their objectives. Many academics and business professionals believe that Artificial Intelligence (AI) has significantly improved the tax administration process through various practical tax applications.

Artificial Intelligence aims to develop computer technology to the point where it can sense its environment, similar to how humans do and respond by analyzing various internal and external factors. Artificial Intelligence (AI) will allow us to process data for precise decision-making. Thus, thanks to the convergence of faster computers, better networks, and recent scientific advancements, new tools are now accessible to tax professionals.

Even though Artificial Intelligence (AI) has undeniable benefits, it may pose a risk if implemented incorrectly. Kelnar (2019) explained that AI could lead to job displacement, biased algorithms could increase unfairness, and artificial media will undermine faith; it gives states immense power and offers privacy and security trade-offs, and autonomous weapons could lead to more global conflict. Implementing AI in the tax system requires careful consideration of internal activities, such as human resources and management functions, and external activities, such as the business community and the nation's overall health.

1.2 THE USE OF INFORMATION TECHNOLOGY BY TAX ADMINISTRATIONS

Brautigam et al. (2008) said that constructing a sound tax system is comparable to constructing a solid nation. In fact, if both activities are done simultaneously, they are likely to go faster and better. Most countries' tax administration procedures include figuring out how much tax people owe and how much they pay, going after people who do not pay their taxes, and taking penalty actions. So, building tax administration in such optimal activities greatly helps a country to build its nation on significant revenue sources.

Although information technology is not a "miracle cure" for resolving all problems with a nation's tax system, recent reform projects in tax administration in different nations have traditionally centered on IT. In addition, every country's tax authority is trying to get a standardized integrated tax administration system, which is a way to run taxes so taxes can do more for national development. We all know that tax administration is a whole process that includes understanding who pays taxes, making tax systems that work well and efficiently, and making sure tax laws make sense (Cotton & Dark, 2017; Merima et al., 2015).

Many things need to be set up to do this, like receiving and processing tax payments. These processes either generate data or demand data. Therefore, it makes sense that a company processing many data could benefit significantly from computer power. Computers can store vast amounts of information and have replaced huge paper archives. Modern tax administration processes have been digitalized by workflow management software, which has replaced manual tax calculations with new computing power.

Tax administrations are also suitable for data analysis; since they can make the required investments. Because such large sums of money are involved, even a tiny efficiency improvement can benefit a tax authority. Additionally, most tax administrations have a sizable Information and Communication Technologies (ICT) department on staff, making accessing the necessary technical resources easier (Pijnenburg, 2020).

Baltzan (2012) said that all information technology should be evaluated by its information quality, including accuracy, completeness, consistency, uniqueness, and timeliness. Furthermore, Hacker (2018) also described that system quality of an information system should be evaluated by its functional suitability, performance efficiency, compatibility, usability, reliability, security, maintainability, and portability.

Generally, a traditional manual system cannot handle the growing complexity of the tax system. Instead, Information Technology (IT) is needed. As a result, tax administrations are now investing heavily in developing their IT capabilities.

1.3 ARTIFICIAL INTELLIGENCE FOR TAX ADMINISTRATION AND COLLECTION

According to Milner & Berg (n.d.), the term "analytics" encompasses everything from business analysis and displays to more advanced issues such as machine learning, data mining, and Artificial Intelligence. Real applications, on the other hand, engage with us in a subtle, smooth, and valuable way. They do this to enhance our lives, make routine activities simpler, and assist us in making difficult decisions with fewer errors.

Many research scholars and company experts believe that Artificial Intelligence entered the tax administration with numerous practical tax applications and diversely benefits the system. Even though it may seem unlikely that AI will ever take over human responsibilities completely, its applications will probably play a role in the tax function of the future by assisting tax experts in identifying errors, classifying transactions, estimating audit risk, and proposing good tax strategies within increasingly complex global legal frameworks (Bernard & Rao, 2021; Collosa, 2020; Cotton & Dark, 2017; Drew, 2018; Milner & Berg, n.d.; Petrosovitch, 2020a–e; Pijnenburg, 2020; Volkenburgh, 2020).

1.4 DEFINITION OF ARTIFICIAL INTELLIGENCE IN TAXATION

Despite the fact that different authors interchangeably use the terms Robotic Process Automation (RPA), Machine Learning (ML), and Artificial Intelligence (AI), some authors provide distinct contextual definitions for each term. Although the distinctions between them can sometimes be hazy, Volkenburgh (2020) defined each term:

1. **Robotic Process Automation (RPA):** It is a software program that executes highly analytical automated tasks. If there are specific requirements for completing the task, these kinds of tasks can be efficiently completed.
2. **Machine Learning (ML):** It is the science of teaching computers to improve their performance on a task progressively. In contrast to RPA, which is logical and condition-oriented, machine learning necessitates some level of cognitive ability on the part of the computer.
3. **Artificial Intelligence (AI):** These systems are computer programs with capabilities similar to those of humans. There is no teaching involved; instead, the objective is to construct a neural network that can take in a large amount of data and create algorithms on its own to aid it in determining how to perform a task correctly.

We used to believe that artificial intelligence was only used in science fiction, but now it is being applied to a broader range of practical activities than we previously thought. Artificial Intelligence directly affects how countries and organizations achieve their goals. John McCarthy first used "Artificial Intelligence" at the Dartmouth Conference in 1956. He defines it as "the science and engineering of making intelligent machines, especially intelligent computer programs." On the other hand, Brad Smith (2019) said that AI is a computer system that can learn from experience and recognize patterns in data. Then, these patterns can be used to offer advice and make recommendations for actions.

AI uses several technologies, such as different software, different algorithms, many input data, and different interfaces for the senses. The technology will interact, learn, decide, and recommend things to the users based on how these inputs interact.

Although it can be challenging to define AI generally, academics all agree that it is a technology that can carry out cognitive functions such as learning, interacting, creating, and replicating that were previously only attributed to humans (Milner & Berg, n.d.; Smith & Browne, 2019).

The goal of Artificial Intelligence is to develop computer technology to the point where it can sense its environment, similar to how humans do and respond by analyzing various internal and external factors.

It is the process of developing a quick and accurate human-machine system. This means that the technology will have an automated learning process from patterns that can recognize a problem, analyze a situation based on variables related to the problem, predict the outcomes, offer a workable solution based on the analysis result, and finally react to the problem for the next time when a similar situation is encountered.

The objective of Artificial Intelligence is to create computer programs that can correctly adapt to changing inputs without external guidance. As a result, it was first observed in science fiction, motion pictures, academic research facilities, and government laboratories. However, this technology is now showing up in various daily tasks and addressing a wide range of challenging issues, including identifying taxpayers, choosing audited documents, and detecting business transactions, among other things.

Accordingly, it is accurate to say that Artificial Intelligence heavily relies on computer science techniques, psychological principles, and neurobiological ideas and that the system is built to mimic brain functions (Milner & Berg, n.d.).

A country's tax administration, like other governmental institutions, will have access to many data about business transactions on various company websites. Using Artificial Intelligence will allow them to process many data for precise decision-making. Therefore, new tools are now available to tax professionals thanks to the convergence of faster computers, better networks, and recent scientific advances.

1.5 ROLE OF ARTIFICIAL INTELLIGENCE IN TAXATION

Artificial Intelligence (AI) in tax administration aims to transform data into a knowledge asset and influence tax and customs management. Because a significant amount of taxpayer data is being collected and analyzed in real-time, that will benefit various administrative areas, and the combination of IT and data analysis will greatly benefit from this (Collosa, 2020).

According to Milner & Berg (n.d.), the tax administration could create a statistical model that would predict whether certain events would occur or not. However, using AI allows the administration to process all organizational data as well as other outside factors, making it, if used properly, a much more promising strategy. In contrast to human decision-making, Artificial Intelligence is transparent, has superior speed, gives consistent results, and is easily understood.

Volkenburgh (2020) claims that Artificial Intelligence can be used in tax administration to categorize data, extract the necessary data from the record, extract crucial data from tax documents, organize tax-sensitive transactions, analyze notices from tax regulators and make tax forecasts.

Collosa (2020) also discussed the main advantages advantage of AI, including:

1. **Enhance Tax Revenue:** Artificial intelligence (AI) enables the processing of large amounts of financial data, the categorization of data much faster and with high fairness and accuracy than humans, the identification of non-compliance taxpayers, improvement controls, and the prevention of tax fraud.

2. **Categorizing of Taxpayers:** Artificial Intelligence (AI) can classify taxpayers more effectively and efficiently than other systems based on the revenue amount, the type of business, the type of tax, the source of tax, and other criteria.

3. **Artificial Intelligence (AI):** These can detect tax evasion or avoidance that taxpayers may engage in. Artificial Intelligence (AI) enables the tax administration to receive the necessary feedback and identify any irregularities in business transactions.

4. AI assists higher officers in making decisions by providing very concrete information and processing significant input at the macro-economic level.
5. AI is an efficient calculator that can save time and resources depending on the quality of the input.

1.6 RISKS IN THE USE OF ARTIFICIAL INTELLIGENCE

Understanding the drawbacks of every technological advancement are essential not only for categorizing them as good or bad but also because idealistic thinking can lock us in a grave from which we might never be able to escape. In light of this, it is imperative to consider the practicality of all information and feedback.

It is well known that Artificial Intelligence is a revolutionary idea in many organizations and contains a great deal of power to change the nature of organizational working processes. Therefore, when using it, care must be taken to ensure that it is used responsibly and that the necessary safety measures are taken to prevent any unintended adverse effects.

Collosa (2020) said that using AI responsibly involves more than just abstaining from illicit activity. It entails using Artificial Intelligence in way that respects human rights, does not oppress interests, and does not purposely widen the inequality gap. Furthermore, divergent futures are becoming more and more possible thanks to AI; the degree to which dangers manifest will rely on the decisions and actions made by individuals, groups, businesses, and governments.

Kelnar (2019) explain that AI could lead to job displacement, biased algorithms could increase unfairness, artificial media will undermine faith, give states immense power and offer privacy and security trade-offs, and autonomous weapons could lead to more global conflict.

There are risks associated with using AI that is intrinsically related to data and extrinsically related to society's adoption of AI. At least four intrinsic risk categories must be taken into account during the phases of AI design, programming, and implementation: fairness and inclusivity, system reliability and security, user data privacy and security, and transparency and accountability. In terms of extrinsic hazards, one of the concerns is the future of labor. According to the OECD, 14% of jobs worldwide will be impacted, with 32% significantly impacted (Collosa, 2020).

Although it is commonly considered that intrinsic and extrinsic side effects are unavoidable, the authors can minimize them via proper planning, control, and administration. Consequently, suitable AI frameworks are necessary for the transparent adoption of processes that permit achieving their accountability expectations, taking into account the organization's values and social laws and norms at all times.

Towards artificial intelligence (AI), the OECD (2023) identifies five essential criteria for the responsible governance of trustworthiness:

- The purpose of artificial intelligence (AI) should be to promote equitable growth, sustainable growth, and human well-being.
- Artificial intelligence (AI) algorithms should be created in a manner that recognizes the legal system, civil rights, democratic principles, and pluralism and must incorporate the necessary protections.
- Transparency and responsible disclosure must permeate AI platforms so that individuals can comprehend Artificial Intelligence (AI) based results and criticize them.
- Artificial intelligence (AI) systems must operate reliably and securely throughout their lifecycles, and possible risks must be regularly assessed and mitigated.
- Individuals and corporations responsible for the design, implementation, and operation of Artificial Intelligence (AI) systems must be made responsible for their systems' compliance with the aforementioned standards.

In line with these values-based principles, the OECD has five suggestions for policymakers: invest in AI and research and development; create a digital ecosystem for AI; create an environment where AI can thrive; build human capacity; get ready for the change in the labor market; and encourage international cooperation for trustworthy AI.

Regarding taxation, the authors share what Dr. Adolfo Iriarte Yanicelli (2020) affirms "In the age of knowledge, the central right that the taxpayer will have will be the right to know how the Artificial Intelligence (AI) reaches a conclusion, perhaps controversial." This necessitates an updating and incorporation of taxpayer rights into the digital age.

According to Blanco (2020), there are dangers related to potential AI misapplication. It requires adopting a set of guiding principles that should direct administrative action and conducting an adequate assessment from an ethical standpoint. In order to ensure its security, the author claims that AI in tax administration must adhere to the principles of caution, non-discrimination, proportionality, transparency, and data governance.

1.7 REQUIREMENTS TO IMPLEMENT AI IN TAXATION

Collosa (2020) said that for a proper AI operation, the tax administrations must have the people and technology resources with the capability to:

- Compile and present all the information the organization has saved in a standard way.
- Enact all associated intelligence processes that convert the data into information that can be used to make decisions.
- Start the succeeding procedures, and control feedback on the information that has been spread.
- Implement extensive data analysis and AI-based systems using commercial solutions and open-source tools.

Generally, the creation of Artificial Intelligence (AI) systems in tax administration requires various platforms, concepts, and interconnected algorithms, relying on the nature of the issue and the solution's area. Those organizations that opt to build solutions internally must consult and develop their teams, both in terms of the number and type of profiles, by establishing a group with expertise in the administration of open-source software and AI-related skills.

1.8 ARTIFICIAL INTELLIGENCE APPLICATIONS IN THE TAX SYSTEM

The tax collection capacity of a nation determines its ability to function efficiently. So, tax is the most complex concept that affects everyone, from large corporations to individuals. As a result, the seamless integration of this idea with Artificial Intelligence will guide a new era of excellent efficiency and effective performance in tax administration. However, implementing AI in the tax system requires careful consideration of internal activities, such as human resources and management functions, and external activities, such as the business community and the nation's overall health.

For the adoption of AI in tax administration, clarification of the following issues is needed:

1. **Proposal Preparation:** Precise definitions of the goals to be met, the data processing needed, and the results anticipated.
2. **Filling the Necessary Human Power Gap:** Artificial Intelligence (AI) requires human power to process the function, fill in the data,

and interpret the outcome. There should be enough human resources, both in terms of quantity and quality of expertise, to properly implement Artificial Intelligence (AI).

3. **Access to Data:** It is necessary to access both public data, which is available to the general public, and private data, which is kept within a single company, to gather the required amount of data and obtain accurate predictions from AI processes.
4. **Confidentiality:** Because the tax administration has access to many private documents, the implemented AI must protect such documents from unauthorized users. Therefore, the tax administration must specify the kinds of financial and non-financial data that are transmitted in AI.
5. **Rules and Regulation:** The tax administration must establish a legal framework overseeing the proper operation of AI. It is crucial to comprehend the governing rules and regulations, which describe the purpose of AI, the requirements of those impacted by the implementation, and the rights and obligations of various stockholders. Therefore, it is imperative that the government and business society have the necessary rule-based attachment.

1.9 CATEGORIES OF AI AND ITS APPLICATION IN THE TAX SYSTEM

The technical operation of AI necessitates knowledge of information technology and computer science, which is beyond the scope of this work. However, Milner & Berg (n.d.) classifies the AI function in the following ways in order to illustrate the general procedure of AI with regard to tax administration:

1. **Forecasting:** It is the most basic form of learning algorithms and forecasting. In essence, the program evaluates a trend and then may interpolate or extrapolate the trend using new data to generate a forecast. It is essential to keep in mind those strategies and methods to identify these characteristics are readily available and can result in far more accurate tax provisioning projections.
2. **Clustering:** With precise algorithms, computers can quickly and accurately identify clusters while performing tax-related

tasks on massive amounts of transactional and detailed data. Clustering is a basic essential mechanism for tax data processing. Whenever adopting a strategy for a more extensive data set, it is often advantageous for tax analysts to test by executing machine learning and evaluating the findings to choose the most effective method.

3. **Prediction (Classification):** The algorithm looks at a set of data in the beginning and categorizes groups of behaviors that result in different outcomes or results. This result will aid in determining how each result will affect the situation. The tax administration can thus use this classification to learn about the amount of revenue collected, the impact of each business transaction on revenue collection, and the risk levels for tax audit activities, which aid in the detection of tax evasion and avoidance practices.
4. **Expert Support-Systems:** AI assists tax officials by breaking down complex issues into simpler ones. Tax experts may receive guidance from AI in various ways, including justifications based on rules and logic.
5. **Optical Character Recognition (OCR):** These technologies can digitize paper-based material, such as tax filings, handwritten photographs, textbooks, agreements, and pictures. These documents are now instantly accessible for comprehensive searches and interaction with other AI applications.
6. **Natural Language Processing (NLP):** It aims to automatically detect "context" in the text, which refers to what the text says, what it means, and what the choice of particular words implies. This work is at the intersection of Artificial Intelligence (AI) and linguistics.

1.10 RESULTS AND DISCUSSION

The review of different literature shows the following specific results:

- A country's ability to work well depends on how well it can collect taxes. So, tax is the most complicated idea affecting everyone, from large businesses to people living independently. So, when this idea is combined with Artificial Intelligence smoothly, it will lead to a new era of excellent efficiency and performance in tax administration.

However, putting Artificial Intelligence (AI) in the tax system requires careful thought about both internal things, like human resources and management, and external things, like the business community and the health of the country as a whole.

- Creating artificial intelligence (AI) systems for tax administration requires different platforms, ideas, and algorithms that work together. The requirement depends on the nature of the problem and the area where the solution will be used. Organizations that want to build their solutions must consult and build their teams, both in terms of the number of profiles and types, by putting together a group with skills in managing open-source software and Artificial Intelligence (AI).
- Creating artificial intelligence (AI) systems in tax administration requires different platforms, ideas, and interconnected algorithms, depending on the problem's nature and the solution's area. Organizations that want to build their own solutions must consult and build their teams, both in terms of the number of profiles and types, by creating a group with expertise in managing open-source software and AI-related skills.

1.11 CONCLUSION

In conclusion, Artificial Intelligence (AI) is now influencing tax administration to support the expansion of tax collection. Several organizations have approved its prototype test, including research facilities, academic institutions, and governmental organizations.

Artificial Intelligence (AI) will therefore deal with more challenging issues in the future that the government encounters when trying to collect money from the commercial world. Thus, the combination of tax and Artificial Intelligence (AI) will succeed in every nation. Therefore, tax and computer science experts will develop a system that optimizes government taxes' efficient and effective collection. Therefore, if the government implements Artificial Intelligence (AI) for taxation with a creative study, it will succeed. The blending of tax and Artificial Intelligence (AI) will intensify.

KEYWORDS

- **amalgamation**
- **artificial intelligence**
- **data science**
- **machine learning**
- **robotic process automation**
- **taxation**

REFERENCES

Baltzan, P., (2012). *Business Driven Information Systems* (3rd edn.). McGraw-Hill.

Barnay, A., Davis, J., Dimson, J., Gibbs, E., & Korn, D., (2018). *Four Innovations Reshaping Tax Administration* (pp. 1–10). McKinsey & Company. https://www.mckinsey.com/industries/public-and-social-sector/our-insights/four-innovations-reshaping-tax-administration (accessed on 03 October 2023).

Bernard, R. N., & Rao, A., (2021). *What is Artificial Intelligence?* https://www.pwc.com/us/en/tech-effect/ai-analytics/artificial-intelligence.html (accessed on 03 October 2023).

Blanco, G. H., (2020). *The Use of Artificial Intelligence by Tax Administrations, a Matter of Principles?* CIAT Blog.

Brautigam, D., Fjeldstad, O., & Moore, M., (2008). *Taxation and State-Building in Developing Countries: Capacity and Consent.* Cambridge University Press.

Collosa, A., (2020). *Artificial Intelligence in Tax Administrations: Benefits and Risks of its Use.* https://www.gccfintax.com/articles/artificial-intelligence-in-tax-administrations-benefits-and-risks-of-its-use-1685.asp (accessed on 03 October 2023).

Collosa, A., (2021). Artificial intelligence in tax administrations. In M. F. Verdi (Ed.), *Tax Administration Review* (pp. 72). Inter-American Center of Tax Administrators (CIAT). https://www.ciat.org/Biblioteca/Revista/Revista_48/Ingles/2021_TAR_48.pdf

Cotton, M., & Dark, G., (2017). *Use of Technology in Tax Administrations 1: Developing an Information Technology Strategic Plan (ITSP).* IMF Working Papers.

Drew, J., (2018). Merging accounting with "big data" science. *Journal of Accountancy*. https://www.journalofaccountancy.com/issues/2018/jul/big-data-and-accounting.html (accessed on 03 October 2023).

Hacker, N., (2018). *Quality Attributes in Software Architecture*. https://www.sciencedirect.com/science/article/pii/B9780123819727000026 (accessed on 03 October 2023).

Kelnar, D., (2019). *The State of AI 2019: Divergence*. https://www.stateofai2019.com/introduction (accessed on 03 October 2023).

Merima, A., Abdulaziz, S., Abebe, S., & Bekele, F., (2015). *Information Technology and Fiscal Capacity in a Developing Country: Evidence from Ethiopia.* ICTD Working Paper 31. https://doi.org/10.2139/ssrn.2587857.

Milner, C., & Berg, B., (n.d.). *Tax Analytics: Artificial Intelligence and Machine Learning – Level 5*. https://www.pwc.no/no/publikasjoner/Digitalisering/artificial-intelligence-and-machine-learning-final1.pdf (accessed on 03 October 2023).

OECD, (2023). *OECD AI Principles Overview*. https://oecd.ai/en/ai-principles (accessed on 03 October 2023).

Petrosovitch, K., (2020a). *Digital Tax Framework is Poised to Become Tax Reality by the End of 2020*. https://www.linkedin.com/pulse/digital-tax-framework-poised-become-reality-end-2020-petrosovitch/ (accessed on 03 October 2023).

Petrosovitch, K., (2020b). *Global Tax Reporting Framework for Digital Platforms in the Sharing and Gig Economy on its Way*. https://www.linkedin.com/pulse/global-tax-reporting-framework-digital-platforms-gig-its-katrina/ (accessed on 03 October 2023).

Petrosovitch, K., (2020c). *How Can Artificial Intelligence Enhance Taxation?* https://www.linkedin.com/pulse/how-can-artificial-intelligence-enhance-taxation-katrina-petrosovitch/.

Petrosovitch, K., (2020d). *How Can Blockchain Enhance Taxation?* https://www.linkedin.com/pulse/how-can-artificial-intelligence-enhance-taxation-katrina-petrosovitch/ (accessed on 03 October 2023).

Petrosovitch, K., (2020e). *Internet of Things (IoT) and Taxation – What to Consider?* https://www.linkedin.com/pulse/internet-things-iot-taxation-what-consider-katrina-petrosovitch/ (accessed on 03 October 2023).

Pijnenburg, M., (2020). *Data Science for Tax Administration*. https://scholarlypublications.universiteitleiden.nl/access/item%3A2912751/view (accessed on 03 October 2023).

Smith, B., & Browne, C. A., (2019). *Tools and Weapons*. Penguin Press.

Volkenburgh, B. V., (2020). *Artificial Intelligence and Taxes: 10 Ways It's Being Used*. https://www.crowdreason.com/blog/artificial-intelligence-stax (accessed on 03 October 2023).

CHAPTER 2

A Retrospection of Business Intelligence in the Era of Big Data Analytics and Artificial Intelligence for Fintech

RACHANA JAISWAL

Department of Business Management, HNB Garhwal (A Central) University, Srinagar, Uttarakhand, India

ABSTRACT

At the moment, Business Intelligence (BI) systems are extensively employed in a range of corporate domains that are based on the process of decision-making in order to produce value. This is because BI systems are able to analyze large amounts of data quickly and efficiently. What we mean when we talk about BI is the process of identifying, analyzing, and projecting information that is crucial to running a firm. The traditional approach to business intelligence places an emphasis on the collection, extraction, and organization of data in order to enable efficient and professional query processing to derive insights from historical data. This approach also places an emphasis on the use of data warehouses.

BI has become a process that is more crucial and significant, and it has garnered more great attention in the domains of industry and academia as a result of the existence of big data, the Internet of Things (IoT), Artificial Intelligence (AI), and Cloud Computing (CC). Figuring out how to put these new technologies to use in order to deliver data-driven value for modern business intelligence is the key obstacle that must be overcome. This chapter will present and investigate the importance of employing Big Data Analytics (BDA), data mining, and AI while establishing and refining existing business intelligence to handle the problem that has been identified. In addition, the

Advanced Digital Technologies in Financial and Business Management: Unleashing the Power of Artificial Intelligence, Machine Learning, Blockchain, and the Internet of Things. Jyoti Batra Arora, Nitish Pathak, and Neelam Sharma (Eds.)

opportunities and challenges related to the development of value from data via the implementation of modern business intelligence techniques in the context of Fintech will be discussed.

2.1 INTRODUCTION

When first introduced in 1989, the term "business intelligence and analytics" (BIA) has since gained widespread acceptance in the academic and IT professional communities. BIA is the process by which a company gains insight into its operations and the marketplace by analyzing data collected from internal and external sources (Al-Khowarizmi et al., 2022). BI has traditionally been used to refer to methods for improving business decision-making with data-driven decision-support tools. BI encompasses not only the systems and software used to collect and analyze data, but also the underlying architectures, tools, databases, applications, and methodologies. BI aims to provide business managers and analysts with the tools they need to perform the necessary analyzes and take the appropriate actions by providing them with interactive and simple access to different types of data, allowing for their manipulation and transformation, and providing them with the results (Bany Mohammad et al., 2022; Božič & Dimovski, 2019). In the most recent phase of the fourth industrial revaluation, an enormous quantity of data has been recently produced and generated by computer machines such as GPS, sensor systems, websites or application systems, or by individuals through social media, i.e., twitter, Facebook, Instagram or LinkedIn, etc. These methods of manufacturing and generating have just emerged during the last several decades (Božič & Dimovski, 2019). On the servers that are used to store this data, large amounts of new data are continually being saved, despite the fact that these servers are already full. This massive quantity of data comes from a wide range of sources, such as websites, social media, monitoring, the IoT, sensors, and online news articles. As a consequence of improvements in information and communication technology, it is now much easier to compile vast amounts of heterogeneous data from a variety of sources into a single coherent whole. This collection of data includes both organized and unstructured data, as well as information that is both sophisticated and basic in nature. At this point in time, the analysis of data that is in an unstructured form may account for up to 80% of a company's total revenue. As a consequence of this analysis of unstructured data, which contains significant pieces of information, the firm will be able to improve the productive process of the business (Al-Khowarizmi et al., 2022; Zhou et al., 2022). This will allow the company to be more competitive. In addition to this, its significance rests in the areas of manufacturing, security, healthcare, and education. This may be accomplished by the use of analytics on vast volumes of data, in conjunction with both natural and AI, and data. Management is essential in order for the BI to be completed successfully.

BI is an umbrella term that encompasses a wide variety of technologies, tools, systems, and applications that are used for the collection, analysis, and presentation of business data. In order to make it easier for companies to put their choices into action, we will perform analysis, integration, and presentation of the business report using an interactive format. This strategy will be of inexhaustible aid in the process of acquiring, studying, and exercising control over their data in order to promote decision-making for the aim of creating corporate processes and procedures. In addition, BI refers to an organization's capability of deriving meaningful information from the data that is continually acquired as a consequence of day-to-day operations and business processes. This definition of BI When it comes to providing assistance with decision making, the BI system plays a crucial role marker in order to get the insights for the goal of improving one's productiveness or making better judgments more rapidly (Božič & Dimovski, 2019). In addition, BI has the potential to improve not only the effectiveness of operational rules but also the impact that those rules have on the decision-making process at the corporate level. It also has the potential to improve the supervision system, administration, budgeting, and recording of financial data. Because of this, the strategic alternatives that may be used in changing company situations are enhanced. BI has the potential to improve an organization's performance in a variety of other ways as well, including the identification of previously unknown opportunities and business insights, the enhancement of decision-making procedures, and the drawing of attention to potential risks. These are but a few of the many benefits that BI offers.

In this era of Big Data, it is feasible to make rapid development in a variety of experimental approaches, as well as to increase the efficacy and accomplishment of a variety of organizations by analyzing vast volumes of data pertaining to the availability of data. These goals can be achieved by conducting research on the available data. Big Data organizations have the potential to gain more depth and sharper perspicacity as a result of this, which will facilitate decision-making, expand the client's knowledge, and encourage exploration. Companies are so taken aback by the quantity of data and the types of data, in addition to their own operations, that they have made it a priority to store data and to evaluate, comprehend, and present it in a significant manner. This is because the amount of data and the types of data are growing at an exponential rate. There is more to what is meant by the phrase "Big Data" than just data that has been sorted and matched with agreements.

Business Intelligence (BI) is needed for fintech for several reasons:

1. **Data-Driven Decision Making:** In fintech, there is a vast amount of data generated every day from various sources such as customer interactions, transactions, and market data. BI helps fintech companies to collect, analyze, and interpret this data to make informed decisions about their business strategies, product development, and marketing.
2. **Real-Time Insights:** With BI, fintech companies can get real-time insights into their business operations and customer behavior. This helps them to identify opportunities and risks as they emerge and respond quickly to changing market conditions.
3. **Competitive Advantage:** In the highly competitive fintech industry, BI can provide a competitive advantage by enabling companies to analyze customer behavior, market trends, and competitor activities. This helps fintech companies to develop better products, services, and marketing strategies.
4. **Risk Management:** Fintech companies deal with sensitive financial data, and it is essential to have robust risk management policies and procedures in place. BI can help fintech companies to monitor transactions, detect fraud, and identify potential risks.
5. **Compliance Reporting:** Fintech companies are subject to a wide range of regulations and compliance requirements. BI can help fintech companies to monitor compliance activities and generate reports for regulatory agencies.
6. **Improved Operational Efficiency:** BI can help fintech companies to streamline their operations by identifying inefficiencies, automating processes, and optimizing resource allocation.

BI is essential for fintech companies to make data-driven decisions, get real-time insights, gain a competitive advantage, manage risks, and comply with regulatory requirements. BI helps fintech companies to unlock the full potential of their data and drive growth and profitability.

2.2 LEGACY BUSINESS INTELLIGENCE

In order to improve business processes and operations, BI automates the creation of models and insights from previously unstructured data compiled from a variety of sources and organized in a logical fashion. Separating the data collection and data organization processes tied to the back-end architecture from the data analysis and user-facing display processes is considered best practice in enterprise BI architectures. Information gleaned from BI's transaction processing is stored in operational data sources known as online transaction processing servers (OLTP). Data is extracted and transformed with OLTP before being placed in a data warehouse, which is a structured data repository. Data warehouses can use a variety of query optimization methods to run analytics queries and analyze data more quickly. To accomplish this speed boost, the data warehouse will create data marts as subsets of the data warehouse. In addition, conventional BI tools get at transactional data stored in data warehouses via reporting mechanisms. As a result, by analyzing these transaction records, we can detect trends and make predictions about the future of the business.

Data from sensors and mobile devices, company intranet web messages, and individual employee and customer profiles are just some of the newer additions to the BI data source landscape in recent years. Sensor data and messages shared on OSNs are just two examples of the vast majority of unstructured data sources currently available. As a result, the main challenge is maximizing query efficiency while continuing to store these cutting-edge data sources in the same relational format as in the past. When it comes to data analysis, more data means more potential for discovering novel insights (Bany Mohammad et al., 2022). However, the challenges posed by big data remain the primary concern from an analytical perspective. Since there is now a larger volume of data, more possibilities exist in the field of BI (Basile et al., 2022). If users use sensors and other real-time personal information in conjunction with historical data trends, they can get insights from situational BI that aren't readily available otherwise. Real-time insights into business operations, such as immediate feedback for a call center's operation as a result of their work, are provided by operational BI, which is BI for business operations. As an added bonus, self-service BI allows users to construct analytics rules using the metadata of the data at their disposal. These novel BI approaches need careful management to ensure they don't compromise enterprise governance and compliance models.

2.3 CONTEMPORARY BUSINESS INTELLIGENCE (CBI)

In response to the question "What happened?" BI software's primary purpose is to deliver insightful analyzes to the user. CBI platforms offer responses to the questions "What is happening, what will happen, and why?" in order to facilitate the monitoring and attainment of a continuous development of an organization within the realm of fast analytics, as well as the completion of mission objectives through the use of predictive analytics. To this day, the most useful features of legacy BI platforms are the comprehensive historical reports and straightforward ad hoc analysis tools they've provided for the past two decades. Access to BI features is made possible by a data architecture that includes a repository for all relevant information, such as an enterprise data warehouse (EDW). EDWs are the structural foundation of conventional data management platforms, as they connect vast network systems of data sources into a central data warehouse. Data from the EDW is converted to show historical business information such as weekly revenue metrics or quarterly sales, and is then consolidated, refined, and pulled into a number of reports and dashboards. However, these dashboards and interim reports rely on conventional BI to function (Bany Mohammad et al., 2022).

2.3.1 ASPECTS OF CONTEMPORARY BUSINESS INTELLIGENCE

1. **Near-Real-Time Business Intelligence (NRTBI):** It is more important than ever before in today's cutthroat economic climate. A key goal of NRTBI is to reduce the lag time between data collection and analysis. The system's responsiveness to events improves as response time decreases. Using NRTBI realization, businesses can analyze their operational data streams for trends or patterns over time.

2. **Situational Business Intelligence (SBI):** With the help of situational BI, Users can keep tabs on their immediate environment. Business intelligence (BI) positioning is essential when positions have rapidly shifted, often as a result of external business trends. However, this external data is typically unstructured because it was collected from the Internet, an external vendor, or the company's internal network. Combining this unstructured information with structured data from the company's local data warehouse is essential for supporting real-time decision marking. A company may care if its customers and users are generally positive or negative about

the most recent updates, for instance. Through the analysis of these comments, businesses are able to provide immediate feedback to the development team, enhancing the product's competitiveness and qualification. Another example is the importance of knowing the effects natural disasters have had on any suppliers' company relies on. Business owners who are aware of the risks posed by natural disasters are better able to prepare for them.

3. **Self-Service Business Intelligence (SSBI):** Users can generate their own analyzes and analytical queries with Self-Service BI (SSBI) without involving the IT department. Applications in SSBI should have easy-to-navigate user interfaces so that users can access the data without having to learn the ins and outs of the storage system. Non-traditional data sources, as well as those organized by IT, should be available to the user, and potentially expanded.

2.3.2 BIG DATA

In the last decade, the "big data" phenomenon has led to significant changes in the way databases are designed and used. In this context, "extraordinary" refers to the vastness and global scope of current data sets, the vast majority of which were amassed with the help of computers, which have largely superseded other forms of media in people's daily lives (Basile et al., 2022; Elia et al., 2022; Niu et al., 2021; Mikalef et al., 2019; Aydiner, 2019; Jacobs, 2009). In one minute, nearly 400 hours of video are added to YouTube. Big data is a term used to describe a variety of large and complex data sets that are difficult to manage using conventional application processing and data management techniques. Big data is a large quantity of data, either structured or unstructured, that has been gathered, stored, analyzed, and used for analysis or decision-making (Huang et al., 2022a, b; Goel et al., 2022). Users can get all of this information from browser history, location, their social media accounts, medical records, and past purchases. Because of the complexity of the data it contains, traditional, simple database systems will be unable to keep up with the demands of big data. In particular, big data is characterized by the following three features:

1. **Volume:** It is a characteristic used to characterize the vast quantities of data utilized by big data. Data sizes typically start at 1 GB and go up to YouTube. Big data, despite its rapid expansion, should be able to process any size data set.

2. **Variety:** The use of a wide range of data sources is what is meant by "variety" in the context of a large data analytics system. There are many different file formats in use among computers today. An example of a structured data format is the information stored in a database. Text messages, videos, CSV files, and Excel spreadsheets. Information in handwritten notes may be disorganized. When properly implemented, Big Data Analytics will make use of data from all of these places.
3. **Velocity:** To describe how quickly information is being produced, we can use a property known as velocity. It is also used to characterize the rate at which newly created data is processed. With just a few clicks, an online store can access massive amounts of data about a single customer. Speed is also important for making sure data is updated and updated in real time, which is necessary for the system to function optimally. Data that can be generated in real time is essential to helping businesses streamline their processes that can have serious economic repercussions for establishments.

It is essential to understand the various practical issues that have arisen in BI systems in the past, as more businesses show an interest in using big data technologies to support their BI (Mikalef et al., 2019). Modern BI platforms collect environmental data and use it to make accurate predictions and give advice. As real-time BI systems are created, there is an immediate increase in the need for data collection, integration, processing, and visualization. Sensors, such as those found in smartphones, computers, and health trackers, as well as Internet of Things (IoT) technologies are designed to provide contextual and semantic sound to entities that could not previously contribute Intelligent in crucial decisions, and this is what sets BI systems apart. Therefore, many companies are currently engaged in big data analysis (Li & Wong, 2022; Aydiner, 2019).

Since data sets are frequently dispersed, machine learning methods necessitate big data analytics. Distribution methods, in which data is stored on platforms with varying computing capabilities and networks, are a solution to privacy and storage space issues. It's not easy to reap the benefits of big data analytics and application diversity. As an example, every hour Walmart's servers process more than a million customer transactions, and this information is stored in databases that hold more than 2.5 petabytes of data, which is equivalent to 167 times the volume of books in the Library of Congress.

Many sectors, including academia, healthcare, the media, insurance, industry, and government, have begun utilizing big data analytics. Numerous healthcare networks have implemented big data analyzes of business intelligence and decision support systems to facilitate the use of empirical evidence in making decisions and taking action. These systems make it possible for healthcare organizations to analyze large, varied datasets at lightning speed. Consequently, it is clear from the discussion that big data analytics and data management are critical for business intelligence, and the following reasons support this claim. BDA can look at both current and past information to predict the future, which is a huge help when it comes to making decisions (Li et al., 2022; Nguyen et al., 2022). This allows companies to better prepare for the future and make informed decisions in the present. Significant savings can be made through the use of big data technologies like cloud-based analytics and Hadoop for the storage of massive amounts of data.

The rapidly expanding business intelligence and analysis sectors attracted a lot of attention from academics. The exponential growth of data has forced businesses to abandon their reliance on outdated methods of operation. To leverage this massive data set for organizational development, sophisticated analytic approaches are required (Nguyen, 2022; Trieu et al., 2022). Business intelligence and analysis is a cutting-edge approach to making sense of this data deluge in order to make more informed strategic decisions, make more accurate predictions, and seize emerging opportunities (BI&A). BI&A is obligatory in the vast majority of businesses. BI&A has been proven to be an effective method for making important decisions. As an added bonus, it is plain to see that efficient BI&A procedures have an effect on data and technology systems. Institutions and industries alike have come to rely on data collected through business intelligence and analysis tools because of their usefulness and significance (Zhang & Chen, 2020). By analyzing and visualizing internal data, BI&A helps businesses make more informed decisions. Methodologies and data analysis like these help businesses not only improve their performance and productivity, but also keep their competitive edge over their rivals.

With the help of BI&A, a unified framework can be constructed, which can help speed up the performance of the organization. Numerous factors and technological advancements have influenced both past and present BI&A trends. Since technology is progressing so rapidly, using traditional methods of analysis is no longer adequate. The future of business analytics and intelligence will be less homogenous (Qiu et al., 2022; Rana et al., 2022; Aydiner, 2019). Success possibilities associated with data analysis technologies have piqued future interest in business intelligence and analytics. In addition, the many practices and methodologies that make up BI&A have applications in fields as diverse as e-government, market intelligence, healthcare, and security. Future-oriented systems are being helped by BI&A (Rashid et al., 2022). BI&A has quickly developed into biotechnology in developing areas by enabling real-time data that will transform nations into smart cities. One of the most important steps in data mining is deciding on a suitable method of data extraction. The best methods can be determined with the help of the work's specifics, such as the object's type and level of difficulty.

AI has made great strides forward in recent years due to a number of factors, one of which is the availability of vastly more computing power than ever before. The previously trained AI model can now be completed by machine learning in a matter of hours rather than days. One more thing to think about is expanding access to data. Information may have been called "new oil" or something similar (Zhang & Chen, 2020). Data processing tools like analyzes and machine learning algorithms are required to extract actionable insights from the data. AI in BI is most effective during the processing phase (Srivastava & Dhamija, 2022; Trieu et al., 2022). Machine learning is at the core of AI systems. AI is improved by analyzing large data sets. Machine learning enhances models by using a body of acquired rules and knowledge to examine large, complex data sets. The machine learning model learns from both large amounts of data and frequent human interaction in order to provide the user with information and responses that are tailored to their specific needs. Large datasets, or "big data," can be mathematically analyzed to reveal patterns, trends, and correlations, often pertaining to human behavior and interaction. AI has made great strides thanks to deep learning. In order for a device to make a decision or carry out an instruction, programmers create a code that tells the device how to interpret a set of words, images, or commands (Tripathi & Tabassum, 2022). The user then presents the entry (data), which may be subject to further rule definition by internal engineers. To cap it all off, the system produces results (analysis) that are in line with the inputs and rules.

2.4 CASE STUDIES OF FINTECHS LEVERAGING BI

This study found below fintechs that have successfully leveraged BI to achieve their business goals:

1. **Robinhood:** It is a commission-free trading platform that has been using BI to provide personalized investment recommendations to its users. By analyzing data on user behavior, such as trading patterns

and risk tolerance, Robinhood is able to make personalized investment recommendations to its users and improve their overall investment experience.

2. **Nubank:** It is a Brazilian digital bank that has been using BI to improve its customer service operations. By analyzing data on customer interactions, Nubank is able to identify common issues and provide faster and more efficient customer service. Nubank's BI system also enables the company to identify potential fraud and security risks.
3. **Stripe:** It is a payment processing company that has been using BI to improve its fraud detection capabilities. By analyzing data on transactional behavior, Stripe is able to detect potential fraud in real-time and prevent losses. Stripe's BI system also enables the company to identify opportunities for revenue growth and expansion into new markets.
4. **TransferWise:** It is a global money transfer company that has been using BI to improve its customer experience. By analyzing data on customer feedback and usage patterns, TransferWise is able to identify areas for improvement and enhance its product offerings. TransferWise's BI system also enables the company to monitor currency exchange rates and provide customers with the best possible rates.
5. **Funding Circle:** It is a peer-to-peer lending platform that has been using BI to improve its risk management processes. By analyzing data on borrower credit scores and loan performance, Funding Circle is able to assess the creditworthiness of borrowers and set appropriate interest rates. Funding Circle's BI system also enables the company to identify potential defaults and take proactive measures to mitigate risk.
5. **PayPal:** A leading fintech company, has been using BI to enhance its fraud detection capabilities. By analyzing large volumes of transactional data, PayPal is able to identify fraudulent transactions in real-time and prevent losses. PayPal's BI system also enables the company to track customer behavior, identify spending patterns, and personalize marketing campaigns based on customer preferences.
6. **Lending Club:** It is a peer-to-peer lending platform that connects borrowers with investors. The company has been using BI to improve its risk management processes. By analyzing data on borrower credit

scores, income levels, and other factors, Lending Club is able to assess the creditworthiness of borrowers and set appropriate interest rates. The company's BI system also enables it to monitor loan performance and detect potential defaults.

7. **Square:** It is a payment processing company that enables merchants to accept credit card payments. The company has been using BI to improve its customer service operations. By analyzing data on customer interactions, Square is able to identify common issues and trends, and take proactive measures to resolve them. The company's BI system also enables it to track customer satisfaction levels and identify opportunities for improvement.

8. **Kabbage:** It is a fintech company that offers small business loans to entrepreneurs and small business owners. Kabbage uses BI to assess the creditworthiness of borrowers and provide real-time funding decisions. Kabbage uses BI to automate its underwriting process, allowing the company to process loan applications quickly and efficiently. This approach has helped Kabbage to scale its lending operations rapidly while maintaining high levels of accuracy and consistency.

9. **Social Finance (SoFi):** It is a fintech company that offers personal finance products and services, including student loan refinancing, mortgages, and investment management. SoFi uses BI to analyze customer financial data and provide personalized financial advice and recommendations to its users. By leveraging BI, SoFi can offer customized investment recommendations, retirement planning advice, and debt management strategies based on individual customer needs. It uses BI to improve its underwriting processes and assess the creditworthiness of potential borrowers. By analyzing data from a variety of sources, including social media profiles and educational backgrounds, SoFi can make more informed lending decisions and offer more competitive interest rates. It also uses BI to monitor its loan portfolios and identify potential risks and default trends. This helps SoFi to mitigate risk and minimize potential losses. Further, it also uses BI to optimize its marketing campaigns and improve customer acquisition and retention. By analyzing customer behavior and demographic data, SoFi can tailor its marketing efforts to target specific customer segments and improve conversion rates.

10. **ZestFinance:** It is a fintech company that offers machine learning-based underwriting and credit scoring solutions to lenders. ZestFinance has successfully leveraged BI to achieve its business goals in several ways, including:

    i. **Advanced Underwriting Models:** ZestFinance uses BI to analyze vast amounts of data and create advanced machine learning models for underwriting and credit scoring. This allows ZestFinance to offer more accurate credit scores and risk assessments to its customers, enabling lenders to make more informed lending decisions and reduce the risk of defaults.

    ii. **Customized Credit Scoring:** ZestFinance uses BI to create customized credit scoring models for different lenders and credit products. This allows lenders to tailor their credit products to specific customer segments and offer more competitive interest rates and loan terms.

    iii. **Risk Management:** ZestFinance uses BI to monitor its loan portfolios and identify potential risks and default trends. This helps ZestFinance to minimize risk and improve the accuracy of its underwriting models.

    iv. **Product Development:** ZestFinance uses BI to develop new underwriting and credit scoring solutions based on customer feedback and usage patterns. By analyzing customer data, ZestFinance can identify areas where it can offer new products or features that meet customer needs and preferences.

    v. **Improved Efficiency:** ZestFinance uses BI to automate its underwriting and credit scoring processes, enabling the company to process loan applications quickly and efficiently. This has helped ZestFinance to scale its lending operations rapidly while maintaining high levels of accuracy and consistency.

ZestFinance's use of BI has enabled the company to create advanced underwriting models, customize credit scoring, manage risk, develop new products, and improve efficiency. This has helped ZestFinance to become one of the leading providers of machine learning-based underwriting and credit scoring solutions in the fintech industry.

These case studies demonstrate how BI can be used to achieve a variety of business goals in fintech, from improving customer service to enhancing fraud detection and risk management capabilities. By leveraging the power of data, fintech companies can stay ahead of the competition and deliver better experiences for their customers.

2.5 ARE BIG DATA AND ANALYTICS CRUCIAL FOR FINTECHS?

Differentiating themselves from traditional banks, new fintech companies are leveraging big data to make predictions about customer behavior and create sophisticated risk assessments. Disruptive fintech and challenger banks benefit from real-time data because it allows them to quickly adjust to changes in the market. The large banks are unable to keep up with their rapid implementation of aggressive strategies. If traditional financial institutions are like powerful diesel-powered tanks, then data-driven fintechs are like maneuverable electric scooters. By analyzing massive amounts of data, fintechs can better serve their clients and create tailored services (Mikalef et al., 2019; Aydiner, 2019). Utilizing big data, fintechs can learn everything there is to know about their clientele, eliminating the need to "shot in the dark" or "cover their backs" with conservative risk assessments (Zhou & Shen, 2022; Tripathi & Tabassum, 2022; Varma et al., 2022; Zhang & Chen, 2020). As a result of applying big data analysis, four major benefits accrue to the field of emerging fintechs.

2.5.1 CUSTOMER-FOCUSEDNESS

In order to meet the specific requirements of their clients, fintechs can now leverage the wealth of information provided by big data to develop in-depth profiles of their users and precise methods of customer segmentation. Advanced modeling methods allow for the provision of individualized services that take into account factors such as the risk tolerance, age, gender, socioeconomic status, geographical location, and even the existence of romantic partnerships (Yu et al., 2022; Yuan et al., 2022; Watson, 2007). Market segmentation is a marketing strategy that divides a potential customer base into smaller, more manageable groups for the purpose of collecting more precise data. Researchers can learn more about the customer experience, new product development opportunities, customer retention strategies, and more through market segmentation. BI can be a valuable tool for customer segmentation, which involves dividing a customer base into groups based on common characteristics, behaviors, or preferences. Here are some ways in which BI can be applied to customer segmentation:

1. **Data Collection:** BI can be used to collect and analyze customer data from various sources, such as transaction history, demographic data, and social media. This data can then be used to identify patterns and trends in customer behavior.
2. **Behavioral Analysis:** BI can be used to analyze customer behavior, such as purchase history, website activity, and social media interactions. This enables companies to understand how customers interact with their products and services and identify opportunities to personalize offerings.
3. **Customer Profiling:** BI can be used to build customer profiles based on various factors such as demographics, interests, and behavior. This enables companies to segment customers based on their unique characteristics and tailor their marketing efforts accordingly.
4. **Segmentation Analysis:** BI can be used to analyze customer segments to identify commonalities and differences between them. This enables companies to better understand their customers' needs and preferences, and tailor their offerings accordingly.
5. **Predictive Modeling:** BI can be used to build predictive models that can identify which customer segments are most likely to purchase certain products or services. This enables companies to optimize their marketing efforts and maximize revenue.

BI can be a valuable tool for customer segmentation by enabling companies to collect and analyze customer data, understand customer behavior, build customer profiles, analyze customer segments, and build predictive models. By leveraging BI, companies can personalize their offerings, optimize their marketing efforts, and improve customer satisfaction. Therefore, this helps in achieving the below benefits:

- Gaining a competitive edge;
- Accelerating and refining product development;
- Improving the effectiveness of advertising campaigns.

2.5.2 ENHANCED SECURITY

Big data aids fintechs in the development of trustworthy fraud detection systems, which is especially important given the prevalence of fraudulent activity in the world of digital banking. As an added bonus, digital apps provide fintechs with an easy way to notify customers of security threats and keep money safe. BI can be an effective tool for fraud detection in various industries, including financial technology (fintech). Here are some ways in which BI can be used for fraud detection:

1. **Anomaly Detection:** BI can be used to identify anomalies in transaction data that may indicate fraudulent activity. By analyzing transaction data and identifying unusual patterns or outliers, BI can flag suspicious transactions for further investigation.
2. **Predictive Analytics:** BI can be used to build predictive models that can detect potential fraud before it occurs. By analyzing historical data and identifying patterns, BI can identify potential fraud and alert companies to take preventive measures.
3. **Real-Time Monitoring:** BI can be used to monitor transactions in real-time and flag potentially fraudulent activity as it occurs. By setting up alerts and triggers based on certain conditions or thresholds, BI can identify and prevent fraudulent activity in real-time.
4. **Social Network Analysis:** BI can be used to analyze social networks and identify potential fraud rings or organized crime. By analyzing the connections between individuals and organizations, BI can identify suspicious patterns that may indicate fraud.
5. **Data Visualization:** BI can be used to visualize transaction data and identify potential fraud visually. By creating visual representations of transaction data, BI can identify patterns and outliers that may be difficult to identify through other methods.

BI can be a powerful tool for fraud detection in fintech and other industries. By leveraging BI to identify anomalies, build predictive models, monitor transactions in real-time, analyze social networks, and visualize data, companies can detect and prevent fraud before it occurs.

2.5.3 IMPROVED CAPABILITY TO EVALUATE RISK

Companies that focus on big data analytics in the fintech sector can pool information from a wide variety of sources to uncover any possible avenues. Fintechs can operate with more stability, better manage their cash flow, and charge their customers competitive rates thanks to more accurate risk assessments. How banks evaluate risk is changing as a result of predictive analytics (Varma et al., 2022). Fintech firms that rely heavily on data collection and financial trends have found predictive analytics to be especially beneficial – one of the largest and most prevalent applications of predictive analytics is to improve cyber security and prevent fraud – the market in which fintech companies operate is extremely cutthroat, with intense competition. There is no doubt that technology is altering the financial landscape. The widespread use of big data, particularly in the burgeoning field of predictive analytics, is largely responsible for this astounding transformation (Trieu et al., 2022).

Predictive analytics, a relatively new branch of data science, has proven particularly useful for fintech companies that rely heavily on data collection and financial trends. In addition to data mining, computer science, and AI, Special Counsel notes that the science behind predictive analytics employs a variety of machine learning techniques. These techniques are applied to numerous fintech solutions, including blockchain, crowdfunding, and mobile payments. Therefore, the following are some of the ways in which predictive analytics is revolutionizing the fintech industry. Improving cyber security and thwarting fraud are two of the most common and widespread applications of predictive analytics. The banking sector is particularly vulnerable to cybercrime because of the proliferation of digital transactions and the increasing prevalence of automated processes (Niu et al., 2021). Data from millions of user transactions can be analyzed with predictive analytics to reveal and record regular habits. Any behavior outside of these norms will immediately notify the bank of potentially fraudulent activity, long before the user files a report or complaint (Wang, 2022). These procedures, made possible by predictive analytics, strengthen cyber security systems and strategies across the finance industry and especially in fintech solutions like bitcoin, blockchain, and mobile payments. As a result of its usefulness in vetting prospective borrowers, predictive analytics is now being adopted by insurtech firms for use in their own risk analysis algorithms. BI can be a powerful tool for risk management, which involves identifying, assessing, and managing potential risks to an organization. Here are some ways in which BI can be applied to risk management:

1. **Data Collection:** BI can be used to collect and analyze data from various sources, including financial data, operational data, and external data sources such as news and social media. This data can be used to identify potential risks and trends in real-time.

2. **Risk Assessment:** BI can be used to assess the likelihood and potential impact of identified risks and prioritize them based on their severity. This enables organizations to focus their resources on the most critical risks.
3. **Scenario Analysis:** BI can be used to conduct scenario analysis, which involves simulating potential risk scenarios to understand their potential impact on the organization. This enables organizations to identify potential mitigation strategies and plan for potential outcomes.
4. **Monitoring and Alerting:** BI can be used to monitor potential risks in real-time and send alerts when certain conditions or thresholds are met. This enables organizations to take immediate action to mitigate potential risks.
5. **Predictive Modeling:** BI can be used to build predictive models that can identify potential future risks based on historical data and trends. This enables organizations to take proactive measures to mitigate potential risks before they occur.

BI can be a powerful tool for risk management by enabling organizations to collect and analyze data, assess potential risks, conduct scenario analysis, monitor risks in real-time, and build predictive models. By leveraging BI, organizations can make informed decisions, mitigate potential risks, and improve overall business performance.

2.5.4 INVESTMENT ANALYSIS

Business Intelligence (BI) can be a valuable tool for investment analysis, which involves evaluating investment opportunities and making informed investment decisions. Here are some ways in which BI can be applied to investment analysis:

1. **Data Collection:** BI can be used to collect and analyze data from various sources, including financial statements, market data, and news articles. This data can be used to identify investment opportunities and evaluate potential risks.
2. **Financial Analysis:** BI can be used to conduct financial analysis, including ratio analysis, trend analysis, and valuation analysis. This enables investors to assess the financial health of potential investments and evaluate their potential for growth.

3. **Portfolio Analysis:** BI can be used to analyze the performance of investment portfolios, including the allocation of assets, returns, and risks. This enables investors to identify areas for improvement and optimize their portfolio.
4. **Market Analysis:** BI can be used to conduct market analysis, including market trends, industry analysis, and competitor analysis. This enables investors to identify emerging trends and evaluate the competitive landscape.
5. **Predictive Modeling:** BI can be used to build predictive models that can forecast future market trends and evaluate potential investment opportunities. This enables investors to make informed investment decisions and maximize returns.

BI can be a valuable tool for investment analysis by enabling investors to collect and analyze data, conduct financial and market analysis, analyze investment portfolios, build predictive models, and make informed investment decisions. By leveraging BI, investors can identify investment opportunities, manage risk, and optimize their investment portfolios.

2.5.5 REGULATORY COMPLIANCE ACTIVITIES

Business Intelligence (BI) can be a valuable tool for compliance reporting, which involves monitoring and reporting on regulatory compliance activities. Here are some ways in which BI can be applied to compliance reporting:

1. **Data Collection:** BI can be used to collect and analyze data from various sources, including financial data, operational data, and regulatory reports. This data can be used to identify potential compliance issues and track compliance activities.
2. **Regulatory Reporting:** BI can be used to automate regulatory reporting processes, including data collection, analysis, and report generation. This enables organizations to streamline their compliance reporting activities and reduce the risk of errors.
3. **Monitoring and Alerting:** BI can be used to monitor regulatory compliance activities in real-time and send alerts when certain conditions or thresholds are met. This enables organizations to take immediate action to mitigate potential compliance issues.

4. **Auditing:** BI can be used to conduct auditing activities, including compliance audits, risk assessments, and internal control testing. This enables organizations to assess their compliance posture and identify areas for improvement.

5. **Performance Monitoring:** BI can be used to monitor the performance of compliance activities and identify areas for improvement. This enables organizations to track their progress towards compliance goals and optimize their compliance activities.

BI can be a valuable tool for compliance reporting by enabling organizations to collect and analyze data, automate regulatory reporting, monitor compliance activities in real-time, conduct auditing activities, and monitor performance. By leveraging BI, organizations can improve their regulatory compliance posture, reduce the risk of compliance issues, and optimize their compliance activities.

2.5.6 PERFORMANCE TRACKING

Business Intelligence (BI) can be a valuable tool for tracking the performance of fintech companies, which involves measuring key performance indicators (KPIs) and identifying areas for improvement. Here are some ways in which BI can be applied to fintech performance tracking:

1. **Data Collection:** BI can be used to collect and analyze data from various sources, including financial statements, customer data, and market data. This data can be used to identify KPIs and track performance over time.

2. **Performance Measurement:** BI can be used to measure KPIs, including revenue growth, customer acquisition cost, customer retention rate, and market share. This enables fintech companies to assess their performance relative to industry benchmarks and identify areas for improvement.

3. **Dashboard Reporting:** BI can be used to create real-time dashboards that visualize KPIs and enable fintech companies to monitor performance in real-time. This enables organizations to make data-driven decisions and take corrective actions as needed.

4. **Predictive Modeling:** BI can be used to build predictive models that can forecast future performance based on historical data and market

trends. This enables fintech companies to identify potential growth opportunities and evaluate risks.

5. **Benchmarking:** BI can be used to benchmark performance against industry peers and competitors. This enables fintech companies to identify areas where they are falling behind and identify best practices from other companies in the industry.

BI can be a valuable tool for tracking the performance of fintech companies by enabling them to collect and analyze data, measure KPIs, create real-time dashboards, build predictive models, and benchmark performance. By leveraging BI, fintech companies can make data-driven decisions, identify growth opportunities, and optimize their performance.

2.5.7 SUPERIOR CUSTOMER SERVICE

Competition in the fintech industry is fierce. Consequently, those who wish to remain competitive must now place a premium on lead conversion rates and customer retention achieved through superior user experience (Zhou & Shen, 2022). The use of ML and AI in the field of predictive analytics has proven to be extremely fruitful. Chatbots are a common example of how AI and ML are being put to use today. The apparent simplicity of chatbots belies their power, which is why more and more companies are adopting them. Small Business Trends' research into the global market predicts that the chatbots industry will be worth $1.25 billion by 2025. This is due to not one but two factors. To begin with, chatbots allow companies to respond to customers around the clock, seven days a week, cutting down on downtime and the need for extra human customer service representatives. To continue, the artificial intelligence that helps chatbots gather customer information can also use it for pattern analysis. In the end, these analyzes provide more accurate and nuanced insights into customer behavior and preferences, letting fintech companies tailor their financial products and services to each individual (Yu et al., 2022; Yuan et al., 2022). Predictive analytics and fintech solutions together improve financial services in many ways, including security, efficiency, and overall competitiveness. More fascinating developments are unquestionably on the horizon, thanks to the ongoing cycle of AI and ML learning. This bodes well for consumers and businesses alike, as it will spur the development of novel approaches that facilitate quicker, less complicated financial dealings with reduced opportunities for fraud or theft in the digital realm (Yalcin et al., 2022; Niu et al., 2021; Watson, 2007).

BI can be a valuable tool for delivering superior customer service, which involves meeting or exceeding customer expectations and providing a positive customer experience. Here are some ways in which BI can be applied to customer service:

1. **Customer Feedback Analysis:** BI can be used to collect and analyze customer feedback from various sources, including surveys, social media, and customer service interactions. This enables organizations to understand customer needs and preferences and identify areas for improvement.
2. **Real-Time Analytics:** BI can be used to monitor customer interactions in real-time and identify potential issues or opportunities for upselling or cross-selling. This enables organizations to provide proactive support and personalized recommendations to customers.
3. **Customer Segmentation:** BI can be used to segment customers based on their unique characteristics, behaviors, and preferences. This enables organizations to tailor their customer service offerings to meet the specific needs of different customer segments.
4. **Predictive Modeling:** BI can be used to build predictive models that can anticipate customer needs and preferences based on historical data and trends. This enables organizations to proactively provide support and personalized recommendations to customers.
5. **Performance Monitoring:** BI can be used to monitor the performance of customer service agents and identify areas for improvement. This enables organizations to provide targeted training and coaching to improve the quality of customer service.

BI can be a valuable tool for delivering superior customer service by enabling organizations to collect and analyze customer feedback, monitor customer interactions in real-time, segment customers, build predictive models, and monitor performance. By leveraging BI, organizations can deliver personalized support, anticipate customer needs, and improve overall customer satisfaction.

2.6 PRACTICAL IMPLICATIONS

BI has become increasingly important for companies, especially those in the financial technology (fintech) sector, as they seek to stay competitive in the era of BDA and AI. Here are some practical implications of BI in the era of big data analytics and AI for fintech:

1. **Improved Decision-Making:** BI provides valuable insights into customer behavior, market trends, and other important data points that can inform business decisions. In the fintech sector, this data can help financial institutions better understand their customers and tailor their products and services to meet their needs.
2. **Enhanced Risk Management:** Fintech companies can use BI to identify and mitigate risks more effectively. By analyzing large data sets, BI can help identify patterns that indicate potential fraud or other types of financial crimes, allowing companies to take proactive measures to prevent them.
3. **Increased Efficiency:** BI can help fintech companies automate many of their processes, reducing the need for manual data entry and analysis. This can save time and resources and help companies respond more quickly to market changes.
4. **Improved Customer Service:** BI can help fintech companies gain a better understanding of their customers and their needs, allowing them to provide more personalized and relevant services. This can lead to higher customer satisfaction and loyalty.
5. **Better Marketing Strategies:** BI can help fintech companies identify the most effective marketing channels and messages for reaching their target audiences. By analyzing data on customer behavior, preferences, and demographics, companies can optimize their marketing efforts and improve their ROI.
6. **Competitive Advantage:** BI can give fintech companies a competitive advantage by helping them stay ahead of market trends and better understand their customers. This can help companies identify new opportunities and develop innovative products and services.

Overall, BI is an essential tool for fintech companies looking to succeed in the era of BDA and AI. By leveraging the power of data, fintech companies can make more informed decisions, reduce risks, improve efficiency, enhance customer service, develop better marketing strategies, and gain a competitive edge.

2.7 POLICY IMPLICATIONS

BI has become an integral part of the decision-making process in the era of big data analytics and AI. Some of the policy implications of BI in fintech are:

1. **Data Privacy and Security:** As fintech companies collect large amounts of data, policymakers need to ensure that data privacy and security regulations are in place to protect the consumers' personal information. This includes developing policies around data sharing, data retention, and data breaches.
2. **Fair Lending Practices:** Fintech companies often rely on big data analytics and AI to make lending decisions. However, the use of these technologies can lead to unintentional discrimination against certain groups of people. Policymakers need to ensure that fintech companies are using these technologies in a fair and unbiased manner.
3. **Cybersecurity:** With the rise of big data analytics and AI in fintech, the risk of cyberattacks increases. Policymakers need to develop policies to ensure that fintech companies have robust cybersecurity measures in place to protect against cyber threats.
4. **Consumer Protection:** Fintech companies have the potential to disrupt traditional financial services. As such, policymakers need to ensure that consumers are protected from any harm caused by fintech companies. This includes developing policies around transparency, disclosure, and accountability.
5. **Regulation of AI:** As AI becomes more prevalent in fintech, policymakers need to develop regulations around the use of AI. This includes developing policies around explainability, bias, and accountability.

Policymakers need to ensure that fintech companies are using BI in a responsible and ethical manner. This requires developing policies around data privacy and security, fair lending practices, cybersecurity, consumer protection, and regulation of AI. By doing so, policymakers can help foster an environment where fintech companies can thrive while also protecting consumers.

2.8 SOCIAL IMPLICATIONS

While the era of BDA and AI has brought numerous benefits to the Fintech industry, it has also raised several social implications that need to be considered. Some of the social implications of BI in the era of Big Data Analytics and AI for Fintech are:

1. **Data Privacy and Security:** The collection and analysis of vast amounts of data by Fintech companies raise concerns about data privacy and security. Consumers may be uncomfortable with the amount of data that is being collected about them and may not trust Fintech companies to safeguard their data.
2. **Algorithmic Bias:** The use of AI in Fintech raises concerns about algorithmic bias, where AI systems may discriminate against certain groups of people based on their race, gender, or other characteristics. This could result in unfair treatment of some customers and could harm their financial well-being.
3. **Job Displacement:** As AI systems become more sophisticated, they may replace some human jobs, leading to job displacement and unemployment. This could have social and economic implications, particularly for vulnerable populations.
4. **Financial Exclusion:** While AI and Big Data Analytics can provide Fintech companies with valuable insights into consumer behavior, there is a risk that some segments of the population may be excluded from these insights, leading to financial exclusion.
5. **Lack of Transparency:** The use of AI and Big Data Analytics in Fintech could make decision-making processes less transparent, making it difficult for consumers to understand why certain decisions are being made. This could lead to a lack of trust in Fintech companies and their decision-making processes.

Overall, the social implications of BI in the era of Big Data Analytics and AI for Fintech need to be considered to ensure that these technologies are used in an ethical and responsible manner. Fintech companies must work to address these social implications by developing transparent and accountable decision-making processes, ensuring data privacy and security, and mitigating the risk of algorithmic bias. By doing so, Fintech companies can build trust with their customers and enhance the overall social and economic impact of these technologies.

2.9 FUTURE RESEARCH AGENDA

As the era of BDA and AI continues to shape the landscape of the Fintech industry, there are several areas that future research could focus on to enhance BI in this field. Potential research agendas are:

1. **Ethical Considerations of Using AI in Fintech:** With the rise of AI-powered systems in Fintech, future research could investigate the ethical considerations of using these systems, such as bias and privacy concerns. This research could aim to identify potential risks and develop frameworks for addressing these ethical concerns.
2. **Integration of Human Expertise and AI:** Although AI has advanced significantly, human expertise and intuition remain critical in many aspects of the Fintech industry. Future research could investigate ways of integrating human expertise and AI to improve decision-making processes and overall system performance.
3. **Real-Time Analytics:** It is becoming increasingly important in the Fintech industry, as companies seek to gain insights into consumer behavior and preferences in real-time. Future research could explore ways of enhancing real-time analytics to enable faster decision-making and better customer experiences.
4. **Data Quality and Governance:** As the volume of data in Fintech continues to grow, ensuring data quality and governance becomes increasingly important. Future research could focus on developing frameworks and tools for managing data quality and governance in Fintech, ensuring that data is accurate, reliable, and secure.
5. **Explainable AI:** As AI systems become more sophisticated, their decision-making processes become increasingly opaque. Future research could investigate ways of developing Explainable AI systems that enable users to understand how AI systems make decisions, improving transparency and accountability in the Fintech industry.

Overall, these research agendas could help enhance BI in the era of BDA and AI for Fintech, ultimately leading to better decision-making, enhanced customer experiences, and improved overall system performance.

2.10 CONCLUSION

In order to set themselves apart from conventional banks, fintech startups are increasingly turning to big data in order to forecast customer behavior and create complex risk assessments. Disruptive fintech and challenger banks can adjust quickly to a changing market thanks to the availability of real-time data. They could at any time employ competitively damaging tactics, rendering the major banks obsolete. When compared to data-driven fintech, big banks are like lumbering diesel-powered tanks, but electric scooters can jump over obstacles and make tight turns. Fintechs' ability to process massive amounts of data allows them to make better decisions and provide more individualized service to their clients. Fintechs may use big data to learn about their customers on an individual level, rather than relying on guesswork or safe risk assessments. The financial technology sector is developing quickly. As a result, customers now have different requirements and requirements from their banking institutions. Customers may now benefit from a more customized and individualized service thanks to AI, ML, and big data. Now more than ever, the quality of the service a customer receives is what sets them apart and what they expect from a company. Therefore, customers have been drawn away from banks and toward Fintech. Analysts believe that the improved customer service provided by fintech firms and alternative financial institutions contributes to their growing popularity.

KEYWORDS

- **artificial intelligence**
- **auditing**
- **business disruptions**
- **business intelligence**
- **data collection**
- **investment analysis**

REFERENCES

Al-Khowarizmi, A., Syah, R., & Elveny, M., (2022). The model of business intelligence development by applying cooperative society based financial technology. In: *Proceedings of Sixth International Congress on Information and Communication Technology* (pp. 117–125). Springer, Singapore.

Aydiner, A. S., Tatoglu, E., Bayraktar, E., Zaim, S., & Delen, D., (2019). Business analytics and firm performance: The mediating role of business process performance. *Journal of Business Research*, *96*, 228–237.

Bany, M. A., Al-Okaily, M., Al-Majali, M., & Masa'deh, R. E., (2022). Business intelligence and analytics (BIA) usage in the banking industry sector: An application of the TOE framework. *Journal of Open Innovation: Technology, Market, and Complexity*, *8*(4), 189.

Basile, L. J., Carbonara, N., Pellegrino, R., & Panniello, U., (2022). Business intelligence in the healthcare industry: The utilization of a data-driven approach to support clinical decision making. *Technovation*, 102482.

Božič, K., & Dimovski, V., (2019). Business intelligence and analytics for value creation: The role of absorptive capacity. *International Journal of Information Management*, *46*, 93–103.

Elia, G., Stefanelli, V., & Ferilli, G. B., (2022). Investigating the role of FinTech in the banking industry: What do we know? *European Journal of Innovation Management.*

Goel, P., Kulsrestha, S., & Maurya, S. K., (2022). Fintech unfolding: Financial revolution in India. *Thailand and The World Economy*, *40*(2), 41–51.

Huang, S. C., Wu, C. F., Chiou, C. C., & Lin, M. C., (2022). Intelligent FinTech data mining by advanced deep learning approaches. *Computational Economics*, *59*(4), 1407–1422.

Huang, Z. X., Savita, K. S., & Zhong-Jie, J., (2022). The business intelligence impact on the financial performance of start-ups. *Information Processing & Management*, *59*(1), 102761.

Jacobs, A., (2009). The pathologies of big data. *Communications of the ACM*, *52*(8), 36–44.

Li, F., & Wang, L., (2022). Research on fintech based on big data technology. *International Journal of Economics and Management Systems*, *7*.

Li, J., He, Z., & Wang, S., (2022). A survey of supply chain operation and finance with FinTech: Research framework and managerial insights. *International Journal of Production Economics*, *247*, 108431.

Lin, C. Y., (2022). Exploring the spatialities of institutional entrepreneurship in Taipei's FinTech industry. *Regional Studies*, 1–13.

Mikalef, P., Pappas, I., Krogstie, J., & Pavlou, P., (2019). *Big Data and Business Analytics: A Research Agenda for Realizing Business Value*.

Nguyen, D. K., Sermpinis, G., & Stasinakis, C., (2022). Big data, artificial intelligence, and machine learning: A transformative symbiosis in favor of financial technology. *European Financial Management.*

Nguyen, V. P., (2022). Evaluating the FinTech success factors model to achieve a sustainable financial technology business: An empirical study in Vietnam. *Cogent Engineering*, *9*(1), 2109317.

Niu, Y., Ying, L., Yang, J., Bao, M., & Sivaparthipan, C. B., (2021). Organizational business intelligence and decision making using big data analytics. *Information Processing & Management*, *58*(6), 102725.

Qiu, Z., Huo, X., & Dai, Y., (2022). The development of FinTech in China. In: *Fintech and Financial Risk in China* (pp. 1–21). Springer, Singapore.

Rana, N. P., Chatterjee, S., Dwivedi, Y. K., & Akter, S., (2022). Understanding dark side of artificial intelligence (AI) integrated business analytics: Assessing firm's operational inefficiency and competitiveness. *European Journal of Information Systems*, *31*(3), 364–387.

Rashid, F. R., & Julaihi, M. Z. H., (2022). Big data, green growth, and technology disruption in Asian companies and societies: Application of fintech in Brunei Darussalam–embracing e-wallet in the retail sector. In: *Handbook of Research on Big Data, Green Growth, and Technology Disruption in Asian Companies and Societies* (pp. 38–57). IGI Global.

Srivastava, K., & Dhamija, S., (2022). FinTech: Application of artificial intelligence in Indian banking. In: *Proceedings of International Conference on Communication and Artificial Intelligence* (pp. 601–613). Springer, Singapore.

Trieu, V. H., Burton-Jones, A., Green, P., & Cockcroft, S., (2022). Applying and extending the theory of effective use in a business intelligence context. *MIS Quarterly*, *46*(1), 645–678.

Tripathi, N., & Tabassum, I., (2022). Growth of fintech unicorns in India: Recent trends. *Global Journal of Management and Business Research*.

Varma, P., Nijjer, S., Sood, K., Grima, S., & Rupeika-Apoga, R., (2022). Thematic analysis of financial technology (fintech) influence on the banking industry. *Risks*, *10*(10), 186.

Vinoth, S., (2022). Artificial intelligence and transformation to the digital age in Indian banking industry–A case study. *Artif. Intell.*, *13*(1), 689–695.

Wang, J., (2022). Performative innovation: Data governance in China's fintech industries. *Big Data & Society*, *9*(2), https://doi.org/10.1177/20539517221123312.

Watson, H. J., & Wixom, B. H., (2007). The current state of business intelligence. *Computer*, *40*(9), 96–99.

Yalcin, A. S., Kilic, H. S., & Delen, D., (2022). The use of multi-criteria decision-making methods in business analytics: A comprehensive literature review. *Technological Forecasting and Social Change*, *174*, 121193.

Yu, P., Lu, S., Sampat, M., Li, R., & Ahuja, A., (2022). How AI-enabled agile internet of things can enhance the business efficiency of China's FinTech ecosystem. In: *AI-Enabled Agile Internet of Things for Sustainable FinTech Ecosystems* (pp. 190–223). IGI Global.

Yuan, B., (2022). Fintech and financial regulation in the context of big data. In: *The 2021 International Conference on Machine Learning and Big Data Analytics for IoT Security and Privacy: SPIoT-2021* (Vol. 1, pp. 875–881). Springer International Publishing.

Zhang, C., & Chen, Y., (2020). A review of research relevant to the emerging industry trends: Industry 4.0, IoT, blockchain, and business analytics. *Journal of Industrial Integration and Management*, *5*(1), 165–180.

Zhou, Z., & Shen, Z., (2022). *An Open Big Data Policy and Fintech Lending in a Platform Ecosystem*. Available at SSRN 4052500.

CHAPTER 3

From Data to Insights: How AI and IoT Are Reshaping Financial Services?

NEHA A. KANTIKAR and P. NANDISH

Department of Electronics and Communication Engineering, M.S. Ramaiah Institute of Technology (Affiliated to VTU), Bangalore, Karnataka, India

ABSTRACT

Digital processes have played a major role in the evolution of the banking and financial sector. But the outbreak of COVID-19 not only affected the world economy but also led to a crisis. Here's where AI (artificial intelligence) and IoT (Internet of things) play a crucial role. AI helps in imitating human intelligence and IoT involves internet-based communications. While both of these technologies contribute to the development of financial services individually, the amalgamation of both can be a huge boon in reshaping the existing framework. The integration of AI and IoT leads to the creation of smart machines optimizing available processes, hence minimizing financial industry-specific hazards. In this regard, the chapter focuses on the Amalgamation of AI and IoT in the financial industry, discussing its evolution, use cases, and benefits of the same along with a little briefing about the contribution of AI and IoT as individual emerging technologies.

3.1 INTRODUCTION

AI (Artificial Intelligence) and IoT (Internet of Things) are inextricably linked. With an annual surge in enterprise installations, both of them are growing in popularity. Both of them have the power to change the banking and financial industries. The Internet of Things (IoT) is a fast-growing

Advanced Digital Technologies in Financial and Business Management: Unleashing the Power of Artificial Intelligence, Machine Learning, Blockchain, and the Internet of Things. Jyoti Batra Arora, Nitish Pathak, and Neelam Sharma (Eds.)

network of interconnected objects with integrated sensors that allows for real-time data collection and exchange (Dinesh Reddy et al., 2016). The best way to describe the Internet of Things is as the internet-grounded interconnection of computer devices found in common things. In the corporate world, the introduction of the Internet of Things (IoT) has generated a lot of commotion. As businesses look to create new methods to provide services and satisfy the demands of their customers, IoT is fueling a new wave of innovation in the banking and financial sectors. The genuine meaning of AI has always been debated because standards for what constitutes "real intelligence" are constantly evolving. A broad definition of AI as a domain is any method that enables robots to complete duties like humans (Stephan Bredt, 2019). Artificial intelligence is modernizing the processes for dealing with finances in the sector of finance. Financial due diligence is being helped by artificial intelligence to automate and improve processes that range from credit determinations to a quantitative transaction and corporate risk management (Haitham Nobanee et al., 2020). Remodeling of business processes, operation of industries is now possible due to the summation of AI and IoT. They produce intelligent services that help in making decisions wisely. Being beneficial to both industries and customers, the amalgamation of AI and IoT have opened the gateways of development in the field of finance (Satya Suneetha et al., 2021).

The chapter begins with giving insights about individual contributions of both the emerging technologies, i.e., AI and IoT in the financial domain, their use cases and benefits. It further explains about the Amalgamation of AI and IoT in finance and its evolution. The chapter also covers different use cases and benefits of the blend of AI and IoT in the field of finance and banking.

3.2 LITERATURE SURVEY

Artificial Intelligence has taken huge steps in recent years. Having been used by every industry on the globe, AI is now one of the growing technologies in the forefront. IoT finds its application in gathering, selecting, and interpreting huge volumes of data which humans find impossible to handle (El-Aziz et al., 2022) Thus, IoT can be defined as a technology which involves the connection of devices using internet protocols to communicate and perform tasks with least intervention of humans (Irmak et al., 2018).

The entire industry of finance has evolved into a digital industry. These digital trends encourage a good number of banking operations such as transferable models, custom-made services, management of risks and many more.

Researchers looked at how AI is affecting commercial banks' day-to-day operations, and their findings suggested that the use of AI has advanced the traditional banking industry. The Indian banking industry is figuring out a new way to utilize AI, which will increase their operational effectiveness and client pleasure (Jewandah, 2018). El-Aziz et al. (2022) findings show that intention of users and security behave like mediating factors and efficiency like moderating factors. These factors impact the enthusiasm of applications of IoT.

3.3 ARTIFICIAL INTELLIGENCE (AI)

Artificial intelligence is advancing as a technology, making things smarter every day, encouraging more sectors to use AI in the creation of their goods and services. Following the same, the financial industry now uses AI for a variety of tasks thus making their services simpler and user-friendly. Banks are also experimenting with and applying the technology in a variety of ways, much like other industries. "The Global AI in Financial Services Survey," a report published in 2019, which was funded by EY and Invesco, shows how AI is altering ways financial institutions gather and use data insights. This has a ripple effect on new business model innovation, competitive settings, workforces, risk dynamics, and new problems for businesses and policymakers. Artificial intelligence helps financial businesses spot dangers, stop fraud, automate tedious processes, and boost service quality with timely deployment. All of it results in greater effectiveness and more earnings.

3.3.1 AI IN FINANCE

The emergence of AI in the financial sector demonstrates how swiftly it is altering the commercial landscape, even in more traditional sectors. Here are a few of the most well-known applications of AI in banking (Anil et al., 2020):

1. **Fraud Prevention:** With the development of digital processes like online transactions and cybercommerce, AI now is contributing towards detection of frauds. To examine multiple data points pertaining to consumer behavior and transaction patterns, the machines employ cutting-edge algorithms. The location, amount, time of day, frequency, and kind of the transaction, among other details, could all be included in this data. The computers then make use of this information to find trends and abnormalities that might be

signs of fraud. The algorithm might identify something as suspicious if, for instance, a customer regularly conducts business from one place but suddenly conducts a sizable transaction from another.

2. **Personalized Banking:** In an effort to reduce traditional call centers, AI offers chatbots helping customers gain solutions within no time. The algorithms applied detect income, calculate expenses and their patterns generating effective budgets. Thus, largest to smallest banks are embracing AI in their applications which provide services like good communication, on-time bill payments, etc.
3. **Process Automation:** Artificial Intelligence services like recognition of characters have resulted in automation of processes that consume more time. Financial industries provide AI software that checks, processes, and evaluates. RPA (Robotic Process Automation) processes automate repetitive chores, eliminating extra consumption of time and manpower, enabling automation in finance.
4. **Risk Management:** Facilities like cognitive computing manage both structured and unstructured data and processing power handles huge chunks of data. AI algorithms examine and analyze risky situations and help in the early detection of problems. Thus, Artificial intelligence plays a major role in the management of risks in finance.

3.3.2 USE CASES OF AI IN FINANCIAL SERVICES

According to the Fintech 5×5 survey conducted by Tribe payments in the year 2021, 67% of financial organizations believe that artificial intelligence will have the biggest impact on the industry in the coming 10 years. Ignoring a financial technology transition means denying your company the chances for growth and development that artificial intelligence in finance may offer.

The use of data to inform judgments about the most likely outcome in the future is known as predictive analytics. Credit rating is said to be one of the best real-world examples of financial services. With the application of AI, customer credit scoring can be more apt and precise. Ford Motor Company uses machine learning to assess the credit risk of candidates with scant credit histories. Another financial company, ZestFinance is now branded as ZestAI due to the shifting nature of their business. Even in cases when a borrower has no credit history, they can use predictive analytics to uncover answers (Fernandez et al., 2019).

Algorithms that use machine learning can monitor user activity and identify trends that stand out from the norm. These algorithms can analyze enormous amounts of data across numerous channels in real-time, providing a workable answer for the expanding digital environment.

Kount is one such instance of a successful AI-driven platform. The platform's algorithms are capable of combining millions of transactions from different payment sources. It offers real-time alerts with a risk assessment when a customer is ready to complete a transaction. The institution can then decide with advice whether to approve or reject the transaction.

Investments and automated trading platforms are driven by machine learning algorithms. The advanced algorithms analyze data from various sources and offer suggestions and forecasts regarding the likelihood that an investment decision would succeed.

Bloomberg already makes use of AI to analyze the market and anticipate upcoming trade trends. For traders to make the most effective investing decisions, they can rapidly and accurately recognize certain tendencies. One of the market-leading trading technology platforms is called AlphaSense. It uses Natural language processing (NLP), which is a type of AI that analyzes words in news, studies, and transcripts to forecast financial events. A human would need weeks instead of seconds to review the same amount of data.

Chatbots are ideal for handling straightforward rule-based inquiries, freeing up finance employees to concentrate on more difficult customer issues. There are several instances of chatbots in use today in the banking sector. Allianz has a chatbot named Allie and Mia that provides 24/7 online service and responds to inquiries from the Co-op Banking Group.

One of the most popular banking programs to date is Erica. Customers can receive assistance and guidance from the Bank of America smart bot for a variety of their services.

3.3.3 CASE STUDIES OF AI IN FINANCIAL SECTORS

1. **Enova:** To encourage responsible financing, Enova created the Colossus platform, which uses AI and machine learning to provide non-prime clients, businesses, and banks with improved data and technology. Colossus offers assistance to individuals and small businesses by providing practical solutions for financial challenges, such as unexpected expenses or securing bank loans, while ensuring that neither a lender nor the borrower is put in a difficult position.

2. **4Front Credit Union:** In Traverse City, 4Front Credit Union is a community banking cooperative that serves customers from all around Michigan. To strengthen its loan platform, 4Front Credit Union has adopted Scienaptic's AI-established underwriting portfolio which assists in advancing loan decisions using artificial intelligence. A portal for underwriting that increases transparency for banks and other financial organizations while reducing losses is one of the financial services offered by Scienaptic Solutions. By connecting structured and unstructured data, processing the data, understanding from each encounter, and delivering context underwriting expertise, Scienaptic's AI has prevented over $200 million in credit risk.
3. **Cross Riverbank:** Software for processing documents that blends machine learning and human verification is available from Ocrolus. Cross River, one of the 10 largest banks in New Jersey eliminated a lot of their older manual procedures by empowering their pay verification and fraud protection features in collaboration with Ocrolus. It issued more than 198,000 PPP loans through its partnership with Ocrolus, totaling more than $6.5 billion in SBA funding.
4. **Kasisto:** KAI, a conversational AI platform used to enhance client experiences in the finance sector, was developed by Kasisto. By offering consumers self-service alternatives and solutions, KAI assists banks in reducing the number of call centers. The AI-powered chatbots also assist customers with the other everyday economic matters and offer them thoughtful tips. The website of the business claims that Kasisto is used by financial companies like TD Bank, J. P. Morgan, and Standard Bank.
5. **HDFC Bank:** Eva, a chatbot powered by AI, was created by Bangalore-based Senseforth AI Research for HDFC Bank. Eva, which stands for Electronic Virtual Assistant, has answered more than 2.7 million customer inquiries, actively engaged in interactions with more than 530,000 different clients, and held 1.2 million discussions since its inception.

3.3.4 BENEFITS OF AI IN FINANCE

1. **Evaluation of Risks:** According to Towards Data Science, businesses and banks are using machine intelligence algorithms to present customized solutions in addition to identifying a person's financing choices.

The advantage is that the AI can determine loan eligibility more quickly and accurately and without bias (Arshi Naim et al., 2022).

2. **Financial Consultancy Services:** AI algorithms can evaluate a person's portfolio, the most current trends, or the majority of types of crucial financial information to give you the information you need as quickly as feasible.
3. **Personalized Financial Banking:** The need to wait on hold for a customer care agent has been reduced as well as eliminated by chat-bots and personal assistants. Customers may now view their account activity, make payments, check their balance, ask any questions of a virtual assistant, and receive personalized financial advice wherever it is most suitable.
4. **Prevention of Cyber Attacks:** AI helps customers who want to be sure that their financial and personal data will be kept as secure as possible. Up to 95% of cloud breaches may be the result of human error (Arshi Naim et al., 2022). By analyzing and spotting common data trends and patterns as well as warning them of irregularities or strange activity, AI may be able to assist businesses in enhancing their security.
5. **Efficient Prediction and Evaluation of Loan Risks:** Artificial intelligence analyzes a customer's past purchasing patterns and current spending habits to predict their future borrowing patterns for loans. This is definitely important in areas where cell phone access is available but there is none to traditional credit.

3.4 INTERNET OF THINGS (IOT)

Due to recent advancements in communication technology and sensor manufacturing technology, the Internet of Things (IoT) has sparked a revolution in the modern technological period that is intensifying quickly. The Internet of Things is the linking of physical objects like consumer electronics, cars, and other items that have software, sensors, and actuators. Connecting the physical and digital worlds is the primary goal of IoT. As a result, the physical environment is typically made up of a network of sensors, and the perceived information is converted into processable information that must then be converted into orders for actuators to carry out. The number of areas designed to enable IoT has greatly increased as a result of its growing importance. The Internet of Things (IoT) is being globally and quickly adopted, amplifying the connections of the modern world. With the creation of ARPANET, the first connected network and the ancestor of the modern Internet, the development of the Internet of Things as we know it today got underway only a few decades ago (Jianxin Wang et al., 2021).

The abundance of opportunities that the future looks to hold only serves to further demonstrate how far IoT development and IoT technology advancement have progressed. Today's technology not only overcomes barriers that we once believed to be impenetrable, but also advances us closer to a society in which everyone will have equal access to the internet and the technical wonders that flow from it. IoT will keep developing in a variety of ways that will surprise and astonish us, ultimately generating genuinely boundless potential for everyone.

3.4.1 USE CASES OF IOT IN FINANCE

A straightforward IoT use case in the financial sector is the elimination of debit cards through the use of a smartphone or smartwatch. Another possibility is for retail banks to implement sensors in stores similar to how merchants are developing to do so with the aim of providing customers with discounts, recommendations, and product details via their cell phones. According to recent research, customers are roughly 20 times more likely to make a purchase when they receive personalized messaging. Banks could expand cross-selling opportunities and improve services by directly integrating retail banking systems with clients' personal systems (Butler, 2020).

For lending, collecting debt from individual and business borrowers requires a lot of work and overhead expenses. Using IoT sensors and networks, FSIs may monitor the operations and supply chain activities of debtor enterprises to assess their preparedness to pay without incurring the high overhead costs associated with check failures. Similar to this, an Internet of Things (IoT) network of ATMs, card readers, and several other point-of-sale devices can be utilized to evaluate a borrower's expenses and income aiming to determine their ability and willingness to repay, and furthermore spending by defaulters can be restrained until repayment (Vijay Kumar et al., 2019).

IoT devices monitor the condition of insured products and alert insurers to any abnormalities which would help them to act quickly and implement the appropriate safety measures to reduce risks. Insurance businesses foresee events and implement a preventive approach using IoT-generated data. For example, an insurer could be able to spot an asset failure and notify a policyholder before it results in damage. This method assists in reducing insurance claims while guarding against insurance fraud. The software used by CPAs and the clients' payment systems can communicate with one another via the Internet of Things, automating basic bookkeeping operations like data input, reconciliation, invoicing, and other similar processes. IoT has made it possible to gain insights into how commercial enterprises operate and assists accountants in keeping track of current financial data. IoT also significantly contributes to increased transparency and automation in auditing, assisting CPAs in tracking daily transactions and overseeing audit trials on-site to identify data anomalies and prevent fraud (Lande et al., 2018).

Banks benefit from the ability to evaluate user data collected through connected networks and devices and offer specialized solutions. Customers' locations may be tracked by the bank, which may then recommend particular services that are available nearby. The bank may monitor consumer spending patterns and overall expenditure trends, and depending on overspending and underspending, it can provide tailored suggestions to its clients (Saxena et al., 2017).

3.4.2 CASE STUDIES OF IOT IN FINANCIAL SECTORS

1. **State Bank of India (SBI):** The biggest bank in India, has used IoT to cut down on energy usage and to boost branch operations. To track energy use and environmental factors like temperature, humidity, and light, the bank has put in sensors and monitoring systems. This has assisted the bank in reducing its carbon impact and optimizing its energy usage.
2. **HDFC Bank:** One of the biggest private sector banks in India, HDFC Bank, has adopted IoT in its ATMs to enhance their functionality and lower downtime. The bank has placed sensors to keep track of the condition of its ATMs, foresee future problems, and proactively plan maintenance. This has assisted the bank in reducing ATM downtime and enhancing client satisfaction.
3. **ICICI Bank:** To provide real-time visibility and control over cash flow and inventory management, ICICI Bank, another significant private sector bank in India, has integrated IoT into its corporate banking services. To monitor the movement of goods and money throughout its supply chain, the bank has implemented sensors and RFID tags. As a result, the bank's fraud risk has decreased, inventory levels have been optimized, and cash management has been strengthened.

4. **Bank of America:** One of the biggest banks in the US, Bank of America, has incorporated IoT into its branch network to enhance customer service and lower operating expenses. In order to tailor customer encounters, offer on-the-spot support, and monitor consumer flows at its branches, the bank has installed beacons and sensors. This has helped the bank to improve customer satisfaction and reduce staffing costs.
5. **BBVA:** The Spanish multinational bank BBVA has integrated IoT into its mobile banking app to give each of its clients individualized financial guidance. To gain insight into consumer behavior and financial patterns, the bank has combined sensors and data from wearable devices. As a result, the bank is better able to engage its customers and provide them with financial products and services that are customized for them.

3.4.3 BENEFITS OF IOT IN FINANCE

The Financial Institutions and Banks can bring in a lot of improvement in their operations by making use of IoT in a systematic manner. The Benefits of the IoT in Financial Institutions and banking are mentioned below:

1. **Risk Management:** Through the collection of real-time information on customer assets, IoT can assist financial institutions in enhancing risk management.

   By implementing round-the-clock security monitoring, CCTV cameras, intelligent alarm systems, and other security-related technology, banks, and financial institutions can increase the security of their branches. The relevancy of IoT stands upright due to its capability to enable remote management and connectivity of smart gadgets. Hence, the locking up of the branch can occur smoothly by the security team, if necessary, else required actions might be taken to detect incursions (Jagadeesha et al., 2023).
2. **Analysis of Raw Data:** IoT technology may compile data from a variety of sources via digital sensors, mobile apps, and other means. Mobile apps are used for almost all banking transactions, allowing the banking and financial sector to study customer behavior and make decisions (Dong et al., 2017).
3. **Planning of Products:** Banks may present much better and more focused service offers with the help of data obtained from numerous

sources, including internet browsing history, mobile apps, and online purchasing behavior. With the use of IoT, the launch date, key demographics, products, and services can be properly selected, and success rates are increased (Agnihotri et al., 2017).

4. **Data Security and Prevention of Fraud:** To enhance security and stop potential fraud, financial institutions make significant investments in IoT. Each client account is secured by a risk mitigation strategy that is developed using the information gathered from different scenarios. Biometrics can then be used to secure the accounts, enabling easier payments with higher security. It enhances data protection procedures and fosters client confidence. IoT also stops fraud by immediately identifying anomalous activities. IoT devices alert customers to bogus login attempts and prevent hackers from accessing client accounts. Analytics provide information on how customers interact with the bank's website and mobile app. With the use of the data, they are able to stop fraudulent transactions before it's too late and take fast action in the event of any suspicious activity (Fadoua Khanboubi et al., 2019).

IoT has the potential to revolutionize the financial sectors by improving efficiency, enhancing security, optimizing resource management and providing better customer experience.

3.5 AMALGAMATION OF AI AND IOT IN FINANCE

The world of finance has definitely evolved through the application of artificial intelligence and the Internet of things. IoT aids in the smart acquisition of data from numerous sources. But performance of tasks such as processing of data is hard due to the large flow of data to and from the devices. Here's where AI plays its role as the brain of these devices which genuinely aids in making decisions and simulating how machines will react or act.

The integration of AI and IoT is called Artificial Intelligence of Things (AIoT). IoT and AI's amalgamation is proved to be capable of reframing the operations of businesses and industries. AI enabled IoT produces smart devices assisting making decisions. AI helps devices analyze data wisely whereas IoT communicates among them through the internet (Zhou et al., 2019).

IoT mainly consists of sensors which are implemented by machines and help in providing data through the internet. Thus, the fundamental stages followed by IoT services include Data Collection, Transmission, Processing,

Prediction, and Action. AI plays its role in the prediction phase, thus helping generate effective actions (Figure 3.1).

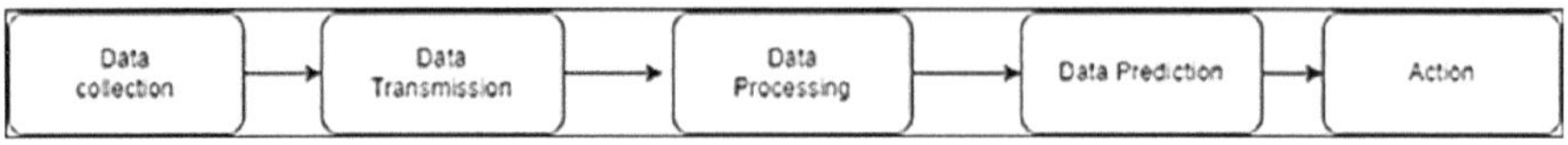

FIGURE 3.1 Steps followed by IoT devices.

1. **Collection of Data:** Sensors that are built into IoT devices are used to collect data. These sensors are a component of the actual devices, and different sensors may be connected to a single device in order to collect various sorts of data.
2. **Transmission of Collected Data:** Due to its enormous volume, the captured data is subsequently typically transferred to the cloud for storage. Because businesses do not need to invest heavily in deploying hardware for keeping massive volumes of data, the cloud helps to reduce the cost of storage.
3. **Processing of Transmitted Data:** If the data is not processed, it has no use being saved in the cloud. The steps involved in processing the data include retrieving the pertinent information from the cloud, cleaning it to remove any anomalies, transferring it to a common format, and finally using algorithms to generate insights.
4. **Prediction and Analyzation of the Processed Data:** Artificial Intelligence and Machine learning algorithms are applied on the processed data to predict and analyze thus supporting smart decision making.
5. **Action:** The final stage after producing predictions is for the machines to behave in accordance with the generated insights.

The steps described provide a clear explanation of the value of fusing IoT with AI. While the former aids in gathering data from various sources, the latter enables the devices to make useful inferences from the data gathered and take wise action. The steps are universal despite the domain. Hence, the process of amalgamation of AI and IoT in the financial sector follows the same as above.

3.6 FRAMEWORK OF AMALGAMATION OF AI AND IOT IN FINANCIAL SECTOR

AI enabled IoT technology improves the usage of smart ATM, wearables, mobile banking, block chain, security, frauds, benefitting both the customer and the financial organizations. The consumers benefit with convenience, security, services, real time planning and the organizations benefits with real time data, quality of services, customer satisfaction, etc., thus overall developing and improvising the efficiency of banking and financial services. The flow chart of the role of Amalgamation of AI and IoT in the financial sector (Mishra et al., 2022).

3.6.1 GROWTH OF AMALGAMATION OF AI AND IOT IN FINANCE

1. **Early Adoption:** Routine task automation and fraud detection were the primary goals of the first iterations of AI and IoT in finance.
2. **Data Analytics Advancements:** The emergence of big data analytics and cloud computing has made it possible to use AI for more complex financial analyzes.
3. **Increased Investment:** Due to the potential financial advantages of AI and IoT, there has been a rise in funding for R&D.
4. **Solutions that Put the Customer First:** More recent research has concentrated on using AI and IoT to give clients individualized financial advice and solutions.
5. **Regulation:** As AI and IoT are used more frequently in finance, regulations are required to assure the responsible and moral application of these technologies.

3.6.2 USE CASES AND APPLICATIONS OF INTEGRATION OF AI AND IOT IN THE DOMAIN OF FINANCE

With the growth of these technologies, Banking and financial services have already begun adopting and improvising them. The first humanoid branch assistant launched by HDFC is called "Ira." Other examples include City Union Bank's "Lakshmi," Canara Bank's "Mtra," are one of many examples of adaptation of AI and IoT in banking and financial organizations.

1. **Digital Banking:** Financial institutions have been investing heavily in AI and IoT over the past couple decades to reduce costs and improve customer service. In order to provide consumers with the

finest quality services possible, banks now provide a variety of digital banking channels, including ATM, internet banking, mobile banking, and UPI payments.

2. **Wearables:** This technology has been implemented incredibly well thanks to IoT and AI. A prime example of information everywhere is the wearable. Apple Pay, the company's first wearable device, allowed for payments to be made using a wristwatch. Soon enough, Android Pay and Samsung Pay also went down the same road.
3. **Smart ATM:** One of the most recent advancements in the thriving financial service industry is the web ATM system. Modern banking and financial institutions view the internet as a potent weapon that is effectively leveraging the delivery of services and goods to a greater number of potential customers at a comparable lower cost. Smart ATMs make it possible to leverage technologies like AI and IoT to improve customer service and lessen the likelihood of fraud. For gaining access to ATM services, one Russian bank has already begun implementing facial and biometric identification options. Diebold Nixdorf, which is arguably best known for its ATM innovations, provides software for ATM maintenance, ostensibly allowing banks to be informed when an ATM needs maintenance before it breaks down (Agarwal, 2019).
4. **Retail Analytics:** Numerous data points from cameras and sensors are used in retail analytics to track consumer activity and anticipate when they will arrive at the checkout line. Thus, the system can recommend dynamic staffing levels to cut short checkout times and hence, boost productivity of the cashier. According to Arimo, its retail solution uses data from customer eCommerce behavior to develop predictions. This data includes a record of each time a customer clicks on a product link or other website feature.
5. **Cyber-Security:** Technology development has increased the likelihood of cybercrime. AI algorithms can get all the data about clients' interests and behavior. However, institutions are investing more in AI and creating new security measures like biometric authentication, compliance monitoring, voice assistants, etc., to guard against cyber-attacks and to improve consumer interactions and experiences. IoT technologies including neural networks machine learning, linear regression and decision trees are expanding thanks

to AI, and these technologies have been included into IoT cybersecurity applications to guard against risks and prospective assaults.

6. **Fraud Detection:** By leveraging anomaly detection, Arimo believes its software, Behavioral AI for Financial Services, may assist financial institutions in identifying suspicious or anomalous consumer behavior. Arimo calls their products "Behavioral AI for IoT" (Arshi Naim et al., 2022), which implies that IoT devices can use their machine learning algorithms to collect and analyze data for the sectors they claim to serve.
7. **Vehicle Insurance:** TrueMotion provides behavior change algorithms, claiming that these algorithms can enable vehicle insurance firms to use predictive analytics to deliver more individualized products to clients based on their behavior. To spot changes in driving behavior, insurance companies might ask their customers to utilize the TrueMotion mobile app or a company app that has been connected with TrueMotion. The system makes use of sensors included in the majority of cellphones to determine when a driver is touching or using their phone, how many harsh brakes they apply each day, and how much mileage they log each day. In accordance with the frequency of the activity and time the driver spends using their phone each time, this activity is then utilized as data to estimate the level of risk the driver poses to the insurance.

3.6.3 CASE STUDIES OF AMALGAMATION OF AI AND IOT IN FINANCE SECTOR

1. **JPMorgan Bank:** To enhance the functionality of their ATMs, JPMorgan Chase is utilizing AI and IoT. They have put in place predictive maintenance solutions that gather data from the machines using IoT sensors, and then utilize AI algorithms to forecast when repair is required. As a result, downtime has decreased, and customer satisfaction has increased.
2. **Commonwealth Bank of Australia:** To give consumers tailored financial advice, Commonwealth Bank of Australia is utilizing AI and IoT. They have created a virtual assistant that analyzes client data and provides tailored recommendations using machine learning and natural language processing technologies.

3. **Citigroup:** To enhance risk management, Citigroup is utilizing AI and IoT. They have put in place a smart-contract platform that keeps track of supply chain performance using IoT sensors and blockchain technologies. The data gathered by the sensors is then analyzed by AI systems to spot potential dangers, enabling Citigroup to make better judgments.
4. **Mastercard:** To enhance fraud detection, Mastercard is utilizing AI and IoT. They have created a platform for fraud detection that employs machine learning algorithms to examine data from social media, IoT devices, and other sources in order to spot fraudulent activity.
5. **Barclays Bank:** To enhance the client experience, Barclays Bank is utilizing AI and IoT. They have created the idea of a "smart branch," which employs IoT sensors to gather information on client behavior and AI algorithms to optimize the branch's design and services.

3.6.4 EVOLUTION AND BENEFITS OF AMALGAMATION OF IOT AND IN FINANCE

Combining AI and IoT has the potential to totally transform the financial sector and how services are offered to customers. The only way to accomplish this, though, is if banks and insurers train their staff to develop goods and services that work effectively with smart devices. The banking sector has the chance to transform any Internet connection into a commerce experience since consumers are relying on smart appliances and devices to make their lives easier. In recent years, the application of AI and IoT in banking financial institutions has grown substantially, resulting in increased productivity, cost savings, and more individualized consumer experiences. Using IoT-enabled devices, some specific applications include fraud detection, algorithmic trading, and smart financial management. As more financial institutions employ AI and IoT technology, the trend is anticipated to continue. The use of amalgamation of AI IoT in finance has advanced in a number of significant ways as described below:

1. **Fraud Detection:** To identify and stop fraud, AI algorithms are analyzing data from IoT devices like smartphones, smartwatches, and other connected gadgets.
2. **Trading Using Algorithms:** Market data is gathered by IoT devices and sent to AI algorithms that can execute trades automatically in real-time.

3. **Smart Financial Management:** IoT devices with assistance of AI are being utilized for smart financial management to collect information on consumer spending patterns and offer individualized financial guidance.
4. **Risk Management:** To identify potential hazards and make better investment decisions, a lot of financial data is being analyzed using AI and IoT.
5. **Customer Experience:** Financial services such as mobile banking and voice-activated financial management are tailored and convenient for customers thanks to the application of AI and IoT.

Overall, the use of AI and IoT in banking has increased productivity, reduced costs, and improved client experiences. As financial institutions continue to use these technologies, the trend is anticipated to continue.

3.7 CONCLUSION AND FUTURE WORK

The Internet of Things and artificial intelligence are both developing quickly, and it is highly likely that soon everything that we do on any digital device will be connected to every other digital device we use. It's anticipated that the use of AI and IoT together would significantly develop and improve the financial sector. A lot of financial data may be analyzed with the use of AI, which can then offer insights to help with better decision-making. IoT can make it possible to monitor and trace financial transactions in real-time, lowering the risk of fraud. The effectiveness and precision of financial services and products, ranging from digital payments and banking to investment management, could be enhanced by this combination. Additionally, chatbots and voice assistants powered by AI can enhance the client experience by offering immediate assistance and financial guidance. Integrated Artificial Intelligence and the Internet of Things can revolutionize the field of financial services. In future, the amalgamation of AI and IoT can be seen improving its accuracy in providing security to both customers and financial companies, with the increased adoption of cryptocurrency and blockchains, as well as improvising custómer-client relationship thus providing an advanced level of transparency.

KEYWORDS

- **artificial intelligence**
- **blockchains**
- **financial guidance**
- **financial services**
- **internet of things**
- **risk management**
- **smart financial management**

REFERENCES

Agarwal, P., (2019). Redefining banking and financial industry through the application of computational intelligence. In: *2019 Advances in Science and Engineering Technology International Conferences (ASET)* (pp. 1–5). Dubai, United Arab Emirates. doi: 10.1109/ICASET.2019.8714305.

Agnihotri, S., & Ramkumar, K. R. (2017). A survey and comparative analysis of the various routing protocols of internet of things. *International Journal of Pervasive Computing and Communications*. ISSN: 1742-7371.

Anil, B. M., & Gopalakrishnan, S., (2020). Application of artificial intelligence and its powered technologies in the Indian banking and financial industry: An overview. *IOSR Journal of Humanities and Social Science (IOSR-JHSS), 25*(4), *Series. 6*, 55–60. e-ISSN: 2279-0837, p-ISSN: 2279-0845.

Arshi, N., (2022). Benefits of artificial intelligence (AI) in financial practices. *International Journal of Studies in Business Management, Economics and Strategies, 1,* 1–12.

Butler, T., (2020). What's next in the digital transformation of the financial industry? In: *IT Professional* (Vol. 22, No. 1, pp. 29–33). doi: 10.1109/MITP.2019.2963490.

Dinesh, R. V., & Gangadharan, G. R., (2016). Towards an "internet of things" framework for financial services sector. In: *2016 3rd International Conference on Recent Advances in Information Technology (RAIT), Dhanbad, India* (pp. 177–181). doi: 10.1109/RAIT.2016.7507897.

Dong, X., Chang, Y., Wang, Y., & Yan, Y. (2017). Understanding usage of internet of things (IoT) systems in China: Cognitive experience and affect experience as moderator. *Information Technology & People*. ISSN: 0959-3845.

El-Aziz, R., El-Gamal, S., & Ismail, M., (2022). Mediating and moderating factors affecting readiness to IoT applications: The banking sector context. Social science research network, Rochester, NY, SSRN, doi: 10.1109/ISCON52037.2021.9702445. In: *Conference: 2021 5th International Conference on Information Systems and Computer Networks (ISCON).*

Fadoua, K., Azedine, B., & Mohamed, T., (2019). Impact of digital trends using IoT on banking processes. *Procedia Computer Science, 151*, 77–84. ISSN 1877-0509.

Fernandez, A., (2019). *Artificial Intelligence in Financial Services.* Banco de Espana Article 3/19, Available at SSRN: https://ssrn.com/abstract=3366846 (accessed on 03 October 2023).

Haitham, N., & Al-Booshi, L., (2020). Applications of artificial intelligence in financial management decisions: A mini-review. *SSRN Electronic Journal.*

Irmak, E., & Bozdal, M., (2018). Internet of things (IoT): The most up -to- date challenges, architectures, emerging trends, and potential opportunities. *International Journal of Computer Applications (0975 – 8887), 179*(40).

Jagadeesha, R. B., Salman, A. A., & Maziar, N. Q., (2023). FinTech enablers, use cases, and role of future internet of things. *Journal of King Saud University – Computer and Information Sciences*, *35*(1), 87–101. ISSN 1319-1578.

Jewandah, D. S., (2018). How artificial intelligence is changing the banking sector: A case study of top four commercial Indian Banks. *International Journal of Management, Technology and Engineering, 8*(VII). ISSN No: 2249-7455.

Jianxin, W., Ming, K. L., Chao, W., & Ming-Lang, T., (2021). The evolution of the internet of things (IoT) over the past 20 years. *Computers & Industrial Engineering, 155*, 107174, ISSN 0360-8352.

Lande, R. S., Meshram, S. A., & Deshmukh, P. P., (2018). Smart banking using IoT. In: *2018 International Conference on Research in Intelligent and Computing in Engineering (RICE)* (pp. 1–4). San Salvador, El Salvador. doi: 10.1109/RICE.2018.8627903.

Mishra, P., & Tatavarty, G., (2022). *Role of Artificial Intelligence and Internet of Things in Promoting Banking and Financial Services During COVID-19: Pre and Post Effect.* 10.1109/ISCON52037.2021.9702445.

Satya, S. G., & Naga, S. N., (2021). Amalgamation of internet of things with artificial intelligence. *Advances and Applications in Mathematical Sciences, 20*(12), 3071–3076. Mili Publications.

Saxena, S., & Al-Tamimi, T., (2017). Big data and internet of things (IoT) technologies in Omani banks: A case study. *Foresight, 19*, 409–420. 10.1108/FS-03-2017-0010.

Stephan, B., (2019). Artificial intelligence (AI) in the financial sector—Potential and public strategies. *Front. Artif. Intell., Sec. Artificial Intelligence in Finance, 2.*

Vijay, K. S., (2019). *IoT Applications in Finance and Banking.* 10.6084/m9.doi.one, IJRAR19K3720.

Zhou, J., Wang, Y., Ota, K., & Dong, M., (2019). AAIoT: Accelerating artificial intelligence in IoT systems. In: *IEEE Wireless Communications Letters* (Vol. 8, No. 3, pp. 825–828). doi: 10.1109/LWC.2019.2894703.

CHAPTER 4

Blockchain for Insurance Claims Management

MASOODA MODAK,[1] KALYANI PAMPATTIWAR,[1] NAMRATA PATEL,[1] and NEELAM SHARMA[2]

[1]*Department of Computer Engineering, SIES Graduate School of Technology, Nerul, Navi Mumbai, Maharashtra, India*

[2]*Maharaja Agrasen Institute of Technology, GGSIPU, New Delhi, India*

ABSTRACT

Insurance is a substantial market where an amazingly high percentage of funds is lost to fraud and inefficiency. Despite the Indian insurance market's size, growth, and importance, it suffers from ancient systems and broken processes that are opportunistically exploited by all parties involved. The insurance claim process is a series of manual steps and the data required for it might be stored in silos that do not communicate with each other. Fraud is a potential issue. For the insurer, it might be a costly process because of manual administration, reconciliations, and settling disputes. For the policyholder, claiming in times of need or distress is an inconvenience. These issues drive us to propose a blockchain-based insurance claims management solution. Blockchain technology may offer a practical solution for managing the claims process while ensuring integrity, accountability, and non-repudiation. This chapter aims to focus on the current process of claims management and its drawbacks along with a blockchain solution for it. This chapter will discuss how consensus methods, smart contracts, and machine learning algorithms can be used to simplify the claims process, protect claim transactions, and prevent fraud. Furthermore, this chapter also discusses a

Advanced Digital Technologies in Financial and Business Management: Unleashing the Power of Artificial Intelligence, Machine Learning, Blockchain, and the Internet of Things. Jyoti Batra Arora, Nitish Pathak, and Neelam Sharma (Eds.)

blockchain-based IoT approach in the insurance domain along with recent advances in blockchain.

4.1 INTRODUCTION

4.1.1 BLOCKCHAIN TECHNOLOGY

In recent years Blockchain technology got more attention because of its decentralized, distributed, immutable digital ledger. As this is a decentralized mechanism for storing transactions; there is no central authority involved in it. These transactions are stored in the form of blocks and chains of these blocks from the blockchain. The size of the blockchain keeps on increasing when blocks are added to the chain. Since this technology avoids the need of third parties or intermediaries; it is used in various application domains like finance, digital assets, the Insurance sector, Supply chain, healthcare, and so on. The drawback of a single point of failure in the case of the centralized system can be removed with the use of a decentralized, Peer-to-Peer (P2P) blockchain system. In this, each user acts as a node which is responsible for performing various operations like initiating and validating transactions. All these nodes are connected with each other in a decentralized fashion as shown in Figure 4.1. Each node has a copy of the blockchain maintained with them which keeps on updating on regular basis.

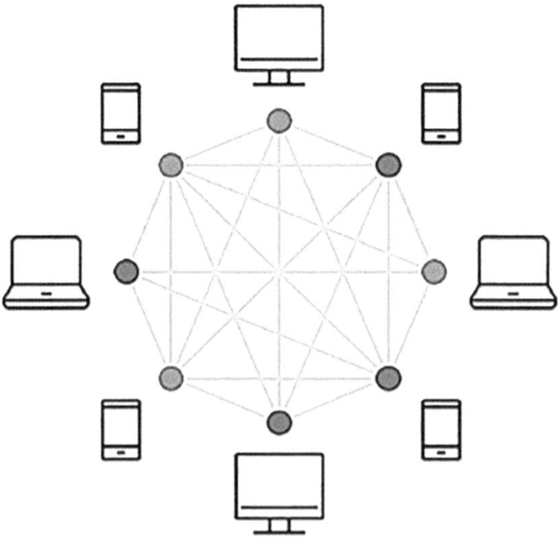

FIGURE 4.1 Blockchain architecture.

Source: Adapted from Jaradat et al., 2022

4.1.2 BLOCK STRUCTURE

The sequence of Chains of blocks forms the blockchain. In this, any block can initiate a transaction and broadcast this transaction to all nodes in a network. Network nodes perform validation of the transaction. A number of transactions occurring at one particular time are grouped together to form the block and this block is then added to the blockchain. Each block is made up of two parts namely block header and the block body. The Block header is the metadata of the block and is made up of the following components:

- **Block Version:** It tells which set of block validation rules to follow.
- **Merkle Tree Root Hash:** The hash computed from all the transactions in the block.
- **Timestamp:** Current time.
- **Nonce:** It is a 4-byte field, which usually starts with 0 and increases for every hash calculation.
- **Previous Block Hash:** 256-bit hash of the previous block is computed and inserted in a new block in the blockchain which makes the blockchain tamperproof.

4.1.3 ORGANIZATION OF THE CHAPTER

Section 1.1 introduces Blockchain technology and the insurance claim process. Section 1.2 discusses the convergence of Blockchain technology with the Internet of Things (IoT). Section 1.3 mentions the current insurance process and the drawbacks of the traditional claim process. Section 1.4 summarizes about how blockchain technology adds new features to the insurance sector. Section 1.5 discusses the Blockchain-based solution to insurance claim management. Section 1.6 summarizes the challenges faced with the adoption of Blockchain Technology and Section 1.7 mentions the advances in Blockchain with IoT.

4.1.4 INSURANCE CLAIM PROCESS

For decades, insurance fraud has had a huge detrimental influence on the insurance industry. Because of the large number of false claims paid out by motor insurance companies, rates have been raised by hundreds of dollars to compensate for the fraudulent payouts, lowering insurance companies' competitiveness and quality of service. As a result, there is a compelling need to provide quick and effective insurance claim process, reinsurance, and swapping, autonomous insurer, digital identity, fraud detection, risk measurement, and safe data management systems that strike the right balance between client personal data preservation, loss prevention savings, and false alarm detection expenditure.

Because of claims leakage, insurance companies are currently losing a significant amount of money. Insurance companies have a significant and costly problem in the form of fraudulent claims, which could cost the sector billions of dollars each year. To create the basis for false claims, insurance fraudsters frequently exaggerate or manufacture circumstances. Insurers have traditionally relied on mathematicians to assess risk and determine premium rates for policy underwriting, ensuring that payouts are reasonable without jeopardizing the company's financial health. Traditional methods of detecting insurance fraud are time-consuming and difficult. Expert scrutiny, adjusters, and special investigation services are the mainstays of their operations. Furthermore, manual detection incurs additional costs and yields inaccurate findings. Moreover, insurance companies may incur additional losses as a result of late decisions (Kirlidog et al., 2012).

4.2 CONVERGENCE OF BLOCKCHAIN AND IOT

IoT provide a future vision where computing systems, users, and things interact for practicality and financial gains by connecting online and offline objects with the help of the right communication technology. Such a concept necessitates a high level of security, data privacy, authentication, and assault resistance. Blockchain, a distributed ledger that keeps an immutable log of network transactions, can introduce these characteristics. IoT is playing an increasingly significant part in our daily lives, occupying a large amount of our home automation, medical life, and mobile healthcare, among other areas. The failure of the centralized server, accountability, and traceability, maintenance, processing massive amounts of data, lack of confidence, and transparency are all issues that centralized IoT architecture faces. All of these problems could be solved with Blockchain technology. The integration of blockchain with IoT is meeting the needs of a wide range of businesses, from the energy sector to supply chain management. Hyperledger fabric, IOTA, Bitcoin, and Ethereum are some of the blockchain technologies that can be utilized with IoT (Bhushan et al., 2021, p. 90). Besides the obvious benefits of integration of IoT and blockchain, blockchain faces numerous hurdles in its advancement and adoption in the IoT. These difficulties can be divided into three categories: In a resource-constrained setting, scalability, privacy protection, and utilization are all important considerations (Bhushan et al., 2021).

4.2.1 BLOCKCHAIN WITH IOT FOR E-HEALTHCARE

The deployment of sustainable electronic healthcare infrastructure has transformed healthcare services and made it possible for E-health technology to quickly and effectively meet the demands of all parties involved in the delivery of healthcare. The issue of protecting the security and privacy of the patients' data remains the main roadblock to the success of E-health, despite the tremendous improvement in current healthcare services. Healthcare information continues to be the most sought-after resource by cyber intruders, according to a detailed review of multiple research papers. Researchers have used a variety of strategies and techniques to protect digital healthcare services (She et al., 2021). Blockchain is one of the approaches.

By offering decentralized computation and storage for IoT data, blockchain can address such critical issues. As a result, combining IoT and blockchain technology may be a viable option for designing decentralized IoT-based e-healthcare systems. The IoT refers to the spread of Internet connectivity to physical devices and ordinary objects. These gadgets, which are equipped with electronics, Internet connectivity, and other types of technology, may communicate and interact with others through the Internet while also being watched and controlled remotely. Given the demanding criteria for IoT networks, blockchain appears to be an excellent fit for 1) safeguarding the network from data manipulation attacks and 2) offering a secure platform for all network devices to connect with one another.

The scope of communication between remote devices connected to the internet for data and access transfer has multiplied due to continuous developments in the IoT. As a result, practically every business on the planet has been changed and disrupted by IoT, from the education sector to supply chain management. IoT has also performed admirably in the healthcare industry, making diagnostic procedures easier and effectively observing patient activity. The main benefit of IoT, which is what the authors are focusing on, is that it facilitates patient monitoring even during inactive patient hours, which is sometimes very difficult to achieve with a conventional system.

Drawbacks of current IoT systems:

- The majority of today's IoT networks are based on the server–client model, in which all devices are recognized, authenticated, and connected through cloud servers, which necessitates massive processing and storage capacity. Furthermore, even if the devices are close to each other, all conversations between them must transit through the Internet. While this strategy works well for tiny IoT networks, it does not scale well. For large-scale IoT networks, the expense of constructing a large number of communication links, maintaining centralized clouds, and networking all equipment is also significant.
- Aside from the financial implications, relying on cloud servers exposes the design to a single point of failure. Furthermore, IoT devices must be resistant to data breaches and physical tampering. While some existing solutions safeguard IoT devices, they are complex and unsuitable for resource constrained IoT devices with low compute power.

4.2.1.1 OVERCOMING IOT'S SHORTCOMINGS WITH BLOCKCHAIN

Blockchain creates a peer-to-peer network, which reduces the expense of setting up and maintaining centralized clouds, data centers, and networking equipment by dispersing computing and storage requirements throughout the network's devices. The single-point-of-failure problem is solved with this communication model. The use of cryptographic methods in blockchain addresses the privacy concerns for IoT networks. It also addresses the issue of IoT network dependability by employing tamper-resistant ledgers.

4.2.2 IOT-BASED BLOCKCHAIN ARCHITECTURE FOR E-HEALTHCARE

The general IoT-based blockchain architecture for e-healthcare is shown in Figure 4.2. The operations are separated into four tiers in the architecture: 1) IoT e-healthcare; 2) blockchain platform; 3) connection; and 4) IoT devices. Within the IoT ecosystem, the blockchain platform is critical for the transmission of block data. Authentication is critical for a variety of services, protocols, and resources. The two-factor and multi-factor authentication can be used for authentication. Both authentication approaches will allow users of the blockchain environment to communicate with blocks effectively while allowing for the legitimate usage of authenticity. As a result, the current state of cyber-physical communication will be well established and realized. The aforementioned approaches have been shown to be the most appropriate for an IoT-based blockchain-centric environment (Ray et al., 2020).

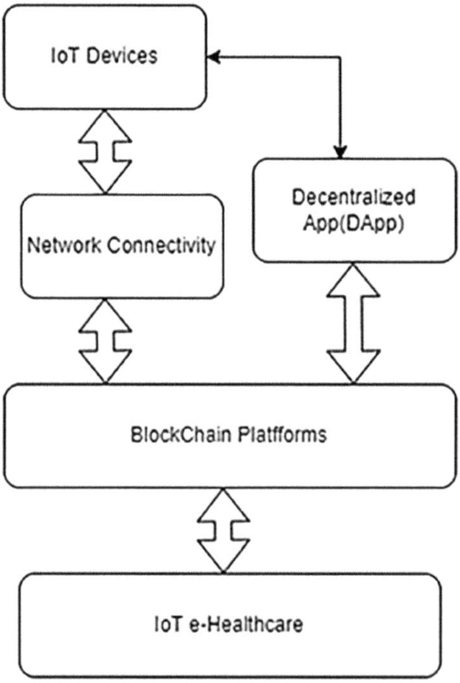

FIGURE 4.2 IoT-based blockchain architecture for e-healthcare.

Source: Adapted from Ray et al., 2020

Further, blockchain-based IoT model for managing transactions made by medical sensors and devices was proposed by Dey et al. (2017) for a more organized approach. Using the MQTT protocol was suggested by the architecture, which is capable of serving as the main conduit for tying the IoT platform's biosensors to it. Furthermore, the architecture included IPFS (InterPlanetary File System), which can filter out state information or changes in the blocks when certain transactions are added to the blocks to lessen deduplication of the stored transactions. The work proposed by Budida et al. (2017) provides an interactive environment with relation to an IoT-controlled healthcare system. The cornerstone of the suggested architecture is essentially the ingestion of generating data from smart wearables and biosensors, followed by providing patients with clear feedback and simple solutions.

Further extension to e-healthcare model is proposed by Sabyasachi et al. (2019). The foundation of the entire system is the IoT, Blockchain, and Machine Learning integration for anomaly identification in the patient's health data's behavior. The methodology presented is essentially a system that calls for the employment of an IoT module to intercept and retrieve the data produced by the patient's wearable devices. The Blockchain system pictured is best used to store and retain patient data in the form of multiple transactions and to support access control to various stakeholders. Additionally, the Blockchain architecture is utilized to enhance medical research by retaining the pseudo-anonymity of the patient's identification and by providing validated and trusted data for more precise research. By analyzing the data based on the parameters provided by the doctors for the fundamental identification of the conditions that the patients are facing, the Machine Learning model is primarily used for the detection of anomalies and to forecast specific scenarios that may arise in due course of time.

4.2.3 PRIVACY CONCERN FOR PATIENT DATA ANONYMITY ON EHR SYSTEM

Different security techniques can be used by healthcare providers to protect communications between various entities. They can implement blockchain security in either their back-end systems, which house the eHealth Records (EHRs), or their front-end systems, which are in charge of interacting with doctors and nurses. With the aid of this technology, patients now have complete, unchangeable records and unrestricted access to their electronic health records (EHRs). In terms of anonymity, the authors discovered that the Blockchain only permits pseudonymity. Blockchain can also alter how medical transactions were conducted. It might ensure the quality assurance for supporting CRUD (Creating, Retrieving, Updating, and Deleting) functions for electronic health records. Shaimaa Badr et al. (2018) provide the Pseudonym-Based Encryption with Different Authorities (PBE-DA) strategy to ensure the validity of Electronic Health Records (EHRs) contained in blockchain and satisfy anonymous access to these records from cloud providers. PBE-DA relieves IoT devices from the computational strain involved with producing cryptographic data by moving the logic for key generation and authentication from the IoT nodes to the relevant gateway (GW). Additionally, there are numerous authority (Private Key Generation: PKG), which eliminates the escrow issue and complies with the Blockchain's distributed data storage model, to produce and distribute public/private keys for the patient system. Additionally, PBE-DA will be used to develop a virtual patient database.

The findings as well as results for PBE-DA demonstrated that it is an appropriate paradigm for obtaining a high level of efficiency and security in such complex platforms for EHRs systems that deal with Blockchain in IoT infrastructure design.

Figure 4.3 represents a framework for a multi-tier blockchain which broadly classified into 3 tiers. Tier 1 is represented as Level A which is a Blockchain-based platform for the edge part that acts as a base for EHR record creation. This tier consists of sensors (devices) with complete initial

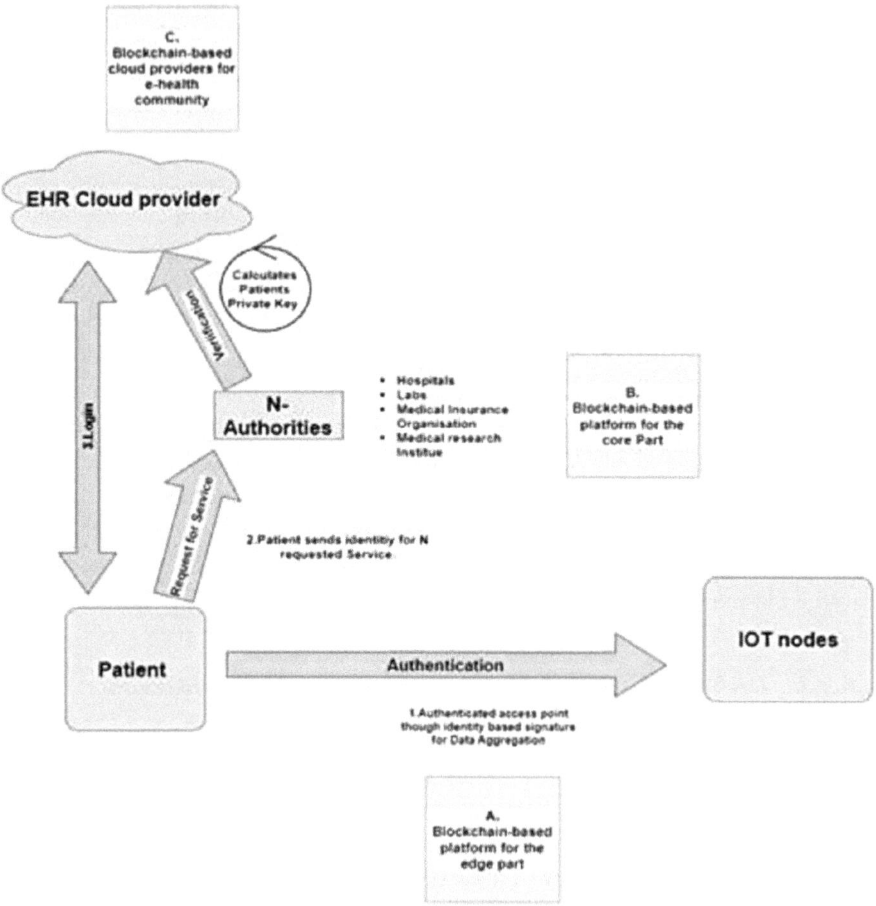

FIGURE 4.3 Framework for a multi-tier blockchain.

Source: Chakraborty et al., 2019

registration, for example patient ID, Pseudonym, public key and other services which the patient can use for authentication. Second Tier represents as Level B as Blockchain-based platform for the core Part which represents Authorities like Hospital, Pharmaceutical, insurance, research department or others which look over Patients Health record for storing and securing patient treatment, anonymity, and other sensitive attributes. Third tier represented as Block C as Blockchain-based cloud providers for e-health community for authentication, access policies for cloud users and providers.

4.3 CURRENT INSURANCE PROCESS

Insurance policies traditionally are processed using paper contracts, which imply that the claims process as well as payment process are prone to errors and may directly or indirectly require human intervention. This evolves to be a risk factor for all the bodies involved, namely, the customer, the insurance agent, the insurance company.

The insurance claim process tends to combine a number of manual steps, right from the person who is holding a policy requiring filling an application form, which is then verified by the insurer verifying the proofs submitted for the insured event. The insurer may then pay the claim after receiving all the details pertaining to the claim. The claim process may take even longer if there happens to be some disagreement over any factor. Figure 4.4 discusses traditional insurance claim management process in which, first customer needs to fill the form and pay for the policy. The insurer then issues the policy and receipt to the insured, i.e., customer who has purchased the policy When the insured suffers from loss, he/she file the claim. The insurer verifies the claim and does the cost estimation for the claim to be processed. If the claim is covered in the policy, it will be processed, and insurer pays compensation to the claimant else claim will be rejected.

4.3.1 DRAWBACKS OF TRADITIONAL INSURANCE PROCESS

The information needed to process a claim could be kept in separate silos that don't communicate with one another. Flaw in the claim procedure in terms of information asymmetry and data silos further could lead to a fraud, which is a possible risk. From the insurer's perspective, the claim process can be costly because it involves laborious paperwork, administration, conformation, and resolving arguments, while from the insured's perspective, claiming at times of need is inconvenient.

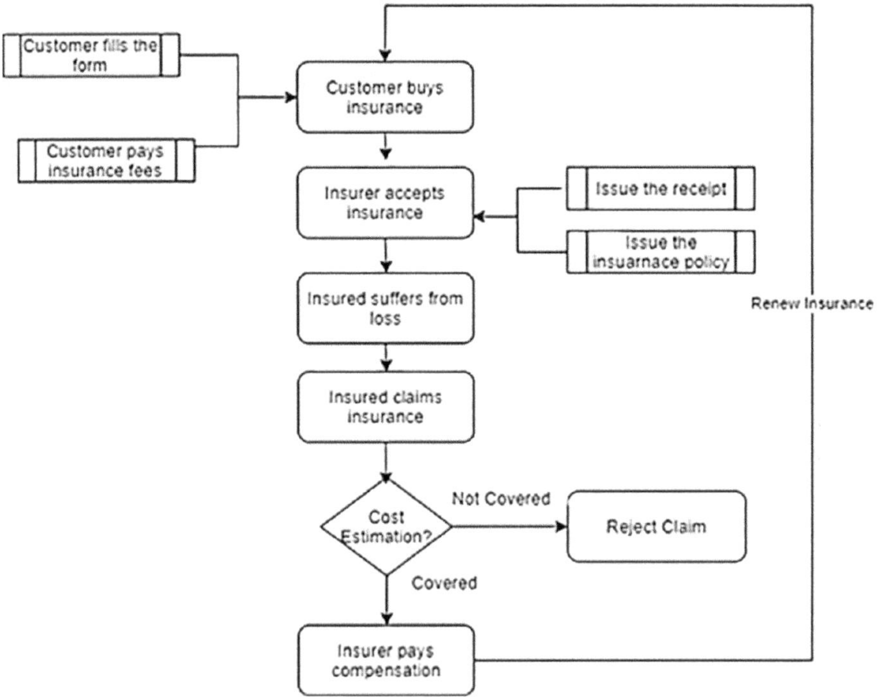

FIGURE 4.4 Insurance claim process.
Source: Adapted from Cousaert et al., 2021

The information required for processing the insurance claim may be stored in a secure way by the insurer so as to avoid any sharing and to avoid any communication among each other. But yet, fraud is a probable event which is likely to occur, and the weaknesses of the claim process could be exploited by the customer. Thus, because of manual processing and administration, this may prove to be a pricey process for the insurer. The policy holder may also suffer botheration and suffering in the process of claiming the insurance amount.

In the case of swaps and reinsurances, there are some difficulties which are faced. A settlement for reinsurance account takes around 2 to 3 months, right from its time when the insurer pays a claim till the time when the insurer receives the recovery from the reinsurer. The involved time includes time to collect the data regarding the claims, calculation of the reinsured claims or the premiums, reconciliation of the claims or settling of disputes. Thus, it can be seen that multiple parties are trying to access the same data. This data as mentioned before is stored in a secure way by the insurer so as to avoid any sharing and to avoid any communication among each other. This leads to the delay in the process of reinsurance and at the same time it also becomes error prone.

When trying to conclude a contract (e.g., a bulk annuity), a lot of effort is spent purifying data, which could entail missing out on a sale if the data isn't ready. Collateral transactions necessitate the use of a third party to manage the collateral assets. This comes at a cost, and these assets may be pledged again. Due to a lack of shared data, tracking postponed lifetimes for bulk annuities is challenging. It's difficult to novate swaps for longevity risk transfer since the new transacting party normally doesn't have access to the entire claims history.

In case of tokenization of insurance risk (removes sensitive data entirely swapping it with a mathematically unrelated "token") (Cousaert et al., 2021), fees from securitizing insurance risk are extracted by intermediaries, lowering the cash raised and the profit earned. Thus, the administration of the securitized book of business costs insurers a lot of money. Often, investors do not have a clear picture of the underlying insurance risk.

It is a fact that privacy protection of data and Know-Your-Customer (KYC) rules are costly and time-consuming to adhere with. Furthermore, customers have no control over who has access to their personal information.

Due to the necessity to return cash to shareholders and high operational costs, the existing insurance business and operating model is not optimized for the benefit of policyholders.

4.3.2 SHALL THE INSURANCE SECTOR BE BLOCKCHAINED?

Recently, the insurance industry demonstrated a strong interest in blockchain. To investigate its commercial possibilities, several big corporations made sizeable investments, while consulting companies looked into whether it applied to the insurance industry. The tasks that are anticipated are listed below:

- Utilizing smart contracts to enhance customer experience and reduce operating costs could result in excellent experiences for customers who receive their money before they actually claim it. This is possible because smart contracts have the ability to self-execute, which could speed up claim processing and require less human effort. For instance, smart contracts for auto insurance may be set up to only transmit funds to consumers whose vehicles are repaired by licensed technicians.

- A side benefit of smart contracts is that because all of their clauses are hard-coded, they can eliminate any ambiguities that might exist in conventional text-based contracts. This fact may increase transparency and reduce the frequency and severity of legal disputes.
- A global group of signatories to a defined set of blockchain recording rules. Together with information that may originate from other fields (medical records, police theft reports, etc.) can be used to spot fraud throughout the claims processing procedure.
- While renewing rules, blockchain-based identity verification solutions might reduce the amount of data entry required from clients. Customers must first go through an identification procedure where approved intermediaries examine their IDs and associated with their wallets. Smart contracts might then use this information to validate and automatically retrieve ID papers. In a more complex situation, other data (such as health tests, asset ownership, etc.) might be saved and acquired by smart contracts for automatic and accurate premium computations.
- Pay-per-use insurance coverage might be made possible by smart contracts, which rely on IoT for automatic approval. Only if clients' GPS coordinates (e.g., those obtained by their smartphone) show they are traveling outside of the country might travel insurance premiums be collected. Similar to this, clients may only pay their auto insurance rates when they are really driving.
- Peer-to-peer insurance is not a new idea appeared few years ago. Nonetheless, smart contracts could provide wide innovations in this field, since they could allow the creation of DAOs whose functioning rules are hard-coded. With DAOs, insurers groups would be able to manage themselves without the need of external control.

In case of fraud prevention, a common database that was created by several individuals (doctors, police officers) may be useful. Data entered should be connected to the customer's digital identity and should not be altered by outside parties. Despite the fact that reliable middlemen might ensure the accuracy of recorded data, their existence will raise the costs. Thus, Blockchain is advantageous in such cases.

In the case of Identity verification, a shared ledger would be required, much like in fraud protection, to record client papers, certificates of ownership, etc., by various writers and link them to their digital identity. It should be forbidden for writers to change data that has already been inserted by others. Disintermediation may result in cost savings similar to fraud prevention. If the aforementioned problems are effectively handled, blockchain may be a useful option for facilitating the authoring and exchange of knowledge.

In case of peer-to-peer insurance, disintermediation is necessary, and smart contracts might control communication between several unreliable parties collaborating on a database. It would also profit from related transactions, for example, to verify client identity and record claims. So, depending on blockchain could be a wise decision.

4.4 HOW CAN BLOCKCHAIN HELP?

There is no one definition of blockchain and any effort at one frequently leads to semantic squabbles. The working group employs the following definition to provide a baseline and common understanding for the purposes of this report.

Blockchain is a distributed database/ledger on which the state (i.e., the current snapshot of data) is certified and verified without the need for a trusted centralized authority. Blockchain, in its most basic level, is a database that is shared by various users. Instead of a single organization, data is verified by several groups. Each participant then propagates and stores the data.

The following are the distinguishing characteristics of blockchain/DLT (Distributed Ledger Technology) that set it distinct from other technologies:

- It provides a single source of truth, allowing for digital value exchange without the requirement for a central authority, which is frequently used as an intermediary.
- Smart contracts applied on a blockchain can automate business logic, reducing operational frictions and expenses, and thereby improving business process efficiencies.

When compared to manual processing, blockchain, and smart contracts, which specify the rules between different actors in the insurance sector, could be utilized to enhance claim processing speed and lower costs, as well as reduce errors caused by human interaction and inattention. Smart contracts could be used to encode the rules for claims processing and enable the company's reimbursement process in this scenario. The blockchain allows for a highly distributed ledger to be used for recording transactions and putting them in chronological order.

To summary, blockchain technology adds new features to the insurance sector through its innovative concepts of sharing, verifying, and securing data between different nodes participating in the network. Furthermore, combining blockchain with AI has the potential to alter the global insurance sector. In reality, the recent revolution of those technologies and their rapid adoption in numerous industries allows insurance businesses and the insurance industry in general to rethink about rescheduling existing operations and merging those technologies into one solid architecture.

4.4.1 BLOCKCHAIN FOR CLAIM PROCESSING

The provisions of the insurance policy are encoded in a smart contract, which pays out claims automatically once the proper parameters are received. This is feasible for simple "parametric" insurance products where the claim trigger event, such as flight delays, extreme weather, natural disasters, or death of a person (via ubiquitous biometric sensors), can be easily verified using reliable publicly available data. Claims are recorded on the blockchain for auditability to prevent multiple claims on the same insured event. It also enhances the client experience and eliminates double claiming on the same occurrence, preventing insurance fraud (Popovic et al., 2020).

4.4.2 BLOCKCHAIN FOR REINSURANCE

The provisions of reinsurance treaties/swaps are written into a smart contract, which executes payments (premiums and claims) to and from reinsurers when pre-determined conditions are met:

- Experience data is stored on the blockchain, which is tamper-proof and auditable right away.
- Data is recorded on the blockchain by all stakeholders (insurers, reinsurers, third-party data providers, asset managers, and consultants) so that everyone has access to a single version of the truth.
- For large-scale annuity transactions, cleansed data might be placed on the blockchain, which is tamper-proof and allows all parties to see what has been changed. Any and all transactions (reinsurance premiums and claims).
- All reinsurance premiums and claims are recorded on the blockchain for future transacting parties' visibility.
- Contracts are less complicated (because to the fact that contract rules are programmed rather than written in legal prose), and Reinsurance market that is more liquid and transparent.

- Makes it easier to trade insurance-linked securities on the secondary market.
- In the long run, once a standard/platform is established, standardized data collection and verification will result in more trustworthy data, shorter time between data submission and price quotes and simplified regulatory reporting requirements.

4.4.3 BLOCKCHAIN FOR SECURITIZATION

Smart contracts are utilized to trigger payouts to investors when predetermined conditions are met, and blocks of insurance business are escrowed on the blockchain. This is a capital market application of the reinsurance use case.

The ILS is packaged as a "token," or a digital version of the ILS, which could broaden the investor pool. It involves no costs to intermediaries, which makes it a cost-effective option to raise funds and transfer risk (e.g., investment banks). It also improves information flow to investors by recording and auditing cashflows emerging from a block of company. As a result of greater information flow to investors, the ILS market's liquidity improves through informed price discovery.

4.4.4 BLOCKCHAIN FOR DIGITAL IDENTITY

Regulatory KYC criteria are written into a smart contract and automated; customers' private information is kept and maintained locally by customers; blockchain operates as a trusted conduit of data from customers to insurers. Customers' personal information may not be stored by insurers. As a result, it minimizes the attack surface, reducing the danger of a data breach. It also reduces the onus of complying with data privacy standards.

Customers retain complete ownership of their data and have complete discretion over who they share it with customers may share the same data with numerous insurers, allowing for frictionless quotation production; and any changes to personal data could be communicated to insurers in real time. Customers could share minimum personal data for KYC checks thanks to advanced encryption techniques like zero-knowledge proofs (ZKPs).

4.4.5 BLOCKCHAIN FOR AUTONOMOUS INSURER

When different technical developments (Big Data, artificial intelligence (AI), and Blockchain) attain maturity, they form a Decentralized Autonomous Insurer (DAI).

Insurance products are priced using Big Data by Al-based algorithms; automatic compliance with KYC rules via decentralized digital identity; peer-to-peer risk pooling via blockchain, in which people, societies, and businesses can transact risk directly; premium and claim payments are managed using smart contracts; funds are determined and prepared to invest by Al-based algorithms; all transaction information is stored on the blockchain and made accessible to the regulator;

But at the same time, it should be noted that this technology has some issues. They can be summarized as below:

- There are no established standards or platforms.
- A lack of reliable third-party data (oracles) to trigger a claim on increasingly complex covered events.
- Blockchain and smart contracts may not offer an obvious advantage over current technology.
- The security laws and regulations governing digital asset representation are unclear.
- The enabling technology is still in its infancy; digital identification is a public utility; and private businesses are the least motivated to build the infrastructure required for the technology to function.
- Customers would need to alter their mentality about how they manage and maybe monetize their personal data since data is not stored by the insurer;
- Insurers would need to change their mindset about how they consume data because data is not retained by the insurer. They must have the confidence and motivation to reveal their personal information in exchange for more benefits, such as lower premiums, customized products, and speedier underwriting.

4.5 BLOCKCHAIN SOLUTION FOR CLAIM MANAGEMENT

Classical insurance policies are frequently managed on paper contracts, which makes claims and payments vulnerable to inaccuracy and frequently necessitate human oversight. This is made worse by the fact that traditional insurance's inherent complexities, which are consumers, brokers, insurers, and reinsurers, as well as insurance companies, are all involved in the insurance industry and risk is the major product. As a form of decentralized ledger, the blockchain technology boosts the efficiency of the insurance sector by a four-fold namely fraud prevention, claims automation, and data analysis with Reinsurance and the IoT.

In case of insurance sector, it is the need of the time:

- To eliminate intermediaries from the value transmission or exchange process.
- To create a tamper-resistant record that is trusted by all stakeholders and multiple participants.
- To reduce the value chain's operational friction and costs (Popovic et al., 2020).

Blockchain paves the way to address these issues. The next section addresses the many techniques to dealing with the claim procedure proposed by researchers.

4.5.1 SMART CONTRACTS AND HYPERLEDGER FABRIC

Smart contracts, which are part of the blockchain, are self-executing codes. The business logic in a smart contract is executed when specific circumstances are met. The immutability of a smart contract is one of its indispensable features. Many blockchain-based apps can be constructed utilizing smart contracts, which are an integral part of the Ethereum blockchain (Mertz et al., 2018). In the realm of insurance claims, several academics proposed a range of frameworks. Transparency, security, and non-repudiation are the focal points of these frameworks (Gera et al., 2020). Traditional claim process suffers from difficulties such as a policyholder giving incorrect information when filing a claim and the alteration or deletion of customer data to demonstrate prejudice. The insurance company/staff, the agent, and the police are all involved in the claim procedure. Each member in the peer-to-peer blockchain network will have their own peer node. The insurance peer is a tool used by insurance companies and their employees to process claims. For the verification process to be completed, police need a peer. The claim verification process can be aided by an agent peer. For blockchain implementation, IBM's platform is employed.

Hyperledger Fabric generates certificates for the peers as part of the process. It also launches the insurance network and creates Docker images for the network. The application interacts with three types of peers namely police peers, insurance peers, and agency peers. When it comes to settling an insurance claim, the peers reach a consensus. These peers will be allowed to take part in claim processing, and the transactions will be kept on a distributed ledger. Every transaction is digitally signed and recorded in the blockchain. In a distributed context, an immutable collection of transactions is thus preserved. Figure 4.5 demonstrates the framework for integration of blockchain with the insurance application.

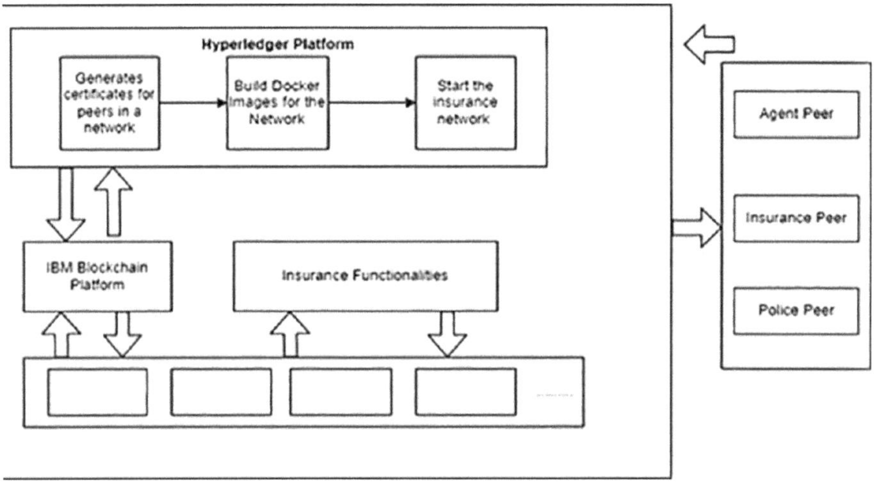

FIGURE 4.5 Framework for integration of blockchain with the insurance application.

Source: Adapted from Gera et al., 2020

4.5.2 BLOCKCHAIN-BASED ARTIFICIAL INTELLIGENCE DRIVEN INSURANCE NETWORK FRAMEWORK

When compared to manual processing, blockchain, and smart contracts, which specify the rules between different actors in the insurance sector, could be utilized to increase claim processing speed and reduce expenses as well as errors caused by human participation and lack of attention. The regulations for claims processing are contained in smart contracts, which also facilitate the insurer's return process. The blockchain allows for a highly distributed ledger to be used for recording transactions and putting them in chronological order. This method uses permissioned blockchain as a network for insurance companies to store and distribute various customer and claim-related data.

As shown in Figure 4.6 client data and records are collected from the blockchain network and used as features to estimate client risk rate and other metrics such as the future claim amount in this technique (Dhieb et al., 2020). As a result, the authors can forecast the client's behavior and vulnerability in the future. The fraud detection module analyzes and verifies claims in order to detect and classify different types of fraud. The blockchain network classifies and stores submitted claims. Machine learning algorithms are used in the fraud detection module. The claims that have been extracted from the shared ledgers can then be manually verified. The confirmed data can be used as training data for the classifier in future iterations to enhance its accuracy (Ilinca et al., 2020).

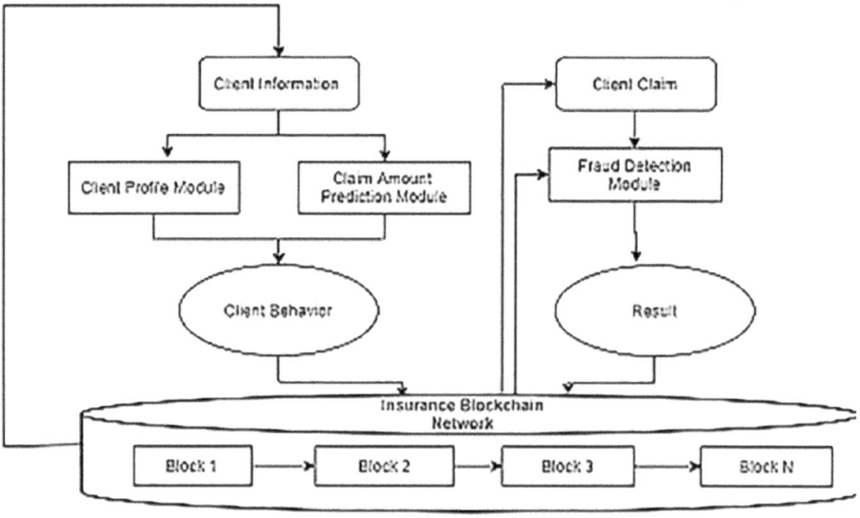

FIGURE 4.6 Blockchain based artificial intelligence insurance network framework.

Source: Dhieb et al., 2020

4.5.3 INSURANCE CLAIM USING ETHEREUM ON MISTORE

The authors demonstrate how MIStore works. MIStore comes with two parts Transaction and block in MIServer. Transaction divided into two things one is header and other is payload. Transaction header contains Hash, block number, Order, Timestamp, sender, Receiver, and Payload. Block headers consist of Name, Hash, Parent Hash, Parent Hash, Proof of work, Timestamp, Merkle root, Nonce (Zhou et al., 2018). Figure 4.7 shows the Insurance claim using Ethereum on MIStore.

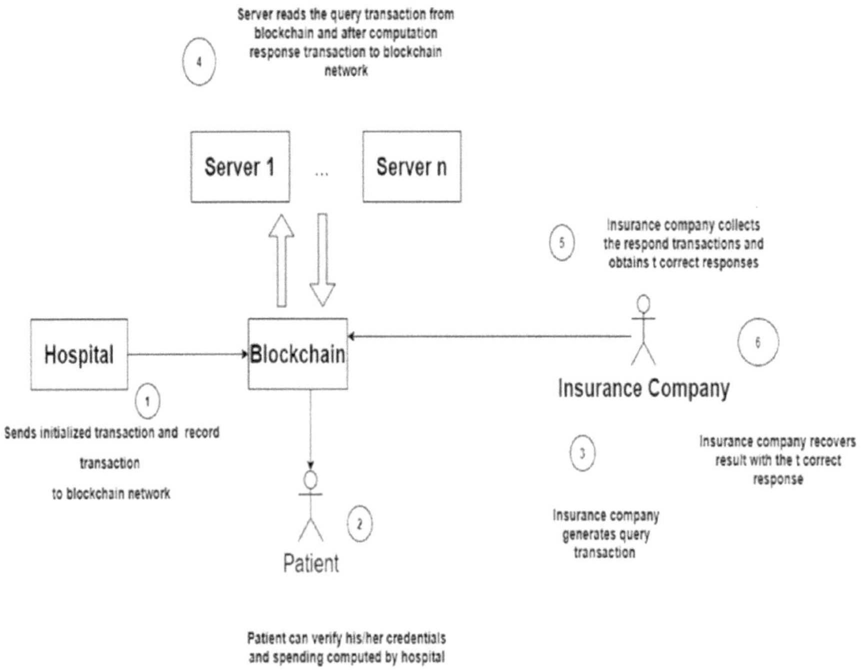

FIGURE 4.7 Insurance claim using Ethereum on MIStore.

Source: Adapted from Zhou et al., 2018

4.6 CHALLENGES IN ADOPTION OF BLOCKCHAIN TECHNOLOGY

As shown in Figure 4.8, challenges in adoption of blockchain are divided into varied factors.

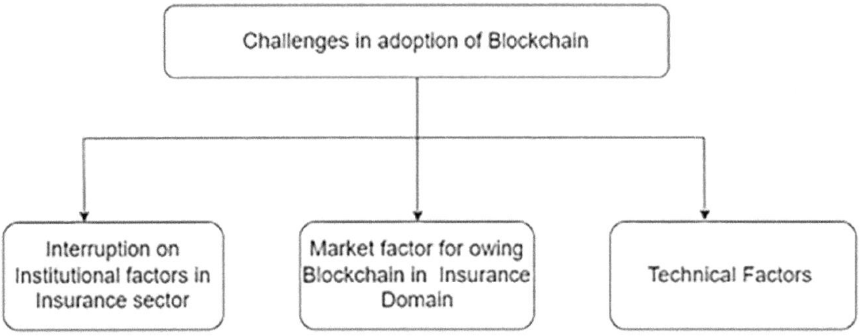

FIGURE 4.8 Typical challenges in blockchain adoption.

Source: Adapted from Janssen et al., 2020

4.6.1 INTERRUPTION ON INSTITUTIONAL FACTORS IN INSURANCE SECTOR

Institutional factors can be interpreted as an important protocol for regulating transaction or communicating between entity.

The main perspective about challenges in adopting blockchain is:

- Market resistance to change the medium of transaction.

  Example: Customer to agent or agent to company.
- Change of platform.
- New players approaching new ideas and motto.

Validating above points is challenging and understanding each business process and transforming it on digital platform is challenging. However, understanding business requirement, business strategies and its impact on societal arena is challenging (Janssen et al., 2020).

4.6.1.1 NEED OF REGULATION AND LEGISLATION IN INSURANCE SECTOR

As being one of the blooming phases still many sectors are not advent on Blockchain standards on contrary Government also on slower node for adopting Blockchain standards.

Altogether negligence and streamlining rules and regulations in insurance sector is time consuming. On top of It many countries do resist to imbibe it. Blockchain endorsement in insurance sector will lead to collaborative governance which will provide stability and trust in market which is also relied upon collaborative rules and protocol thus benefiting people and various stakeholders and government for streamlining the process. Due to collaborative approach will also need of Law and regulations for monitoring the insurance sector in market. As the result false document, false claims can be bow downed by having such system. Main contribution will be taken by policy maker which will set the regulations to incorporate blockchain technology in existing framework. As looking at blockchain advantage of its existence is due to its features as mentioned like distributed ledger, immutable, smart contracts, right to be forgotten, etc. Main the perception of blockchain has to overcome the mis concepts that blockchain is only a bitcoin. Its far more matured and enriched for its smart contracts and ledger which will be very helpful to rid of insurance mafia and fraudulent. As people should make aware that Bitcoin is simply one of the incarnations of blockchain as cryptocurrency. In order to adapt blockchain technologies policy makers and several other participants should dig down appropriate governance framework which includes provision of approves or disapprove for authorized participants, any correction mechanism and supporting law in cases of disputes.

4.6.1.2 GOVERNANCE

Although blockchain must be managed, it is also a governance tool in and of itself. Insurance players should put in place appropriate governance frameworks, which include provisions on the respective parties' liability, rules to approve/reject authorized participants, correction mechanisms, applicable law in case of disputes, and so on, in order for blockchain technologies to be adopted. These governance frameworks should also be customized to the roles and characteristics of blockchain technologies. Insurance manipulation and unfair behaviors could also be avoided by good governance. Due to a lack of adequate security, certain individuals may gain access to information stored in blockchain and use it for unfair purposes such as front-running competitors or pricing manipulation. As a result, a clear balance between the need to protect sensitive information through privacy standards and the amount of transparency should be struck (Al-Saqaf et al., 2017).

4.6.2 MARKET FACTOR FOR OWING BLOCKCHAIN IN INSURANCE DOMAIN

In aspect of operating an organization in its blockchain environment it is necessary to make smart contracts in view of buying a policy or selling policy for creating trust and necessary value generation. Blockchain is such lace which ties up desired people in one single chain irrespective of inter domain.

4.6.2.1 STRUCTURES OF MARKETS

Blockchain adoption necessitates a high level of computerization. As a result, some countries (e.g., developing or least developed) are not ready to adopt blockchain-based solutions. Because blockchain technology mandates data dissemination across multiple nodes, the severity of the challenges to consider grows because of the high bandwidth, storage demand, and computing power necessary to be an active node. As a result, some groups and areas may be unable to take advantage of the benefits of blockchain technology for national services. Financial marks' structure and sturdiness may also be disrupted by blockchain-based innovations. The European Securities and Markets Authority published a report in 2017 that highlighted the benefits as well as potential risks of Digital Ledger Technologies (DLTs) for financial market applications, including the possibility of increased market volatility and the still-controversial role that smart contracts could play as the size of the blockchain-based securities asset base grows, due to their embedded automated triggers that can cause one-directional market routs (Androulaki et al., 2018).

4.6.2.2 CHALLENGES IN UNDERSTAND BUSINESS PROCESS

Traditional business processes in Insurance company may not appear to be applicable to blockchain because it is founded on the "cutting the middleman" idea, which eliminates the need for intermediate transaction costs. In the short term, the costs of adopting and implementing blockchain technologies for existing businesses can be prohibitively high, particularly for incumbents with large existing back-office processes, complex legacy IT systems, and processes created to conform to existing standards that may require costly redesign. Some back-office operations may be removed or replaced with blockchain technologies, which may cause issues.

4.6.2.3 MATURED SMART CONTRACTS AND AGREEMENTS

There is currently a lack of transparency surrounding smart contracts, limiting them to simple agreements. "Computer protocols that facilitate, verify, execute, and enforce the terms of a commercial agreement" is how smart contracts are defined. The rules of a smart contract, on the other hand, are integrated in software. As soon as the information is added, and all parties agree that the outcome is satisfactory. If all of the conditions are met, the contract will be completed automatically. For a while, in order for a smart contract to be implemented, it must be self-monitoring and self-enforcing via a mix of scripting and mechanisms put up to keep track of important off-blockchain data and information to the smart contract's rules being carried out effectively thus leads to programming challenge (Chernet & Jilledi, 2021).

4.6.3 TECHNICAL FACTORS: AN IMPORTANT CONSIDERATION

Looking at technical aspect having blockchain in insurance company can take varied sizes and shapes. Private or public closed blockchains (also known as private/public permissioned blockchains) and private or public open blockchains (also known as permissionless blockchains) form the basis of a typology.

4.6.3.1 TIME FACTOR

Time is important factor for any business process and imbibing blockchain will lead to many other challenges w.r.t. transaction process. For example: In comparison to other transaction processing networks such as VISA (2,000 tps typical, 10,000 tps peak), Twitter (5,000 tps typical; 15,000 tps peak), and advertising networks (>1,00,000 tps typical), the time to process transactions for a Bitcoin network is only one transaction per second (tps).

4.6.3.2 SIZE FACTOR

Size of the blockchain is the other challenging note to be considered. As size increases further processing time also increases.

4.6.3.3 SCALABILITY

Because the transactional volumes required by services like T2S are bigger than those required by Bitcoin transactions, the blockchain is not yet mature enough to handle them. As a result, the degree of difficulty will be determined by the applications. Relatively it depends upon market segments and its verticals. Because there are various "back doors" via which the system can be attacked, distributing access and management over multiple nodes can provide a security risk.

4.6.3.4 SHARING INFRASTRUCTURE

Infrastructure plays an important role in terms of arranging distributed ledger. Arranging decentralized storage, communication protocol, Network administrator is challenging task. In the blockchain economy, it is critical to build standard infrastructure components so that insurance industry may concentrate on producing value-added services rather than fundamental infrastructure. Because the blockchain economy involves the complex and sensitive engineering features of decentralized networks, it is critical to have a well-developed and secure infrastructure (Rouse et al., 2010).

4.7 ADVANCES IN BLOCKCHAIN WITH IOT

Blockchain and IoT are two concrete pillars in Computer science which leads in new path of advancement when integrated as Blockchain with IoT (Atlam et al., 2018). There are still numerous other open advances as listed below:

4.7.1 ADVANCES IN SMART CONTRACTS

- Integrating smart contracts with IoT System will make a system to attain reliability and integrity of Data.
- Smart contracts will lay as a base to execute all functions of IoT assuring assurance and wholeness. • Due to continues changing environmental condition of IoT smart contract should be dynamic in nature.
- Emergence platform for integrating IoT with Smart contract is considerable need.

4.7.2 IMBIBING REGULATING LAWS

- Advancement by imbibing regulatory rules in practice of blockchain with IoT.
- Enhancing security: Elevation in safeguarding low capability IoT devices under the umbrella of secured environment.
- Building of IOTA: IOTA designed especially for IoT and its application and still there is a requirement for decentralized technology of IOTA.

KEYWORDS

- **artificial intelligence**
- **blockchain**
- **claims**
- **consensus algorithms**
- **distributed ledger technology**
- **e-healthcare**
- **Ethereum**
- **insurance**
- **internet of things**
- **know your customer**
- **smart contracts**

REFERENCES

Al-Saqaf, W., & Seidler, N., (2017). Blockchain technology for social impact: Opportunities and challenges ahead. *Journal of Cyber Policy*, 1–17.

Androulaki, E., Barger, A., Bortnikov, V., Cachin, C., Christidis, Yellick, J. (2018). Hyperledger Fabric: A Distributed Operating System for Permissioned Blockchains. *Proceedings of the Thirteenth EuroSys Conference* (EuroSys '18), Article No. 30, 1–5 pages. Association for Computing Machinery (ACM).

Atlam, H. F., et al., (2018). Blockchain with internet of things: Benefits, challenges, and future directions. *International Journal of Intelligent Systems & Applications, 10*(6).

Bhushan, B., et al., (2021). Unification of blockchain and internet of things (BIoT): Requirements, working model, challenges, and future directions. *Wireless Networks, 27*(1), 55–90.

Bhushan, B., et al., (2021). Untangling blockchain technology: A survey on state of the art, security threats, privacy services, applications, and future research directions. *Computers & Electrical Engineering, 90.*

Budida, D. A. M., & Mangrulkar, R. S., (2017). *Design and Implementation of Smart HealthCare System Using IoT* (pp. 1–7). IEEE.

Chakraborty, S., Aich, S., & Hee-Cheol, K., (2019). *A Secure Healthcare System Design Framework Using Blockchain Technology*, 260–264.

Chernet, H. F., & Jilledi, S. K. (2021). A next-generation smart contract and decentralized blockchain platform: a case study on ethiopia. *International Journal of Economics and Management Systems, 6*, 253–260.

Cousaert, S., Nikhil, V., & Jiahua, X., (2021). *Token-Based Insurance Solutions on Blockchain, 2109*, 07902.

Dey, T., Jaiswal, S., Sunderkrishnan, S., & Katre, N., (2017). *HealthSense: A Medical Use Case of Internet of Things and Blockchain* (pp. 486–491). IEEE.

Dhieb, N., Ghazzai, H., Besbes, H., & Massoud, Y., (2020). A Secure AI-Driven Architecture for Automated Insurance Systems: Fraud Detection and Risk Measurement, in *IEEE Access*, *8*, 58546–58558, doi: 10.1109/ACCESS.

Gera, J., Palakayala, A., Rejeti, V., & Anusha, T., (2020). *Blockchain Technology for Fraudulent Practices in Insurance Claim Process*, 1068–1075.

Ilinca, D. (2020). Applying blockchain and artificial intelligence to digital health. *Digital Health Entrepreneurship*, 83–101.

Janssen, M., Weerakkody, V., Ismagilova, E., Sivarajah, U., & Irani, Z., (2020). A framework for analyzing blockchain technology adoption: Integrating institutional, market and technical factors. *International Journal of Information Management, 50*, 302–309.

Jaradat, A., Ali, O., & AlAhmad, A., (2022). Blockchain technology: A fundamental overview. In: Muthu, S. S., (eds.), *Blockchain Technologies for Sustainability. Environmental Footprints and Eco-design of Products and Processes*. Springer, Singapore. https://doi.org/10.1007/978-981-16-6301-7_1.

Kirlidog, M., & Asuk, C., (2012). A fraud detection approach with data mining in health insurance. *Procedia – Social and Behavioral Sciences, 62*, 989–994.

Mertz, L., (2018). *(Block) Chain Reaction: A Blockchain Revolution Sweeps into Health Care, Offering the Possibility for a Much-Needed Data Solution* (Vol. 9, pp. 4–7). IEEE.

Popovic, D., Avis, C., Byrne, M., Cheung, C., Donovan, M., Flynn, Y., Fothergill, C., et al., (2020). Understanding blockchain for insurance use cases. *British Actuarial Journal, 25*.

Ray, P. P., et al., (2020). Blockchain for IoT-based healthcare: Background, consensus, platforms, and use cases. *IEEE Systems Journal, 15*(1), 85–94.

Rouse, R., (2010). The financial services regulatory landscape. *Journal of Corporate Accounting & Finance, 21*, 113–115.

Shaimaa, B., Ibrahim, G., & Abd-Elrahman, E., (2018). Multi-tier blockchain framework for IoT-EHRs systems. *Procedia Computer Science, 141*, 159–166. ISSN 1877-0509, https://doi.org/10.1016/j.procs.2018.10.162.

She, A. H., Al-Amri, J. F., Subahi, A. F., Agrawal, A., Pathak, N., Kumar, R., & Khan, R. A., (2021). An analysis of integrating machine learning in healthcare for ensuring confidentiality of the electronic records. *Computer Modeling in Engineering and Sciences, 130*(3), 1387–1422.

Zhou, L., Wang, L., & Sun, Y., (2018). MIStore: A Blockchain-based medical insurance storage system. *Journal of Medical Systems, 42*.

CHAPTER 5

Industrial Automation: 6G with Artificial Intelligence

S. MAHESWARAN,[1] R. D. GOMATHI,[2] S. SATHESH,[1] S. NANDITA,[1] I. MOHAMMED SHAFIQ,[1] P. RITHIKA,[1] and Y. SYAMALA[3]

[1]*Department of Electronics and Communication Engineering, Kongu Engineering College, Perundurai, Tamil Nadu, India*

[2]*Department of English, Kongu Engineering College, Perundurai, Tamil Nadu, India*

[3]*Department of IoT, Seshadri Rao Gudlavalleru Engineering College, JNTUK, Kakinada, Andhra Pradesh, India*

ABSTRACT

Sixth generation (6G) network uses a higher frequency than 5G. In 6G, sub-mm waves are used. Research has been started on 6G technology, even though 5G technology is currently in the process of development. In a few years, 6G technology will grow and it needs some time to develop. Some of the goals in this research are the maximum speed of one terabit per second (Tbps) on an internet device, very low latency, a very large number of connected devices, and lowering the energy consumption with battery-free IoT devices. Many summits, conferences, and symposiums have been held regarding 6G. As it is a known fact that artificial intelligence works where machines operate without human control. It is also predicted that AI is the future technology. In combination with 6G, it has wide applications in industries. In the study, the main focus is on artificial intelligence in the 6G network. In addition to that, artificial intelligence has drastically improved 6G. AI has an important role in network optimization and new waveforms

Advanced Digital Technologies in Financial and Business Management: Unleashing the Power of Artificial Intelligence, Machine Learning, Blockchain, and the Internet of Things. Jyoti Batra Arora, Nitish Pathak, and Neelam Sharma (Eds.)

are designed. It has the potential to attain higher speed and other benefits. It is applied in autonomous vehicle networks, cybersecurity, scientific discovery, healthcare applications, industrial security, and event identification by avoiding damage to both human beings and machines. It can also be applied when both of them are in contact, avoiding shipment loss during transporting industrial products.

5.1 INTRODUCTION

As we know that 6G is faster than 5G we use this technology in various places, especially in industries. The industries are large so it is necessary to identify if any problem occurred, only then we can prevent the total damage to the industry. So, artificial intelligence with 6G is important. Artificial intelligence enables the machine to perform human intelligence required tasks based on experience and modifying to present input data. Artificial intelligence is used for identifying the problem and a high speed 6G network is needed to transfer the data to the cloud or server so that the industrial men can identify the problem and rectify it. For example, in a biscuit factory, if a problem occurs in any one of the areas, it will affect the production. So, the problem should be identified as soon as possible to avoid the loss. It is used in industrial security. For example, identifying the temperature of the place and the cooler fans can be operated accordingly. By using these images of the people entering the industry can be recorded and the unknown people who entered can be identified easily. It is also applied in other areas such as event identification where the event has to be identified and the information has to be sent to the cloud to solve the problem. Using artificial intelligence and image processing we can say the exact event happening in the industries namely firing, fighting, giddiness, theft, etc. In industries, there may be several problems which cannot be identified manually. In such situations, artificial intelligence with a 6G network can be used. Also, this technology is used in transportation purposes. As this technology has more speed and accuracy, it will be an unavoidable one in the future. Nowadays, industries are fully automated. Artificial intelligence is very important because it reduces human usage. As the latency is very low, 6G is the best network currently which can be used everywhere especially in places where it requires high security and high precision. During human machine contact while working, this technology can be used for proper monitoring of both machine and human beings. Due to proper monitoring, there will not be any damage to machines and health damages to human beings. Transportation plays a major role in the lives of people. Artificial Intelligence with 6G in the transportation field gives a sophisticated life for the people. The industries run with a lot of data. The data handling can be made easier and quicker with the 6G. The data are stored in the cloud. Cloud is nothing but the server where the data is stored, and the data can be accessed all the time. Cloud is one of the greatest advantages in the modern era because it can store many data. It is not like a hard drive because it has limitations. By using this cloud computing, companies and users don't need to maintain physical servers by themselves. The speed of transmitting the data to the trained model is made faster using 6G. The utilization of industrial applications is discussed below. This type of technologies enhances the production of the industries and reduce the losses so that the economy of the industries is increased, and the GDP of a country is increased. Artificial intelligence with 6G will produce a great impact in the industrial field.

5.2 PROBLEM STATEMENT

In industries, it is necessary to maintain the temperature of the surrounding environment of the industry, to maintain the temperature of the human beings and machines. So, monitoring the temperature is important. Here, artificial intelligence with 6G can be used. By using thermal camera, temperature of the human beings can be monitored, and the cooler fans can be operated accordingly. There is a problem of unknown person entering the industries. With the help of these scanners and cameras, the people can be monitored. This is related to security. Another problem is event identification. If an event (problem) is occurred, the situation should be analyzed, and proper steps should be taken. If a problem is occurred in a certain place, the requirements should be identified in terms of medical support, etc. (Figures 5.1 and 5.2).

In industries, humans and machines are working together. Sometimes due to the contact of the machines, human beings are affected, and machines are also damaged. For this, a solution should be found to maintain the distance between the machines and human beings such as sensor alarm, etc. So that there will not be any damage to both human beings and machines. Another problem that is found in industries is damage during shipping. In containers, the industrial products are carried to various places. Sometimes the speed and vibration of the vehicle may affect the product. The product may be damaged. So, a solution should be found for this problem. Speed and

FIGURE 5.1 Image indicates whenever human comes close to the machine, the machine automatically stops.

Source: https://i.ytimg.com/vi/nU6JdDijyMo/maxresdefault.jpg.

FIGURE 5.2 In this transportation vehicle, for proper safety cameras are used and for damage protection of the goods, vibration sensors are kept for detecting the vibration level.

Source: https://www.freepik.com/premium-photo/truck-trailer-container-docking-load-shipment-goods-pallets-warehouse-freight-industry-logistics-transport_6094136.htm.

vibration limit can be found and according to that, the load can be carried out. The face of the person while getting inside the container, should be captured for security reasons. If any unofficial person is entered, it should be recognized, and the information should be stored. Here, the cloud can be used for storing the information because it is a source for data storage.

5.3 OVERVIEW OF THE EXISTING SYSTEM

In this study (Kamruzzaman, 2021), they proposed the method to develop a smart city with a networking architecture for its environments employing light weight security model (SCNM-LSM). They also used artificial intelligence to construct architecture design with light weight security model. In this security model, most of the algorithm was based on the mathematics and the model was tested and verified.

In this research (Nayak & Patgiri, 2021), they proposed the healthcare method using artificial intelligence and 6G network. Using the image processing (neural network), the human body will be scanned and for that image, histogram value is generated and according to the histogram value the treat is taken by the artificial intelligence.

In the study (Padhi & Charrua-Santos, 2021), they proposed a method to improve the industrial Internet of Everything (advanced level of IoT) and it also connects devices, machines, sensors, IoTs, etc., They said that all the machines and mechanisms are connected to the internet, i.e., 6G. In addition to that, they explained 6G IIoE priorities, challenges, and applications.

In this paper (Letaief, Chen, Shi, Zhang, & Zhang, 2019), they proposed the uses and advantages of 6G. 6G can enable the artificial intelligence application, 6G network design, artificial intelligence enabled methodologies and 6G network optimization. And this data can be transferred very fast because of using 6G.

This study (Han, Tu, Liu, Martínez-García, & Peng, 2021), says about the proposed method to detect the anomaly on multidimensional data processing vital devices using 6G with massive Industrial Internet of Things (IIoT). They try to develop a model for industry that will connect with 6G and artificial intelligence.

In this study (Aslam et al., 2021), they proposed 6G to Cognitive Radio Network (CRN) application, key challenges, securities, requirements. They used artificial intelligence for CR network and to empower 6th generation in all forms, server-based communication, physical layer, data mining, etc.

In this research (Lin et al., 2020), they proposed a security-based model using 6G enabled NIB for industrial applications. They are same as us, but they did not use artificial intelligence. Instead of using artificial intelligence they used image processing and lot of mathematical equations in the algorithm.

This research (Zhang, Cao, Cui, Zhang, & Chen, 2021), proposed a model for a vehicular network for enhancing security. This model has lots of data to store and share. So, they use 6G network to transfer it in a faster manner. Their main objective is the detection model of CAN bus message that is proposed. It also solves some problems such as weight (overload), balance, etc. They used mathematical and logical equations in the algorithm to cater the above requirement.

In this study (Ali et al., 2020), they proposed a machine leaning in 6G and by using that, they had improved the wireless communication networks. They used 3 layers, which included physical, medium control layer and the application layer. These layers were on the basis of ML.

All the referred researches have used 6G and artificial intelligence for the communication, home appliances, healthcare, security enhancement, Internet of Things, etc., By understanding and attaining the knowledge from these references, it is the trained model in artificial intelligence for the security enhancement in the industries, event detection, transportation system monitoring and the human detection in industries by using 6G networks.

5.4 APPLICATION OF AI IN INDUSTRIES

5.4.1 INDUSTRIAL SECURITY

6G and Artificial Intelligence (AI) are introduced. Artificial intelligence means machines are working automatically, without the help of human beings. Artificial intelligence is to qualify the computer or machine to perform the tasks such as recognition of speech and image, decision making and problem solving according to the situation, perception, and reasoning. It enables the machine to perform human intelligence that required tasks based on the experience and modifying to present input data. 6G (6th generation) is the fastest network compared to all and also, it has very low latency (delay). The latency of the 6G network is nearly 0.01 μs (microsecond). In real time, latency cannot be seen, so it helps to increase the speed and efficiency. Only, the industrial development decides the economic growth of the country. Industries contribute to national income, increase in employment and maintain a balanced economy. Industries face lag in the security systems. They require a security system to maintain and protect their assets, information about products and workers, safety

(Maheswaran et al., 2021) and health of workers, etc., So, using artificial intelligence and 6G network, a security system can be formed for industries. This system is stronger, faster, stores large data and analyze larger data in a short time. Artificial intelligence is used to communicate to users, make algorithms, make programs and IoTs (internet of things) (Sathesh et al., 2020). Here, three cameras are used for the security purposes.

5.4.1.1 THERMAL CAMERA

It is used to find the body temperature of the human beings (Figure 5.4) entering into the industry and this temperature of human beings is stored in a cloud to find or predict the average room temperature and according to this data, the cooler will operate. If the temperature is quite high from the normal level, it will inform the manager of that industry and it would not allow the person to get in. In the algorithm, the average temperature of those working machines is already noted (stored in a cloud) and processed. And the temperature of the human beings who have got in are also stored in the clouds. These data are processed using the formula (which is given below). Using this formula, the exact room temperature is predicted. If the room temperature increases, it will inform the manager of the industry and it will also find where the problem lies and why this temperature rise occurs. It is also conveyed to the manager of the industry. This process will occur within 0.7 ms (milliseconds). It is very less time, so we can prevent that accident or any issue before it happens. This camera also monitors the temperature of the machines which are working. If the temperature of the machines increases across the normal level, it will turn off the machine and inform the workers and manager of the industry and prevent the blast or explosion of the machine (Maheswaran, Sathesh, Priyadharshini, & Vivek, 2017). These algorithms and programs are in a separate place. This single algorithm can handle 50–100 cameras even more than that. Using 6G network, the data can be uploaded or transferred in a faster way so that, all the thermal cameras could transfer its data to the central server algorithm (Figure 5.5). This algorithm will receive those data from the camera and process that raw data to convert into information about that data. The result of the process will transfer to that respective block. According to that information, the data will be given to the machines, workers, and manager. The block diagram is given in Figure 5.3.

$$Average\ temp = \frac{Room\ temp\ +\ \Sigma(Machine\ temp) + \left(No.Of\ human * bodytemp\right)}{No.of\ machines + No.of\ humans}$$

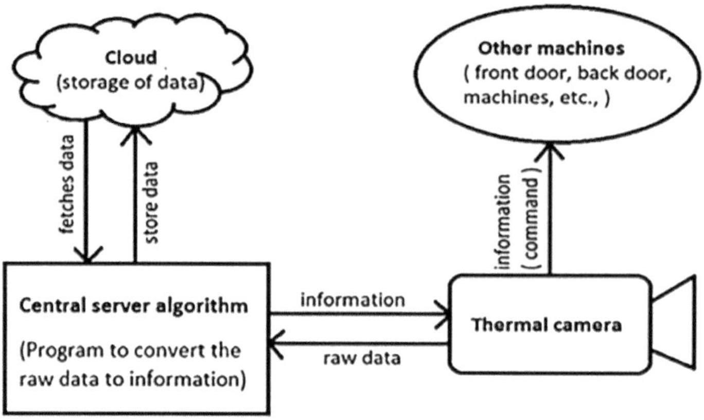

FIGURE 5.3 Representation of mechanism of thermal camera.

5.4.1.2 SCANNER

Identity cards of the employees are crucial in industries for security, employee confidence, company morale, customer relations, employee accountability, branding, and professionalism. So, it is important to verify the ID of the employee. Scanner is used to scan the ID card (Identity card) and fetch the information about the card that is used for further processing (Figure 5.8). It scans the barcode in the employee ID to get data about that person. Like the above thermal camera, this scanner also does not have any personal algorithm. It will transfer the data to the central server algorithm, that algorithm fetches the data from all the cameras and processes that raw data to make useful information about the ID card (Noguchi, Niibori, Zhou, & Kamada, 2015; Yang et al., 2020). The ID card contains the information about the particular person such as name, worker ID, address, DOB (Date of Birth), photo of the person, etc., and this information is already uploaded in the cloud. Thus, while scanning the ID card, all that information is fetched from the cloud and make use of that data for further use. If the person who is entering doesn't have an ID card or having an invalid ID card means it sends the information to the door to close and manager about the person who was entered. Due to 6G network, it conveys the information in 10 ms. The artificial intelligence will communicate to the person by asking questions about him/her and why he/she wants to get in. It also makes a confirmation about that person according to the perception if it satisfies with that further, it will open the door. Or else it doesn't open the door until it gets the information from the manager (Figures 5.6–5.8).

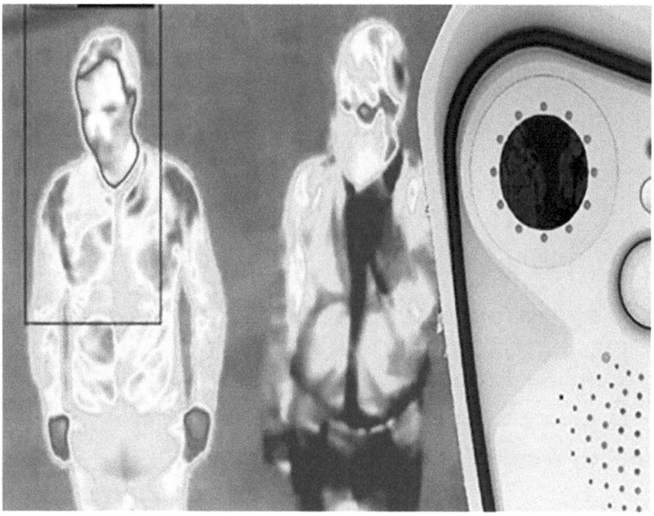

FIGURE 5.4 Human at thermal camera.

Source: Mobotix. https://www.mobotix.com/sites/default/files/styles/media_image/public/2020-03/mx_thermalm16_people_930x550.jpg?h=c4a9cdb7&itok=6uFJdeMX.

FIGURE 5.5 Normal vs. thermal camera.

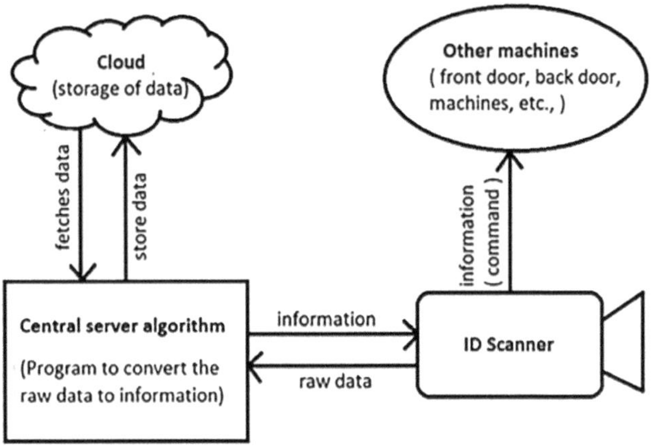

FIGURE 5.6 Representation of mechanism of ID scanner.

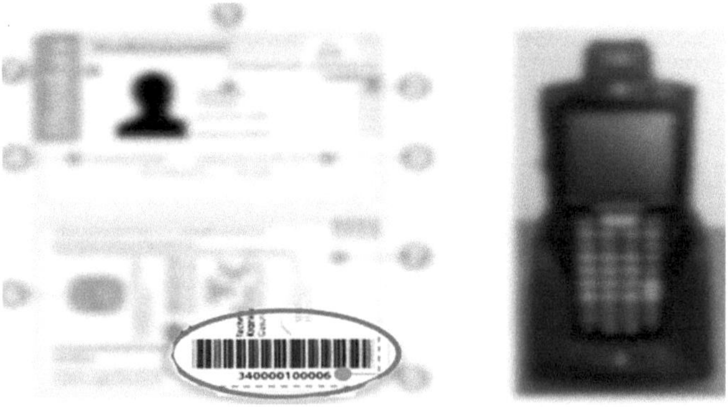

FIGURE 5.7 Bar code.

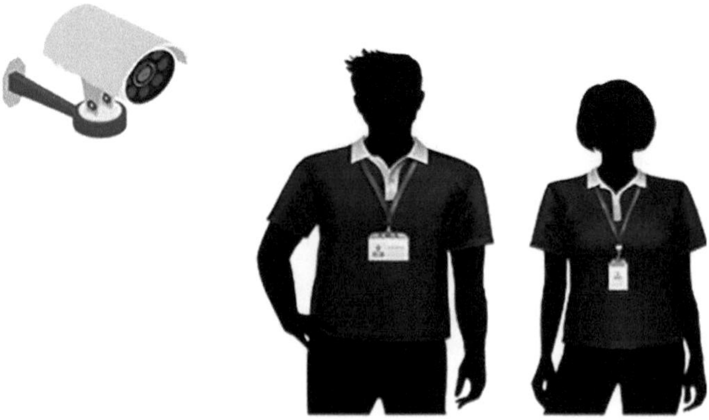

FIGURE 5.8 Camera observation.

5.4.1.3 NORMAL CAMERA

Nowadays, impersonation is increasing everywhere. Normal camera is used for the image processing to recognize the face of the human being who is entered as shown in Figure 5.9. This camera is used to identify the face of the employee and match it with the ID card which is worn by him/her. If the face is matched to the ID card, the camera will send the time and data about the person to the database of the industry. Then, it will calculate the working process. If it doesn't match, both front and back doors are closed, and artificial intelligence will interact with the person about why he/she wants to enter and why he/she is wearing another person's ID card. This information will also be transferred to the manager of the industry. Like the above thermal camera, it does not have any personal algorithm or program. It will transfer the data to the central server algorithm that fetches the data from normal cameras and scanners. After that it processes both normal camera data and scanner data together and makes an information about the link between the two data. This information will transfer to a normal camera. If the person's face doesn't match with the ID card, it will search the person on the internet to fetch the Aadhar details about the person and it will also check whether the name of the person is in the FIR or not. All this information is sent to the manager of the industry within 10 to 15 ms (millisecond) (Figure 5.10).

FIGURE 5.9 Camera observation.

FIGURE 5.10 DocFace+.

Source: Medium. https://miro.medium.com/v2/resize:fit:1200/1*3YU0QHDcHnNa7deSH3N5hQ.png.

5.4.1.4 WORKING

It is seen from Figure 5.11 that how the camera works, the algorithm and how all the three cameras are working together. All the three cameras are fixed at the entrance of the industry. When a person is entering into the entrance all the three can scan the person simultaneously (i.e., Thermal camera scans the person to check the temperature of the person, an ID scanner checks the ID card and scans its details, the normal scanner scans the face of the person). All the three cameras fetch the data from the person and send it to the central server algorithm (using 6G we can transfer the data faster with low latency). The server algorithm checks whether the temperature of the person is normal or not (Figure 5.11). If the temperature is high, then the front door (entrance of the industry) is closed. It will not allow the person to get in. Then the person will be noted as leave for the day in the database of the industry and this information will be transferred to the manager of the industry. Scanner scans the ID card and fetches the data of a person from the cloud. It scans the barcode in ID. The face scanner (normal camera fetches the face using image processing) detects the face and checks it with the ID card. If the face doesn't match, then both the front and back door (Way to out) are closed. He/she will be stuck inside the gates and artificial

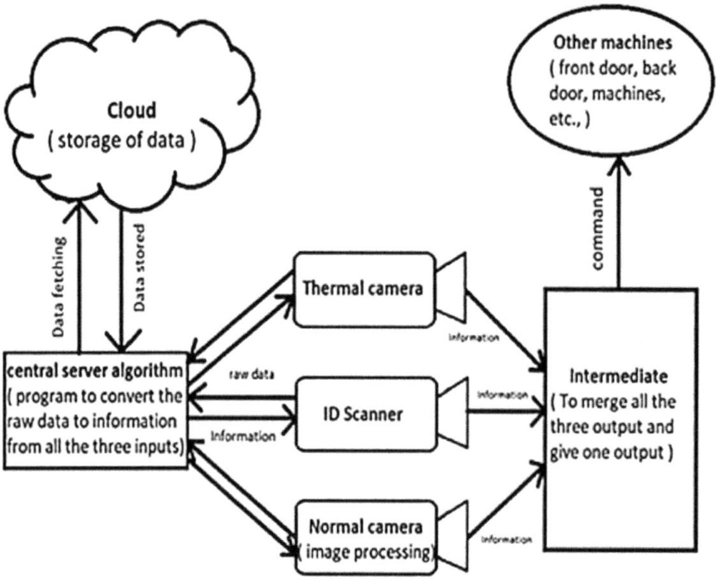

FIGURE 5.11 Representation of mechanism of all the three cameras.

intelligence will interact with the person by asking questions for confirmation and simultaneously the other side using the person's face, his/her Aadhaar card will be found on the internet. And it also checks whether the person is committed in any criminal cases by comparing the FIR copies with him/her data. All this information is transferred to the manager of the industry. If the person doesn't wear any ID card, then the front door is closed. After this, artificial intelligence will interact with the person and get the information about why he/she wants to get inside the industry and who they are. This information is transferred to the manager of the industry. If the manager said to permit, the artificial intelligence will permit them and they are considered as a visitor and their information are saved in the cloud like date, time, face, Aadhar ID, name, etc., This information is erased after a particular time which was decided by the owner or the high post officer of the industry. We can also change all these settings by communicating with artificial intelligence with some initial command or a password, etc.

5.4.2 INDUSTRIAL SECURITY

Event detection using image processing is explained. This topic fully depends on the image processing. In industries, everyone is busy with their work, they are unable to notice all the incidents happening around us. Nowadays, theft is highly increased. Many of the industries are suffering due to this issue, it requires many people to notice the problems, instead of that, a new model is introduced to overcome the above issue. Using artificial intelligence and image processing, the exact event happening is done in industries such as firing, fighting, giddiness, theft, etc., It will be informed that from all the emergency situations to their respective teams such as medical team, safety team, etc., From this, severe damage is prevented. In image processing, it is to train the model for each and every situation several times. If we increase the number of trainings, it helps to increase the efficiency of the process. After we developed the model, it is able to identify the event happening in the industry. Another method is to count the number of people who are all inside the industry. Once a person is entering through the entry gate, he/she is taken into account. And this total count is continuously updated to the central server algorithm. If they are less than the total count, it doesn't make any problem, if they are more than the total count, it means an unknown person is entering into the industry and so, it may make a problem. The major aim of this concept is to avoid theft in industries. Its objective is to find the theft occurrence and inform the higher manager to avoid or prevent the theft. It doesn't store or process the data; it actually transfers the data to the central server algorithm. In that place, only the processing of data is carried out. It works in two ways.

5.4.2.1 NUMBER OF PEOPLE METHOD

According to the above statement, in the entry of the industry, there is a security system to check whether the entering person is a worker or not. It also counts the number of people entering and number of people leaving. Actually, this data is required to calculate the average temperature of the room. So, this data must be stored in the cloud. This data (number of people entered) can be considered from the cloud. All the cameras which are placed inside the industry will transfer (using 6G (6th generation) the data can be transferred in a very fast manner) its data to the central server algorithm. It fetches all the data from the cameras which are inside the industry and calculates the number of people who are working inside the industry. The identification of human being is done by the image processing (using CNN model which is explained above). The algorithm will check whether the number of people working must be less than or equal to the number of people entered (Figure 5.12). If the number of people working is greater than the number of people entered, ensure that someone is entered through the wrong way and so, it has more possibilities of the person who might be a thief. So that if this case happened the algorithm will intimate the manager of the industry. Once the intimation is sent, all the doors are closed automatically and only one door will be opened to exit. All the workers those who are inside the industry have to gone through a security system to check them. In this way, the thief can easily be identified and also theft can be prevented. It is the simplest and easiest way to detect the theft (Figures 5.12–5.14).

5.4.2.2 IMAGE PROCESSING METHOD

In this method, all the events such as firing, fighting, giddiness, theft, etc., using image processing has lots and lots of algorithms and training data. It follows the steps such as acquisition of image, pre-processing, training the model using CNN and identification of events. In this method, there are some security cameras that capture all the activities of the workers inside the industry. All those cameras transfer all the data to the central server algorithm. All the data is processed only in this place and using a high processor, it can be possible. For transferring all the data in high speed, 6G network is used.

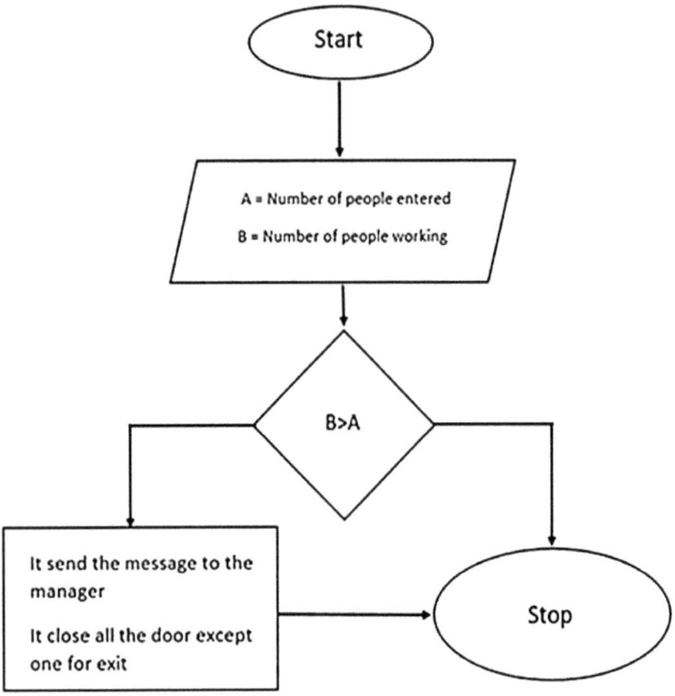

FIGURE 5.12 Representation of algorithm for theft detection.

FIGURE 5.13 Detection sample representation.

FIGURE 5.14 Animated representation.

All the trained data is stored in the cloud. While processing all the data, all the training data is taken from the cloud using 6G network. It compares both real-time data and the trained data. According to that, it can find the events. After finding, the event will send the information to the respective teams and the manager of the industry (Figure 5.15). It also sends the problem where it occurred. If an accident occurs like above, all the processes are taken, and this information will be transferred to the safety team, manager, and medical team. In case, the injury is quite heavy, or the person needs any operations. It is not possible to get him/her to the hospital. Because industry will release lots of pollution. So, it must be placed out of the city. Due to this situation, getting him/her to the hospital is quite difficult within the respective time. Artificial intelligence can connect with the doctor who is in the hospital, and it will work according to the instructions of the doctor. Similarly, if the doctor wants to raise the hand, the artificial intelligence hand will rise with very low latency because of using 6G (it is very fast). The data will reach the artificial intelligence in 0.001 μs (microsecond). In real time, the latency cannot be seen through the natural eyes. So, if any emergency case occurs, the doctor can do any operation in the hospital to the patient who is in the industry through artificial intelligence which is present in the industry. And that, all algorithms and data are changeable. It can be changed by giving some command to the artificial intelligence or he/she can create a password to change all those things. This can only be operated by the owner or the higher manager of the industry (Figure 5.15).

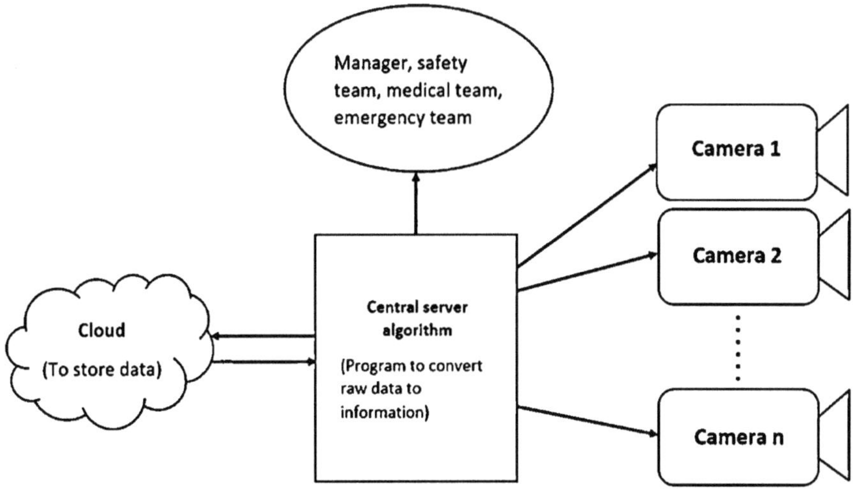

FIGURE 5.15 Representation of mechanism of security camera using image processing.

5.4.3 HUMAN DETECTION IN INDUSTRIES

Artificial Intelligence plays a vital role in the industrial field as it reduces the human consumption in the working place. Nowadays technologies have attained a drastic growth and the utilization and application of each development in the world is increasing. As the world is moving towards wireless communication, 5G has played a major role in today's technologies. The application of 5G in every field is integrated and without 5G in the current scenario humans cannot survive. Even though 5G has all the sophisticated technology improvements it couldn't meet the rising demands. So, 6G has been emerging to compete with the 5G demands in all aspects. The development of the 6G network is based on large scale, multi handling of huge data in all the environment. As the industries run with a lot of data the data handling is made easier and quicker with the 6G. The speed of transmitting the data to the trained model is made faster using the 6G. It is the key factor in the utilization of 6G in industrial application. As artificial intelligence has the influential learning ability, recognition ability and analysis ability the employment of AI into 6G network will optimize the performance of the model and also enhance the knowledge discovery and the decision-making ability. So, if the trained model has the highest efficiency and accuracy, the utilization of this model will be more useful for the industries in the detection of humans in the machine working areas. Large scale industries use heavy machines and machines which are in movement. In those industries, the role of human in those areas are too dangerous for both humans and machines. If any damage caused to human or to the machine, it is a great loss. In order to reduce or omit the loss, a model is being trained along with the application of 6G network. The proposed solution for the above-mentioned problem is, if any human being gets into the machine working areas, an alert or any intimation should be passed to the machine that there is a danger near x meters. Humans are portrayed as a danger to the machine. When the machine gets intimated, it should immediately stop its working. In order to make this happen, a model was trained with artificial intelligence using Convolutional Neural Network (CNN), image processing and Deep Learning techniques.

5.4.3.1 TRAINING A MODEL USING ARTIFICIAL INTELLIGENCE

Here two models are trained and at last both the models are combined to perform the task. One model is trained to identify the human and another model is trained to identify the machine. Firstly, a model is trained for human identification. To train a model, at first, it is needed that the datasets are to be collected. Different images of humans at different ages are collected and are grouped into datasets. Before feeding the images into the model, image processing techniques are to be applied.

5.4.3.2 *IMAGE PROCESSING FOR THE HUMAN IDENTIFICATION*

The images of different human beings are collected using smartphones and normal cameras. Each collected image is stored in PNG format. The image pre-processing techniques such as normalization, vectorization, image resizing, and augmentation of images are carried out in the Jupyter and Keras package using python. These techniques are followed to produce clear images.

5.4.3.3 *DATASET CREATION*

After the image processing techniques have been completed, the images collected are partitioned into datasets. In order to create the datasets for the partition, data augmentation is used. K-Fold cross validation is used for the partition of datasets as it is more optimized methodology for the machine learning technique. The value of K taken here is 10 so it is 10-fold cross validation. The collected images are divided by 10 and the resulting value is taken as the number of folds. Nearly 250 images of humans at different ages are collected and hence D=250/10=25 (25 folds). Here 200 images are used for training and the remaining 50 images are used for testing.

5.4.3.4 *CNN MODEL*

A CNN algorithm is developed to train the model. Here CNN is designed with the maxpooling layer. All the layers are listed one by one along with the filters, size, and shape. Different values are given for the filters and for each convolutional layer, a maxpooling layer is given. In the next layers, the values for the filters are increased. The values of the filters used are 32, 64, and 80. After giving the values for the datasets in the convolutional architecture, the model is compiled with the training datasets and numbers of epoch used to validate the training dataset are 30, 50, and 75. The best accuracy is obtained at the 50th epoch in the validation dataset. The same procedure is followed to evaluate the testing dataset, but the difference is each and every image should be cross checked with the training datasets. Therefore, every single image is first read by the model and according to the application of the algorithm, the evaluated results are obtained.

Thus, a model is trained for the identification of human of different ages using the image processing technique and Convolutional Neural Network (Figure 5.16). This model has an efficiency of about 98.8% in the detection of human.

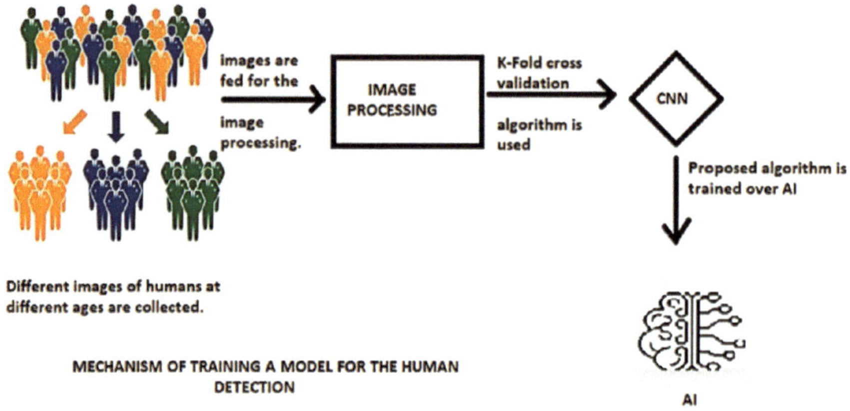

FIGURE 5.16 AI model for human detection.

Secondly, another model is going to be trained for the identification of machine. In this, training the model is bit easier when compared to training the model for the human identification. Since each human being is different from each other, different aged humans are captured, and the captured images are then processed. But in the case of machine, no such different types of images are needed. So, collecting the number of images to train the model is reduced and hence the efficiency is also high as it doesn't have much complexity in identifying the machine.

5.4.3.5 *IMAGE PROCESSING FOR MACHINE TRAINING MODEL*

As per the above trained model, the images of machines are collected from the CCTV camera and smartphone. These images are then stored in PNG format and the image processing techniques are applied to get more cleared and unbiased images. All these techniques are carried out in the Jupiter and keras package.

5.4.3.6 *DATASET COLLECTION*

Training and the validation dataset are generated with the help of the image data generator in the Jupiter. An array matrix is created for the RGB values, and it is modified to 0 to 1. Two classes are created for training dataset one is training and another one is validation. Now the training images are converted into datasets to feed into the convolutional neural network. For both training and validation dataset, target size, batch size and class mode are given. And the names of the labels will be the names of the folders used to store the collected images for training.

5.4.3.7 CNN ARCHITECTURE MODEL

The procedure followed for the CNN model in the identification of the human is followed for this model. The algorithm for the CNN model is followed up with the max pooling layer. Each layer is listed one by one below with the corresponding max pooling layer along with the filters. The number of filters needed, and the size of the filters are given as input. At last, 2 dense layers are given for the multiclass classification. The values of the filters used here are 16, 32, and 64. The values for the filters are in an increased manner due to the increase in the number of channels. After the process of compilation, the steps per epoch and the number of epochs is given for the training dataset. The epoch used are 15, 30, and 45. The highest efficiency is seen in the 30th epoch as 99.5%. The same steps in the identification of the human after compilation is followed for testing datasets.

Therefore, a model is trained (Figure 5.17) for the identification of machine using CNN and image processing with the efficiency of 99.5%.

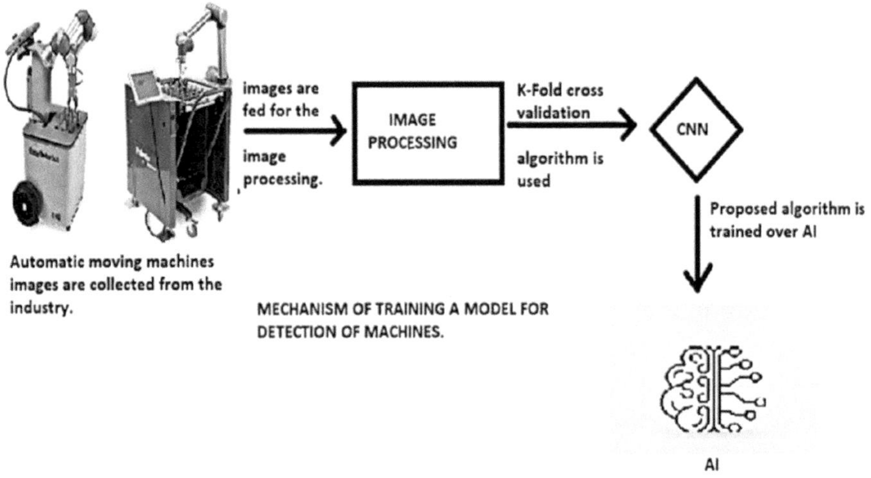

FIGURE 5.17 AI model for machine detection.

5.4.3.8 TRAINING A MODEL TO CALCULATE THE DISTANCE

Final step of this proposed method is to calculate the distance between the machine and the human when the human is detected by the trained model. As per the solution of the problem statement, when the human is detected within x meters, the machine is to stop working so that no damage or harm will happen both for humans and machine. Training a model to calculate the distance between the objects using the normal cameras is not possible. So, to implement the idea a camera is needed with a depth infrared sensor like interior sensor, it can be a camera with a lidar sensor. There are multiple options to be used. For this, the intel RealSense camera is to be used. The specification of this camera is, it has a RGB camera so the normal video can be seen with colors. Additionally, it has two stereo cameras which will get the depth of each specific pixel of the frame along with this, there is also an infrared projector. So, the first thing needed is to check the distance of the object and the depth of the object. Second thing we need is object detection. This is needed because only if the object is detected, the distance between the objects can be calculated. To perform these functions, two library functions are needed. One is an Intel RealSense camera and the second one is OpenCV. Along with that, it is to have a mask RCNN which is an eastern segmentation Arduino that will provide the detection of the object. And also, it will have a precise segmentation at the pixel level of the object.

5.4.3.9 IMPLEMENTATION IN OPENCV

Load the RealSense camera and get the frame from the real sense camera. From the RealSense camera, three things are obtained, one is retted next, second is BGR frame and the last one is depth frame. Ret is used to say whether a frame is true (frame is present) or false (frame is not present). To make sure whether the interior sense is getting the frame correctly, it is to get first the BGR frame. By getting the BGR frame, the video frame from the intel RealSense camera will be obtained. In this, 1st step is the attainment of video frame with the objects, but the depth details are not known. So, in the 2nd step, the depth of the objects is to be obtained. In the depth frame, the size of the frame is same as the size of the original frame, but the only difference is instead of showing the pixel of the frame with color, it shows the distance from the camera in millimeters (mm). Thus, to get a particular object distance, it is declared that the distance is equal to the depth frame and by mentioning the particular x and y axis values of the pixel that needed. In order to differentiate the particular pixel, the other pixels are searched in a circle or any shape that is drawn over the required pixel. Now to detect the object, MRCNN is used. These are the objects that are detected from the BGR frame. This mask CNN is to provide four different arrays. The first one is the boxes, second one is the classes, third one is the contour and the fourth one is the center. Boxes is nothing but the rectangle of where the object is located, and classes is what's the object is whether it is a person or things or anything. Contour is the precise boundaries of the detected objects. By using the contours, the mask is obtained and finally, the centers are nothing but the center point from which it is used to get the distance. From this point, the information will be provided from the depth camera. After getting this information, masks are going to be drawn on the BGR frame. So, for each different detection of the object, different colored mask is shown to differentiate the objects. Along with the mask, the depth of the object (distance) is also drawn as in Figure 5.20. Thereby, the distance of the objects is calculated.

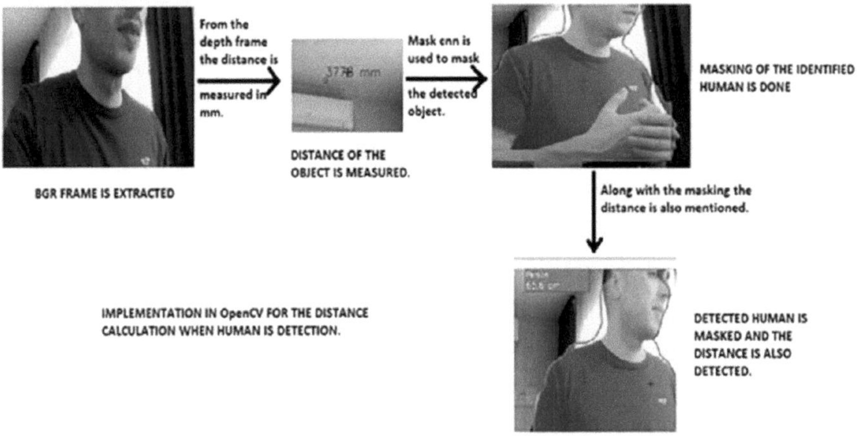

FIGURE 5.18 Implementation in OpenCV.

5.4.3.10 INTIMATION OF DANGER

The distance of the object is calculated from the machine. So, by placing the intel RealSense camera over the machine, the distance between the machine and the human if detected can be calculated. If the calculated distance between the machine and the human is 2 meters (i.e., meter as mentioned above. Here x=2) then the machine should be stopped from working. The distance calculating the data is passed actively to the trained model. The model is trained to intimate an alert message to the machine whenever the model gets the distance data less than or equal to 2 meters. So, the artificial intelligence model will use the 6G application in getting the transmitted data from the Intel RealSense camera. And 6G will make the transmission of data faster within a fraction of seconds. Since it is a live data, a faster data transmitting system is needed which will only merge along with the model. By utilizing 6G, the model can be made to react more efficiently. After the machine gets alert intimation from the trained model, it is designed to stop its working function. Thereby, at the distance of 2 meters, the machine will stop moving and working when the human is detected.

The overall algorithm for this trained model is shown in Figure 5.19. Therefore, overall efficiency of the model is about 98.9% to calculate the distance between the human and the machine and the intimation of danger is done correctly when the model id by detecting the human.

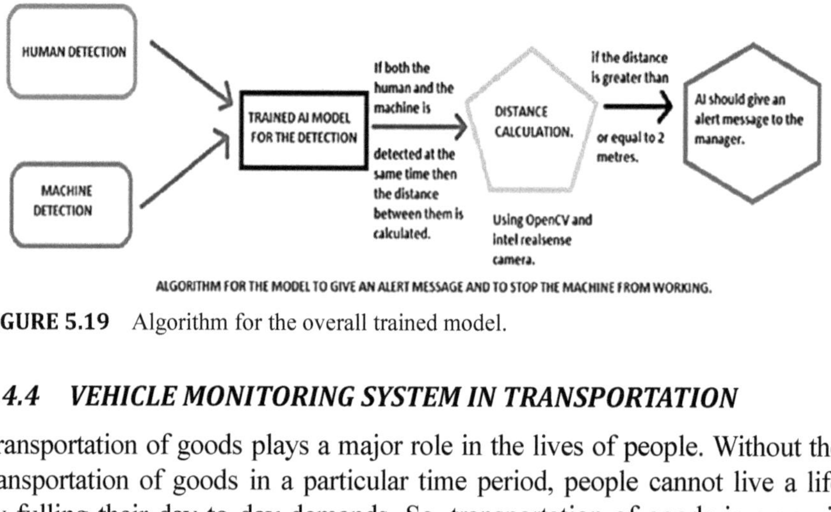

FIGURE 5.19 Algorithm for the overall trained model.

5.4.4 *VEHICLE MONITORING SYSTEM IN TRANSPORTATION*

Transportation of goods plays a major role in the lives of people. Without the transportation of goods in a particular time period, people cannot live a life by fulling their day to day demands. So, transportation of goods in a specified timeline is the most important factor. Most of the industrial cities such as Chennai, Bangalore are facing the issues in the transportation field due to heavy traffics across the cities. To manage the transportation systems in the industries, artificial intelligence along with the emerging 6G networks is implicated. Artificial Intelligence is an emerging technology in all the fields and the efficiency of using artificial intelligence in the transportation industry is much higher and gives a sophisticated life for the workers in the industry and also the economical profit of industry is increased. Here, the role of 6G is in the data transformation to the trained model. As 6G is the fastest communicating network with the lowest lagging, the model can get the data within a second and thereby the transporting system can be maintained according to the algorithm proposed. In order to make a real time information transporting system, it is to look around the parameters such as location, speed, theft detection, etc. In this study, a model is to be trained for intimation of the live location of the vehicle, speed of the vehicle, vibration of the vehicle, date, and in time of the vehicle in the industry and date and out time of the vehicle in the industry, working hours of the engine (Engine status), total run time of the vehicle and total off time of the vehicle. The above-mentioned data are collected separately and are fed to the trained model. If the data feeding into the model has differences from the algorithm in the trained model, an alert message or a notification should be passed by the model to the manager of the company and also the driver to overcome the issue.

5.4.4.1 LOCATION DETECTION

In each of the vehicle, a GPS location tracker is fitted to give the live location of the vehicle. The GPS is activated when the engine is started, and the vehicle starts moving. From the starting place of the vehicle, the location data is fetched using GPS. It also gives the last activated location of the vehicle. These live data are directly inserted into the model (Figure 5.20). This model is trained to give an intimation to the manager if the vehicle stops for a long time before reaching the destination. If the vehicle is lost, GPS location will not be tracked or whenever there is no data fetching from the GPS tracker, at that point an intimation or an alert message is to be passed to the higher officials (manager). Apart from that, the data of the GPS should always be displayed so as to check the current location of the vehicle or the activation status of the vehicle. Also, the higher officials who can have the access can check the location of the vehicle.

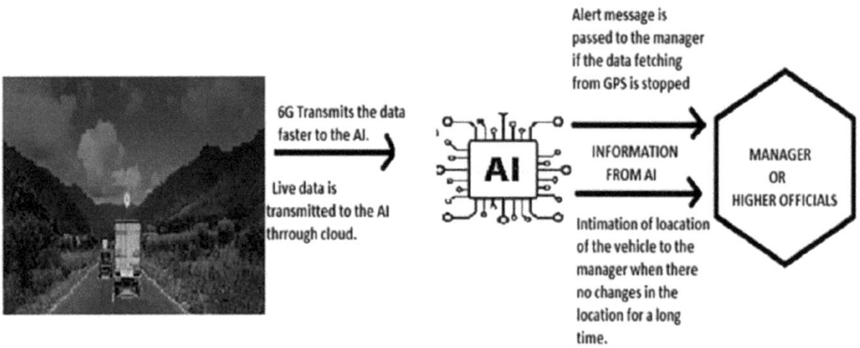

FIGURE 5.20 Mechanism of location intimation of AI.

5.4.4.2 SPEED DETECTION

Nowadays the percentage of accident occurring is increased in each and every seconds. Moreover, during the daytime, the accident happening rate has increased. The cause of these accidents is the unconsciousness of the driver, vehicle fault which leads to non-controlment of the vehicle of the driver, sleepiness of the driver or other unexpected situations happening in the environment (Sathesh et al., 2020). The safety of the driver is very must as it is a life (Koopman & Wagner, 2017). It's not a negligible one as the family of the driver greatly depends on the driver and also, along with the safety of the driver, the safety of the goods is also must. If the goods are delivered with damage, there is loss for the corresponding company and also for the consumers. So, in order to ensure the safety measures, digital speedometer is attached with the vehicles of the heavy vehicles. The data is extracted from digital speedometer. These live data are then fed into the model. Here the model is trained as when the speed of the vehicle increases across 100 Kmph and then, it should leave an intimation or an alert message to the driver and the manager as the speed of the vehicle is high as in Figure 5.21. Even after this intimation, if the speed of the vehicle is high, there is a continuous alert message to the manager to make the vehicle to stop immediately.

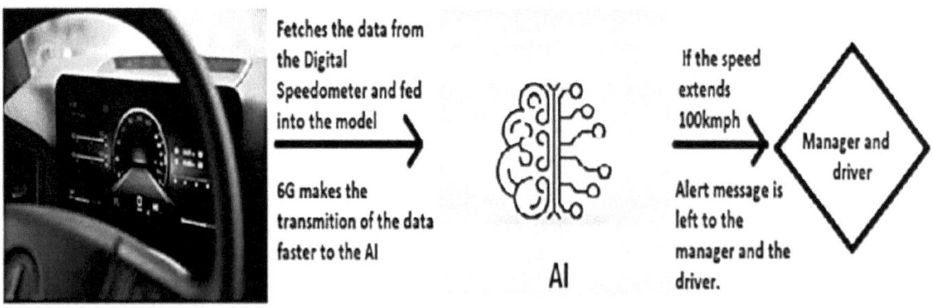

FIGURE 5.21 Mechanism of speed detection and representation of AI algorithm for intimation.

5.4.4.3 THEFT DETECTION AND VIBRATION SENSING

In this generation, the fear of theft of vehicles and the theft of goods in the container is increased. Artificial Intelligence has also grown in the areas of security management, and it plays a major role in industrial applications like transport systems. So, in order to reduce the theft happenings, the implementation of Artificial Intelligence along with the 6G in the transport system of the industry will play a vital role. Before feeding the data to the model, a surveillance camera or thermal camera is inserted or fixed in the container of the vehicle to detect the objects or the human other than the goods to be transported. The image processing techniques are followed to create the dataset for training the model and a CNN algorithm is proposed to detect the objects other than the goods. The live data from the camera inserted in the vehicle are directly taken from the image processing technique and after these processing, it is fed into CNN model (Figure 5.22). So, if the model detects any other objects or humans or if the present object is missing, an intimation message should be sent to the driver as well as the manager of the industry.

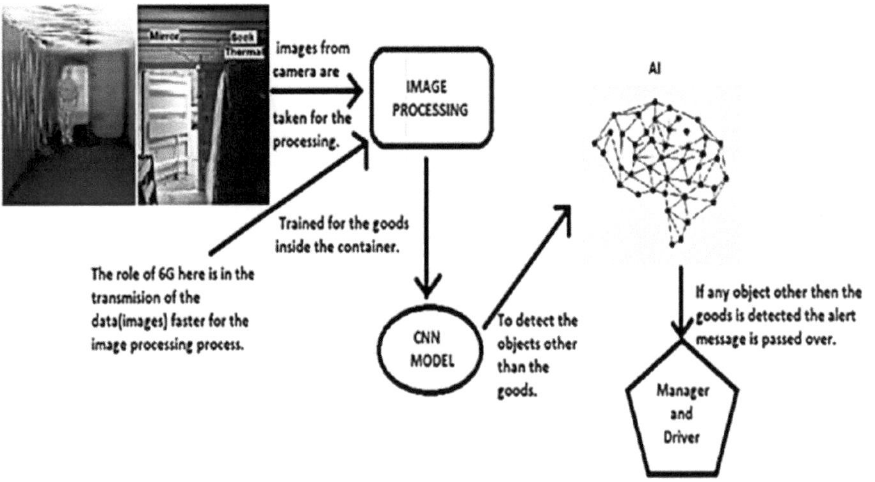

FIGURE 5.22 Theft detection model trained using image processing and implementation of 6G in the transformation of data.

5.4.4.4 VIBRATION SENSING

Another security application is the fix of vibrational sensors into the container. The vibrational sensor used is vibrational data logger. Here the data driven from the data logger is analog, so as to get the value from the analog signals, a test instrument is connected to mA meter or signal converter or to a data system is used to convert the data into digital. Now the data for the model are transmitted from the test instruments and the digital values are passed into the model. Here the model is trained to leave an intimation message to the driver if the frequency value exceeds the limit (limit=100) as shown in Figure 5.23. Even after the intimation if the data value is higher than the limit, an intimation should be passed to the manager or to the higher officials. The application of this implementation is if the vibration of the goods is higher, there will be a cause of damage to the goods. So, this implication will help in overcoming the damage caused in the goods.

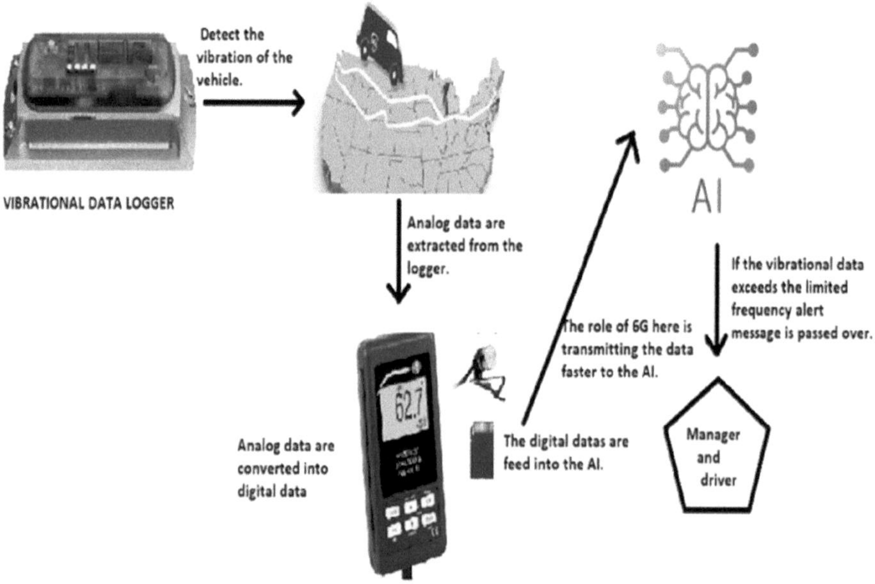

FIGURE 5.23 Detection of vibration using data logger and AI model is trained to leave an alert message.

5.4.4.5 ON DATE OFF DATE DATA COLLECTION

The data for the vehicle leaving and entering the industry along with the timings are noted at the security gate which are not manually recorded. It is also recorded in the digital format as in Figure 5.24. Now the data which are stored digitally are passed into the model. This data storing will help us whenever the information is needed to fetch or missed due to malfunctioning of the vehicle transportation system if any malfunctioning happened after once the vehicle left out the industry according to the data collected in the entry and the exit check out, it can approximately be detected where the vehicle is.

5.4.4.6 DATA TABLE

INDUSTRY NAME: TRANSPORT DEPARTMENT																		
VEHICLE MONITORING SYSTEM																		
VEHICLE NUMBER: 12						SPEED (Km/h)												
Sl. No.	ON DATE	ON TIME	OFF DATE	OFF TIME	ENGINE RUN DURATIN (MM:SS)	ENGINE OFF DURATIN (MM:SS)	IOLE	less_5	5_10	11_30	31_50	51_70	71_85	86_100	101_110	above 110	GPS Loss	Remarks
1	15-01-2022	21:17:56	15-01-2022	21:18:55	0:59	3:26	0:41	0:7	0:11	0:0	0:0	0:0	0:0	0:0	0:0	0:0	0:0	TO
2	15-01-2022	21:14:10	15-01-2022	21:14:30	0:20	3:44	0:12	0:4	0:4	0:0	0:0	0:0	0:0	0:0	0:0	0:0	0:0	TO
3	15-01-2022	21:10:08	15-01-2022	21:10:26	0:18	2:41	0:11	0:5	0:2	0:0	0:0	0:0	0:0	0:0	0:0	0:0	0:0	TO
4	15-01-2022	21:07:05	15-01-2022	21:07:27	0:22	2:43	0:12	0:10	0:0	0:0	0:0	0:0	0:0	0:0	0:0	0:0	0:0	TO
5	15-01-2022	21:03:59	15-01-2022	21:04:22	0:23	3:54	0:22	0:1	0:0	0:0	0:0	0:0	0:0	0:0	0:0	0:0	0:0	TO
6	15-01-2022	18:33:06	15-01-2022	21:00:05	146:59	11:52	13:19	6:49	7:3	22:54	41:38	55:4	0:11	0:0	0:0	0:0	0:1	TO
7	15-01-2022	16:57:55	15-01-2022	18:21:14	83:19	9:56	9:37	3:54	2:8	6:57	12:37	47:6	1:0	0:0	0:0	0:0	0:0	TO
8	15-01-2022	16:47:20	15-01-2022	16:47:59	0:39	4:3	0:16	0:9	0:14	0:0	0:0	0:0	0:0	0:0	0:0	0:0	0:0	TO
9	15-01-2022	16:41:06	15-01-2022	16:43:17	2:11	5:37	1:35	0:36	0:0	0:0	0:0	0:0	0:0	0:0	0:0	0:0	0:0	TO
10	15-01-2022	15:22:50	15-01-2022	16:35:29	72:39	7:13	6:21	2:13	1:18	4:48	8:47	47:37	11:35	0:0	0:0	0:0	0:0	TO
11	15-01-2022	13:02:18	15-01-2022	15:15:37	133:19	9:22	13:59	7:52	5:45	17:37	31:24	55:45	0:57	0:0	0:0	0:0	0:0	TO
12	15-01-2022	11:03:37	15-01-2022	12:52:56	109:19	7:7	3:36	1:56	2:41	13:58	26:28	59:13	1:25	0:0	0:0	0:0	0:2	TO
13	15-01-2022	09:39:27	15-01-2022	10:56:30	77:3	11:56	10:4	2:14	1:30	5:34	9:7	47:24	1:10	0:0	0:0	0:0	0:0	TO
14	15-01-2022	09:26:50	15-01-2022	09:27:31	0:41	16:20	0:19	0:14	0:8	0:0	0:0	0:0	0:0	0:0	0:0	0:0	0:0	TO
15	15-01-2022	08:00:46	15-01-2022	09:10:30	69:44	11:43	3:56	1:20	1:3	5:4	10:8	46:10	1:35	0:0	0:0	0:0	0:0	TO
16	15-01-2022	05:36:45	15-01-2022	07:49:03	132:18	17:16	16:4	5:54	3:16	14:7	28:16	62:48	1:30	0:0	0:0	0:0	0:23	TO
17	15-01-2022	05:18:48	15-01-2022	05:19:29	0:41	4:24	0:24	0:17	0:0	0:0	0:0	0:0	0:0	0:0	0:0	0:0	0:0	TO
18	15-01-2022	05:13:59	15-01-2022	05:14:24	0:25	3:25	0:23	0:2	0:0	0:0	0:0	0:0	0:0	0:0	0:0	0:0	0:0	TO
19	15-01-2022	05:03:19	15-01-2022	05:10:34	7:15	10:11	5:55	0:23	0:21	0:36	0:0	0:0	0:0	0:0	0:0	0:0	0:0	TO
20	15-01-2022	04:45:37	15-01-2022	04:53:08	7:31	254:25	7:15	0:16	0:0	0:0	0:0	0:0	0:0	0:0	0:0	0:0	0:0	TO
21	15-01-2022	00:29:48	15-01-2022	00:31:12	1:24	0:5	0:37	0:22	0:10	0:14	0:1	0:0	0:0	0:0	0:0	0:0	0:0	TO
22	15-01-2022	00:28:54	15-01-2022	00:29:43	0:49	3:18	3:43	0:5	0:1	0:0	0:0	0:0	0:0	0:0	0:0	0:0	0:0	TO
23	15-01-2022	00:24:28	15-01-2022	00:25:36	1:8	12:43	0:25	0:5	0:16	0:22	0:0	0:0	0:0	0:0	0:0	0:0	0:0	TO
24	15-01-2022	00:11:02	15-01-2022	00:11:45	0:43	3:40	0:18	0:14	0:11	0:0	0:0	0:0	0:0	0:0	0:0	0:0	0:0	TO
25	15-01-2022	00:07:04	15-01-2022	00:07:22	0:18	5:2	0:12	0:5	0:1	0:0	0:0	0:0	0:0	0:0	0:0	0:0	0:0	TO
26	15-01-2022	00:00:59	15-01-2022	00:02:02	1:3		0:45	0:18	0:0	0:0	0:0	0:0	0:0	0:0	0:0	0:0	0:0	TO
					TOTAL RUN TIME	14:11:50	01:37:41	00:35:45	00:26:51	01:32:11	02:48:26	07:01:07	00:09:23	00:00:00	00:00:00	00:00:00	00:00:00	
					TOTAL OFF TIME	07:06:06												

FIGURE 5.24 The data collected by the management system with the utilization of 6G network.

5.4.4.7 OVERALL MECHANISM OF THE VEHICLE MANAGEMENT SYSTEM`

All the parameters which were trained separately are combined together into a single model (Figure 5.25). If any one of the parameters needed to be intimated to the manager or the driver, that particular data alone is passed to the manager.

This model also enables the manager to check the data at the intermediate time. So, by combining all these parameter training of the model for separate parameters is reduced and all together one model is trained. This model has the efficiency in working along with 6G network as 97.6% and this implication system in the industries will help the transportation management system in the industries to work easier and faster and it also reduces the workload of the workers. This also reduces the number of workers needed to collect and maintain all these data. There will be no lagging of data detection as we use the most efficient technologies such as artificial intelligence and 6G.

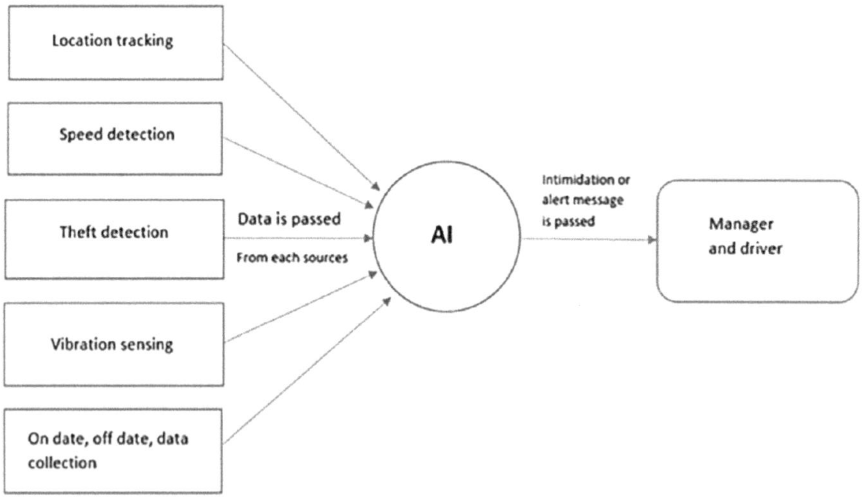

FIGURE 5.25 Process of AI.

5.4.5 *IMPLICATIONS OF AI IN INDUSTRIES*

By using artificial intelligence with 6G, the production can be increased because problems are identified earlier and solved. In industries, the securities have improved. Thermal cameras, normal cameras and scanners are used here for security purposes. The thermal camera is used to find the body temperature and the information are stored in the cloud. All these cameras sense the information, and these are stored in the cloud. The stored information is accessed by the people and can be solved quickly. While driving, to ensure the safeties of the people, speedometer devices are used. For monitoring the location of the vehicle, GPS location tracker is fitted in vehicle monitoring system. Intel real sense camera is used to monitor the distance between machines and humans. The distance is calculated by this device, and it stops working if the distance between them is reached the permissible limit. In the transport system of the industries, the fear of theft is more. In the transportation vehicle, camera is fixed, image processing is done and artificial intelligence with 6G is used here for prevention of theft. Moreover, the information is sent to the driver and the manager. In industries, to check the entry of the workers, there is a security system to count the number of people and by using this system, it can be identified who is entering the industry. The information about the vehicles entering and leaving the industry is noted at the security gate in digital format. If there is any problem occurred, the data is accessed, and the problem can be solved. During transportation, inside the containers, the vibrational sensors are kept identifying the vibration level. This system is for protection of goods from damages. And the vibration limit is set and if the vibration level crosses the limit, the information is sent to the manager or to the higher officials. The data from the vibrational sensor is analog. To convert the analog signal to digital signal, ADC converter is used. In the above techniques, the information is stored in the cloud. Cloud is nothing but a source of data storage. The information can be accessed anywhere and anytime. As 6G can use high frequencies, high capacity and very low latency, the information is passed very quickly. Due to high-speed network, raw materials are not wasted, there is a proper usage of raw materials because there will be monitoring of it. Everything is organized and the works are standardized. Equipment failures can easily be managed. Employees are properly engaged and monitored. From documents, AI collect the information and the review time is reduced. Future decisions are informed by AI so that, the operational efficiencies are improved. By using artificial intelligence, the productivity is increased by 40% or more. By using these techniques, time is saved, production is increased, and importantly without any problem and interruption, production will be in progress. In short, the efficiency of the whole industry is improved. If the production gets increased, the economy will be increased. In 6G, various research is going on regarding the applications in the industries. This updated technology will be useful in many industries.

5.5 CONCLUSION

Artificial intelligence with 6G in industries helps us to achieve 96% efficiency in production and it can reduce the extra spending. Artificial intelligence performs the task within the given time. Moreover, it works 24×7 without any interruption and breaks and it does not have downtime. Artificial intelligence creates the working place for next generation which reduces the human usage. It can perform higher level tasks and make the work easier for humans. Also, it reduces the work of differently abled people and transforms the job at ease. Artificial intelligence has a great potentiality that raise the efficiency of every industry.

AI can even play an important role in many fields like marketing, healthcare, finance, and data analysis. Recently, in combination with more technologies, AI enhances those applications and technologies empowering them to a great extent. Within a few years, AI will dominate each and every field and it will replace many tedious jobs. 6G is a network where research is going on to find suitable solutions for complex tasks. Artificial intelligence with 6G creates an impact in many places especially in industries where high manpower and high accuracy is needed. This technology in industries reduces the usages by human beings and reduces the mistakes done by them. In case the mistakes are very less, there will not be any losses and also no need to get panic of thefts. It could assure for proper monitoring. Also, there will be a proper protection when artificial intelligence is used. By using the above techniques in industries with the help of artificial intelligence in 6G, profits could definitely be increased which helps in the increase of overall GDP of the country.

KEYWORDS

- **artificial intelligence**
- **cloud**
- **data collection**
- **industrial automation**
- **IoT devices**
- **security**
- **thermal camera**
- **vehicle management system**
- **vibrational data logger**

REFERENCES

Ali, S., Saad, W., Rajatheva, N., Chang, K., Steinbach, D., Sliwa, B., Wietfeld, C., et al., (2020). *6G White Paper on Machine Learning in Wireless Communication Networks*. arXiv preprint arXiv:2004.13875.

Aslam, M. M., Du, L., Zhang, X., Chen, Y., Ahmed, Z., & Qureshi, B., (2021). Sixth generation (6G) cognitive radio network (CRN) application, requirements, security issues, and key challenges. *Wireless Communications and Mobile Computing.*

Han, G., Tu, J., Liu, L., Martínez-García, M., & Peng, Y., (2021). Anomaly detection based on multidimensional data processing for protecting vital devices in 6G-enabled massive IIoT. *IEEE Internet of Things Journal*, *8*(7), 5219–5229.

https://blogger.googleusercontent.com/img/b/R29vZ2xl/AVvXsEj7uitAR0T2Q1ALbHcdlipdle114VioONjIoljmzgYIEIzJY2ahxuIr3xqncrpoKajRJr90Y_SMmb7qD20DDdIl_U426AzI_rfMxX3W2YMgStUBrvMRyT3AucDFZpso H9MnbYGZWot Tsl7VSI8 Qx5w5daNlS5jnDmOcUeUYJatQXhRTSzniFA79mPIZ/s4745/AdobeStock_183573395.jpeg (accessed on 03 October 2023).

https://docplayer.biz.tr/docs-images/73/69056085/images/27-0.jpg (accessed on 03 October 2023).

https://i.ytimg.com/vi/nU6JdDijyMo/maxresdefault.jpg (accessed on 03 October 2023).

https://miro.medium.com/v2/resize:fit:1200/1*3YU0QHDcHnNa7deSH3N5hQ.png (accessed on 03 October 2023).

https://www.freepik.com/premium-photo/truck-trailer-container-docking-load-shipment-goods-pallets-warehouse-freight-industry-logistics-transport_6094136.htm (accessed on 03 October 2023).

https://www.mobotix.com/sites/default/files/styles/media_image/public/2020-03/mx_thermalm16_people_930x550.jpg?h=c4a9cdb7&itok=6uFJdeMX (accessed on 03 October 2023).

Kamruzzaman, M., (2021). *6G-Enabled Smart City Networking Model Using Lightweight Security Module.* Researchsquare preprint 10.21203/rs.3.rs-954242/v1.

Koopman, P., & Wagner, M., (2017). Autonomous vehicle safety: An interdisciplinary challenge. *IEEE Intelligent Transportation Systems Magazine*, *9*(1), 90–96.

Letaief, K. B., Chen, W., Shi, Y., Zhang, J., & Zhang, Y. J., (2019). A. The roadmap to 6G: AI empowered wireless networks. *IEEE Communications Magazine*, *57*(8), 84–90.

Lin, H., Garg, S., Hu, J., Kaddoum, G., Peng, M., & Hossain, M. S., (2020). A blockchain-based secure data aggregation strategy using 6g-enabled nib for industrial applications. *IEEE Transactions on Industrial Informatics*.

Maheswaran, S., Sathesh, S., Karthik, R., Murugesan, G., Gomathi, R., & Duraisamy, P., (2021). An innovative method for identification of artificially ripened banana using single board computer. In: *2021 12th International Conference on Computing Communication and Networking Technologies (ICCCNT)* (pp. 1–7).

Maheswaran, S., Sathesh, S., Priyadharshini, P., & Vivek, B., (2017). Identification of artificially ripened fruits using smart phones. *International Conference on Intelligent Computing and Control 2017 (I2C2)., 4*, 178–183.

Nayak, S., & Patgiri, R., (2021). 6G communication technology: A vision on intelligent healthcare. In: *Health Informatics: A Computational Perspective in Healthcare* (pp. 1–18). Springer.

Noguchi, S., Niibori, M., Zhou, E., & Kamada, M., (2015). Student attendance management system with Bluetooth low energy beacon and android devices. In: *2015 18th International Conference on Network-Based Information Systems.*

Padhi, P. K., & Charrua-Santos, F., (2021). 6G enabled industrial internet of everything: Towards a theoretical framework. *Applied System Innovation*, *4*(1), 11.

Sathesh, S., Pradheep, V. A., Maheswaran, S., Premkumar, P., Gokul, N. S., & Sriram, P., (2020). Computer vision based real time tracking system to identify overtaking vehicles for safety precaution using single board computer. *Journal of Advanced Research in Dynamical and Control Systems*, *12*(7), 1551–1561.

Yang, H., Alphones, A., Xiong, Z., Niyato, D., Zhao, J., & Wu, K., (2020). Artificial-intelligence-enabled intelligent 6G networks. *IEEE Network*, *34*(6), 272–280.

Zhang, Z., Cao, Y., Cui, Z., Zhang, W., & Chen, J., (2021). A many-objective optimization based intelligent intrusion detection algorithm for enhancing security of vehicular networks in 6G. *IEEE Transactions on Vehicular Technology*.

CHAPTER 6

A New Deep Learning Approach for Stock Price Prediction Using CNN-BILSTM and ARIMA-LSTM

PRIYANKA MAHAJAN,[1] PRABHPREET KAUR,[2] and NEELAM SHARMA[3]

[1]*Research Scholar, Department of Computer Engineering and Technology, Guru Nanak Dev University, Amritsar, Punjab, India*

[2]*Faculty, Department of Computer Engineering and Technology, Guru Nanak Dev University, Amritsar, Punjab, India*

[3]*Faculty, Department of Artificial Intelligence and Machine Learning, Maharaja Agrasen Institute of Technology (MAIT), GGSIPU, New Delhi, India*

ABSTRACT

Investment in stock markets is a large percentage of the economy of any country. If stock market trends can be predicted with proper methodology, investors can maximize returns. Predicting the stock market's behavior has become a critical requirement, making it one of the active study topics. In order to propose answers to this challenging issue, data modeling and machine learning have been widely used. Deep learning has shown success in recent years in handling such difficult tasks. In the literature, time series prediction was done using autoregressive integrated moving average (ARIMA) models. This study's goal is to employ a ground-breaking technique for stock price forecasting by making use of machine learning models and then comparing them with time series models like ARIMA, Seasonal Auto-Regressive Integrated Moving Average with exogenous factors (SARIMAX). Besides this, two hybrid model approaches named ARIMA – with long short-term memory

Advanced Digital Technologies in Financial and Business Management: Unleashing the Power of Artificial Intelligence, Machine Learning, Blockchain, and the Internet of Things. Jyoti Batra Arora, Nitish Pathak, and Neelam Sharma (Eds.)

(ARIMA-LSTM) and Convolution Neural Network-Bidirectional LSTM (CNN-BiLSTM) are also proposed for forecast purposes. The proposed strategy outperforms more conventional machine learning techniques in terms of both prediction accuracy and speed. ARIMA-LSTM shows an accuracy score of approximately 97.4%, while CNN-BiLSTM shows an R2 score of 0.963150. Investing in stocks can be made easier by comparing the predictions given by each of the seven different models.

6.1 INTRODUCTION

The client as well as the stockbroker can make a lot of money if they correctly predict the stock market. Due to the inherent uncertainty and non-linearity of the financial markets, effective stock market return forecasting is a significant challenge. Time dependence is a crucial factor in stock price prediction movement. Time series analysis is a popular method for describing data that changes over time. Auto-Regressive Integrated Moving Average (ARIMA) models, proposed by Kumar & Thenmozhi (2014), are the most widely utilized technique for modeling time series data. Nevertheless, the inherent volatility and fluctuating variance of stock prices are ignored by this linear model. Due to this, ARIMA is not considered a good fit for predicting stock prices. But, with the latest technological advances in computing and data science, machine learning has become popular and suitable method for prediction purpose.

Non-linear and non-stationary stock market data are extremely difficult to break down and forecast because of their high heteroskedasticity (Wadi et al., 2018). Shares may be down for a long period with no returns. During the 2008, stock market meltdown, intraday trading of the DJIA (Dow Jones Industrial Average) lost 777.68 points. Sensex fell around 1,500 points after Corona Virus strikes global stock markets. Investing at the wrong moment can quickly lower rewards. Supporters of the efficient market hypothesis theory claim that it is impossible to anticipate future stock values with any degree of precision. But studies show that it is feasible, to accurately estimate the price of stocks (Sen et al., 2021). The approaches followed for the stock market forecasting (Yadav et al., 2022) are described below (Figure 6.1):

1. **Fundamental Analysis:** It focuses on the business of a stock rather than simply analyzing the stock itself. This technique uses the past success of the firm and the trustworthiness of its financials to make predictions about the stock's future value.
2. **Technical Analysis:** These techniques don't take into account the company's underlying business model; instead, they rely on stock price

trends and patterns. Methods like AR, MA, and ARIMA fall within this group. These techniques work best for making short-term forecasts.

3. **Machine Learning:** Time series forecasting is becoming increasingly challenging, but AI is emerging as a powerful answer. Over the past decade, several AI (Artificial Intelligence) and ML (Machine Learning) approaches have been applied to stock market forecasting. This is due to its ability to extract data characteristics from high-frequency raw data without requiring any specialized previous knowledge.

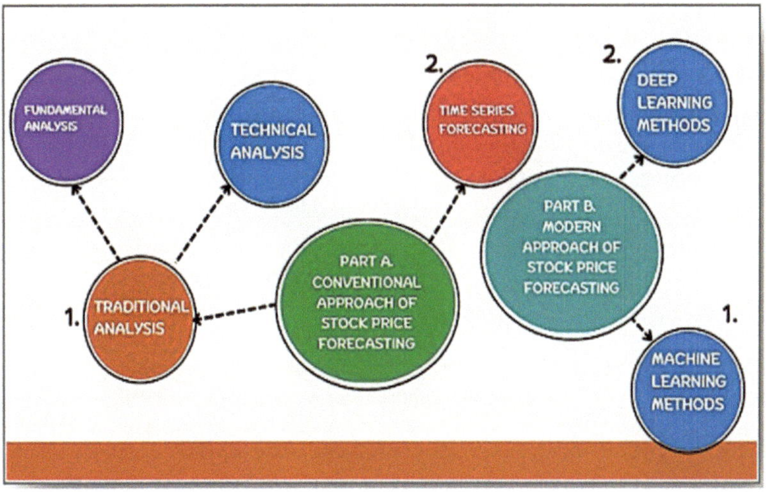

FIGURE 6.1 Categories of various stock market prediction (SMP) techniques.

Historically, stock price forecasts have depended on segmenting the stock price time series (Pratheeth & Vishnu Prasad, 2021). Technical analysts have used a variety of approaches for the examination of stock prices. There are always highs and lows in the stock market. Investors now see the market and its risks; quite differently than they did in the past.

In the study, the model for the stock price forecasts problem are tried to be built using several methodologies and algorithms. Statistical, machine learning and deep-learning models have been created but none has worked. News data from NSE (National Stock Exchange), Economic Times, and even Twitter are not being considered (Prasad et al., 2022).

The rest of the paper is organized as follows. Conventional techniques for predicting the stock market are briefly discussed in Section 2. Section 3 makes familiar to the research gaps which are found in previous literature. Section 4 discusses the thorough objective of this study. Section 5 describes the dataset and the platform on which prediction can be easily performed without any error. Finally, Section 6 shows the result and discussions followed by the conclusion in Section 7.

6.2 LITERATURE REVIEW

In this section, the research conducts a literature analysis on the topic of predicting stock market data using machine learning and deep learning architectures. The literature review of individual models for Stock price predictions is specified in Table 6.1.

TABLE 6.1 Enlisted Studies Where SMP is Carried Out Using ML and Deep Learning Models

Author of the Research Study/Published Year	Technique Implemented	Brief Methodology
Tay & Cao/2001 (Cao & Tay, 2003)	SVM	Compared SVM with BP neural network and regularized RBF.
Nassar; Okwuchi (Nassar et al., 2020).	LSTM	Compared conventional ML models to statistical models and then finally compared DL models with conventional ML approaches.
Sen; Mehtab/2021 (Sen & Mehtab, 2021)	Gamut of 10 deep learning algorithms.	Designed deep learning regression models to accurately forecast daily stock prices. Six models take advantage of LSTM architecture, while four use CNN architecture.
Marah et al./2021 (Thormann et al., 2021)	LSTM with sentiment categorization.	Financial feature engineering, using prior tweets, mood analysis, and technical financial indicators to predict Apple stock values 30 m and 60 m ahead.
Mootha, Sridhar, Seetharaman, & Chitrakala/2020 (Mootha et al., 2020)	Bi-directional LSTM	Sequence to sequence modeling method to predict OHLC.
Liu & Long/2020 (Liu & Long, 2020)	EWT, LSTM, and ORELM	Empirical wavelets transform (EWT) to deconstruct the data, LSTM to forecast and ORELM (outlier robust extreme learning machine) for correction.
Kang et al./2019 (Zhang et al., 2019)	GAN (generative adversarial network) architecture	LSTM as a generator and MLP (multi-layer perceptron) as a discriminator. Also outperforms LSTM, ANN, and SVR.
Bollen et al. (2010, 2011)	Market prediction through twitter moods and SOFNN.	Two mood tracking tools, OpinionFinder and Google-Profile of Mood, examined daily Twitter feeds and predicted values of DJIA.

Presently, the financial market is a chaotic, unstructured dynamic system. Complex, high-dimensional, and noisy stock market data cannot be analyzed accurately using only the conventional econometric methods or statistical methods (Lu, Li, Wang et al., 2020). Hence, some researchers switched towards use of hybrid models for share price prediction movement:

- Abraham et al. (2001) presented one of the earliest hybrid models in 2001, which combined neuro-fuzzy logic with artificial neural networks.
- One such neural network-based time series forecasting strategy was suggested by Sun et al. in 2005. This strategy employs the optimal partition algorithm (OPA) in combination with a radial basis function (RBF) neural network.
- To predict future time series Sallehuddin, Shamsuddin, & Hashim (2008; Sallehuddin et al., 2007), introduced the ANN-ARIMA model, which was built on the GRANN ("Grey relational artificial neural network").
- A strategy combining random walk (RW) and ANN was suggested in 2014 by Adhikari et al. (2014) to predict four financial time series data, and the results demonstrated an increase in forecasting accuracy.
- Another comparable design, developed by Selvin et al. (2017) combines RNNs, CNNs, and LSTMs.
- The slow training speed and low accuracy of the original BP (Back Propagation) neural network training method were ameliorated by the LM-BP neural network stock price forecasting network structure published in 2018 by Zhang et al.
- The ANN-ARIMA hybrid model was shown to provide more accurate results than the conventional ARIMA-ANN model as part of study (Khashei & Hajirahimi, 2019) investigating the usage of hybrid models to manage the complexity of linear and nonlinear components. The timeline of hybrid models is shown as in Figure 6.2.
- In their paper, Eapen et al. (2019) introduced a CNN/Bi-LSTM hybrid model. An individual network-based model outperformed the suggested model by 9%.
- The 2020 predictions for four big US public corporations were made by Kamalov (Alibašić et al., 2019) using MLP, CNN, and LSTM. The experimental findings demonstrated that compared to other research that predicted the direction of price change, these three techniques produced more accurate results.

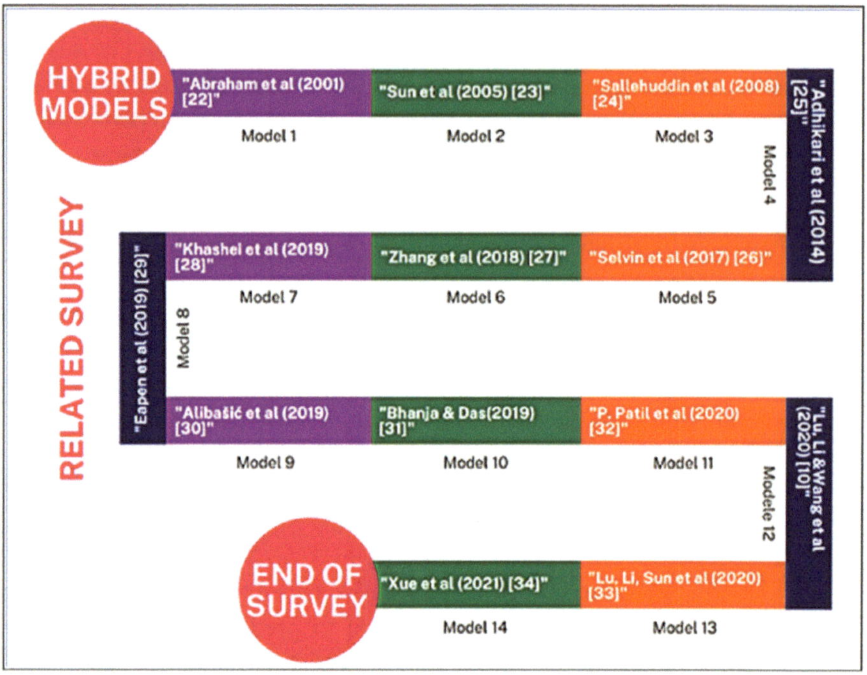

FIGURE 6.2 Hybrid models of deep learning as per the survey conducted.

- To predict future stock values, Bhanja & Das (2019) presented a deep-learning ensemble model that included CNN and LSTM.
- Patil et al. (2020) recommended investigating the possibility of creating a hybrid model for prediction by combining graph theory and machine learning.
- The authors of this research (Lu, Li, Wang et al., 2020) recommend using a CNN-BiLSTM-AM framework in 2020 to predict the stock price at the end of the trading day. Components of this strategy include CNN, bidirectional long short-term memory (BiLSTM), and an attention mechanism (AM).
- Several academic studies, including one by Lu et al. (2020) have proposed the CNN-LSTM model for accurate stock price forecasting. This approach combines the strengths of Convolutional Neural Networks (CNNs), which are good at extracting useful features from the data, with Long Short-Term Memory (LSTM) networks, which are good at discovering dependencies among data points in time series.

- Yan et al. (2021) created a high-precision short-term forecasting model of financial market time series in 2020 using LSTM deep neural networks. They compared it to BP neural networks, ordinary RNNs, and improved LSTM deep neural networks. The results confirmed LSTM's superiority in forecasting accuracy and other measures.

6.3 RESEARCH GAPS

- **RQ1:** Why limited research focuses on the use of deep learning mechanisms for SMP (Stock market prediction) to determine the future prices of the stocks?
- **RQ2:** How technical indicators can influence the irregular term lengths to improve research direction in reliable forecasting of future prices of stocks?
- **RQ3:** How can the latest sentiment analysis techniques be merged with feature engineering to make them a complete prediction system?
- **RQ4:** Which of the models can use a hybrid technique or mechanism to act as accurate predictors of the financial market?

The preceding sections answer some of these gaps in depth by discussing where further study is needed.

6.4 OBJECTIVES

The main objectives and contributions of the current work are as follows:

- Comparative analysis of several machine learning algorithms is carried out.
- The research includes the oldest model named ARIMA for SMP as this model of time series gives the most accurate results in terms of short-time investment.
- The research study also proposes the use of hybrid models based on ARIMA-LSTM and CNN-LSTM for the prediction of time-series data (Khashei & Hajirahimi, 2019).

6.5 METHODOLOGIES

This section gives the main procedure of the methods used as follows. The research workflow diagram of the proposed work is presented in Figure 6.3.

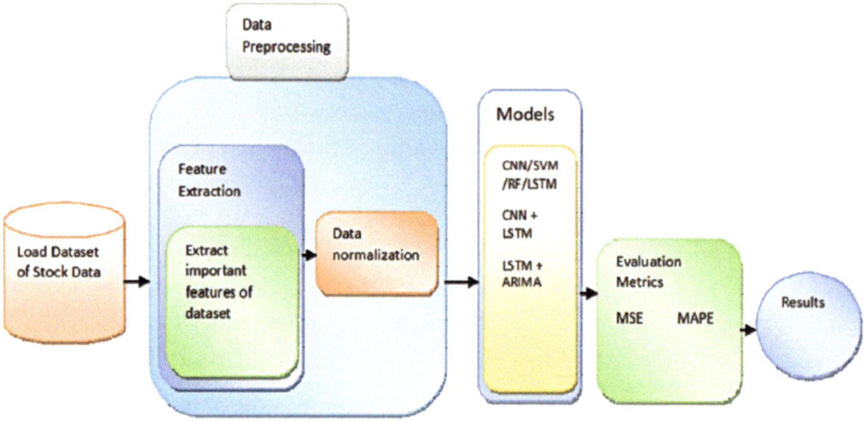

FIGURE 6.3 The workflow diagram of the proposed research study.

6.5.1 DATASET USED FOR RESEARCH

The research study has obtained the dataset or the stock values from Yahoo finance. The dataset uses five common variables provided by Yahoo Finance: OHLCV which includes information about Open price, High price, Low price, Close price, and Volume of one particular stock sold in each day interval.

The research work has included data from "APPLE" company for predictive analysis. Apple develops and sells both computer software and hardware. Based on the past 21 years of stock price data dataset for this study includes the period 01 January 2001 to 31 December 2022, with 5,535 data instances. In this process, the model with the least RMSE is taken as the final model for prediction.

6.5.2 DATA PREPROCESSING

The process of normalizing data aids the model in reaching a minimum, either locally or globally. Adjusted factors, Adjusted Close, etc., are derived from raw data by pre-processing.

Yahoo Finance data is in (.csv) files with four inputs and one output. The attribute Date/Time has been eliminated because it doesn't affect the prediction. The data has been normalized using a min-max scaler as the succeeding Eqn. (1) shows:

$$y^* = (y - \min)/(\max - \min) \tag{1}$$

where; y* represents the new value of data; y represents an old value of data; min is the minimum value of the sample; and max is the maximum value of the sample.

To eliminate randomness, the translation of y* is done to the interval [0, 1]. Next, it's divided into 70% training data and 30% testing data to avoid overfitting and provide a fair evaluation of the models (Al-Bashabsheh & Abu Alasal, 2021).

6.5.3 MODELS USED

To compare the proposed hybrid model with the existing similar models, a few baseline models are initially considered, and then the state-of-the-art models. The following baseline models for the study are considered:

- ARIMA is a widely known model for time series forecasting that works on the concept of Moving Average. It is based on the trend, stationarity and seasonality of the data (Wadi et al., 2018). The limitation with this model is that it cannot be automated for all kinds of stocks, and the need is to set different p, d, and q (number of autoregressive terms, number of non-seasonal differences needed for stationarity, number of lagged forecast errors respectively) values for different stocks.
- LSTM is a well-established model used for time series forecasting and is frequently applied for stock market price prediction. It is a derived RNN with forget gate functionality. LSTMs are very effective for long as well as short-term predictions.
- CNN is a kind of feedforward neural network, which has good performance in image processing and natural language processing, time series. The local perception and weight sharing of CNN can greatly reduce the number of parameters, thus improving the efficiency of model learning (Lu, Li, Li et al., 2020).

6.5.3.1 PROPOSED MODEL

This consists of two hybrid models designed recently and extensively used in stock price prediction. The hybrid models are ARIMA-LSTM and CNN-BiLSTM. The model consists of Time Distributed Bidirectional LSTM.

In first step, individual models namely ARIMA, CNN, and LSTM are tested on data collected. Then in the second step, after contrasting and comparing these predictive models based on RMSE, the research proposals for hybrid models has been carried out for the same dataset.

6.5.4 MODELS EXPLANATION

6.5.4.1 ARIMA MODEL

The classic ARIMA model is still utilized in financial time series (Lee & Jin, 2007; Merh, Nitin, Saxena, Viond, & Pardasani, 2010). The ARIMA model offers several advantages when applied to real-world data, especially for making short-term predictions (Becker et al., 2015). ARIMA forecasts using the Box Jenkin method, which says nonstationary data may be rendered stationary by differentiating the series, Eqn. (2) shows the series Z_t in which θ and φ are unknown values (Prasad et al., 2022).

$$Z_t = \varnothing_1 Z_{t-1} + \varnothing_2 Z_{t-2} + \ldots \varnothing_p Z_{t-p} + \varepsilon_t + \theta_1 \varepsilon_{t-1} + \theta_2 \varepsilon_{t-2} + \ldots . \theta_q \varepsilon_{t-q} \quad (2)$$

where; Z_t is the actual value and ε_t is the random error at t, ϕ_i, and θ_j are the coefficients, and p and q are integers that are greater than zeros and are often referred to as autoregressive and moving average, respectively. Z_{t-1}, Z_{t-2}, …, Z_{t-p} = Response variable at time lag t – 1, t – 2, …, t – p, respectively.

The ARIMA model is a combination of three methods which are namely:

1. **AR:** Time series values are logged before and after regression are applied to them. A symbol for this purpose is 'p.'
2. **Differencing:** It compares successive time series values. Nonstationary time series data are differenced to eliminate trends and turned into stationery. Variable 'd' stands for this case. If d = 1, the difference between the entries in the time series is considered; if d = 2, the difference between the findings obtained at d = 1 is examined.
3. **MA:** This is represented by 'q' which meant how many values in the error term had been delayed.

   ARIMA algorithm for SMP is as in subsections.

6.5.4.1.1 ARIMA Algorithm for Stock Market

- Extract the values of stock market data, i.e., open, close, high, low, volume, adjusted close.

- Normalize and pre-process the data to extract the following values:
    - Low = min. value.
    - High = max value.
    - First, last, median, mean.

    Also, calculate the rolling mean and ewma (Exponential weighted moving average) from the data.

- The time series will be checked for stationarity (p).
- If the data has nonstationarity, the stationarity will be achieved through difference (d).
- Applying Augmented Dickey-Fuller test and calculating p-value.
- Use PACF and ACF, Identity whether to include AR, MA, or both.
    - In ACF:
        - a positive autocorrelation in lagged values, implement AR model.
        - a negative autocorrelation in lagged values, implement MA model.
    - In PACF, If the PACF plot decreases at lagged values, then use the AR model and if the drop in PACF is more gradual then use the MA model.
- Plot the graph for actual versus predicted price and calculate the accuracy of prediction.

This research makes use of two models of ARIMA. One is ARIMA(5,1,0) which is combined with LSTM, a deep-learning Regression model.

6.5.4.2 CONVOLUTIONAL NEURAL NETWORK (CNN)

In 1995, LeCun and his co-workers published a study in which they described Convolutional neural networks for the first time (Shah et al., 2022). CNN is a feed-forward neural network that excels at image processing and Natural language processing (NLP) (Liu et al., 2017). It is possible to use it productively for the task of predicting time series (Kim & Kim, 2019) since it can record both sequential and spatial data simultaneously.

An input and an output layer, as well as several hidden layers, make up a CNN. CNN's hidden layers consist of convolutional and pooling layers organized in a sequence that is compressed and followed by a fully linked network.

Eqn. (3) shows calculating each convolution layer's convolution kernels can be found in the preceding sentence. The features of the data are extracted from the convolution operation of the convolution layer, but the extracted feature dimensions are very large, After the convolution layer, a pooling layer is placed to lower the feature dimension and cut training costs.

$$l_t = tanh\ x_t * k_t + b_t \tag{3}$$

where; l_t represents the convolution output value, tanh is the activation function. The tanh activation function is associated with the range of output values [–1, 1], x_t is the input vector, k_t is the convolution kernel weight, and b_t represents the convolution kernel's bias (Liu et al., 2017). These layers are called hidden layers because the activation function and final convolution hide their inputs and outputs. Backpropagation is employed in the last convolution layer to add weight.

In convolution filters, matrices are employed. In the convolutions layer, the filter examines the image's features to construct a left-to-right feature map (Patel et al., 2015). The kernel matrix is known as a filter is shown as in Figure 6.4.

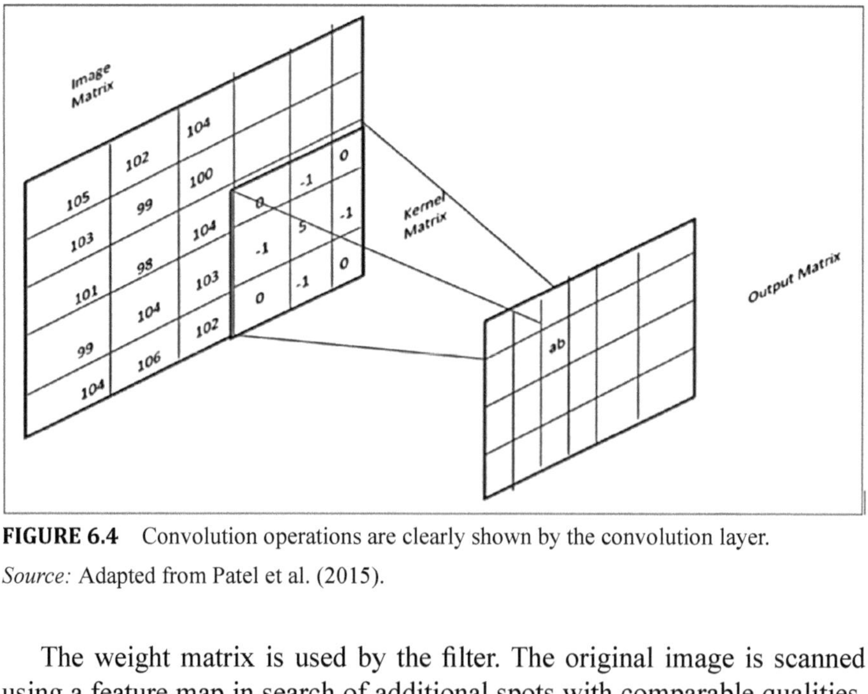

FIGURE 6.4 Convolution operations are clearly shown by the convolution layer.

Source: Adapted from Patel et al. (2015).

The weight matrix is used by the filter. The original image is scanned using a feature map in search of additional spots with comparable qualities.

The feature maps received by the filter should be listed vertically and horizontally to create a single sheet, as illustrated in the center of Figure 6.5. The number of feature maps that may be generated increases exponentially when more than one filter is applied. Compression of feature maps in a CNN pooling layer reduces the number of the model's parameters. Create a new image by re-applying the filter depending on the image.

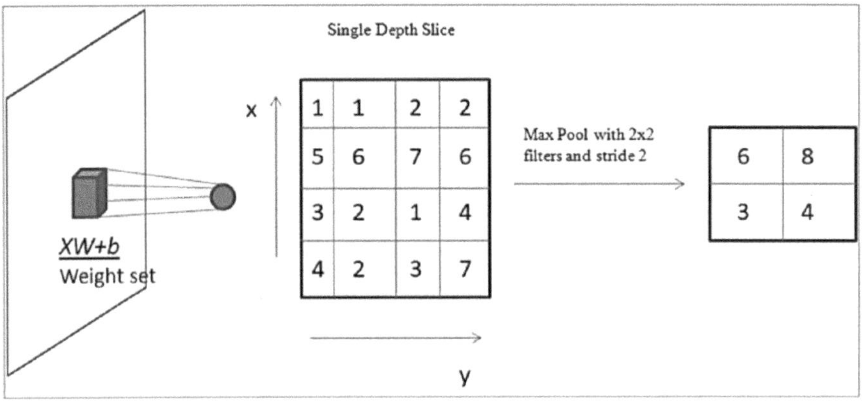

FIGURE 6.5 Operation performed in the pooling layer.

Source: Adapted from Patel et al. (2015).

A CNN can recognize simple data patterns and hence one can use them to generate more complex ones. One can use one-dimensional CNNs to extract interesting features from small (fixed length) pieces of the dataset, and the feature's position in that fragment is not important.

6.5.4.3 LSTM (LONG SHORT-TERM MEMORY)

Recurrent neural networks, such as the long short-term memory (LSTM) kind, are useful for forecasting financial time series such as stock prices because they circumvent the long-term reliance problem. In contrast, LSTMs make minor tweaks to the data by multiplication and addition. In LSTMs, information is disseminated by a process referred to as cell states. Information stored in local short-term memory (LSTMs) can be selectively retrieved or forgotten. What determines a stock's price today is a combination of the following things:

- Whether the stock has been on an upswing or a downswing during the past few days.

- The price of the stock on the previous day.
- Today's potential drivers of the stock price. They are referred to as technical indicators.

The LSTM memory cell consists of three parts: the input gate, the forget gate, and the output gate, as shown in Figure 6.6.

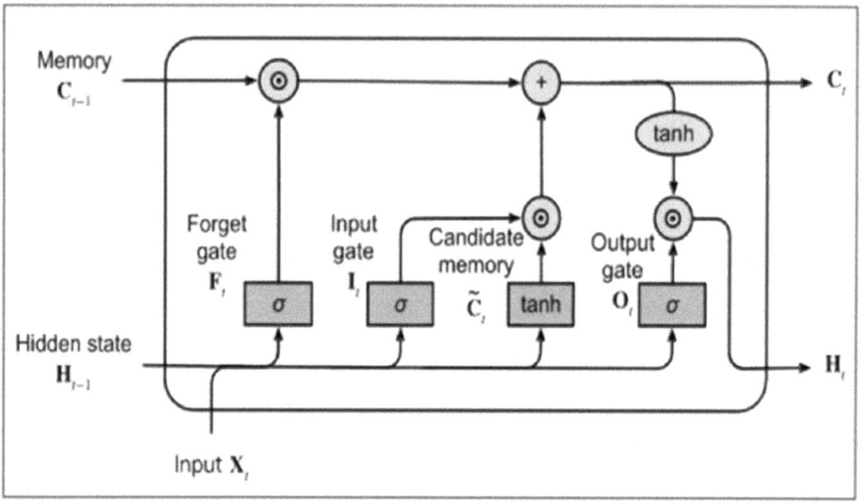

FIGURE 6.6 Architecture diagram of a memory cell of LSTM.

Source: Adapted from Lu, Li, Wang et al. (2020).

The candidate cell state at present is denoted by c_t. Each cell's state information is modified based on its contact with the gate structure. The current input I_t, the preceding cell state c_{t-1}, and the hidden state H_{t-1} are all input to every LSTM cell. The output of the first sigmoid layer—also known as the forget gate Eqn. (4) determines the amount of data to be carried from the previous cell into the present cell.

$$f_t = \sigma(w_f [H_{t-1}, I_t] + b_f) \quad (4)$$

Multiplicating them pointwise, i.e., the preceding cell state yields a value in the interval [0, 1]. If the gate yields a zero, no new data is added to the cell state; a one adds all data. This technique determines the working of forget gate.

$$i_t = \sigma(w_i [H_{t-1}, I_t] + b_i) \quad (5)$$

The second sigmoid layer Eqn. (5) mixes the current input with the hidden state of the preceding cell, much like the first sigmoid layer did.

$$c'_t = \tanh(w_c[H_{t-1}, I_t] + b_c) \tag{6}$$

$$c_t = f_t * c_{t-1} + i_t * c'_t \tag{7}$$

To regulate the network, the previous hidden state, and current input also go into the tanh layer Eqn. (6). After that, the tanh and sigmoid outputs are multiplied pointwise, with the sigmoid output selecting which data to retain from the tanh output. Due to this, the layer is also called the input gate Eqn. (7).

$$o_t = \sigma(w_o[H_{t-1}, I_t] + b_o) \tag{8}$$

$$H_t = o_t * \tanh(c'_t) \tag{9}$$

The present cell state's output Eqn. (8) is the product of a tanh and sigmoid layer. The sigmoid layer determines which part of the cell state is output, whereas tanh layer adjusts output between [–1, 1]. With the use of these gates, control is done on the degree to which the weights are optimized.

6.5.4.4 HYBRID MODELS

The study has proposed the use of two hybrid models for SMP. These models were performed by combining previous models.

6.5.4.4.1 ARIMA + LSTM

This model uses the combination of the statistical time series method and deep learning method for financial market predictions. As ARIMA shows the outstanding performance of SMP before ML and DL models were devised. The ARIMA model is used with the order (5,1,0). Similarly, LSTM also made accurate predictions as compared to ML models. So, their hybridization gives a new model in Figure 6.7 which has a very low RMSE output and gives a more correct observed forecast of the price.

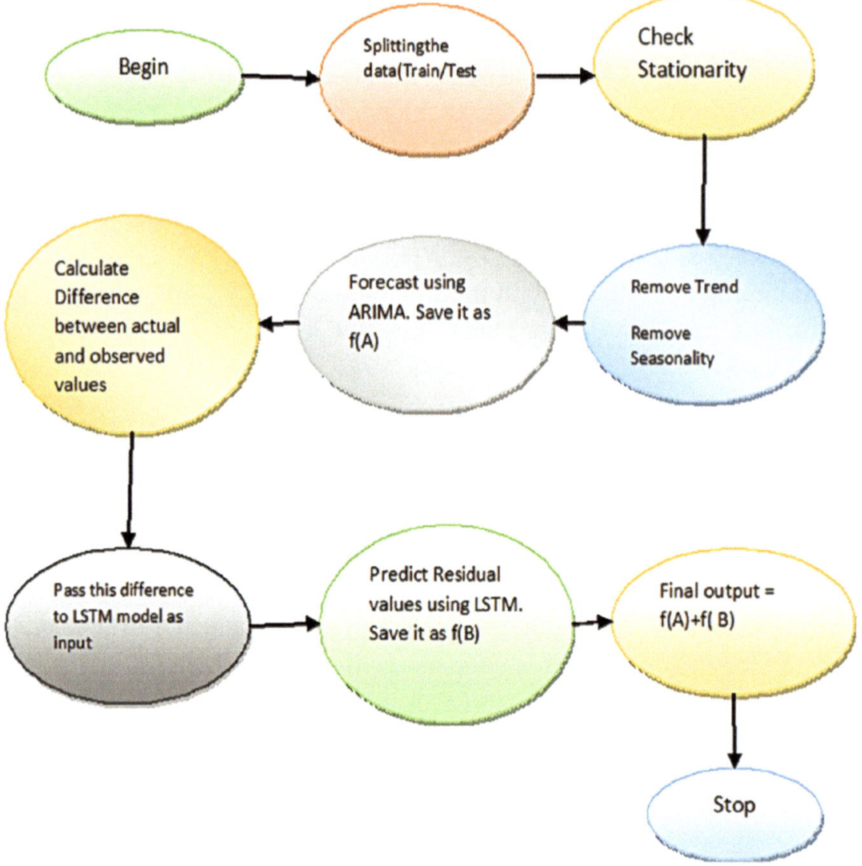

FIGURE 6.7 Working of hybrid model (ARIMA-LSTM).

6.5.4.4.2 CNN+ BiLSTM

1. **Training and Prediction Process:** The proposed model creates a framework by combining two deep learning models named LSTM and CNN. LSTM has several variants; some of the variants include Vanilla LSTM, Stacked LSTM, Bidirectional LSTM, and Time Distributed LSTM. This proposed hybrid model consists of Bidirectional LSTM. Table 6.2 lists important parameters used in this model.

TABLE 6.2 Valuable Parameters Used in the Model (CNN-BiLSTM)

Parameters Used in the Proposed Model	Values of the Parameters
"Number of filters in convolution layer"	64
"Kernel size of convolution layer"	3
"Activation function of CNN layer"	Relu
"Pool size of pooling layer"	2
"Hidden units in LSTM layer"	100
"Activation function of LSTM layer "	Linear
"Batch_Size"	40
"Optimizer"	Adam
"Loss function"	Mean squared error
"Epochs"	100
"Dropout value"	0.5

Source: Adapted from Lu, Li, Li et al. (2020).

2. Pseudocode for CNN and BILSTM Hybrid Approach

i. **Input Data:** Stock market data collected from 'Yahoo Finance Website' from period '01-01-2001' till the date '31-12-2022' using pandas and NumPy libraries.

ii. **Data Normalization and Preprocessing:** Data normalization is carried out by scaling; scaling is necessary as it brings down all the available data into the scale measurable from 0 to 1.

iii. **Initialize the Network:** Give initial values to the weights and biases of each layer of the CNN-BiLSTM.

iv. **Calculation of CNN Layer:** Convolution and pooling layers analyze incoming data and extract features. The final output is computed.

v. **LSTM Layer Calculation:** The BiLSTM layer is utilized to compute the output of the CNN layer, which is subsequently used to decide the output.

vi. **Output Layer Calculation:** The value produced by the BiLSTM layer is sent to the full connection layer, which then produces the output. If one of the final conditions is met, training is complete; otherwise, proceed to Step vii. Update the entire CNN-BiLSTM network, and go to Step viii; otherwise, go to Step vii.

vii. **Error Backpropagation:** Step iv involves retraining the network with new weights and biases based on the predicted error from previous steps.

viii. **Save the Model:** Save the trained model for forecasting.

ix. **Input data:** Input the data in the form of (.csv) files.

x. **Data Standardization:** The input data is standardized.

xi. **Forecasting:** Inputs the standardized data into the trained model of CNN-BiLSTM and then gets the corresponding output value.

6.6 RESULTS AND DISCUSSIONS

This section elaborates on the experimental results conducted using various ML and DL models. Root-mean-square error (RMSE) and R-squared (R2) are two metrics used to compare the accuracy of different models' predictions. Root mean square error (RMSE) is used as the metric for model quality, using the following formula applied to the models:

$$RMSE = \sqrt{\frac{\sum_{t=1}^{n}(actual(t) - predicted(t))^2}{n}} \tag{10}$$

The coefficient of determination (R2) is a statistical metric used in regression analysis to find out how much of the observed variation in the dependent variable can be attributed to the independent variable. A high r-squared value indicates that a regression model well describes the data. In general, R2 might be anywhere from 0 to 1.

The accuracy of a system's classifications is a common statistic. Specifically, it measures how many predictions were accurate relative to the total number of training samples.

$$Accuracy = \frac{Number\ of\ correct\ predictions}{Total\ number\ of\ predictions\ made} \tag{11}$$

It performs optimally only when there are about equivalent numbers of samples from each category.

6.6.1 RESULTS USING LSTM (LONG SHORT-TERM MEMORY)

LSTM models are run with 1,000 epoch values on batch size of 64 values from the Apple dataset. The dataset is discussed in earlier sections. Figure

6.8 shows the summary of the model along with Figure 6.9 showing the observed and predicted forecast.

```
Model: "sequential"
_________________________________________________________________
 Layer (type)                Output Shape              Param #
=================================================================
 lstm (LSTM)                 (None, 100, 50)           10400

 dropout (Dropout)           (None, 100, 50)           0

 lstm_1 (LSTM)               (None, 100, 50)           20200

 dropout_1 (Dropout)         (None, 100, 50)           0

 lstm_2 (LSTM)               (None, 50)                20200

 dense (Dense)               (None, 1)                 51

=================================================================
Total params: 50,851
Trainable params: 50,851
Non-trainable params: 0
_________________________________________________________________
```

FIGURE 6.8 Tabular summary of the LSTM model.

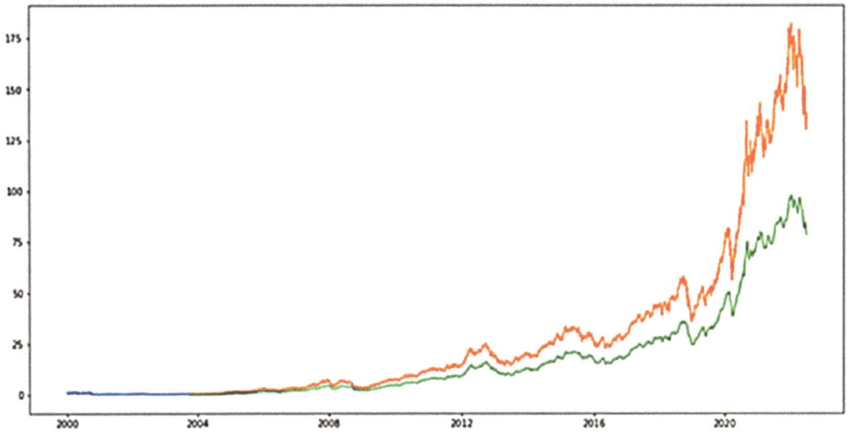

FIGURE 6.9 Graph showing the actual and forecasted values of LSTM.

6.6.2 RESULTS USING CNN

The research also proposes to implement CNN model for SMP. In the proposed CNN model of time-series prediction, the batch size is taken equal to 128. In the previous models, the dataset downloaded from Yahoo Finance is taken from the last two decades. So, the dataset is from the year 2001 till the end of the year 2022.

However, for CNN the dataset is taken from the year 1999 till the end of 2022. The whole dataset is divided into three parts. Before 2015, the dataset is taken as a training set; from the 2015 to 2020 time period, the dataset is known as validating dataset. And the final year, which is from 1 Jan 2021 till 31 Dec 2022, the dataset is taken as a testing dataset. Some parameters of the running model are enlisted as:

Filters = 128, kernel_size = 2, strides = 1, dilation_rate = dilation_rate, padding = "causal" activation = "relu," optimizer = 'Nadam,' Learning rate = 1e–4.

With the help of these parameters the output of the observed forecast is done in the form of a graph as in Figure 6.10.

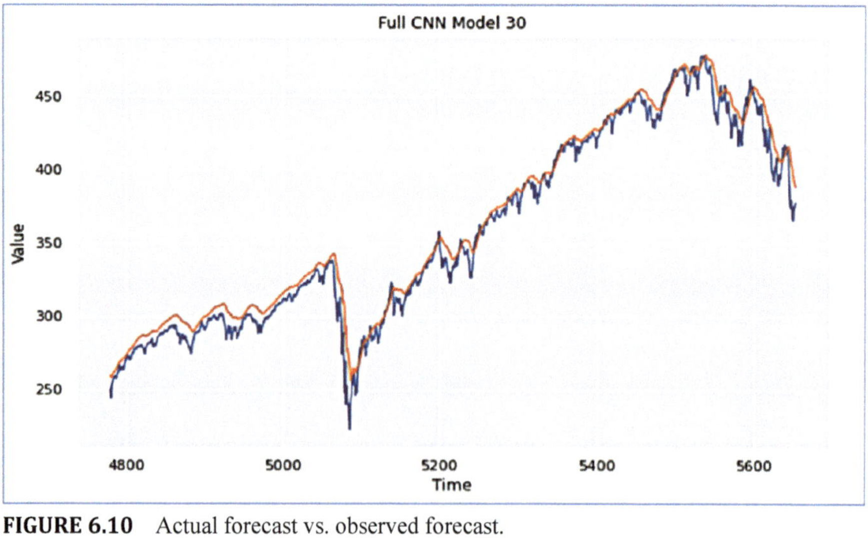

FIGURE 6.10 Actual forecast vs. observed forecast.

After forecasting has been completed, the error values are calculated. This model shows the value of MAE (Mean Absolute error) and MAPE (mean absolute percentage error).

6.6.3 RESULTS USING ARIMA-LSTM

Hybrid model ARIMA-LSTM gives lesser RMSE values and more predictive results as compared to previous models used. Preceding figures show the working of the ARIMA-LSTM hybrid model. Figure 6.11 shows the rolling mean and ewm of the actual data using the ARIMA model.

<matplotlib.axes._subplots.AxesSubplot at 0x7f4e85cdd280>

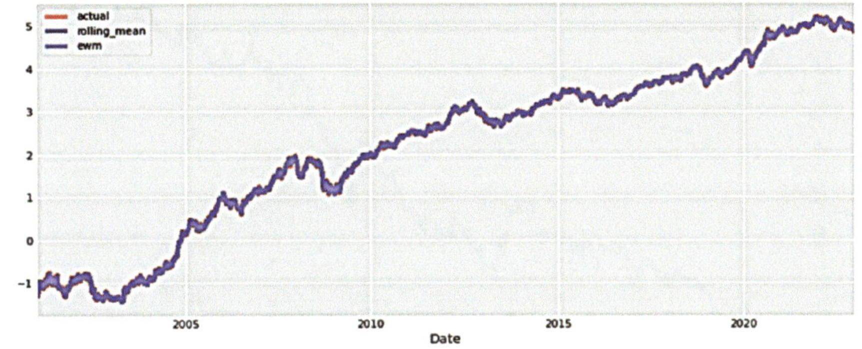

FIGURE 6.11 Rolling_mean and exponentially weighted mean calculated from the actual data.

Figure 6.12 shows the value of comparison of actual and calculated values from the ARIMA model. This model works on the principle of removing trend and seasonality from the actual data.

Date	actual	prediction
2016-05-27 00:00:00-04:00	3.222370	3.223749
2016-05-31 00:00:00-04:00	3.217475	3.223796
2016-06-01 00:00:00-04:00	3.203356	3.219441
2016-06-02 00:00:00-04:00	3.195812	3.205195
2016-06-03 00:00:00-04:00	3.197856	3.197700
...	...	...
2022-12-23 00:00:00-05:00	4.881741	4.884839
2022-12-27 00:00:00-05:00	4.867765	4.883610
2022-12-28 00:00:00-05:00	4.836599	4.870362
2022-12-29 00:00:00-05:00	4.864530	4.838593
2022-12-30 00:00:00-05:00	4.866996	4.865804

1661 rows × 2 columns

FIGURE 6.12 Few of the compared values from results of ARIMA model.

After identification of the trend, the focus of ARIMA is to remove that trend by calculating ACF and PACF. The next, step is to remove seasonality by calculating the difference between actual and predicted values. This difference is passed as input to the LSTM model in the hybridization process. Figure 6.13 shows the final graph of the ARIMA model.

FIGURE 6.13 Final ARIMA model.

LSTM is implemented on the difference values using 500 values of the epoch, along with 100 units of data values, and the optimizer used is 'adam' (Figure 6.14).

```
import math
error2=metrics.mean_squared_error(y_b_test[n_input:] * 10.0, y_b_test_pred * 10.0) **0.5
print(error2)
print (math.sqrt(error2))

0.03420399021514207
0.18494320808059447
```

FIGURE 6.14 Final RMSE values.

6.6.4 *RESULTS USING CNN-BILSTM*

CNN-BiLSTM is the hybridization of two deep learning methodologies, i.e., CNN and BiLSTM. Figure 6.15 shows the graphs of OHLC values plotted. BiLSTM stands for Bidirectional LSTM.

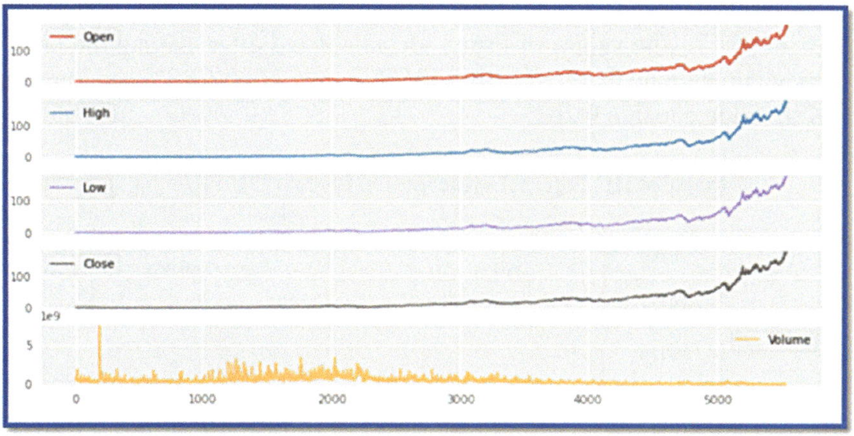

FIGURE 6.15 OHLC values plotted.

The experimentation is carried out using CNN model in coordination with BiLSTM model. The CNN model used is explained.

6.6.4.1 CNN MODEL

The CNN model uses 75% data for training and 15% for testing. It contains six layers: Sequential (an input layer) along with four hidden layers. The very first layer is a Conv1 Dimensional layer with attributes like 64 filters and a kernel size of 3, the conv1D layer is followed by a MaxPooling1D layer with a pooling size of 2, a Flatten layer and at the end, there is an Output layer with a dense single neuron. The model used an Adam optimizer with learning rate=0.1 and a 'Relu' activation function; the model completed 100 epochs with a batch size of 40.

6.6.4.2 BILSTM MODEL

The Bidirectional LSTM model used in the research is time-distributed as well and contains six layers: an input layer (Sequential), two hidden layers (100 Bi-LSTM neurons), two dropout layers after each Bi-LSTM layer, and an output layer (Dense single neuron). The model utilized a linear activation function and Adam optimization function; the model completed 100 epochs with a batch size of 2.

Before calculating the error values, they are plotted as shown in Figures 6.16 and 6.17. The values of Errors are calculated after making the predictions and it is found that CNN-BiLSTM (Figure 6.16) is 96.3% accurate with RMSE value equal to 0.2023.

<matplotlib.legend.Legend at 0x7f406bff7750>

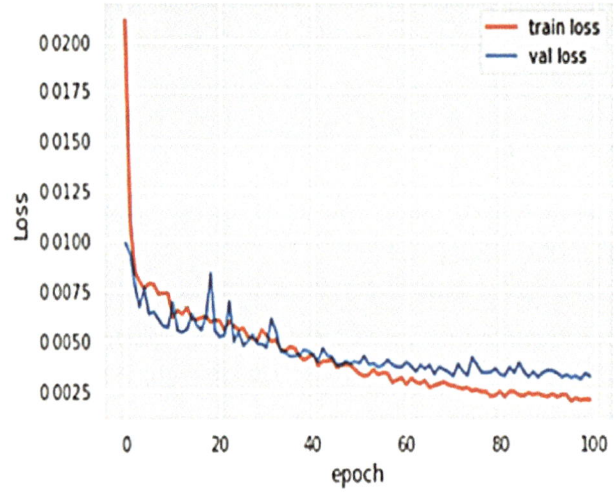

FIGURE 6.16 Plot of train data loss vs test data loss.

<matplotlib.legend.Legend at 0x7f40709c29d0>

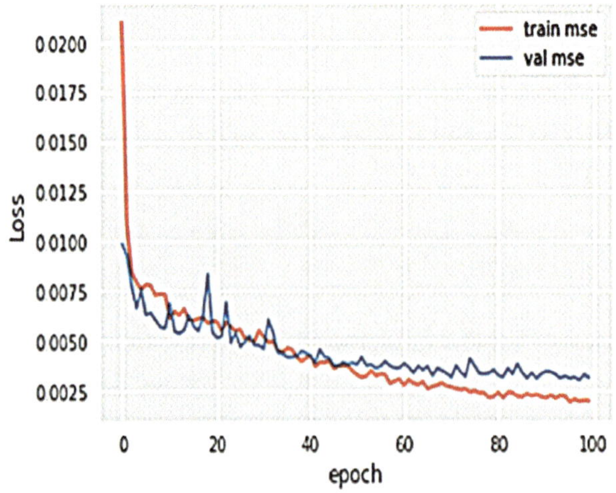

FIGURE 6.17 Plot of train data MSE vs. test data MSE.

6.7 CONCLUSION

According to the algorithms and experimental results, the Hybrid methods have a prediction accuracy of approximately 96%. This accuracy is more than previous ML and DL models. Of the two hybrid models, the prediction accuracy of BiLSTM with CNN is the most fruitful and compared with ARIMA-LSTM. The forecast shows the price movement for the next day with two statuses, indicating whether it will be upward or downward. The clear picture shows that BiLSTM with CNN predicts better accuracy than ARIMA-LSTM (97.4), Random Forest (52.0), and SVM (52.3). This whole picture is clearly shown in Figure 6.18.

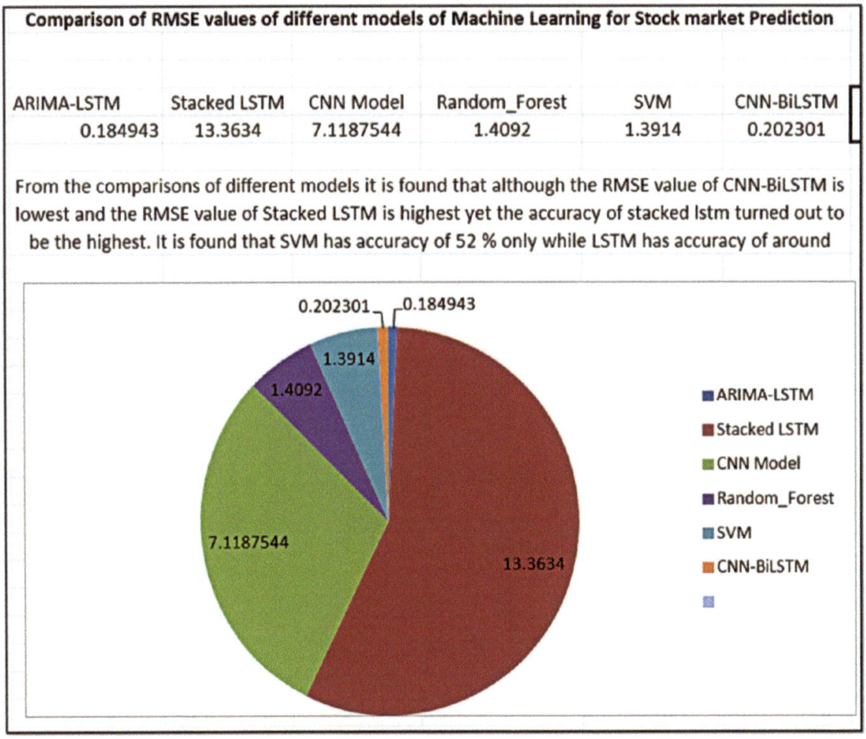

FIGURE 6.18 Pie chart showing all results.

6.8 FUTURE WORK

Deep learning is applied to stock trading and made two main contributions to the applied machine learning literature. First, it is shown that CNN can extract useful features even from low signal-to-noise time series data such as financial asset prices if the inputs are appropriately pre-processed. And the quantitative stock selection strategy is made for judging stock trends by using CNN. Second, the LSTM neural network is used to predict high accuracy in future stock prices, and the predicting outcomes are used as timing signals, which significantly improves the retracement of the CNN stock selection model in the back testing stage. This model easily accommodates returns of different frequencies as well as non-return data and produces investment results that exceed the basic Momentum strategy and Benchmark index in the vast finance literature. The CNN-BiLSTM neural network is applied to modeling and making the quantitative stock selection and timing strategy, which is feasible, robust, and highly profitable. The issue for future work is reducing computational complexity and increasing computation speed so that this method can be applied to hours or minutes data instead of the day's data. Also, if the model is applied to actual investment decisions, there is a need to improve on these aspects, such as feature selection, model construction, and parameter optimization.

KEYWORDS

- **autoregressive integrated moving average**
- **benchmark index**
- **BiLSTMs**
- **convolution neural network**
- **hybrid model**
- **stock price forecasting**
- **stock trading**

REFERENCES

Abraham, A., Nath, B., & Mahanti, P. K., (2001). Hybrid intelligent systems for stock market analysis. *Lecture Notes in Computer Science (Including Subseries Lecture Notes in Artificial Intelligence and Lecture Notes in Bioinformatics)*, *2074*, 337–345. https://doi.org/10.1007/3-540-45718-6_38.

Adhikari, R., & Agrawal, R. K., (2014). A combination of artificial neural network and random walk models for financial time series forecasting. *Neural Computing and Applications, 24*(6), 1441–1449. https://doi.org/10.1007/s00521-013-1386-y.

Al-Bashabsheh, E., & Abu, A. S., (2021). *ES-JUST at SemEval-2021 Task 7: Detecting and Rating Humor and Offensive Text Using Deep Learning*. 1102–1107. https://doi.org/10.18653/v1/2021.semeval-1.153.

Alibašić, E., Fažo, B., & Petrović, I., (2019). A new approach to calculating electrical energy losses on power lines with a new improved three-mode method. *Tehnicki Vjesnik – Technical Gazette*, *26*(2). https://doi.org/10.17559/tv-20170206144804.

Becker, F. G., Cleary, M., Team, R. M., Holtermann, H., The, D., Agenda, N., Science, P., et al., (n.d.). In: *Syria Studies* (Vol. 7, No. 1).

Bhanja, S., & Das, A., (2019). Deep learning based integrated stacked model for the stock market prediction. *International Journal of Engineering and Advanced Technology*, *9*(1), 5167–5174. https://doi.org/10.35940/ijeat.a1823.109119.

Bollen, J., Mao, H., & Zeng, X., (2011). Twitter mood predicts the stock market. *Journal of Computational Science*, *2*(1), 1–8. https://doi.org/10.1016/j.jocs.2010.12.007.

Cao, L. J., & Tay, F. E. H., (2003). Support vector machine with adaptive parameters in financial time series forecasting. *IEEE Transactions on Neural Networks*, *14*(6), 1506–1518. https://doi.org/10.1109/TNN.2003.820556.

Eapen, J., Bein, D., & Verma, A., (2019). Novel deep learning model with CNN and bi-directional LSTM for improved stock market index prediction. In: *2019 IEEE 9th Annual Computing and Communication Workshop and Conference, CCWC 2019*, 264–270. https://doi.org/10.1109/CCWC.2019.8666592.

Khashei, M., & Hajirahimi, Z., (2019). A comparative study of series arima/mlp hybrid models for stock price forecasting. *Communications in Statistics: Simulation and Computation*, *48*(9), 2625–2640. https://doi.org/10.1080/03610918.2018.1458138.

Kim, B. S., & Kim, T. G., (2019). Cooperation of simulation and data model for performance analysis of complex systems. *International Journal of Simulation Modeling*, *18*(4), 608–619. https://doi.org/10.2507/IJSIMM18(4)491.

Kumar, M., & Thenmozhi, M., (2014). Forecasting stock index returns using ARIMA-SVM, ARIMA-ANN, and ARIMA-random forest hybrid models. *International Journal of Banking, Accounting and Finance*, *5*(3), 284–308. https://doi.org/10.1504/IJBAAF.2014.064307.

Lee, K., & Jin, J. J., (2007). Neural network model Vs. Sarima model in forecasting Korean stock price index (Kospi). *Issues In Information Systems*, *VIII*(2), 372–378. https://doi.org/10.48009/2_iis_2007_372-378.

Liu, H., & Long, Z., (2020). An improved deep learning model for predicting stock market price time series. *Digital Signal Processing: A Review Journal*, *102*, 102741. https://doi.org/10.1016/j.dsp.2020.102741.

Liu, S., Zhang, C., & Ma, J., (2017). CNN-LSTM neural network model for quantitative strategy analysis in stock markets. *Lecture Notes in Computer Science (Including Subseries Lecture Notes in Artificial Intelligence and Lecture Notes in Bioinformatics)*, *10635 LNCS*, 198–206. https://doi.org/10.1007/978-3-319-70096-0_21.

Lu, W., Li, J., Li, Y., Sun, A., & Wang, J., (2020). A CNN-LSTM-based model to forecast stock prices. *Complexity*, *2020*. https://doi.org/10.1155/2020/6622927.

Lu, W., Li, J., Wang, J., & Qin, L., (2020). A CNN-BiLSTM-AM method for stock price prediction. *Neural Computing and Applications*, *0123456789*. https://doi.org/10.1007/s00521-020-05532-z.

Merh, N., Saxena, V., & Pardasani, K., (2010). A comparison between hybrid approaches of ANN and ARIMA for Indian stock trend forecasting. *Business Intelligence Journal*, *3*(2014), 23–44.

Mootha, S., Sridhar, S., Seetharaman, R., & Chitrakala, S., (2020). Stock price prediction using Bi-directional LSTM based sequence to sequence modeling and multitask learning. In: *2020 11th IEEE Annual Ubiquitous Computing, Electronics and Mobile Communication Conference, UEMCON 2020*, 0078–0086. https://doi.org/10.1109/UEMCON51285.2020.9298066.

Nassar, L., Okwuchi, I. E., Saad, M., Karray, F., & Ponnambalam, K., (2020). Deep learning-based approach for fresh produce market price prediction. *Proceedings of the International Joint Conference on Neural Networks*. DC. https://doi.org/10.1109/IJCNN48605.2020.9207537.

Patel, J., Shah, S., Thakkar, P., & Kotecha, K., (2015). Predicting stock market index using fusion of machine learning techniques. *Expert Systems with Applications*, *42*(4), 2162–2172. https://doi.org/10.1016/j.eswa.2014.10.031.

Patil, P., Wu, C. S. M., Potika, K., & Orang, M., (2020). Stock market prediction using ensemble of graph theory, machine learning and deep learning models. *ACM International Conference Proceeding Series*, 85–92. https://doi.org/10.1145/3378936.3378972.

Prasad, V. V., Gumparthi, S., Venkataramana, L. Y., Srinethe, S., Sruthi, S. R. M., & Nishanthi, K., (2022). Prediction of stock prices using statistical and machine learning models: A comparative analysis. *Computer Journal*, *65*(5), 1338–1351. https://doi.org/10.1093/comjnl/bxab008.

Pratheeth, S., & Vishnu, P. R., (2021). Stock price prediction using machine learning and deep learning. In: *2021 IEEE Mysore Sub Section International Conference, MysuruCon 2021*, (pp. 660–664). https://doi.org/10.1109/MysuruCon52639.2021.9641664.

Sallehuddin, R., Shamsuddin, S. M. H., Hashim, S. Z. M., & Abraham, A., (2007). Forecasting time series data using hybrid grey relational artificial neural network and auto regressive integrated moving average model. *Neural Network World*, *17*(6), 573–605.

Selvin, S., Vinayakumar, R., Gopalakrishnan, E. A., Menon, V. K., & Soman, K. P., (2017). Stock price prediction using LSTM, RNN and CNN-sliding window model. In: *2017 International Conference on Advances in Computing, Communications, and Informatics, ICACCI 2017, 2017-Janua* (pp. 1643–1647). https://doi.org/10.1109/ICACCI.2017.8126078.

Sen, J., Dutta, A., & Mehtab, S., (2021). This is the accepted version in the second profitability analysis in stock investment using an LSTM-based deep learning model. In: *2021 International Conference on Intelligent Technologies, CONIT 2021*. https://doi.org/10.1109/CONIT51480.2021.9498565.

Shah, A., Gor, M., Sagar, M., & Shah, M., (2022). A stock market trading framework based on deep learning architectures. *Multimedia Tools and Applications*, *81*(10), 14153–14171. https://doi.org/10.1007/s11042-022-12328-x.

Sun, Y. F., Liang, Y. C., Zhang, W. L., Lee, H. P., Lin, W. Z., & Cao, L. J., (2005). Optimal partition algorithm of the RBF neural network and its application to financial time series forecasting. *Neural Computing and Applications*, *14*(1), 36–44. https://doi.org/10.1007/s00521-004-0439-7.

Thormann, M. L., Farchmin, J., Weisser, C., Kruse, R. M., Safken, B., & Silbersdorff, A., (2021). Stock price predictions with LSTM neural networks and twitter sentiment. *Statistics, Optimization, and Information Computing*, *9*(2), 268–287. https://doi.org/10.19139/soic-2310-5070-1202.

Wadi, S. A., Almasarweh, M., & Alsaraireh, A. A., (2018). Predicting closed price time series data using ARIMA model. *Modern Applied Science, 12*(11), 181. https://doi.org/10.5539/mas.v12n11p181.

Yadav, K., Yadav, M., & Saini, S., (2022). Stock values predictions using deep learning-based hybrid models. *CAAI Transactions on Intelligence Technology, 7*(1), 107–116. https://doi.org/10.1049/cit2.12052.

Yan, X., Weihan, W., & Chang, M., (2021). Research on financial assets transaction prediction model based on LSTM neural network. *Neural Computing and Applications, 33*(1), 257–270. https://doi.org/10.1007/s00521-020-04992-7.

Zhang, K., Zhong, G., Dong, J., Wang, S., & Wang, Y., (2019). Stock market prediction based on generative adversarial network. *Procedia Computer Science, 147*, 400–406. https://doi.org/10.1016/j.procs.2019.01.256.

Zhang, L., Wang, F., Xu, B., Chi, W., Wang, Q., & Sun, T., (2018). Prediction of stock prices based on LM-BP neural network and the estimation of overfitting point by RDCI. *Neural Computing and Applications, 30*(5), 1425–1444. https://doi.org/10.1007/s00521-017-3296-x.

CHAPTER 7

Unleashing the Power of AI in Business, Finance, Industry 4.0, and Banking 4.0

SHALLU SEHGAL,[1] NITISH PATHAK,[2] and PRIYANKA GARG[3]

[1]*Associate Professor, Department of Business Management, Shoolini Institute of Life Sciences and Business Management, Solan, Himachal Pradesh, India*

[2]*Bhagwan Parshuram Institute of Technology (BPIT), GGSIPU, New Delhi, India*

[3]*Assistant Professor, Department of Skill Faculty of Management Studies and Research, Shri Vishwakarma Skill University, Gurugram, Haryana, India*

ABSTRACT

Artificial Intelligence (AI), a foundational area of computer science, aims to simulate human cognitive functions to solve real-world challenges. This chapter discusses the role of AI in various business sectors, including healthcare, tourism, retail, and insurance, where it enhances efficiency, personalizes services, and supports decision-making. The chapter traces the evolution of AI, from early problem-solving systems to modern advancements like machine learning and deep learning. It also examines AI's impact on business operations through data collected from 350 respondents in Solan District, Himachal Pradesh, using statistical analysis to test AI's influence on efficiency, growth, and decision-making. The study highlights AI's contributions to optimizing business processes, improving customer experiences, and driving economic progress.

Advanced Digital Technologies in Financial and Business Management: Unleashing the Power of Artificial Intelligence, Machine Learning, Blockchain, and the Internet of Things. Jyoti Batra Arora, Nitish Pathak, and Neelam Sharma (Eds.)

7.1 INTRODUCTION

7.1.1 DEFINITION OF AI

Perhaps the oldest and most comprehensive area of computer science, Artificial Intelligence (AI) deals with all facets of simulating cognitive capabilities for addressing practical problems and creating computers that can learn and think like people (Jarrahi, 2018). To distinguish AI from human intelligence, it is frequently referred to as machine intelligence (Poole et al., 1998; Russell & Norvig, 2011; Tenenbaum et al., 2011). The area was centered on the connection of cognitive science and computer science.

AI systems can be classified into two main categories: narrow or weak AI, which is designed to perform a single specific task, and general or strong AI, which can perform any intellectual task that a human can (Sajja, 2021).

7.1.1.1 APPLICATION OF AI IN DIFFERENT BUSINESS SECTORS

AI technologies may assist healthcare companies in making the most of their data, assets, and resources by analyzing data trends, enhancing efficiency, and improving the performance of clinical and operational workflows, processes, and financial operations. Healthcare information is often fragmented and available in multiple formats (Panesar, 2021).

In the tourism business, Artificial Intelligence (AI) is increasingly being utilized to make tailored recommendations, enhance customer service, and automate repetitive jobs (Leung, 2020). AI can assist in creating more tailored experiences for travelers by learning about their interests and recommending activities, restaurants, cafe, and hotels.

The retail industry is continuously changing because of technological breakthroughs and changing client tastes, which demand that businesses be technologically adept. One of the dominant technologies that multinational brands use for their business processes is Artificial Intelligence for the retail industry. The AI-enabled value chain research, "Most existing theories and models of AI refer to computer systems with human-like intelligence, which encompasses these systems' abilities "to interpret external information accurately, to learn from such data, and to implement those skills and knowledge to achieve specific targets and tasks via flexible adaptation" (Har et al., (2022).

AI is allowing insurers to apply machine learning, data modeling, and predictive analysis to the entire insurance value chain, with positive consequences in the form of greater bottom line and improved customer satisfaction (Kumar et al., 2019).

7.1.1.2 BRIEF HISTORY OF AI

The genesis of Artificial Intelligence is linked in this brief history to philosophy, literature, and imagination. Early advancements in engineering, electronics, and many other fields have inspired AI. Early achievements in problem solving include work on knowledge representation, inference, and basic learning, as well as demonstration programs in language comprehension, translation, theorem proving, associative memory, and knowledge-based systems (Buchanan, 2005).

Researchers like Alan Turing thought about the prospect of a computer playing chess as a test of the machine's intelligence from the very beginning of computer science. So, in 1948, he released "Intelligent Machinery," then in 1950, "Computing Machinery and Intelligence," both of which served as a foundation for further AI research (Turing, 2009). According to Benko & Lányi (2009); Haenlein & Kaplan (2019); and McCorduck et al. (1977), Artificial intelligence (AI) is the use of technology tools to attain goals autonomously while considering any restrictions that may be present.

7.1.1.3 HISTORY: 67 YEARS OF AI

John McCarthy, a retired Stanford University computer science professor, launched AI as a discipline by planning the renowned Dartmouth conference in the summer of 1956 at Dartmouth College, Hanover, with the conviction that there will be systems that would develop intelligence of the human order, he continued to define the area for more than five decades. The seven general categories of AI described by Firschein and Coles in 1973 were language understanding, problem-solving, perception, modeling, learning, and adaptive systems, robotics, and games. They displayed the progress made in AI, the degrees of proficiency that are currently attainable in all seven areas of AI, and a list of 21 hypothetical objects that they predicted will be produced by AI in the future. They foresaw the development of AI services, which are now everyday technology and no longer the stuff of science fiction. In two ways, this has benefited business – first, it has led to a large increase in the amount of money that top technology companies invest in AI and Second, the number of AI start-ups that have been founded in recent years has increased dramatically, which is good for the global economy.

7.1.1.4 TIMELINE OF AI EVOLUTION

Here is a brief outline of the evolution of AI through time:

- **1950s:** The beginnings of AI research, with the Dartmouth Conference that established AI as a field of study.

- **1950s–1960s:** The birth of rule-based AI, where systems were designed to follow specific rules to perform tasks.
- **1960s–1980s:** The advent of expert systems, which could emulate the decision-making processes of human experts in specific domains (Figure 7.1).

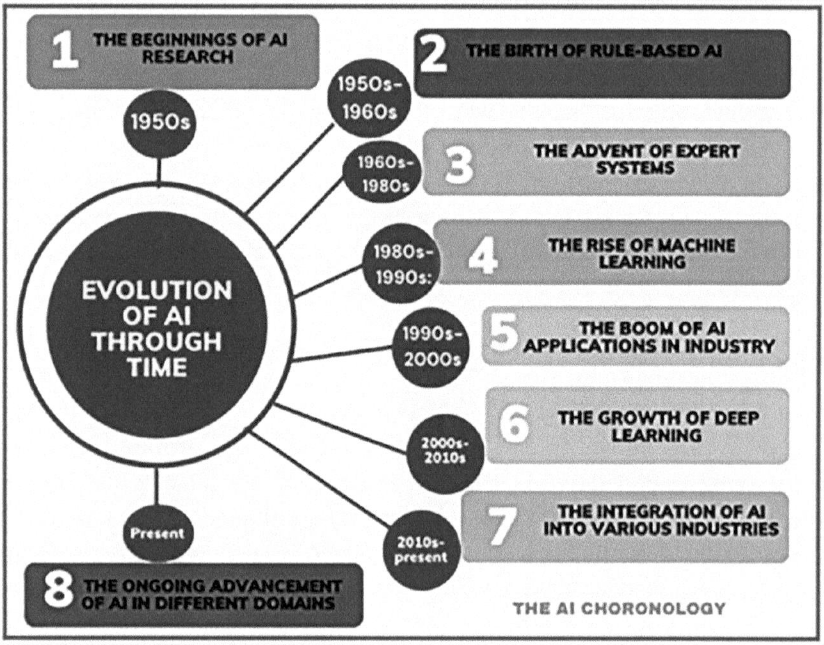

FIGURE 7.1 The AI chronology.

Source: Designed by Shallu Sehgal.

- **1980s–1990s:** The rise of machine learning, with the development of algorithms for learning from data, including decision trees, and artificial neural networks.
- **1990s–2000s:** The boom of AI applications in industry, with the widespread use of expert systems in domains such as finance, healthcare, and customer service.
- **2000s–2010s:** The growth of deep learning, with the development of deep neural networks that revolutionized the field of computer vision and natural language processing.

- **2010s–Present:** The integration of AI into various industries, including manufacturing, retail, and transportation, and the emergence of new AI applications, such as autonomous vehicles and personal assistants.
- **Present:** The ongoing advancement of AI in different Spheres such as generative models, reinforcement learning, and transfer learning, with a growing focus on ethics and responsible AI usage.

7.2 SCOPE OF THE CHAPTER

1. To be familiar with the role of "artificial intelligence" and its uses in business and finance.
2. To find out the impact of "artificial intelligence" on various business segments.

7.2.1 METHODOLOGY

Secondary data from published sources was used to examine the literature already in existence that was pertinent to the present research to achieve the goals of the study. Around 350 respondents working in diverse business sectors of Solan District of Himachal Pradesh were randomly chosen to understand more about the impact, role, uses, and consequences of Artificial Intelligence in different business sectors. The respondents were chosen using the convenience sample criterion. The primary data was gathered via a structured questionnaire using Likert's scale of measurement. Statistical techniques like the mean and t-test were applied to examine, evaluate, and produce the results from the data. The following Null hypotheses were formulated for second objective of the study:

- **H01:** Artificial Intelligence does not ease the work of employees working in different working business sectors.
- **H02:** Artificial Intelligence does not help businesses thrive in the market's fierce or intense competition.
- **H03:** Artificial Intelligence does not provide answers to challenging jobs and aids in Business expansion.
- **H04:** Artificial Intelligence does not train unstructured data models to provide precise forecasts, improved judgment calls, and help modify business procedures.

- **H05:** Artificial Intelligence does not improve efficiency, time, and human mistakes in the workplace.
- **H06:** Artificial Intelligence does not boost economic growth and promote cyber security and privacy.
- **H07:** Artificial Intelligence does not improve decision-making processes, decision-quality, and search operations for various solutions.
- **H08:** Artificial Intelligence does not help in Improving corporate operations, efficient supply chain management, and better consumer experiences.

7.3 ROLE OF AI IN THE BUSINESS AND FINANCE

AI in business refers to the use of computer algorithms, machine learning, and other advanced technologies to automate and improve various business processes, such as decision-making, data analysis, and customer service. The goal is to increase efficiency, accuracy, and customer satisfaction while reducing costs and manual labor. Businesses can use AI for tasks such as predictive analytics, fraud detection, personalized marketing, and supply chain optimization (Kumar, Vaibhav, & L., 2018).

AI is one of the instruments that may take part in marketing activities and improve marketing effectiveness. Considering that AI is crucial to social media marketing (Rose, 2018; Sterne, 2017). It offers the most recent social media marketing technology, which have a good impact on all marketing efforts. Numerous studies have demonstrated a substantial association between social media marketing and AI intelligence (Rauch-Hindin, 1985).

7.3.1 APPLICATIONS OF AI IN BUSINESS ENTERPRISES

1. **Customer Service:** One of the most common applications of AI in businesses is customer service. AI-powered chatbots and virtual assistants have become increasingly popular in recent years, as they are able to handle a high volume of customer inquiries 24 X 7. These tools provide fast and accurate responses, improving the customer experience and saving businesses time and resources that would have otherwise been spent on hiring and training customer service representatives.
2. **Marketing and Sales:** AI algorithms and tools are also being used in marketing and sales to analyze consumer behavior and predict

which products or services they are most likely to purchase. This information can then be used to personalize marketing campaigns and target potential customers with relevant advertisements. This leads to increased efficiency and effectiveness of marketing efforts, as well as higher customer satisfaction and loyalty (Figure 7.2).

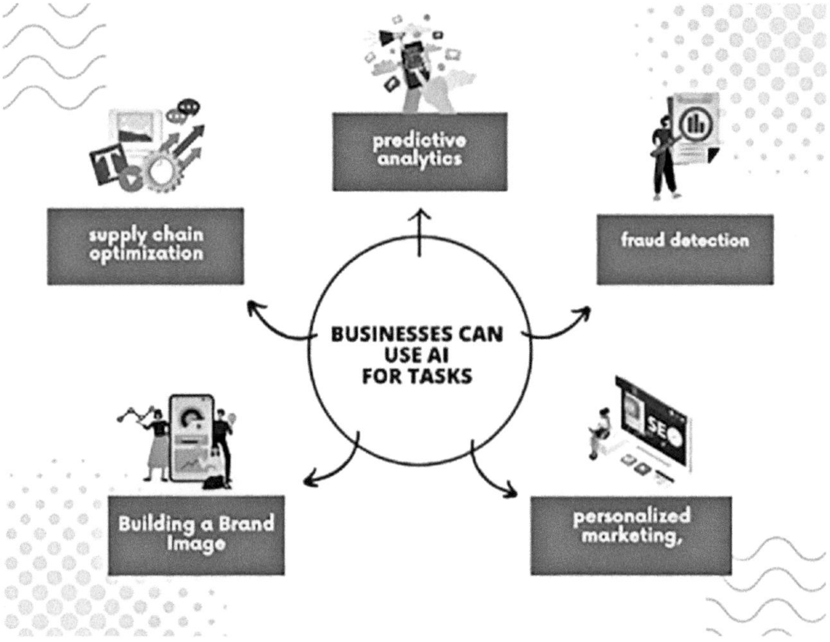

FIGURE 7.2 AI in business.

3. **Automation of Routine Tasks:** AI is being used to automate many routine tasks in businesses, such as data entry and analysis. AI algorithms can quickly and accurately process large amounts of data, saving businesses time and reducing the risk of errors. This also leads to improved decision-making, as AI algorithms can identify patterns and trends in data that might have been overlooked by humans.

7.3.2 BENEFITS OF AI TO SOCIETY

1. **Improved Healthcare Outcomes:** AI has the potential to bring numerous benefits to society, particularly in the field of healthcare. AI algorithms can help to provide doctors with better diagnoses and treatment recommendations, leading to improved patient outcomes.

2. **Addressing Global Issues:** AI can also be used to address pressing global issues such as climate change and sustainable development. For example, AI algorithms can be used to analyze satellite imagery and predict where and when natural disasters are likely to occur, allowing for more effective disaster response.

7.3.3 APPLICATION OF AI IN THE FINANCE INDUSTRY

AI and banking go hand in hand because AI technology may be utilized to enhance various facets of the financial sector (Figure 7.3). Several instances include:

1. **Fraud Detection:** AI can analyze vast volumes of data and seeing unusual trends that might be signs of fraud.
2. **Risk Evaluation:** AI may be used to analyze data and forecast the possibility of loan default.

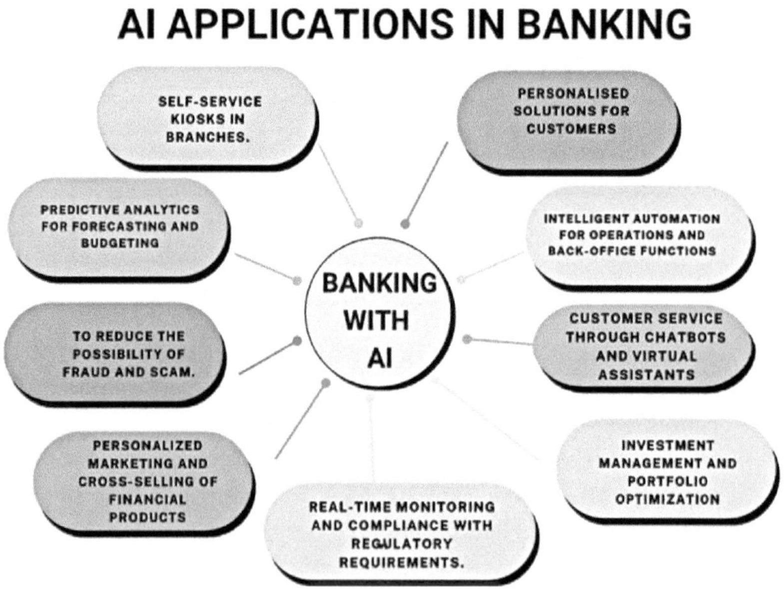

FIGURE 7.3 AI applications in banking sector.

Source: Designed by Shallu Sehgal.

3. **Customer Service:** Chatbots and virtual assistants powered by AI may be used to deliver rapid and effective customer service, answering frequent inquiries, and assisting clients with straightforward tasks.

4. **Investment Management:** Using AI to analyze market data and make investment decisions might result in investors earning greater returns.
5. **Credit Scoring:** Using data from credit histories and income, AI may analyze information to produce a credit score that can be used to assess a person's creditworthiness.

In general, AI can boost banks' productivity, cut expenses, and increase income.

7.3.4 BUSINESSES THAT HAVE USED AI TO TRANSFORM OPERATING MODELS

The usage of AI has been widely embraced by most of the top businesses in the globe. Here are a few of the top businesses using AI to its full potential:

1. **Alibaba:** By incorporating AI into its business processes, Alibaba utilizes the technology to anticipate the things that customers may wish to buy and to automatically generate product descriptions.
2. **Uber:** The world's largest ride-hailing company is only one of several significant corporations using AI to revolutionize business. Uber uses AI to forecast demand, which reduces predicted arrival time and effectively matches passengers with drivers. Uber's AI one-click chat tool enables drivers to interact with passengers by suggesting responses to their comments with only one click.

7.3.5 OTHER OUTSTANDING BUSINESSES THAT HAVE USED AI TO ENHANCE BUSINESS PROCESSES

1. Amazon has automated manufacturing, AI-powered recommendations, and the digital assistant Alexa.
2. Tesla has autonomous vehicles.
3. Azure machine learning platform with Power BI from Microsoft.

On perusal of the available secondary data, it can be concluded that, there are several ways that AI is employed in business and Finance world. Many functions and uses, such as tailoring marketing and advertising, stock management, and computerizing processes. These functions and applications contribute to greater economic growth, internet privacy and security, improved consumer experiences, and efficient supply chain management.

AI has had a significant impact on businesses in recent years and its influence is only expected to grow in the future. AI has revolutionized the way businesses operate by automating routine tasks, improving decision making, and increasing operational efficiency.

7.4 FINDINGS OF THE STUDY

Demographic detail (Table 7.1(a)) of the sample (n=350), shows that 60% of the sample were male and 40% females. Around 34.2% of the population is in the bracket of 20 to 30 years of age. Around 26.4% is between the ages of 30 and 40, 26% of the population falls in 40 to 50 years of age bracket and 13.4% is over the age of 50 years (Table 7.1(b)). Furthermore, 30% of respondents work in the banking and finance industry, followed by 22.5% in retail and business, 18.5% in healthcare and 7.5% and 21.5% are in tourism and Insurance sectors, respectively (Table 7.1(c)) where business analytics employ Artificial Intelligence.

7.4.1 DEMOGRAPHIC DETAILS

A questionnaire of eight questions relevant to the formulated hypotheses for the study was generated and responses from the sample (n = 350) were tabulated (Table 7.2), Likert's scale of measurement was used to gathered responses from the respondents belonging to the semi-urban location of Himachal Pradesh, working in the banking and finance, retail, healthcare, tourism, and insurance sectors.

TABLE 7.1(A) Demographic Details – Gender Wise

Variables		Respondents (%)
Gender	Male	210 (60)
	Female	140 (40)
	Total	350

TABLE 7.1(B) Demographic Details – Age Wise

Variables		Respondents (%)
Age (Years)	20–30	120 (34.2)
	30–40	94 (26.4)
	40–50	88 (26)
	Above 50	48 (13.4)
	Total	350

TABLE 7.1(C) Demographic Details – Working Sector Wise

Variables		Respondents (%)
Working Sector	Banking and finance	105 (30)
	Retail	79 (22.5)
	Healthcare	65 (18.5)
	Tourism	26 (7.5)
	Insurance	75 (21.5)
	Total	350

TABLE 7.2 Responses of Respondents

Questions	Strongly Agree	Agree	Neutral	Disagree	Strongly Disagree
AI ease the work of employees working in different working business sectors.	121	170	2	27	30
AI helps businesses thrive in the market's fierce or intense competition.	72	90	38	133	17
AI provides answers to challenging jobs and aids in Business expansion.	129	155	17	22	27
AI trains unstructured data models to provide precise forecasts, improved judgment calls, and help modify business procedures.	90	197	22	22	19
AI improves efficiency, time, and human mistakes in the workplace.	85	188	12	50	15
AI boosts economic growth and promote cyber security and privacy.	112	97	14	118	9
AI improves decision-making processes, decision-quality, and search operations for various solutions.	119	89	18	57	67
AI helps in improving corporate operations, efficient supply chain management, and better consumer experiences.	181	90	12	50	17

Out of the total sample, 33.3%, 44.7%, 19%, and 2.9% of the respondents in the age groups of 20–30, 30–40, 40–50, and above 50 years, respectively were employed in Banking and Financial sector. Around 34.1%, 30.3%, 7.6%, and 7.8% of the respondents, in the age groups of 20–30, 30–40, 40–50, and above 50 years, respectively were employed in Retail sector. Around 10.7%, 27.6%, 53.8%, and 7.6% of the respondents, in the age groups of 20–30, 30–40, 40–50, and above 50 years, respectively were employed in Healthcare Sector. Around 15.3%, 46.1%, 15.3%, and 2.3% of the respondents, in the age groups of 20–30, 30–40, 40–50, and above 50 years, respectively were employed in Tourism. Around 12%, 45.3%, 36%, and 6% of the respondents, in the age groups of 20–30, 30–40, 40–50, and above 50 years, respectively were employed in insurance sector (Table 7.3).

TABLE 7.3 Age Group versus Working Sector (n = 350)

Age Group of Respondents	Banking and Finance Sector Number (%)	Retail Sector Number (%)	Healthcare Number (%)	Tourism Number (%)	Insurance Number (%)
20–30	35 (33.3)	27 (34.1)	7 (10.7)	4 (15.3)	9 (12)
30–40	47 (44.7)	24 (30.3)	18 (27.6)	12 (46.1)	34 (45.3)
40–50	20 (19)	6 (7.6)	35 (53.8)	4 (15.3)	27 (36)
Above 50	3 (2.9)	22 (27.8)	5 (7.6)	6 (2.3)	5 (6)

The mean scores of the responses to the questions was calculated (Table 7.4) and tested for significance for accepting or rejecting the hypotheses.

TABLE 7.4 Calculation for T-Value and its Significance

Sl. No.	Questions	Number of Respondents	Mean
1.	AI ease the work of employees working in different working business sectors.	350	3.928 †
2.	AI helps businesses thrive in the market's fierce or intense competition.	350	3.191 †
3.	AI provides answers to challenging jobs and aids in Business expansion.	350	3.962 †
4.	AI trains unstructured data models to provide precise forecasts, improved judgment calls, and help modify business procedures.	350	3.905 †
5.	AI improves efficiency, time, and human mistakes in the workplace.	350	3.794 †
6.	AI boosts economic growth and promote cyber security and privacy.	350	3.528 †
7.	AI improves decision-making processes, decision-quality, and search operations for various solutions.	350	3.388 †
8.	AI helps in Improving corporate operations, efficient supply chain management, and better consumer experiences.	350	4.051 †

† *Significant at 0.05 level of significance.*

7.5 RESULTS AND DISCUSSION

- **Hypothesis H01:** It states that the Artificial Intelligence does not ease the work of employees working in different working business sectors. The mean score value is 3.928 (Table 7.4) and the P (0.05) is less than the t-value, the null hypothesis is rejected. So, it is concluded that the respondents belong to the semi-urban location of the Himachal Pradesh, are aware of the benefits of Artificial Intelligence and AI ease the work of employees working in different working business sectors.

- **Hypothesis H02:** It states that the Artificial Intelligence does not help businesses thrive in the market's fierce or intense competition. The mean score value is 3.191 (Table 7.4) and the P (0.05) is less than the t-value, the null hypothesis is rejected. So, it is concluded that the respondents belong to the semi-urban location of the Himachal Pradesh, are aware of the benefits of Artificial Intelligence and AI helps businesses thrive in the market's fierce or intense competition.
- **Hypothesis H03:** It states that the Artificial Intelligence does not provide answers to challenging jobs and aids in Business expansion. The mean score value is 3.962 (Table 7.4) and the P (0.05) is less than the t-value, the null hypothesis is rejected. So, it is concluded that the respondents were working in the various sectors and live in the semi-urban location of the Himachal Pradesh, are aware of the gains of Artificial Intelligence and AI provides answers to challenging jobs and aids in Business expansion.
- **Hypothesis H04:** It states that Artificial Intelligence does not train unstructured data models to provide precise forecasts, improved judgment calls, and help modify business procedures. The processed data with mean score of 3.905 (Table 7.4) and the P (0.05) is less than the t-value, the null hypothesis is rejected. Table 7.3 shows that 33.3%, 44.7%, and 19% respondents in the age bracket of 20–30, 30–40, and 40–50 years, respectively, belonging to semi-urban location of Himachal Pradesh, working in the banking and finance sectors, agree that AI trains unstructured data models to provide precise forecasts, improved judgment calls, and help modify business procedures.
- **Hypothesis H05:** It states that Artificial Intelligence does not improve efficiency, time, and human mistakes in the workplace. The processed data from Table 7.4, with mean score of 3.794 and the P (0.05) is less than the t-value, the null hypothesis is rejected. It also shows that 33.3%, 44.7%, and 19% respondents in the age

bracket of 20–30, 30–40, and 40–50 years, respectively, working in the banking and finance sectors; and 10.7%, 27.6%, and 53.8% respondents in the age bracket of 20–30, 30–40, and 40–50 years, respectively, working in the healthcare sector, belonging to semi-urban location of Himachal Pradesh, significantly agree with that AI improves efficiency, time, and human mistakes in the workplace.

- **Hypothesis H06:** It states that Artificial Intelligence does boost economic growth and promote cyber security and privacy. The processed data from Table 7.4, with mean score of 3.528 and the P (0.05) is less than the t-value, the null hypothesis is rejected. It shows that 34.1%, 30.3%, 7.6%, and 27.8% respondents in the age bracket of 20–30, 30–40, and 40–50 and above 50 years, respectively, belonging to semi-urban location of Himachal Pradesh, working in the retail sector, significantly agree with the Artificial intelligence boosts economic growth and promote cyber security and privacy.
- **Hypothesis H07:** It states that Artificial Intelligence does not improve decision-making processes, decision-quality, and search operations for various solutions. The processed data from Table 7.4, with mean score of 3.388 and the P (0.05) is less than the t-value, the null hypothesis is rejected. It is concluded that the respondents belong to the semi-urban location of the Himachal Pradesh, are aware of the benefits of AI improves decision-making processes, decision-quality, and search operations for various solutions.
- **Hypothesis H08:** It states that Artificial Intelligence does not help in Improving corporate operations, efficient supply chain management, and better consumer experiences The processed data from Table 7.4, with mean score of 4.051 and the P (0.05) is less than the t-value, the null hypothesis is rejected. From Tables 7.3 and 7.4, working in the banking and Finance, healthcare, Retail, Tourism, and insurance sector, with the age bracket of 22 to 30 and 30 to 40, the youth belonging to semi-urban location of Himachal Pradesh, agree that AI helps in Improving corporate operations, efficient supply chain management, and better consumer experiences.

7.6 CONCLUSION

Some of the primary benefits of automation, cognitive technology, and data analysis employing AI algorithms are ease of work, increases productivity, greater efficiency, time and cost efficiency, human factor reduction, consumer preference prediction, and sales maximization. The study examined "artificial intelligence (AI)" and its wide array of potential benefits and drawbacks through responses to posed questions to respondents working in various sectors like banking, retail, insurance, and healthcare, tourism, etc. According to the data presented in the study, there is significant impact of AI on selected sectors in terms of amplified production and greater consumer response, aids in corporate expansion, precise forecasts, improved judgment calls, reduced expenses, time, and human mistakes in the workplace, boosts economic growth, better consumer experiences and improves decision-making processes and decision-quality.

By automating tedious operations and generating insights through data analysis, Artificial Intelligence has significantly increased company productivity and efficiency:

1. As less time and effort are needed to accomplish activities and reach judgments, this improves the ease of work.
2. AI-enabled products and systems also assist businesses in minimizing mistakes, improving consistency and accuracy, and offering clients a more tailored experience.
3. Businesses may run more effectively, make data-driven choices, and gain a competitive advantage by integrating AI across a variety of industries.

In summary, AI is revolutionizing company operations and could completely change the commercial environment. Artificial Intelligence has a lot of promise to improve the world. It will advance in the future and alter the business landscape.

One of the key areas where AI has made a significant impact is in predictive analytics. AI algorithms can analyze vast amounts of data to predict future trends and outcomes, such as customer behavior, market trends, and sales forecasting. This allows businesses to make informed decisions, identify new opportunities, and take proactive measures to mitigate risks.

Another area where AI has made a substantial impact is in customer relationship management (CRM). AI can analyze customer data to personalize interactions and improve customer experience, such as using chatbots and personalized marketing campaigns. This helps businesses to understand their customers better, build loyalty, and increase customer satisfaction.

In addition, AI has also made a significant impact around fraud detection. AI algorithms can detect patterns in transaction data to identify potentially fraudulent activities, which helps businesses to protect their financial assets and reduce the risk of financial loss.

Furthermore, AI has also transformed supply chain management by optimizing processes and reducing costs. AI algorithms can analyze data from suppliers, production processes, and transportation to optimize the supply chain, leading to more efficient and cost-effective operations.

However, there are also critical challenges that need to be considered when applying AI in business. Some of these include bias, data quality, regulation, and explain ability. For example, AI algorithms may be biased towards certain groups, which can result in discriminatory outcomes. It is important for businesses to ensure that AI is used in a responsible and ethical manner, considering these challenges.

Further study can be done that how AI changed the financial status of these business sectors, and how AI impacts the growth and economic development of these business sectors in Solan District of Himachal Pradesh.

7.7 DRAWBACKS

Information technology is advancing, and fewer people are mistrusting it because of its expanding applications. In case of managing complicated commercial systems and helping humans with diverse tasks, it is difficult for Businesses to use AI because of low ability for learning and very low budget. The costs of developing and using Artificial Intelligence might include everything from prospective job losses to potential human lives. There could be hints of more sophisticated technology that haven't been thoroughly studied.

7.8 FUTURE TRENDS IN AI

Soon, based on the fascinating trends in AI, we should anticipate:

1. Songs and movies produced by entertainment firms using AI.
2. Factories that operate entirely without human oversight.
3. the application of AI to create high-quality training data for itself, to deal with bias and data scarcity issues, and many other things.
4. The promise of AI will give us the ability to shape the future in the way we desire for the first time.

KEYWORDS

- **artificial intelligence**
- **banking**
- **computer science**
- **financial services**
- **information technology**
- **manufacturing**
- **retail industry**
- **timeline**

REFERENCES

Akerkar, R., & Sajja, P. S., (2016). Introduction to data science. In: *Intelligent Techniques for Data Science* (pp. 1–30). Springer. Cham. https://doi.org/10.1007/978-3-319-29206-9_1.

Bag, S., Gupta, S., Kumar, A., & Sivarajah, U., (2021). An integrated artificial intelligence framework for knowledge creation and B2Bmarketing rational decision-making for improving firm performance. *Industrial Marketing Management, 92*, 178–189.

Benko, A., & Lányi, C. S., (2009). History of artificial intelligence. *Encyclopedia of Information Science and Technology* (2nd edn., pp. 1759–1762). IGI Global.

Bergeron, F., Raymond, L., & Rivard, S., (2004). Ideal patterns of strategic alignment and business performance. *Information & Management, 41*(8), 1003–1020.

Buchanan, B. G. A., (2005). *(Very) Brief History of Artificial Intelligence* (Vol. 26, pp. 53–60). AI Magazine.

Haenlein, M., & Kaplan, A., (2019). A brief history of artificial intelligence: On the past, present, and future of artificial intelligence. *California Management Review, 61*(4), 5–14. https://doi.org/10.1177/0008125619864925.

Har, L. L., Rashid, U. K., Te Chuan, L., Sen, S. C., & Xia, L. Y., (2022). Revolution of retail industry: From perspective of retail 1.0 to 4.0. *Procedia Comput Sci., 200*, 1615–1625.

Jarrahi, M. H., (2018). Artificial intelligence and the future of work: Human-AI symbiosis in organizational decision making. *Business Horizons, 61*(4), 577–586.

Jumani, A., Laghari, A., Narwani, K., & David, S., (2021). Examining the present and future integrated role of artificial intelligence in the business: A survey study on corporate sector. *Journal of Computer and Communications, 9*, 80–90.

Kaplan, A., & Haenlein, M., (2019). Siri, Siri, in my hand: Who's the fairest in the land? On the interpretations, illustrations, and implications of artificial intelligence. *Business Horizons, 62*, 15–25.

Kumar, N., Srivastava, J., & Bisht, H., (2019). Artificial intelligence in insurance sector. *The Journal of Gujrat Research Society, 21*(7), 79–91.

Kumar, V., & Garg, L. M., (2018). Predictive analytics: A review of trends and techniques. *International Journal of Computer Applications, 182*, 31–37. 10.5120/ijca2018917434.

Kuzey, C., Uyar, A., & Delen, D., (2014). The impact of multinationalism on firm value: A comparative analysis of machine learning techniques. *Decision Support Systems, 59*, 127–142.

Leung, X. Y., (2020). Technology-enabled service evolution in tourism: A perspective article. *Tourism Review, 75*(1), 279–282. https://doi.org/10.1108/TR-06-2019-0229.

Mc Corduck, P., Minsky, M., Selfridge, O. G., & Simon, H. A., (1977). History of artificial intelligence. *IJCAI'77: Proceedings of the 5th International Joint Conference on Artificial Intelligence, 2*, 951–954.

McCarthy, E. J., (1960). *Basic Marketing: A Managerial Approach*. Homewood (Illinois): R. D. Irwin.

McCarthy, J., (1989). Artificial intelligence, logic and formalizing common sense. In: *Philosophical Logic and Artificial Intelligence* (pp. 161–190). Springer.

McCorduck, P., (1979). *Machines Who Think: A Personal Inquiry into the History and Prospects of Artificial Intelligence*. A K Peters Ltd. Natick Massachusetts.

Panesar, A., (2021). What is the future of healthcare? In: *Machine Learning and AI for Healthcare* (pp. 249–291). Apress, Berkeley, CA. https://doi.org/10.1007/978-1-4842-6537-6_9.

Poole, D. L., Mackworth, A. K., & Goebel, R., (1998). Computational intelligence – a logical approach. *Computacion y Sistemas, 2*(2, 3), 146–149.

Rauch-Hindin, W. B., (1985). *Artificial Intelligence in Business, Science, And Industry: Applications* (Vol. II). Prentice-Hall.

Richers, R., (1961). Basic marketing, a managerial approach. *Revista de Administração de Empresas, 1*, 149–152. 10.1590/S0034-75901961000100013.

Rose, D., (2018). *Artificial Intelligence for Business: What You Need to Know About Machine Learning and Neural Networks*. Chicago Lakeshore Press.

Russell, S. J., & Norvig, P., (2011). Artificial intelligence – A modern approach. *Artificial Intelligence* (3rd edn., Vol. 175, pp. 935–937).

Sajja, P. S., (2021). Introduction to artificial intelligence. In: *Illustrated Computational Intelligence; Studies in Computational Intelligence* (Vol. 931, pp. 1–25). Springer, Singapore. https://doi.org/10.1007/978-981-15-9589-9_1.

Singh, K., (2020). Banks banking on ai. *International Journal of Advanced Research in Management and Social Sciences, 9*(9), 1–11.

Sterne, J., (2017). *Artificial Intelligence for Marketing: Practical Applications*. John Wiley & Sons.

Strusani, D., & Houngbonon, G. V., (2019). *The Role of Artificial Intelligence in Supporting Development in Emerging Markets* (Vol. 69, pp. 1–8). E M Compass, International Finance Corporation, Washington, DC.

Tenenbaum, J. B., Kemp, C., Griffiths, T. L., & Goodman, N. D., (2011). How to grow a mind: Statistics, structure, and abstraction. *Science, 331*(6022), 1279–1285. New York, N.Y. https://doi.org/10.1126/science.1192788.

Turing, A. M., (2009). Computing machinery, and intelligence. In: Epstein, R., Roberts, G., & Beber, G., (eds.), *Parsing the Turing Test* (pp. 23–65). Springer, Dordrecht. https://doi.org/10.1007/978-1-4020-6710-5_3.

Wamba-Taguimdje, S., Wamba, S. F., Kamdjoug, J. R. K., & Wanko, C. E. T., (2020). Influence of artificial intelligence (AI) on firm performance: Business value of ai-based transformation projects. *Business Process Management Journal*, 1–45.

CHAPTER 8

Applications of Quantum Machine Learning in Financial Services

S. BHUVANESWARI,[1] A. ABIRAMI,[1] R. DEEPAKRAJ,[2] JYOTI BATRA ARORA,[3] and K. KAARTHIC VARUN[2]

[1]*Assistant Professor, Department of Computer Science and Engineering, Easwari Engineering College, Chennai, Tamil Nadu, India*

[2]*Student, Department of Computer Science and Engineering, Easwari Engineering College, Chennai, Tamil Nadu, India*

[3]*Faculty – IT, Institute of Chartered Accountants of India, Noida, India*

ABSTRACT

An emerging, cutting-edge technology is quantum machine learning. The machine learning algorithms integrate quantum computing, and such algorithms will have the incredible capacity to do any complex non-linear computation in a matter of seconds, which cannot be accomplished by traditional algorithms. Large datasets are difficult for classical algorithms to handle, but they are no match for these quantum algorithms. It helps to resolve the computational and time complexity issues faced by traditional machine learning algorithms. Running quantum algorithms required a quantum computer. Quantum algorithms cannot run on conventional computers, whereas classical algorithms can run on quantum computers. It is applicable to a wide range of groups, including banking, government, finance, social media, and communication media, among others. In the finance sector, huge amounts of financial data can be analyzed using it to detect patterns and anomalies, which can help in identifying fraudulent activities. Quantum algorithms can enhance the security of financial transactions by providing

Advanced Digital Technologies in Financial and Business Management: Unleashing the Power of Artificial Intelligence, Machine Learning, Blockchain, and the Internet of Things. Jyoti Batra Arora, Nitish Pathak, and Neelam Sharma (Eds.)

more secure encryption methods which cannot be broken even by another quantum algorithm. This chapter provides a detailed overview of a few quantum machine learning techniques and their applications to financial services.

8.1 INTRODUCTION

A novel region called "quantum machine learning" combines the ideas of "machine learning" concepts and algorithms with the "quantum computing" to uncover solutions to complicated issues that are either impossible or extremely difficult to solve using conventional techniques. It has many benefits, one of which is its ability to perform the computations 10 times faster than with classical techniques. This is because a quantum computer may carry out several calculations at once thanks to the quantum parallelism principle. For example, a quantum computer can perform a search operation on a database by simultaneously checking all possible answers, whereas a classical computer would have to check each answer one at a time. This makes quantum machine learning particularly useful for tasks such as optimization and unsupervised learning. Quantum machine learning has the significant advantage of processing and analyzing huge and complicated data sets faster than traditional methods. This is caused by a quantum computer's capacity to store and handle a significant quantity of data in a single qubit, whereas on the other side, a classical computer would require multiple bits to process the same amount of data.

8.2 BASIC QUANTUM THEORY

A branch of physics called quantum theory, commonly referred to as quantum mechanics, describes how matter and energy behave at the atomic and subatomic scales. It started out in the first decades of the 20th century as a way to explain phenomena that could not be explained by classical physics, such as the behavior of electrons in atoms. The idea of wave-particle duality, which argues that particles like electrons and photons can act both like waves and like particles, is one of the fundamental principles of quantum theory. This implies that attributes like position and momentum cannot be understood with infinite precision and that particles can exist in multiple states at once. The "uncertainty principle" refers to this. Another important principle of quantum theory is quantum entanglement, which occurs When two particles become entangled, their states become interdependent, regardless of how far apart they are. This allows for the phenomenon of quantum teleportation, in which the state of one particle can be transferred to another particle without physically moving the first particle. Quantum theory also describes the behavior of systems with numerous particles, such as atoms and molecules with the help of quantum states along with its wave functions. The chance of detecting a particle in a specific place or with a specific energy can be determined using these wave functions (Egger et al., 2020).

In the area of quantum computing, quantum theory has one of its most significant applications. Qubits, the quantum bits used in quantum computers, have the ability to exist in several states at once, enabling faster and more effective processing. Other applications of quantum theory include quantum cryptography, quantum simulation, quantum field theory, and in the development of new technologies like transistors, lasers, and memory storage.

8.3 QUANTUM MECHANICS IN COMPUTATIONS

A subfield of computer science is quantum computing which employs the principles of quantum physics to do some forms of computation than traditional computers. The core element of a quantum computing is the quantum bit, or qubit, which can simultaneously exist in several states as shown in Figure 8.1. This property, known as superposition, enables quantum computers to carry out certain tasks, such as navigating to large databases, too quick than classical computers. Quantum entanglement, which enables quantum computers to conduct specific sorts of parallel calculations, or quantum parallelism, is another crucial aspect of quantum computing. The following are a few instances of uses for quantum computing:

- Breaking encryption codes and cryptography;
- Optimizing large-scale machine learning algorithms;
- Simulating quantum systems and materials;
- Developing new drugs and materials.

Cryptography is one of the most significant fields where quantum computing is being used. Factoring huge numbers is difficult on classical computers, which is the basis of many encryption methods. However, Shor's algorithm might factor huge numbers substantially quicker on a quantum computer than on a classical one, potentially breaking encryption codes and making current encryption methods insecure. Another important application is in the field of optimization. Many real-world optimization problems, such as logistics planning and financial portfolio optimization, involve searching through large sets of possible solutions. Grover's approach could be applied to such enormous sets to search them tenfold more quickly than a conventional one.

Quantum computing also has conceivable applications in Machine Learning (ML) and Artificial Intelligence (AI). For example, there are some ML tasks that a quantum computer may be able to execute more quickly than a classical computer by using quantum neural networks. Quantum simulations are another important application of quantum computing. Simulations helps to know how the quantum states like molecules and materials behave on a quantum computer, researchers could gain a better understanding of their properties and potentially discover new materials and drugs (Georgescu et al., 2014). Quantum field theory is also a field that could benefit from quantum computing. On a quantum computer, scientists may simulate the behavior of particles and fields to better comprehend the underlying principles of the universe.

The qubits $|0\rangle$ and $|1\rangle$ are represented as $\begin{bmatrix}1\\0\end{bmatrix}$ and $\begin{bmatrix}0\\1\end{bmatrix}$

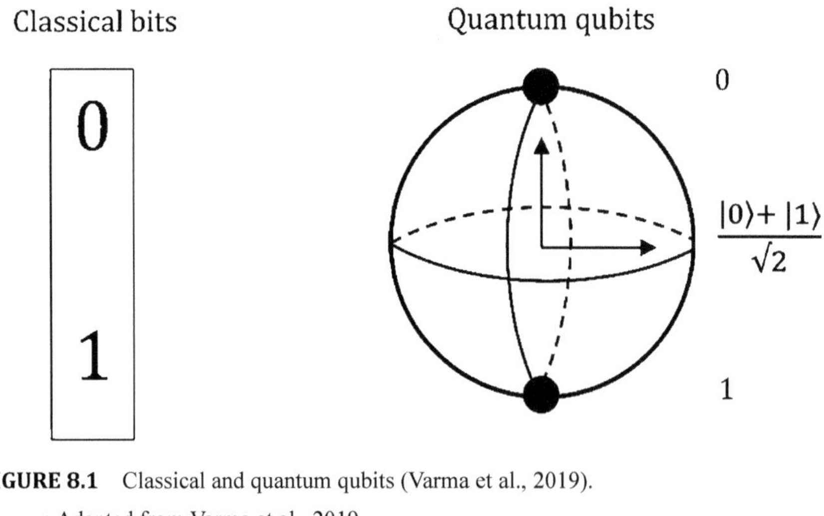

FIGURE 8.1 Classical and quantum qubits (Varma et al., 2019).

Source: Adapted from Varma et al., 2019

8.3.1 SUPERPOSITION

One of the fundamental ideas of quantum mechanics, superposition, enables quantum computers to do some forms of computation more effectively than traditional computers. Only one of two possible states 0 or 1 can a bit has in a classical computer. However, in a quantum computer, as represented in Figure 8.2. A qubit possesses the capability of the superposition of states., which means it can be in multiple states at once. This superposition of states is represented mathematically by a complex-valued wave function, known as a quantum state, in which the possibility of discovering a qubit in an instance is described. The qubit's state can be described by a binary combination of two basic states, 0 and 1, with complex coefficients representing the amplitude and phase of the state.

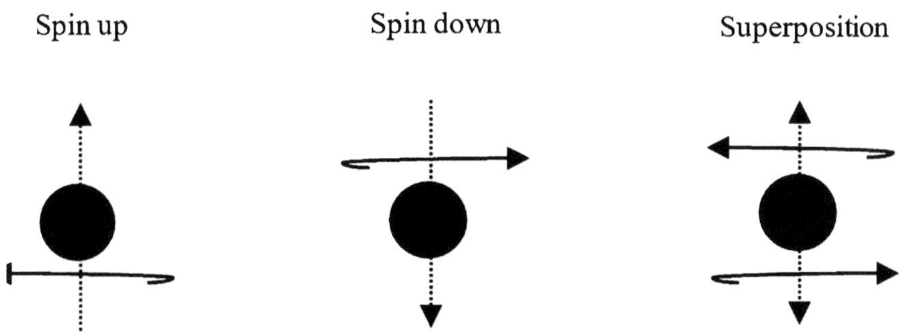

FIGURE 8.2 Representation of superposition.

Because of superposition, quantum computers can perform some operations much quicker than classical computers. For example, a quantum computer can perform a search operation on a database by simultaneously checking all possible answers, whereas a classical computer would have to check each answer one at a time. It enables to perform certain types of computation more efficiently than classical computers, but it also requires a different way of thinking and understanding the system, it is crucial to note that superposition is a fragile state that it is quickly get disturbed by external noise, which is one of the challenges in developing a reliable and stable quantum computer.

8.3.2 QUANTUM ENTANGLEMENT

Another fundamental aspect of quantum mechanics is quantum entanglement, which is used in quantum computing. It happens when two or more quantum systems linked together in such a way that their states are interdependent, even though they are separated by great distances. To put it another way, even if two particles are not directly in contact, their states are nonetheless connected as represented in Figure 8.3.

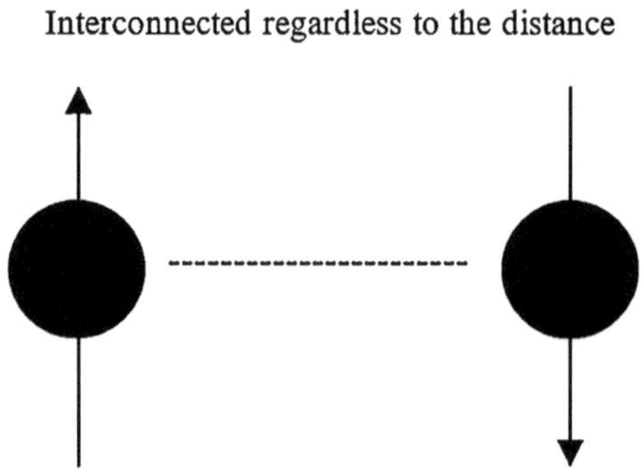

FIGURE 8.3 Representation of quantum entanglement.

Entanglement is utilized in quantum computing to carry out specific calculations in parallel, known as quantum parallelism. For example, a quantum computer can perform a search operation on a database by simultaneously checking all possible answers, using the principle of quantum parallelism. This is made possible by the fact that entangled qubits are able to conduct many calculations at once due to their capability of multiple existence.

Quantum teleportation, which is the transfer of one qubit's state to another without physically moving the original qubit, also makes use of quantum entanglement. This is made possible by the fact that even if they are far away from one another, the state of one qubit depends on the state of the other. Additionally, it is a crucial component of quantum key distribution and quantum cryptography. By sharing a pair of entangled qubits between two parties, they can create a shared secret key that can be used to encrypt and decrypt messages.

8.4 CLASSICAL MODELS VS. QUANTUM MODELS

Classical models as well quantum models are both methods used to analyze and make predictions from data, but there are some significant variations between the two. Among all, the key difference is the type of computation used. Classical machine learning relies on traditional computers, which represent and analyze information using traditional bits. These bits can exist in one of two states, either 0 or 1. Contrarily, quantum machine learning relies on quantum computers, which represent and process information using qubits. Because these qubits can be in numerous states at once, quantum computers can carry out some sorts of operations tenfold quicker than conventional computers.

Another key difference is the type of algorithms used. Classical machine learning algorithms are based on classical mathematical concepts and typically involve optimization, such as gradient descent. Quantum machine learning algorithms, on the other hand, are based on quantum mechanical concepts and may involve principles such as quantum parallelism and quantum entanglement (Figure 8.4). In terms of applications, classical machine learning is well-established and has been used in a broad array of fields such as computer vision, NLP, and speech recognition (Huang et al., 2021). Quantum machine learning, on the other hand, has primarily been used for specific tasks such as optimization and unsupervised learning.

In short, both conventional and quantum machine learning are approaches used for analyzing and forecasting the data, they differ in the type of computation and algorithms used. Classical machine learning relies on classical computers and classical mathematical concepts, while quantum machine learning relies on quantum computers and quantum mechanical concepts (Figure 8.5). Classical machine learning is well-established and has been used in a wide range of fields, while quantum machine learning is still in its nascent stages.

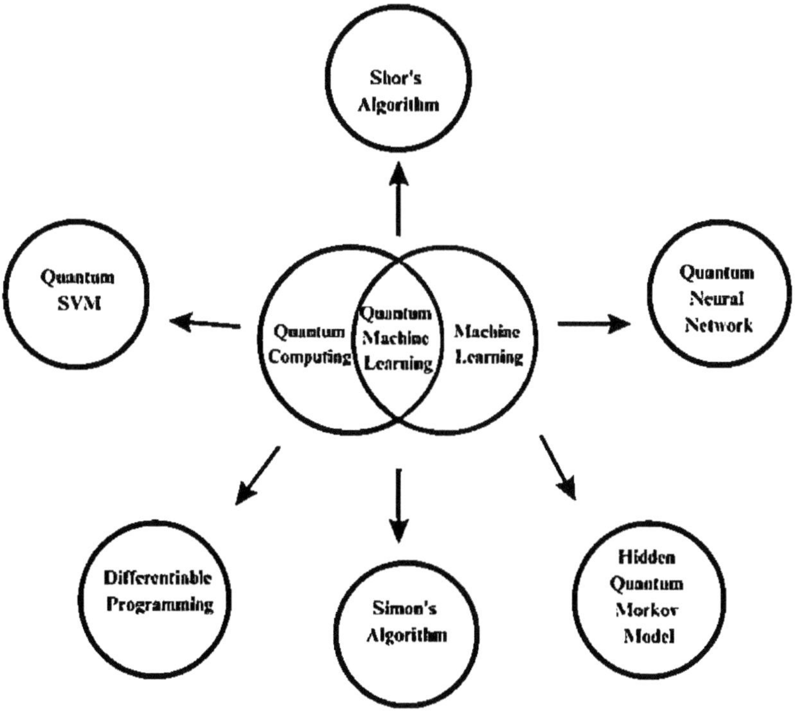

FIGURE 8.4 Quantum machine learning algorithms.

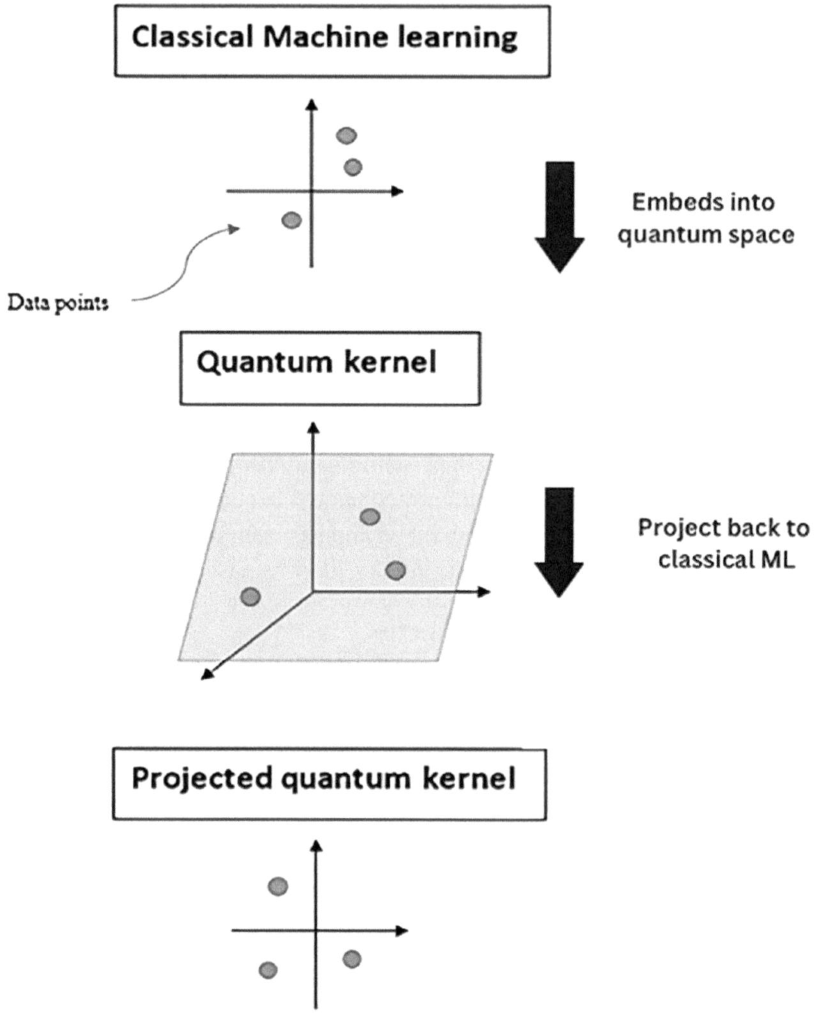

FIGURE 8.5 Conversion from classical to quantum algorithms.
Source: Adapted from Huang et al., 2021

8.5 QUANTUM MACHINE LEARNING IN THE FINANCIAL SECTOR

In recent years, ML has significantly changed how the financial services sector analyzes data, made predictions and automates procedures. The financial services industry has been impacted by ML in the following ways:

1. **Fraud Detection:** ML algorithms can detect fraudulent activity in financial transactions by analyzing patterns and detecting anomalies.

2. **Credit Scoring:** ML can be used to build models that predict creditworthiness depending on past performance and additional factors.
3. **Investment Management:** ML algorithms can forecast future market conditions and trends, assisting investors in making better choices.
4. **Risk Management:** ML can be used to analyze risks and build models that predict potential losses or other risks.
5. **Chatbots and Customer Service:** ML can be used to build chatbots and other customer service applications that provide personalized support and improve customer satisfaction.
6. **Compliance and Regulatory Reporting:** ML can help automate compliance and regulatory reporting by analyzing large amounts of data and flagging potential violations.

In general, ML has helped financial services firms automate procedures, produce more accurate forecasts, and enhance consumer experiences.

8.5.1 QUANTUM MACHINE LEARNING OVER CLASSICAL MACHINE LEARNING

The study of nexus between the ML concepts and quantum computing paves way for the quantum machine learning. Although it is still in its infancy and has not yet gained widespread acceptance, there are some potential advantages of quantum algorithms as represented in Figure 8.6, which include:

1. **Increased Speed:** Information could potentially be processed more quickly on quantum computers than on traditional ones, which could lead to faster training and prediction times for ML models.
2. **Improved Performance:** Some quantum machine learning algorithms have been shown to outperform classical machine learning algorithms, particularly for certain types of problems.
3. **Better Scalability:** Quantum computing could enable the processing of large datasets and high-dimensional feature spaces, which can be computationally expensive for classical computers.
4. **New Applications:** Quantum machine learning could offer new opportunities for ML applications, such as quantum chemistry and drug discovery.

The use of quantum machine learning has the potential to be advantageous, but it also poses significant technical and practical challenges, such as the necessity of particular hardware and software, the difficulty of working with noisy quantum systems, and the requirement for new mathematical and algorithmic frameworks (Egger et al., 2020). Additionally, traditional machine learning is still a potent tool for a variety of applications and will be useful for the foreseeable future.

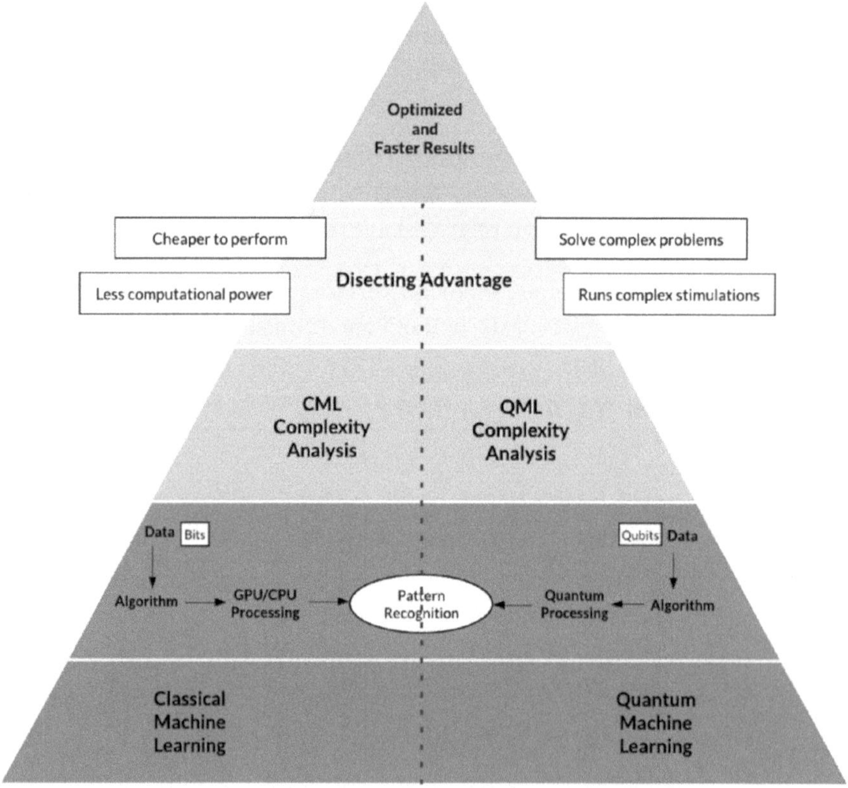

FIGURE 8.6 Advantage of quantum algorithms over classical algorithms.

8.6 FINANCIAL USE CASES

8.6.1 FRAUD DETECTION AND PREDICTION

Fraud detection is an essential practice to monitor and prevent fraudulent activities happened. It is represented in almost many sectors including Sales, health care, business, banking, etc., In all of this fraudulent activity happened in the financial sector has a high impact on financial loss and it happens in various forms such as account theft, redundant applications, banking scams, tax evasion, and money laundering. To prevent all these, machine learning helps to predict and detect fraudulent activities. It uses many complex computational algorithms, and they are:

- Regression;
- Neural networks;
- Principal component analysis (PCA);
- K-nearest neighbors;
- Anomaly recognition.

Neural networks have a large-scale application, and it is used widely because of their adaptive behavior, ability to solve non-linear complex relationships, and fast processing. In addition, Quantum neural networks provide a great leap in the detection and prediction of fraudulent activities. Quantum neural networks are a collection of multiple quantum perceptrons. Figure 8.7 represents the single quantum perceptron.

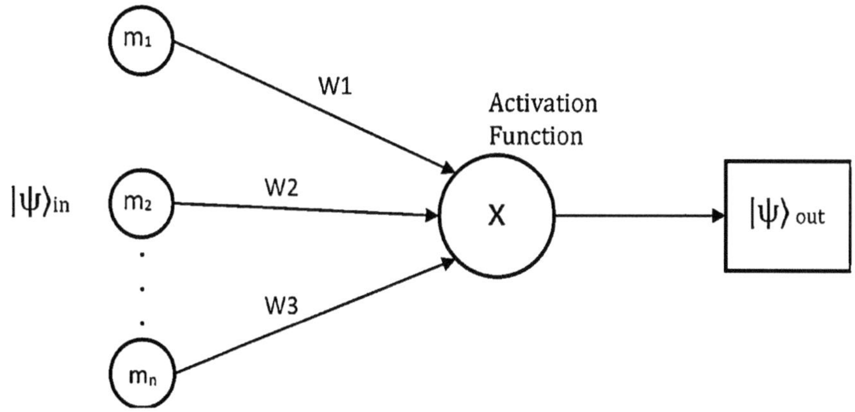

FIGURE 8.7 Representation of single quantum perceptron.

Source: Adapted from Jia et al., 2019

These perceptrons are trained usually either online quantum perceptron training or version space perceptron training. The quantum neural network takes qubits as input from one layer and passes them to the next layer of qubits (Figure 8.8). The superposition states of bits are formed in the inner layer to have a deep insight into the inputs. Encoding the binary inputs into m qubits is the first step. The encoded data is proposed to be a single quantum perceptron. Then the neural network machine learning algorithm is implemented with a quantum state. The n output from the network will be as a dense matrix. The dense matrix is post-processed to get accurate predictions.

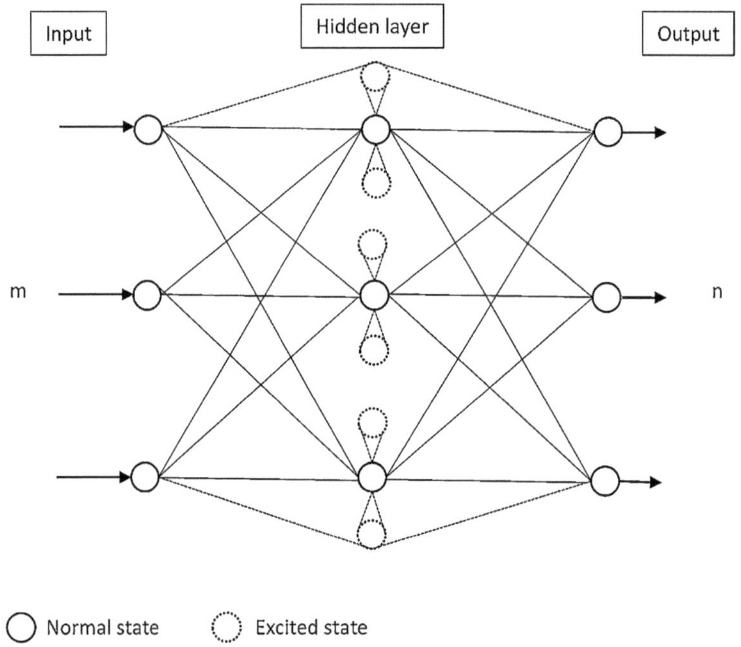

FIGURE 8.8 Representation of quantum neural network.

Source: Adapted from Jia et al., 2019

8.6.2 CREDIT SCORING

Credit scoring is a numerical calculation used in financial services to evaluate an individual or a business's creditworthiness and ability to repay a loan. The calculation is based on several factors such as credit history, payment history, outstanding debts, income, and employment history.

The exact formula used for credit scoring is often proprietary and varies between credit bureaus and financial institutions, but some common factors considered include:

1. **Payment History:** The borrower's history of paying bills on time and avoiding late payments, bankruptcies, and collections.
2. **Credit Utilization:** The proportion of available credit that has been utilized by the borrower.

3. **Length of Credit History:** The duration of open credit accounts for the borrower.
4. **Types of Credit:** The types of credit the borrower has, such as mortgages, credit cards, car loans, etc.
5. **New Credit Applications:** The number of new credit applications made by the borrower.

A decision tree a machine learning technique is used to calculate the credit-scoring individual with the highest precision. The quantum version of the decision tree is a type of machine learning algorithm that leverage the principles of quantum computing to perform decision-making (Figure 8.9). They operate by encoding decision rules into quantum gates, which can then be manipulated using quantum algorithms to produce a final decision. This approach is considered more efficient than classical decision trees as quantum computing allows for parallel processing of information, reducing the time complexity of decision-making tasks. In the quantum decision tree, the internal node splits the input data into two or more subsets concerning discrete functions. This process enhances the way to perform decision-making tasks faster than classical decision trees, due to the parallel processing capabilities of quantum computing. Quantum decision trees are less susceptible to overfitting and can handle noisy or uncertain data better than classical decision trees.

The performance of quantum decision trees may vary depending on the exact use case and the quantum hardware being utilized, despite the fact that these benefits appear promising. This is because it still in its early development stage.

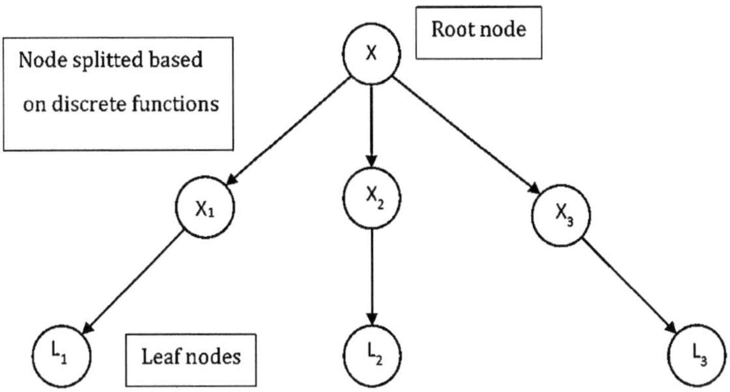

FIGURE 8.9 Representation of quantum decision tree.

8.6.3 STOCK FORECASTING

Stock market forecasting is the process of estimating future stock price changes, based on past market data and other relevant information. There are various methods used for stock market forecasting, including:

- Technical analysis: which uses chart patterns and trends to make predictions.
- Fundamental analysis: which focuses on the financial and economic health of a company.
- Machine learning algorithms: including ANN, SVM, RNN, and others.

It is important to note that stock market forecasting is a difficult task and there is no guaranteed method for accurately forecasting the future stock price movements. It is also influenced by many unpredictable factors, such as global events and market sentiment, making it challenging to make accurate predictions. Support Vector Machines (SVM) give a significant result when compared to others. SVM uses a hyperplane to classify data into different categories and make predictions. The algorithm can handle non-linear and high-dimensional data, making it a good choice for stock market data, which is often non-linear and has many features (Gentinetta et al., 2022). However, the performance of SVM in stock market forecasting depends on several factors such as data quality, feature selection, and model hyperparameter tuning.

The quantum version of SVM leverages the unique features of quantum computers, such as quantum parallelism and quantum interference, to accelerate the learning as well prediction process. In theory, quantum SVM has the potential to provide faster and more accurate stock market forecasts compared to classical SVM. The implementation of quantum SVM requires expertise in both machine learning and quantum computing, as well as a good understanding of the mathematical foundations of SVM and quantum mechanics. The input data is preprocessed and map the stock market data into a high-dimensional quantum feature space to capture the underlying relationships between the data. Then, quantum algorithms are used to detect the optimal hyperplane which separates the data into different segments and makes predictions. Finally, build forecasts based on the developed quantum SVM model (Khodabandehlou et al., 2017).

The classical SVM is converted into quantum SVM by having a quantum feature map $S(\psi(\vec{x}))$ which is used to convert the data from classical data $\vec{x}$ to quantum states as shown in Figure 8.10.

Inner product of feature maps is $S(\vec{x},\vec{z})=|\langle \psi(\vec{x})|\psi(\vec{z})\rangle|^2$ in classical SVM.

The quantum feature map will be:

$$S(\psi(\vec{x})) = K(\psi(\vec{x})) \otimes H^n \otimes K(\psi(\vec{x})) \otimes H^n$$

where; $K(\psi(\vec{x})) = \exp(i\,\{x_1 Z_1 + x_2 Z_2 + (\pi - x_1)(\pi - x_2) Z_1 Z_2\})$; $\psi_{uv}(\vec{x}) = (\pi - x_u)(\pi - x_v)$; $\psi_u(\vec{x}) = x_u$; $K(\psi(\vec{x}))$ is derived from ansatz; and H^n is the Hadamard gate applied to each qubit, where n represents the number of qubits.

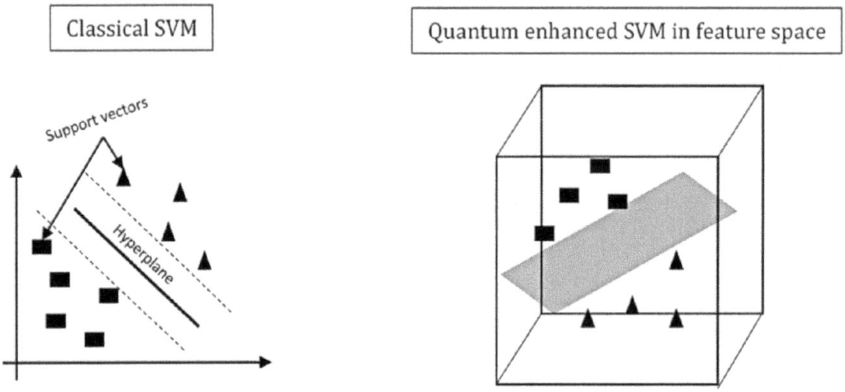

FIGURE 8.10 Quantum SVM.

Source: Adapted from González-Camacho et al., 2018

8.7 STATISTICAL ANALYSIS OF ML IN FINANCIAL SECTOR

A rising corpus of research on machine learning's application in the finance industry indicates that this technology is being used more frequently. Here are some figures on how machine learning is used in the financial sector.

In a 2020 survey of financial institutions by Refinitiv, 78% of respondents said that they were using machine learning for fraud detection, and 69% were using it for anti-money laundering.

By 2025, Accenture estimates that the application of artificial intelligence (AI), which includes machine learning, in the financial services sector could result in productivity improvements of up to $140 billion annually.

According to a 2019 report by Deloitte, 87% of financial institutions surveyed were using machine learning in some capacity, and 63% were intending to boost investment in technological advancement over the following 18 months. In a 2021 report by the Cambridge Centre for Alternative Finance, 25% of surveyed financial institutions said that they were using machine learning for investment management, and 19% were using it for credit scoring.

A 2020 report by FinTech Global found that the total amount of funding for AI and ML for financial sectors had reached $5.5 billion, with 75% of that going to startups.

Quantum computing has a potential application in the field of finance and business sectors (Figure 8.11). Recent research indicates that for some financial applications, quantum machine learning might be superior to classical machine learning in several ways. Examples of these studies are as follows:

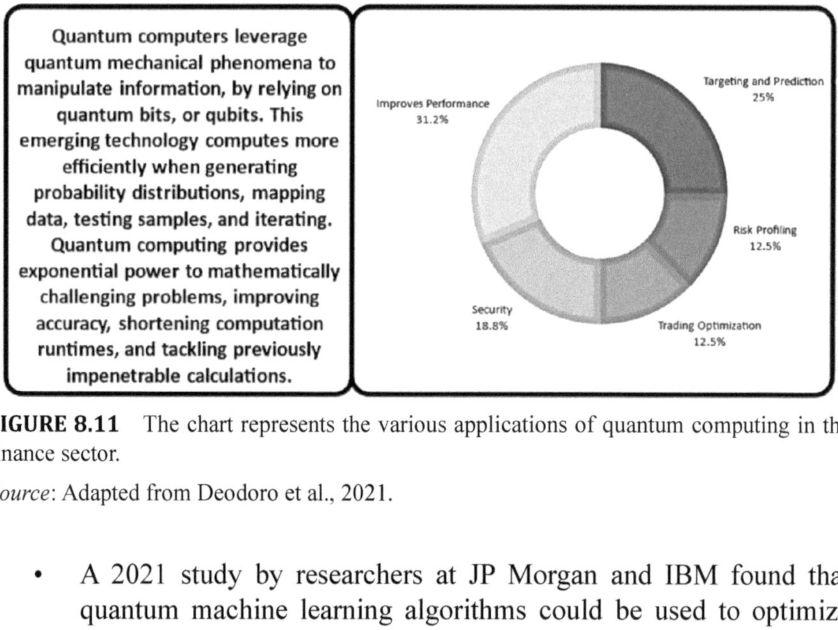

FIGURE 8.11 The chart represents the various applications of quantum computing in the finance sector.

Source: Adapted from Deodoro et al., 2021.

- A 2021 study by researchers at JP Morgan and IBM found that quantum machine learning algorithms could be used to optimize portfolios of financial assets. The researchers used a quantum algorithm to solve the so-called "Markowitz problem," which involves finding the optimal combination of assets to minimize risk for a given level of return. They discovered that in terms of accuracy and speed, the quantum algorithm performed better than classical algorithms.
- A 2020 study by researchers at the University of Oxford and JPMorgan Chase found that a quantum machine learning algorithm could be used to improve the accuracy of credit risk models. The

researchers used a quantum algorithm to train a logistic regression model on credit default data and found that the quantum model outperformed classical models in terms of prediction accuracy.

- A 2019 study by researchers at the University of Sydney and the University of Technology Sydney found that quantum machine learning algorithms could be used to optimize high-frequency trading strategies. The researchers used a quantum algorithm to solve a portfolio optimization problem and found that the quantum algorithm outperformed classical algorithms in terms of risk-adjusted returns.

8.8 FUTURE PROSPECTS

Quantum machine learning has the potential to impact a broad range of disciplines beyond finance, including healthcare, energy, and materials science. In these and other domains, researchers are investigating the possibilities of quantum machine learning in order to create fresh approaches and technologies that can solve some of the most important problems confronting the world today. The active research is made on deploying hybrid quantum-classical algorithms, which integrate classical and quantum machine learning methods. These algorithms may offer more precise and effective solutions for challenging machine learning issues since they are built to capitalize on the advantages of both classical and quantum techniques. Developing new hardware that is more stable and scalable is an active area of research, to make quantum machine learning more practical and accessible.

8.9 CONCLUSION

In this chapter, we have investigated quantum machine learning approaches for financial services such as fraud detection, prediction, credit scoring, and stock market forecasting. Quantum machine learning has several advantages over classical machine learning algorithms. It makes a decision quickly and more precisely. It also handles a huge volume of data that cannot be handled by classical algorithms. At last, it can find a solution for non-linear complex problems. These quantum machine learning algorithms are more powerful and complex to understand. The major drawback of these algorithms is the hardware that is capable to run the quantum algorithms is still in the research phase.

KEYWORDS

- **entanglement**
- **feature map**
- **quantum kernel**
- **quantum machine learning**
- **quantum perceptron**
- **qubits**
- **superposition**

REFERENCES

Ablayev, F., Ablayev, M., Huang, J. Z., Khadiev, K., Salikhova, N., & Wu, D., (2019). On quantum methods for machine learning problems part I: Quantum tools. *Big Data Mining and Analytics*, *3*(1), 41–55.

Acampora, G., (2019). Quantum machine intelligence: Launching the first journal in the area of quantum artificial intelligence. *Quantum Machine Intelligence, 1*, 1–3.

Aïmeur, E., Brassard, G., & Gambs, S., (2006). Machine learning in a quantum world. In: *Advances in Artificial Intelligence: 19th Conference of the Canadian Society for Computational Studies of Intelligence, Canadian AI 2006, Québec City, Québec, Canada, June 7–9, 2006; Proceedings 19* (pp. 431–442). Springer Berlin Heidelberg.

Alcazar, J., Leyton-Ortega, V., & Perdomo-Ortiz, A., (2020). Classical versus quantum models in machine learning: Insights from a finance application. *Machine Learning: Science and Technology, 1*(3), 035003.

Behrman, E. C., & Steck, J. E., (2013). A quantum neural network computes its own relative phase. In: *2013 IEEE Symposium on Swarm Intelligence (SIS)* (pp. 119–124). IEEE.

Boser, B. E., Guyon, I. M., & Vapnik, V. N., (1992). A training algorithm for optimal margin classifiers. In: *Proceedings of the Fifth Annual Workshop on Computational Learning Theory* (pp. 144–152).

Broughton, M., Verdon, G., McCourt, T., Martinez, A. J., Yoo, J. H., Isakov, S. V., & Mohseni, M., (2020). *Tensorflow Quantum: A Software Framework for Quantum Machine Learning.* arXiv preprint arXiv:2003.02989.

Chatterjee, R., & Yu, T., (2016). *Generalized Coherent States, Reproducing Kernels, and Quantum Support Vector Machines.* arXiv preprint arXiv:1612.03713.

Ciliberto, C., Herbster, M., Ialongo, A. D., Pontil, M., Rocchetto, A., Severini, S., & Wossnig, L., (2018). Quantum machine learning: A classical perspective. *Proceedings of the Royal Society A: Mathematical, Physical and Engineering Sciences, 474*(2209), 20170551.

Deodoro, J., Gorbanyov, M., Malaika, M., & Sedik, T. S., (2021). Quantum computing, and the financial system: Spooky action at a distance? *International Monetary Fund Working Papers. 21*(71), 1–33.

Ding, Y., Gonzalez-Conde, J., Lamata, L., Martín-Guerrero, J. D., Lizaso, E., Mugel, S., & Sanz, M., (2019). *Towards Prediction of Financial Crashes with a D-Wave Quantum Computer*. arXiv preprint arXiv:1904.05808.

Egger, D. J., Gambella, C., Marecek, J., McFaddin, S., Mevissen, M., Raymond, R., & Yndurain, E., (2020). Quantum computing for finance: State-of-the-art and future prospects. *IEEE Transactions on Quantum Engineering, 1*, 1–24.

Elsheikh, A., Showaib, E., & Asar, A., (2013). Artificial neural network based forward kinematics solution for planar parallel manipulators passing through singular configuration. *Adv. Robot Autom., 2*(106), 2.

Gentinetta, G., Thomsen, A., Sutter, D., & Woerner, S., (2022). *The Complexity of Quantum Support Vector Machines.* arXiv preprint arXiv:2203.00031.

Georgescu, I. M., Ashhab, S., & Nori, F., (2014). Quantum simulation. *Reviews of Modern Physics., 86*(1), 153.

González-Camacho, J. M., Ornella, L., Pérez-Rodríguez, P., Gianola, D., Dreisigacker, S., & Crossa, J., (2018). Applications of machine learning methods to genomic selection in breeding wheat for rust resistance. *The Plant Genome, 11*(2), 170104.

Huang, H. Y., Broughton, M., Mohseni, M., Babbush, R., Boixo, S., Neven, H., & McClean, J. R., (2021). Power of data in quantum machine learning. *Nature Communications, 12*(1), 2631.

Jia, Z. A., Yi, B., Zhai, R., Wu, Y. C., Guo, G. C., & Guo, G. P., (2019). Quantum neural network states: A brief review of methods and applications. *Advanced Quantum Technologies, 2*(7, 8), 1800077.

Khodabandehlou, S., & Zivari, R. M., (2017). Comparison of supervised machine learning techniques for customer churn prediction based on analysis of customer behavior. *Journal of Systems and Information Technology., 19*(1, 2), 65–93.

Martin, A., Candelas, B., Rodríguez-Rozas, Á., Martín-Guerrero, J. D., Chen, X., Lamata, L., & Sanz, M., (2021). Toward pricing financial derivatives with an IBM quantum computer. *Physical Review Research, 3*(1), 013167.

Mohseni, M., Read, P., Neven, H., Boixo, S., Denchev, V., Babbush, R., & Martinis, J., (2017). Commercialize quantum technologies in five years. *Nature., 543*(7644), 171–174.

Nivelkar, M., & Bhirud, S. G., (2022). Modeling of supervised machine learning using mechanism of quantum computing. In: *Journal of Physics: Conference Series* (Vol. 2161, No. 1, p. 012023). IOP Publishing.

Orús, R., Mugel, S., & Lizaso, E., (2019). Quantum computing for finance: Overview and prospects. *Reviews in Physics, 4*, 100028.

Schuld, M., Sinayskiy, I., & Petruccione, F., (2015). An introduction to quantum machine learning. *Contemporary Physics, 56*(2), 172–185.

Schulte, P., & Lee, D. K. C., (2019). *Huawei and the Global Landscape in 5G and Cloud* (pp. 215–243). World Scientific Publishing Co. Pte. Ltd.

Suzuki, Y., Yano, H., Gao, Q., Uno, S., Tanaka, T., Akiyama, M., & Yamamoto, N., (2020). Analysis and synthesis of feature map for kernel-based quantum classifier. *Quantum Machine Intelligence, 2*, 1–9.

Torrontegui, E., & García-Ripoll, J. J., (2019). Unitary quantum perceptron as efficient universal approximator (a). *Europhysics Letters, 125*(3), 30004.

Uehara, G. S., Spanias, A., & Clark, W., (2021). Quantum information processing algorithms with emphasis on machine learning. In: 2021 *12th International Conference on Information, Intelligence, Systems & Applications (IISA)* (pp. 1–11). IEEE.

Varma, C., Behera, B. K., & Panigrahi, P. K., (2019). *Playing Pong Game on a Quantum Computer* (pp. 1–2).

Wichert, A., (2020). *Principles of Quantum Artificial Intelligence: Quantum Problem Solving and Machine Learning* (pp. 1–14).

CHAPTER 9

Human-Machine Collaboration in Business Process

BRIJMOHAN DAGA,[1] NITISH PATHAK,[2] SRUSHTI SURAJ SHAH,[1] AUSTIN BERNARD FERNANDES,[1] JAYDEN JUDE DSOUZA,[1] and GAYATRI PRAMOD VARMA[1]

[1]*Department of Computer Engineering, Fr. Conceicao Rodrigues College of Engineering (FRCRCE), Mumbai, Maharashtra, India*

[2]*Bhagwan Parshuram Institute of Technology (BPIT), GGSIPU, New Delhi, India*

ABSTRACT

The conveyance and interactivity between a machine, a dynamic technological system, and human that is users with the help of a human-machine interface is termed as human-machine interaction. The closely interacting products like the human-machine system and the human-computer interactions are distinguished by real-time constituents. Research on human-machine interaction has been conducted throughout the previous 50 years. In various employment schemes like industries, transportation, medicine, entertainment systems, a large market value can be attained with the help of appreciable designs of human-machine interaction and systems. In human-machine interactions, controlling and problem-solving are the two primary human job categories. The excessive intellectual processes of accountability management and organizing, are a part of issue resolution, whereas open- and closed-loop operations are continuous and discrete duties in controlling. Natural Language Processing (NLP) approaches have a wide variety of practical and theoretical applications in the discipline of Human-Computer Interaction (HCI) during the past several decades. Human-machine interaction is

Advanced Digital Technologies in Financial and Business Management: Unleashing the Power of Artificial Intelligence, Machine Learning, Blockchain, and the Internet of Things. Jyoti Batra Arora, Nitish Pathak, and Neelam Sharma (Eds.)

made simpler by NLP, which also improves user experience qualitatively. Content abounds in the digital environment. On the Internet right now, there exist 100 trillion words, but not every one of them is equally important. To separate what is significant from what isn't, is an entirely different game. When it comes to summarizing lengthy and tiresome papers, whether they are technical, financial, legal, medical, or even literary, NLP and automated text comprehension have become indispensable tools. Every industry, from academics to business, can gain by using automated text comprehension tools to generate an encapsulation of the important content. Hence this chapter presents the content comprehension as an application of human machine collaboration in business process.

9.1 INTRODUCTION

A user interface is used to facilitate communication and interaction between a machine and a human, which is termed as human machine interaction (HMI). As they enable people to operate machines through instinctive and natural actions, natural user interfaces like gestures are gaining more and more attention in the modern world. Gesticulation-based HMI uses a detector, like Microsoft Kinect, to record human positions and actions, which are then processed to operate a machine. The Gesture-based HMI primarily recognizes the significant explanations of human actions depending on the data supplied by the Kinect, the RGB, the depth and the skeleton data. The challenge of gesture identification for HMI introduces the most recent deep learning techniques for tracking human locomotion analysis and RGB-D-based motion recognition. A number of deep learning frameworks related to the Convolutional Neural Networks are used to identify gestures, utilizing RGB, depth, and skeletal sequences.

The dominant interface, at the time served as a marker for the many historical periods in the growth of the human-robot interface, Batch processing was the most popular method in the 1950s. Users would specify all the requirements for a work on punch cards, carried out by inserting the cards to the machine and receiving the results after the processing got finished. Batch processing was laborious and prone to mistakes. The command-line console, which enabled users to bilaterally input instructions that the system immediately processed and generated results for, came after the batch interface. Although an advance, command-line interface did not fully use human perceptual, cognitive, and learning skills. When graphical user interfaces (GUIs) were created in the midway of the 1960s and the initiation of the 1970s, such skills were put to use. Utilizing a variety of input devices, users of current GUIs engage in rich dialog with the computer. The desktop metaphor or the WIMP (window, icon, menus, pointer) paradigm help users communicate with the virtual environment similar to the physical ones (e.g., files and folders on a disk or a trash on the floor). Later developments of post-WIMP interfaces, such as "graspable" user interfaces and "organic" user interfaces, which were built on flexible displays and permitted new methods of interaction, were made possible by progress in computer technology and understanding of man psychology.

The area of human factors and ergonomics has seen the greatest research into the pattern of input devices and procedures to accommodate restrictions of the human user and even to exploit such limits. The computer's common pointing tools are the mouse, the trackball, the joystick, and the specialized three-dimensional trackers. Other common input devices include different keyboards and keypads. Human intuitive and cognitive capabilities have developed voice based, vision based, touch based, gesture recognizing, and handwritten text recognizing computers (Daga et al., 2017). A user's face in video feeds, together with physiological indications like heart rate, may be used by some computers to implicitly infer things like mood or cognitive load. The actual selection of device and application can frequently be depending on the work, users, or surroundings in which they are to be utilized, given the vast range of inputs available. Cognitive Neural Prostheses and Brain-computer interfaces where the users can operate their Brain routines are developed by Brain sensing technologies, developed by researchers. The people with physical disabilities largely motivate this work. For instance, paralyzed individuals can operate a cursor, write text, or maneuver a wheelchair by just visualizing the movement of various body parts or focusing on certain activities. Regardless of the mechanism used, effective input often calls for sufficient and suitable system feedback to direct actions, validate actuation, and show outcomes. The output is generated in a way the humans can interpret. Visual output through computer displays has historically been the most popular type of output, and the area of information visualization has concentrated on utilizing principles of human vision and cognition to create imagery that effectively communicates ideas. Designers have experimented with the use of aural, tactile or touch, olfactory (smell), and gustatory (taste) interfaces in addition to visual output to benefit from additional human senses. One of the examples of enticing concrete outcome is the Game console controller that wobbles when strike by the antagonist.

The visual displays make use of topological, component-oriented views and dynamic images for computer-generated process visualization. Complementary perspectives can provide useful information. As a way to prevent visual overload, auditory displays are becoming more crucial for alerting users to alerts and providing status information. Multimodal displays are made possible by integration with multimedia. Knowledge-based decision support systems are another cutting-edge way to enhance human-machine interaction. Examples of user-oriented capabilities include procedural help and the avoidance of human mistakes. Application-oriented functionalities are best shown through fault management support, notably the identification of technical faults. Task orientation and various user engagement strategies are defined in the design and assessment of human-robot system components.

Computers can more easily grasp human languages with the help of the scientific discipline of Natural Language Processing (NLP). To extract meaningful knowledge from human languages is the ultimate goal of NLP approaches. Human-Computer Interaction (HCI), on the other hand, is a polymathic research field that draws on the ideas of computer science, cognitive science, and human factors engineering. How human and machines interpret with each other is the main focus of HCI. While a poorly designed HCI produces unforeseen challenges, a good interface becomes an essential component of the daily routines. The magnitude to which the design helps in utilizing the system effectively and efficiently is termed as usefulness of the human-machine interface. Building interfaces based on an awareness and respect for human physical, mental, and behavioral capacities has generally been the goal. However, technological advancements have made computers more reachable and reasonable to a wider range of users, necessitating the need for user-friendly and reliable interfaces regardless of the user's level of skill and the nature of human language. This is because information processing utilizing NLP is frequently challenging, which makes it more challenging for computers to comprehend. In the end, this leads to the challenging usage of computer interfaces like windows, icons, and menus. When this occurs, the human-machine revolution progresses quickly. Through the application of NLP in human-machine interaction, organizations are starting to invest in creative methods to monetize their data. Businesses must comprehend its reality. Organizations must realize that enhanced intelligence is the key to success if they want to succeed. The Business Potential of Human-Machine Interaction, the process of fusing human and machine intellect is what collaboration is all about.

Long before the keyboard and mouse were invented, machines were mostly operated by levers, switches, steering wheels, or buttons. The era of touch screens is currently upon us. Modern interfaces also include body sensors in wearables that gather data automatically. Rapid advancements are being made in voice control as well; users may currently use their voice to interact with digital assistants like Amazon Alexa or Google Assistant. Much less work is required for that. These systems also employ chatbots, and artificial intelligence is helping these machines connect with people more and more effectively.

At the very least, gesture control is as simple to use as voice control. That implies that, in the future, devices like robotics may be turned off with just a simple hand signal. With the use of radar technology, devices may also be controlled remotely or in the dark. Google and Infineon have already created a new sort of gesture control called "Soli." Today, technologies that enhance reality also serve as interfaces. While augmented reality glasses superimpose virtual components on the actual world, virtual reality glasses submerge users in a 3D world that has been artificially made. Due to their high resolution, mixed reality glasses that incorporate both technologies make it possible to portray scenes that are as realistic as possible. To develop their strategy, businesses have up to now studied customer behavior. In order to meliorate the experience for customers, it is now obligatory to go beyond that and comprehend their thoughts. This is made feasible by utilizing the right technology, like NLP, to analyze and interpret consumer attitudes from data sources like social media and mobile data. Natural Language Processing plays a significant part in data science because it can extract insightful information from text, enabling organizations to use this information to improve consumer experiences.

Human-machine system is a technique where human operator and a machine are consolidated together to perform a repetitive or time-consuming task which can be easily done with the help of a machine. Many human exercises, such as health examination, language paraphrasing, and consumer service are already in process of getting done by Artificial Intelligence (AI) in an efficient manner. In business, human-machine system is the integration of technology and humans in the workplace to improve processes, boost efficiency, and improve decision-making. In business, some frequent examples of human-machine systems include.

1. **Chatbots:** These are automated customer support systems that help clients with enquiries and fix simple difficulties.
2. **Robotic Process Automation (RPA):** It is a technology that automates repetitive operations, allowing humans to focus on higher-level

tasks. Data and machine learning algorithms are used in predictive analytics systems to produce forecasts and guide business choices. Collaborative robots (Cobots) work alongside people to execute jobs and boost efficiency. Hence, there are true involvements that AI will eventually replace human jobs across the economy.

9.2 ARTIFICIAL INTELLIGENCE IN INDUSTRY 4.0

Artificial Intelligence (AI) is contributing a lot to the recent development in the industry 4.0. Industries are joining hand to ensure product uniformity, and productivity by reducing the functional cost. This is done by joining hands with machines and humans. AI works by taking data from multiple sources and communicates utilizing AI robotization systems, by apprehending and recognizing all data types. Any traditional business can be transformed in a significant way by the use of AI. The manufacturing industry is constantly expanding as a result of Industry 4.0's advancements in technology. Cutting-edge technologies using AI are being utilized to improve productivity, the quality of products, and cut costs. Most often, AI is used to expedite the work by delivering more accurate outcomes with less manual labor. Digital technology is more advanced than the before being used, making Industry 4.0 cheaper and more efficient. Computing systems that can see, hear, learn have helped to develop cutting-edge platforms that enhance the output, this is made possible only due to the advancement in AI.

Digital revolution has been only possible because of the advancement in the AI sector (Singh et al., 2022). Making use of accurate information with the help of cutting-edge technologies in industries is referred to as Industry 4.0. Humankind has made a great progress, by moving from using steam to making use of sensors at workplace.

The fourth Industrial revolution is in progress currently, which is also known as Industry 4.0, where location, language, gender or age is not a barrier anymore. It mostly aims to do thing which are recurring in an automation manner thereby reducing the human need, and also giving output in a more error free manner as compared to humans. Especially after the change in marketplace which has been brought by COVID-19 pandemic, it has been noticed that Human-machine collaboration can help an organization to grow the business. Not only business but various sectors have been shifted from their traditional methods after the pandemic, like Healthcare, Education, Corporate, Pilgrimage, etc.

9.3 AI IN BUSINESS DEVELOPMENT PROCESS BY THE INDUSTRY 4.0

The term "Artificial Intelligence" was first brought into picture by John McCarthy in 1956 (Rupali et al., 2017). According to him "It is the application of science and engineering for the creation of intelligent devices which will benefit human beings." There are many branches of AI, but some of the most well-known ones are machine learning and natural language processing (Nitish Pathak et al., 2022). Machine learning emphasizes on creating statistical models and algorithms that allow computers learn from data without being explicitly programed. Natural Language Processing (NLP) emphasizes on how computers and human languages interact. It is used to create programs and systems that can decipher, interpret, and produce human language. NLP is used to understand the structure and meaning of the given sentences which are used by human beings to communicate. It does this by checking various elements like syntax, pragmatics, morphology, etc.

There are many applications in this industry, that easily perform a recurring task. Human being tends to get tired after a certain period of time while performing same task again and again. As a result, the repetitive task performed by humans, may contain errors, but the same task if performed by robots, has a less chance of generating errors. An industrial robot may monitor its accuracy and efficiency and also it can plan to improve the mistakes with the help of AI. As it can improve monitoring and safety, most of the organizations are shifting towards AI to reduce their cost of operations and gain maximum profit from the available resources. AI has either contributed to long-term protection measures before they happened or has aided in the diagnosis of the fundamental cause after the event. These solutions may lead to happier employees and safer workplace for any organization. In the manufacturing process, AI not only saves downtime but also ensures high-quality final products.

There are numerous uses of NLP which include sentiment analysis, name-entity recognition, speech recognition, machine translation, and text summarization. One real world example is Gmail where mails are classified as spam, promotions, or social (Daga et al., 2017). This is possible with the help of NLP framework which is called keyword extraction. A machine learns by reading words in the subject line and puts a tag on them accordingly. NLP helps a machine to understand the text which is in human format. Machines only know binary-language, NLP does the main task of converting the language from one form to another. Natural language processing has been upgraded a lot over the last 10 years as a field of study. Technologies like Siri, Alexa, and Google's voice search are heavily dependent on NLP to understand the input and respond to user's requests. NLP systems of today can easily analyze an infinite amount of text-based data in a consistent and unbiased way without getting tired (Nitish Pathak et al., 2021). Given the huge amount of unstructured data fostered every day, from various sources like electronic health records (EHRs) to social media posts, this type of robotization has become very important nowadays for efficiently analyzing text-based data, which if would have been done by traditional methods than it would take more time to deliver the output.

There are many benefits of NLP, but here are some of the real-world advantages that help businesses to upgrade. A firm can conduct extensive analysis. Nowadays massive amount of unstructured text data, in the form of comments on social media, support tickets, online reviews, news articles, and many more are easily available on the internet. These are automatically understood and analyzed by machines that can help organizations to grow their businesses. Search engines, also nowadays, rely on NLP to suggest relevant results based on previous search results. When using google, for example, the search engine automatically predicts what will be the next text based on popular searches. That's why user don't need to write the complete sentences. This saves the time of user and also help in better search while surfing. Sentiment Analysis is another application of NLP. The procedure of diagnosing the emotional tone behind a piece of text, such as a customer review or a social media post, is known as sentiment analysis. Based on the words used, the goal is to classify the text as positive, negative, or neutral. This is accomplished by training machine learning models on large data-sets of annotated text with previously labeled sentiment. Once trained, the model can be utilized to predict the sentiment of new, unseen input data. The model will analyze the text with the help of NLP and assign it a sentiment score ranging from –1 (negative) to 1 (positive). Sentiment Analysis can be used in customer services to measure overall consumer satisfaction with a product or service, by inspecting customer input on reviews, social media, or surveys. A corporation can use sentiment analysis to evaluate if customers are satisfied or dissatisfied with their new product release based on the tweets about their product. In NLP text classification is a process of categorizing text data into pre-defined categories. It involves training a machine learning model on a labeled dataset, where each text data is assigned a label or category, and then using this trained model to predict the category of new, unseen text data with the help of NLP. The goal is to correctly assign a label to a new text data based on its content and context. The categories can be defined based on the specific use case, such as spam vs non-spam email, positive vs negative sentiment, etc. Text classification can be used in various domains such as spam filtering, sentiment analysis, and news categorization.

Nowadays textual data is available on a large scale whether its' a presentation documentation, or even email. And sometimes it takes a lot of time for the user to read the whole article, as the text contained in it might be lengthy and time consuming to read and understand. To overcome this problem, recently, a trending system is used, which has been a blessing for all. With the help of text comprehension using Natural Language Processing, it is possible to get a short and sweet summary of any article without even reading a single part of the text.

Recently autonomous text summarization has got a great pitch because the internet generates humongous volumes of textual data daily, in various forms. Also, existing text data can be accessible easily via the internet at both corporate and personal computers. Hence accessing data is possible easily on a global scale. Content Comprehension system was created to solve the problem of going through long texts, in order to know the main concept, saving time by creating a shorter text version of the original text that contains its summary (Fejer & Omar, 2014). Natural Language Processing makes it easy to reduce the reading time from 10 minutes to 1 minute using various approaches like Abstractive and Extractive summarization methods. It also saves money and time when compared to a talented human comprehension.

Comprehension can be generated using extractive or abstractive summarization methods. Extractive methods manipulate sentences straight away from the original source file based on their significance and generate output as recapitulation which is an aggregate of those sentences. Usually, comprehensions which are generated in this way have a good performance on fluency, grammar, and the summary generated is least deviated from the original content. On the other hand, abstractive approach works just like how humans tend to give highlights in nutshell. Since the summary is generated from scratch it has a bad performance on fluency and grammar. Also, the summary which is generated may be wrong or misleading from the given input (Xiao et al., 2019).

In Extractive approaches, the comprehension is generated by selecting smaller portions of sentences from the original content (Allahyari et al., 2017). Instantaneous representations are created which intend to emphasize or capture the most productive content of the text to be comprehended based on the representations. Mainly there are two types of representations, that is, (I) Topic representation and (II) Indicator representation.

Topic representation mainly emphasizes on highlighting the key-points portrayed in the text. There exists a number of approaches to achieve these representations, one of which includes the Frequency Driven approach where the words are assigned weights depending on their relatability to the topic. The words associated to the topic are assigned 1 and the rest as 0. Frequency Driven Approaches include two common techniques that is Word Probability and Tern Frequency Inver Document Frequency. Word Probability implements the probability of a word calculated against the total number of words in the text as an indicator to derive the importance of a sentence which is drawn by the mean significance of words in the sentence. Tern Frequency Inver Document Frequency is composed as an improvement in the Word Probability technique. Here the most routinely used words that is stop-words like "the" are given low weights and hence discarded. Another approach includes the Topic Word approach where word frequencies and frequency threshold are used to locate the most embryonic words that can best describe the content. The dominance of a sentence is viewed as the number of topic words contained in it.

In Indicator Representations the sentences are given a rank based on their features. Hence the significance of the sentence depends on its features and not the words as in Topic Representations. Indicator Representations involve two methods namely Graph-Based methods and Machine-Learning methods. Graph-Based methods are centered on Page Rank Algorithms. Here the content in the paper-works is represented as connected graphs. The sentences are taken as nodes and the edges indicate the similarity measure between two sentences. In Machine-Learning methods the comprehension problem is viewed as a classification problem. Based on their features the sentences as categorized into summary and non-summary sentence groups. The model is trained with the help of training documents and the respective human recommended extractive comprehensions.

Hence, Extractive comprehension methods are approaches that involve selecting and extracting the most significant sentences or phrases from the original content in order to generate an encapsulation of the original writeup. Some of the examples of algorithms used for Extractive comprehension are Text rank, LexRank, Luhn's Algorithm, Latent Semantic Analysis (LSA) and Latent Dirichlet Allocation (LDA) and many more.

Content comprehension can be used by various users, for instance, researchers can decide easily to weather to read the entire document or not, by just reading the summary of the article in advance. Media groups can use comprehension systems by grouping information, which has been extracted from different sources and summarize them easily with which they don't need to spend their time reading articles from various sources, instead they can just read the summary. Books and literature market also make use of summarization, to help consumers quickly understand the insights of the book and help the customers in deciding whether the book is of their interest or not.

9.3.1 USE CASE: FINANCIAL RESEARCH WITH NLP

Making informed judgments about finances and investments necessitates a thorough analysis and classification of a sizable amount of data. Both individual investors and investment companies may attest to this. This is where an automated text summarizing system made specifically for analyzing and distilling financial data might be useful. Automated text comprehension can be used to provide a succinct summary of financial information for people who are not accustomed with extracting data from financial figures or reports. Asset managers use the Accern No-Code NLP Platform to quickly and accurately extract insights from text data to support timely investment decisions within minutes.

9.3.2 USE CASE: MEDIA MONITORING WITH NLP

Assume, one needs to gather information on a certain industry's state at the moment, from a range of books and media. However, one scarcely has time to read all the headlines, much less time to get to the heart of their arguments. Content Comprehension can assist in this situation by extracting the summary of several news items and other media, allowing one to scan more information.

This chapter emphasizes on extractive approaches for text summarization. In this chapter an application of content comprehension using various Natural Language Processing approaches namely the SpaCy, the Gensim, the Natural Language Toolkit (NLTK), and the Sumy methods, is presented.

9.4 PROPOSED METHODS

There was a necessity for a system to effectively and efficiently generate a quality encapsulation of the original text, irrespective of its length. Hence, in order to achieve a good quality condensation, that successfully interprets what the writer wishes to convey, various Natural Language Processing

Algorithms were implemented. In order to achieve a good quality encapsulation, in this chapter four different summarization algorithms, using the SpaCy, the Gensim, the Natural Language Toolkit (NLTK) and the Sumy Algorithms are compared, to study the quality of comprehension generated by them from the original text. All the four methods of Summarization described here were implemented using Python in Visual Studio Code Integrated Development Environment (IDE). The web-application was created by using FLASK.

Figure 9.1 represents the flow of the working of the Comprehension System using the Natural Language Processing Algorithms. In order to provide easy and comfortable accessibility and convenience a simple user interface is designed. Depending upon the user's convenience the user can provide the input in two ways, i.e., text and URL. The user can select the original text and simply paste it at the text input area, or the user can also select a Web-URL and paste it at the URL input area. The user can then select the summarize option to summarize it. As four different NLP approaches are used, the user can one by one click and select a summarization method and obtain the comprehension generated by the respective summarization method.

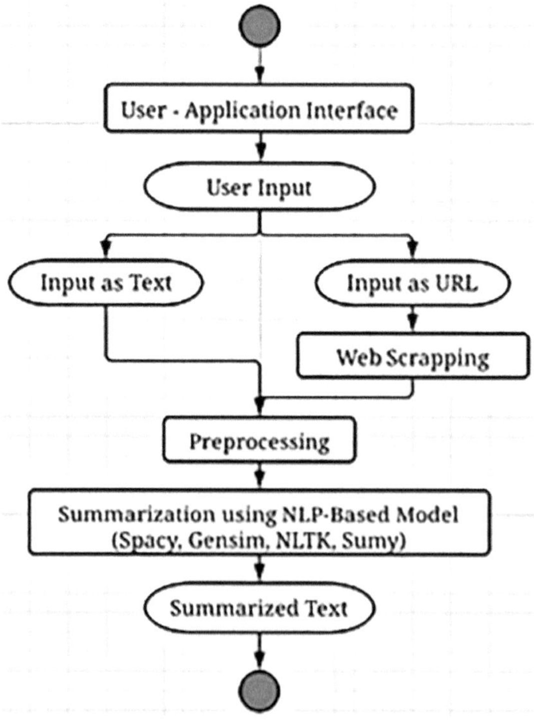

FIGURE 9.1 The flow diagram of comprehension using natural language processing.

For the Web-URL input, the given input very first undergoes web scraping (Khder et al., 2021). Web scraping is a self-regulated approach to acquire enormous quantity of content from website. Most proportion of this data is unstructured which is then metamorphosed into structured data and stored in spreadsheets and databases for its use in various applications. Web Scraping can be performed using online services or by using APIs or running a specific code. The crawler and the scraper are the two main components of web scrapping. By stalking the links over the internet, the crawler being one of the Artificial Intelligence approaches, carry outs web-browsing to search for the required data. Besides the scraper is a mechanism designed specifically to extract content from the website. Depending on the inputs provided and formats specified in the backend code, Web scrapers can withdraw all the data or specific data as desired by the user. Specifying a particular data required makes easier for the web scrapper to pull only those data which is required. As discussed above, the web scraper accepts the Web-URL as the input. The scrapper extracts all the HTML code from the website while advanced scrappers load CSS and JAVA Script elements too. The scrapper acquires all the relevant data from the HTML code and returns in the user-specified formats like excel sheets, CSV files, JSON files and many others.

Python proves to be the most suitable language for Web Scraping as it can manage all the operations comfortably. Python is gifted with two most convenient libraries for executing Web Scraping namely Scrapy and Beautiful soup. Scrapy is quite efficient in Web Scrapping and Data Extraction from APIs. Beautiful Soup retrieves data from website with the help of parse trees.

The data given as input in the form of text, or the data extracted from websites using Web Scraping undergoes various pre-processing stages and then finally gets summarized with the help of the summarization algorithms. Various algorithms have various pre-processing steps, for the processing of the original given data, so that it can be easily summarized and produces quality comprehension using the following algorithms, respectively.

9.5 SPACY COMPREHENSION

The Comprehension algorithm using SpaCy carry outs various steps for the generation of good quality comprehensions (Prakash et al., 2022). The primary step of this algorithm includes Text Cleaning. Many times, the text contains different unwanted symbols or words which do not add up any meaning to the model. Text cleaning is the technique of erasing and modifying certain portions of the text, so that the text results to be effectively and efficiently transparent to the Natural Language Processing frameworks for their easy learning, analyzing, and processing of the text. Text cleaning helps remove all the unhelpful parts of data or noise to boost the gross abundance of the text making it superior for decision making. The first step of text cleaning is the removal of stop-words. The words that are routinely and repetitively used in any language are termed as stop-words. In English Language, the words like "is," "an," "the," "and," "although," "but," and many more are the examples of stop-words. These words are eliminated from the given text as they do not add any meaning or importance to the text, allowing the algorithm to focus on the important words of the text. After the removal of stop-words, the punctuation marks from the text are removed. All the punctuation symbols like comma, colon, semicolon, braces, quotation marks, etc., and Special symbols like copyright symbol, registered symbol, trademark symbol, dollar sign, ampersand sign, etc., are eliminated from the text as they do not add up any meaning to the text. Next all the words in the text are modified to lowercase so that the same words do not get interpreted as different words in the vector space model giving rise to more dimensions (Figure 9.2).

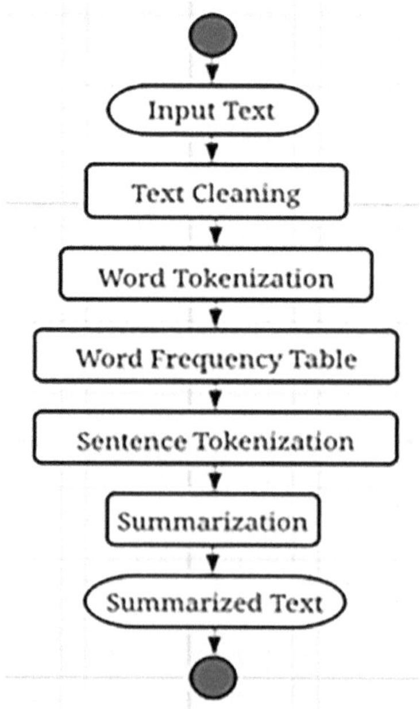

FIGURE 9.2 The architecture of SpaCy comprehension.
Source: Adapted from Prakash et al. (2022).

After the successful completion of Text cleaning, next comes the process of Word Tokenization. Tokenization is the process of splitting large paragraphs and sentences into smaller units for the easy assignment of meaning to the text. Here Large volume of text undergoes tokenization and gets divided into array of paragraphs, further each paragraph undergoes tokenization to get divided into array of sentences. Further each sentence undergoes tokenization and gets split into array of words called word tokens. After the successful generation of word tokens, these word-tokens undergo Word Frequency calculation. The frequency of each word in the entire text is calculated. All the word frequencies are divided by the frequency of the word having the maximum frequency, in order to generate normalized word frequencies. In order to find the most important sentence, the sentence score for each sentence token is calculated by adding the word frequencies with each sentence. In order to retrieve sentences with maximum scores, nlargest from heapq is imported. The nlargest() is a method that helps in finding the particularized number of rows right from the top, from the sorted dataframes, that form the maximum score for a particularized column. Using the nlargest() method 30% of the text with the greatest grade is calculated. Finally, the sentence tokens with the highest score are brought together to form a comprehension of the original text. Thus, the summarized text is displayed as the final output comprehension.

9.5.1 GENSIM COMPREHENSION

The algorithm for comprehension of text using Gensim involves various steps (Ashari et al., 2017). Firstly all the text contained in the input is concatenated to form a single paragraph of text. Concatenation is the process of bring together all the attributes of the available inputs together in order to generate a particular result or effect. Basically, using concatenation, the entire text is brought together as a single log or a single paragraph of text. After concatenation, the text undergoes various pre-processing, similar to the Summarization algorithm in SpaCy. All the stop-words are removed from the text, the punctuation marks are also eliminated from the text. All the words from the text are converted to lowercase for easy processing. The text is then divided into individual sentence units. The entire block of text is converted into an array of sentences. After the generation of sentence tokens, the words in the sentence are converted into word embeddings that is word vectors. The process in which inter word semantics is captured and discrete words are portrayed as true-estimated vectors in inferior dimensional-space. Similar words are given the same representation. Basically, Word Embeddings is providing the words with numeric representations. For the conversion of words into word embeddings the sentences are represented as a collection of words. The numerous occurrences of the words are eliminated, and the words are given a count using the word count method. Word vectors are generated depending on the vocabulary size. The vectors for the original sentences are initialized to 0 and then the values are incremented if the words match with the words in the sentence. The sentence vectors are generated by taking the mean of the respective word vectors (Figure 9.3).

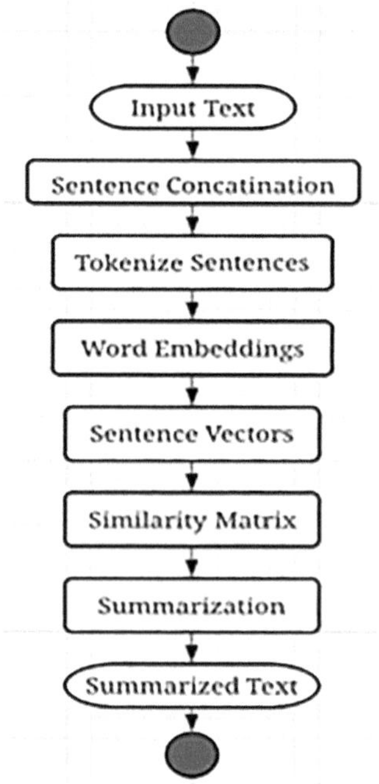

FIGURE 9.3 The architecture of Gensim comprehension.

Source: Adapted from Ashari, Ahmad, & Mardhani (2017).

Using the sentence vectors a similarity matrix is created with the help of cosine similarity. Cosine similarity is the technique of calculating the similarity between the sentences. The cosine of the inclination between two vectors in multi-dimensional space is calculated. The value of cosine similarity lies between 0 and 1. If the value turns out to be close to one, that means the sentences are similar. The value close to zero determines the sentences are not similar. A similarity matrix is prepared based on the similarity score of the sentences. The similar sentences, i.e., the sentences with similarity score more than 0.5 are discarded. The rest of the sentences are combined together, and a final summary is prepared. Hence, the generated summary is yielded as the final comprehension of the original text.

9.5.2 NLTK COMPREHENSION

Content Comprehension using Natural Language Toolkit (NLTK) executes various steps (Swapna et al., 2019). Initially the entire block of text undergoes tokenization. The whole block of text is divided into paragraphs. An array of paragraphs is generated. Each paragraph again undergoes tokenization. Now each paragraph is divided into sentences. Thus, an array of sentences is generated. After tokenization of sentences the next step is Data Pre-processing. In data pre-processing, firstly all the special characters are removed from the text as they do not add any meaning to the text. Next all the stop-words are eliminated from the text as they too, do not affect the meaning or interpretation of the writer. All the words in the text are converted to lowercase for easy processing. Further the sentences undergo tokenization where the sentences are divided into words. The sentences are split into array of words. Thus, a list of words in the text is prepared (Figure 9.4).

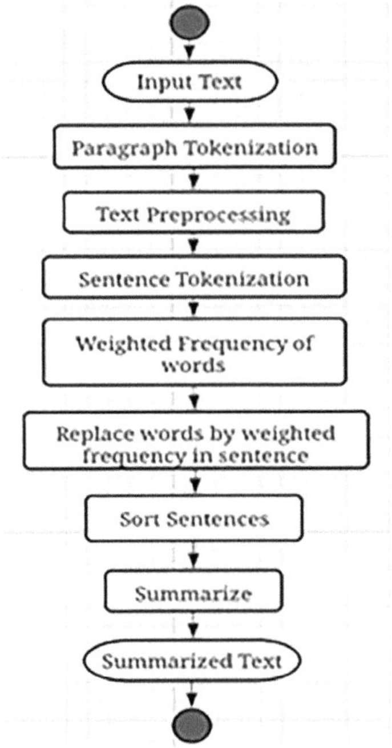

FIGURE 9.4 The architecture of NLTK comprehension.

Source: Adapted from Swapna, Sai Manish, & Rachana (2019).

Next step comes the calculation of weighted frequencies of all the words in the list. The frequency of each word from the entire list of words is calculated. The frequency of the word having maximum frequency is noted. The calculated frequency of each word is divided by the frequency of the word having the highest frequency. The resultant value obtained is termed as the weighted frequency of occurrence. Thus, the weighted Frequency of each word in the text is calculated. Next each word in each sentence of the text is replaced by its respective weighted frequency. Stop-words have zero weighted frequency as they are removed from the text. So, the sentences are free from stop-words. So, all the words in the sentences are replaced by their respective weighted frequencies. Next the sum of the weighted frequency of each word in the sentence is calculated. So, each sentence is represented by the sum of weighted frequencies of words contained in them. All the sentences are arranged in the descending order of their calculated sum. The sentences with the highest sum are placed above, and the sentences having the lowest sum are placed towards the end. A certain set of sentences from the top, i.e., sentences having the highest sum are chosen in the same order. The chosen sentences are concatenated and brought together to form a new block of text. This newly prepared block of text is the summary of the original block of text. Hence, the generated summary is given out as the Comprehension of the inputted large block of text.

9.5.3 SUMY LEXRANK COMPREHENSION

The algorithm for comprehension using Sumy LexRank executes a number of steps (Wu et al., 2015). All the words in the text are converted into word embeddings. A numerical representation of each word is prepared called word vectors. The mean of all the word embeddings of all the words in each sentence is calculated. This calculated mean value for each sentence is then used for comparing the sentences with the other sentences. Further the cosine similarity of all the sentences is calculated. The average value calculated is used to find out the cosine similarity of sentence vectors (Figure 9.5).

After the calculation of similarity value among all the sentences in the text, the similarity value of all the sentences is placed in a connectivity matrix called the Adjacency matrix. Considering a large block of text, could result in a number of similar sentences. Hence, many sentences could be misinterpreted to be similar and thus discarded creating trap for the algorithm. So, in order to solve this problem, Sumy LexRank while focusing on significant sentences also focuses on the sentences nominating them. The

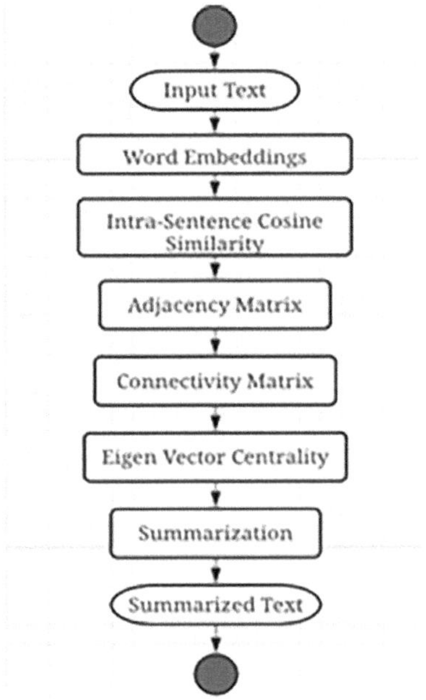

FIGURE 9.5 The architecture of Sumy LexRank comprehension.

Source: Adapted from Wu, Kang, Ping Shi, & Da Pan (2015).

count of connectivity of a sentence with other sentences is calculated. The Sumy LexRank algorithm determines the sentence to be identical to itself only if the calculated cosine similarity is more than 0.3 or 0.1.

Thus, with these calculated values, a connectivity matrix is prepared. In order to discover the important sentences from the whole group of sentences the algorithm executes the power iteration method using the eigen vector centrality. Each row is multiplied by one and the sum is generated. Each row of the matrix prepared undergoes Root Mean Square value calculation. The same procedure is repeated until a normalized unchanging value is found. The sentences with the maximum score are picked and brought together to form a new block of text. Thus, the generated block of text is given as the output. Hence, the comprehension is generated successfully from the original block of text.

Thus, the comprehension using all the respective algorithms is successfully created. The user can click and select the respective summarization algorithm to view the generated summary. Along with the comprehension generated the user can also view the time required to read, both the original text as well as the comprehended content generated respectively. The time required to read the input and output text is calculated using the time library. Hence, victoriously the comprehension using all the four algorithms is generated.

9.6 RESULTS

As observed the application was successfully able to produce summarized output for the given input text as well as for web URL, where the text of the given article was summarized or reduced to the desirable format using the SpaCy summarizer, the Gensim summarizer, the Natural Language Toolkit (NLTK) summarizer, and the Sumy LexRank summarizer. With this application, the users' time to read the entire block of text in articles or documents gets saved. The users can easily understand the context of the whole article in advance with the help of comprehension and do not require to read the entire article and spend time on reading noise and unwanted repetitive parts of the data of the articles, which is widely popular nowadays.

As shown in Figure 9.6, the original article is successfully converted into summarized form using SpaCy summarizer. The reading time of the summarized text is 0.865 min. The reading time of the original text is 2.51 min. This is how the reading time of the original text is reduced from 2.51 min to 0.865 min. Various steps of the algorithm like tokenization of the input text, removal of stop words and punction marks, specials symbols were executed. If such noise data is not removed, the algorithm may not result in a quality comprehension. The words of the text were correctly tokenized. After the generation of quality frequency-table, the sentences were also tokenized properly. Hence finally the process of summarization was executed appreciably resulting in the generation of the comprehension of the original text.

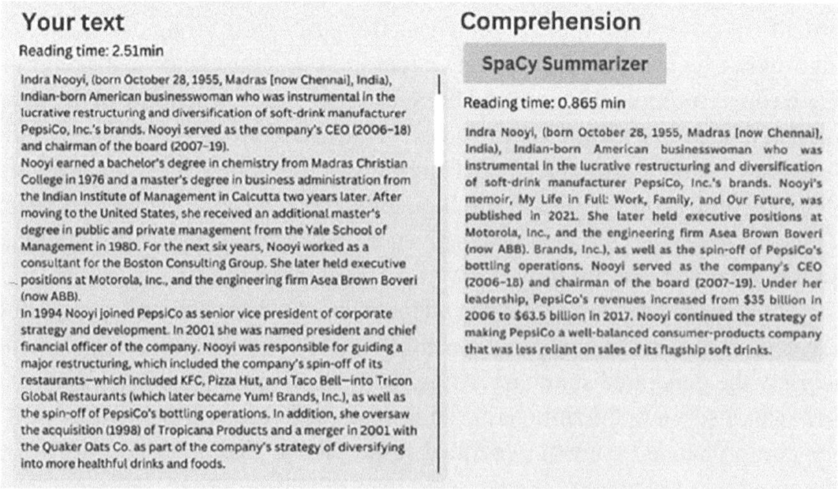

FIGURE 9.6 The comprehension generated using SpaCy summarizer.

As shown in Figure 9.7, for the Gensim summarizer the reading time of the summarized text resulted in 0.57 mins. The time to read the text reduced from 2.51 mins as that of the original text, to 0.57 mins of the comprehended text. The sentences were effectively concatenated. The tokenization of sentences was done perfectly. Word embedding was generated from the sentence tokens and the sentences were perfectly converted to vectors. After the generation of a quality similarity matrix the summarization of the text executed perfectly. Finally, a short and quality comprehension was generated as the output.

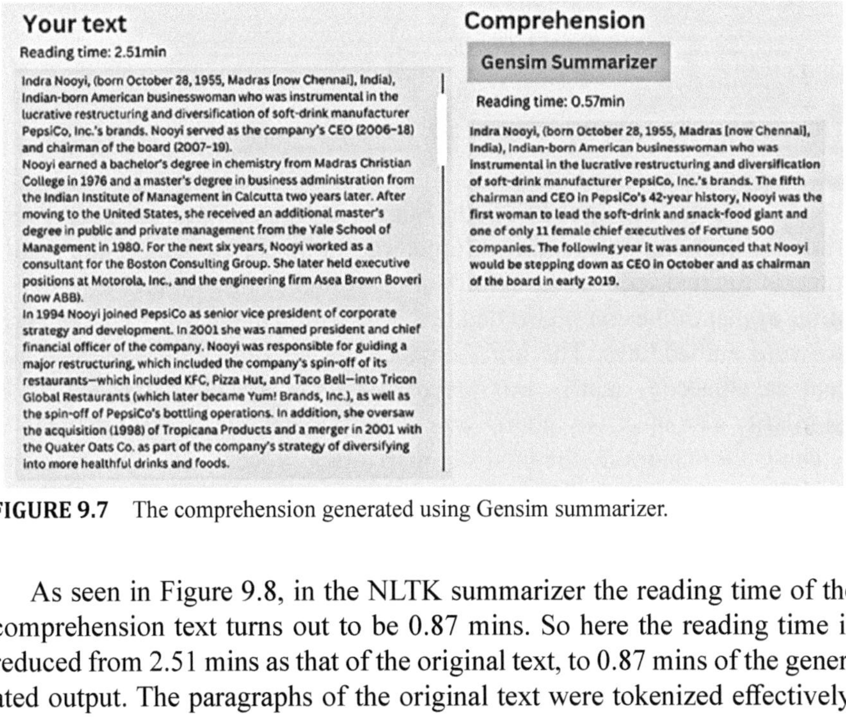

FIGURE 9.7 The comprehension generated using Gensim summarizer.

As seen in Figure 9.8, in the NLTK summarizer the reading time of the comprehension text turns out to be 0.87 mins. So here the reading time is reduced from 2.51 mins as that of the original text, to 0.87 mins of the generated output. The paragraphs of the original text were tokenized effectively. The text underwent a quality text pre-processing. All the irrelevant and unwanted data was eliminated properly. After the tokenization of sentences the weighted frequencies of words were calculated properly. The words were then replaced by their respective weighted frequencies and the sum of all the weighted frequencies was calculated. The sentences were efficiently sorted in the descending order of their sum and the set of sentences with the higher score were selected as the summary. Thus, a good fruitful comprehension was generated with the given algorithm.

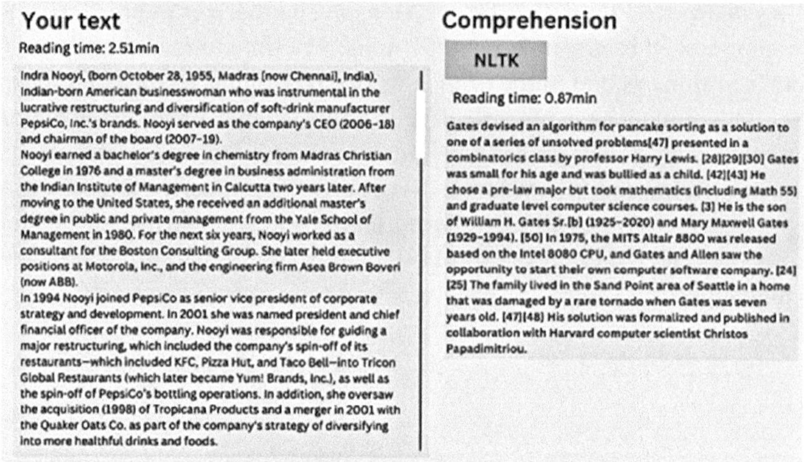

FIGURE 9.8 The comprehension generated using NLTK summarizer.

As observed in Figure 9.9, in the Sumy LexRank summarizer, the reading time for the comprehended text turned out to be 0.27 mins. So, the reading time of the text reduced from 2.51 mins as that of the original text, to 0.27 mins as that of the comprehended text. The words in the text were converted to word embeddings. The intra-sentence cosine similarity was calculated, and an adjacency matrix was prepared effectively. Further based on the similarity a connectivity matrix was efficiently generated. Further using the eigen vector centrality the final summarization process was executed, and a fruitful encapsulation of the original text was generated.

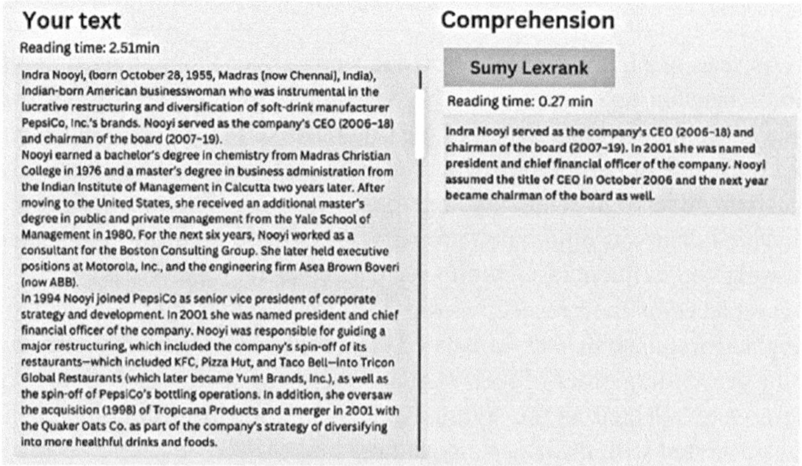

FIGURE 9.9 The comprehension generated using Sumy LexRank summarizer.

As observed from the above results, on comparing the comprehension generated by all the four summarization algorithms that is SpaCy, Gensim, NLTK, and Sumy, the comprehension generated by Sumy LexRank has the least reading time.

9.7 DISCUSSION

When compared to all the four implemented summarization algorithms that is summarization using SpaCy, Gensim, NLTK, and Sumy, it is observed that all the algorithms contain some similarity and also some unique features. All the four algorithms undergo text preprocessing. Some execute text cleaning in the beginning while some in between. As observed Algorithms like SpaCy summarization and also Sumy LexRank perform text cleaning as the initial step. Gensim summarization and NLTK perform text cleaning after the tokenization step.

All the algorithms except the Sumy LexRank perform tokenization of paragraphs and sentences and generate sentence tokens and word tokens respectively. The algorithms SpaCy and NLTK calculate the frequency of each word in the entire text. The NLTK further calculates the weighted frequencies of words. It replaces the words with their weighted frequencies and adds all the values, to calculate the sum value for the sentences. So here the sentences are given rank, based on the sum of the weighted frequencies. Based on this rank the sentences are selected to form the comprehension.

In the case of SpaCy, normalized word frequencies are calculated by dividing all the other frequencies by the maximum frequency. By adding all the normalized word frequencies of each token of sentence, the sentences are given a score. In SpaCy summarization, based on this score the sentences are selected for comprehension generation.

In both Gensim and Sumy, the words are represented with the numerical representations called word embeddings or word vectors. In both the algorithms a similarity score is calculated with the help of cosine similarity. In Gensim, a similarity matrix is prepared while in Sumy an adjacency matrix is prepared. In Gensim, based on the similarity score certain set of unique sentences are brought together to form a Comprehension of the input text. In Sumy, connectivity count of sentences is calculated, and a connectivity matrix is prepared. Important sentences are determined by the score generated for each sentence using the power iteration method and the eigen value centrality. The sentences with the higher score are selected and combined to form the output comprehension of the original block of text.

Table 9.1 shows the reading time of the original text and the comprehension generated by each of the four algorithms for the each given input.

TABLE 9.1 Comparative Study of the Comprehension Generated by SpaCy, Gensim, NLTK, Sumy Algorithms

Input Number	Original Text (Reading Time in min)	Summary Using SpaCy (Reading Time in min)	Summary Using Gensim (Reading Time in min)	Summary Using NLTK (Reading Time in min)	Summary Using LexRank (Reading Time in min)
1	2.51	0.865	0.57	0.87	0.27
2	5.035	0.975	1.695	0.9	0.63
3	3.015	0.92	0.79	0.91	0.48
4	2.445	0.375	0.165	1.015	0.415

Analyzing Table 9.1, it is observed that all the summarization algorithms produce comprehension with less reading time when compared with the reading time of the original text. SpaCy and NLTK result in almost very close reading time except for the last input. For the last input the NLTK produces the highest reading time.

When compared to all the algorithms, Sumy LexRank produces the lowest reading time for all the inputs except the last input. Gensim sometimes produces the highest reading time and sometimes produces a moderate reading time. For the first and the third input Gensim produces a moderate reading time while for the second and the fourth input Gensim produces the highest reading time.

From the yielded results it is inferred that the length of the comprehension produced by all the four algorithms depends just not only the algorithm type, i.e., the steps used in the algorithm but also the original text. The quality of the comprehension using all the four algorithms, is straightly dependent on the quality of the original text. Hence, a good quality content promises to generate a good quality comprehension using all the four implemented algorithms, while a moderate quality content or the content with less important data may generate a moderate quality comprehension irrespective of any of the algorithm used.

Thus, for the generation of a quality comprehension, along with the algorithms the quality of the original content is also very important.

9.8 CONCLUSION

A disciplined procedure should be put in place that consistently takes the standards and recommendations presented into account when designing human-machine interfaces for businesses. Incorporating potential users of machinery into the design process is a good idea, according to field experience. The chapter has made a point of emphasizing how important it is to design interfaces while taking into account the cognitive and physical limitations of people. The consequences of not taking these factors into account might be detrimental to the health of machine users at work, as well as a lack of motivation and productivity.

The process of educating computers to interpret and analyze human informal inputs is described as Natural language processing. Machine learning-based NLP is utilized to produce connections of communication between humans and machines. NLP is always upgrading at the same time it also shows up to be helpful in many different sectors. Many NLP applications may help people and organizations save time, enhance productivity, and improve customer satisfaction.

In the research mentioned above, interaction styles and other technical issues are examined along with the benefits and downsides of each. Human computer interaction literature is also analyzed. The already existing interaction styles are also looked upon for more effective use cases. In terms of interaction, it is discovered that dome "fit" is best between a person and a machine.

While constructing moral, effective, and user-friendly interfaces several disputes need to be taken into account. This highlights the theoretical support for human computer interfaces. In order to achieve the higher score of human-device interaction, the prosperous utilization of human-computer interaction is discussed.

Taking into account potential mankind problems, in order to produce a better-quality human-robot interface, it is significant to select satisfactory interactivity methodologies and the interface kind for the target human group. Therefore, it is advised to use several crucial interactional techniques including parallel input, speech recognition, device compatibility, and handwriting recognition. It is advised designing linked human-computer interactions.

Clearly, in order to improve the effectiveness of gadgets, all currently used human-computer interface strategies are examined. However, putting the recommended interaction models and styles into practice provides a strong foundation for further study. Thus, the chapter concludes by describing the content comprehension as an application of human machine collaboration in the business process.

KEYWORDS

- **artificial intelligence**
- **business process**
- **comprehension**
- **Gensim**
- **human machine**
- **natural language processing**
- **natural language toolkit**
- **SpaCy**
- **Sumy-LexRank**

REFERENCES

Allahyari, M., et al., (2017). *Text Summarization Techniques: A Brief Survey*. arXiv preprint arXiv:1707.02268.

Altinok, D., (2021). *Mastering spaCy: An End-to-End Practical Guide to Implementing NLP Applications Using the Python Ecosystem*. Packt. Publishing Ltd.

Ashari, A., & Mardhani, R., (2017). Document summarization using TextRank and semantic network. *International Journal Intelligent Systems and Applications, 1*, 26–33.

Bird, S., (2006). NLTK: The natural language toolkit. *Proceedings of the COLING/ACL 2006 Interactive Presentation Sessions.*

Butner, K., & Grace, H., (2019). How the human-machine interchange will transform business operations. *Strategy & Leadership, 47*(2), 25–33.

Daga, B. S., & Ghatol, A. A., (2016). Detection of objects and activities in videos using spatial relations and ontology-based approach in video database system. *International Journal of Advances in Engineering and Technology, 9*(6), 640.

Daga, B. S., Ghatol, A. A., & Thakare, V. M., (2017). Facial semantic recognition method for content-based video retrieval systems. *International Journal of Emerging Trends and Technology in Computer Science (IJETTCS), 6*(1), 139–146.

Daga, B. S., Ghatol, A. A., & Thakare, V. M., (2017). Semantic enriched lecture video retrieval system using feature mixture and hybrid classification. Advances in image and video processing. *European Journal of Applied Sciences, 5*(3), 1.

Daga, B. S., Ghatol, A. A., & Thakare, V. M., (2017). Silhouette based human fall detection using multimodal classifiers for content-based video retrieval systems. In: *2017 International Conference on Intelligent Computing, Instrumentation and Control Technologies (ICICICT).* IEEE.

Fejer, H. N., & Omar, N., (2014). Automatic Arabic text summarization using clustering and key phrase extraction. *Proc. 6th Int. Conf. Inf. Technol. Multimedia* (pp. 293–298).

Fejes, L., Johannsen, G., & Strätz, G., (1993). A graphical editor and process visualization system for man-machine interfaces of dynamic systems. *The Visual Computer, 10*(1), 1–18.

Haider, M. M., et al., Automatic text summarization using gensim word2vec and k-means clustering algorithm. *2020 IEEE Region 10 Symposium (TENSYMP)*. IEEE, 2020.

Helander, M. G., Landauer, T. K., & Prabhu, P. V., (1997). *Handbook of Human-Computer Interaction* (2nd edn.). Amsterdam: North-Holland.

Hurwitz, J., et al., (2019). *Augmented Intelligence: The Business Power of Human–Machine Collaboration.* Auerbach Publications.

Johannsen, G., (1992). Towards a new quality of automation in complex man-machine systems. *Automatica, 28*, 355–373.

Johannsen, G., (1993). *Mensch-Maschine-Systeme (Human-Machine Systems, in German).* Berlin: Springer.

Khan, S., & Mustafa, R. R., (2021). Artificial intelligence and NLP-based chatbot for Islamic banking and finance. *International Journal of Information Retrieval Research (IJIRR), 11*(3), 65–77.

Khder, M. A., (2021). Web scraping or web crawling: State of art, techniques, approaches, and application. *International Journal of Advances in Soft Computing & Its Applications, 13*(3).

Li, A., et al., (2016). The mixture of textrank and lexrank techniques of single document automatic summarization research in Tibetan. In: *2016 8th International Conference on Intelligent Human-Machine Systems and Cybernetics (IHMSC)* (Vol. 1). IEEE.

Mohanty, S., & Sachin, V., (2018). *How to Compete in the Age of Artificial Intelligence: Implementing a Collaborative Human-Machine Strategy for Your Business*. Apress.

Nitish, P., Anjani, K. S., & Shams, T. S., (2022). COVID-19 pandemic prediction and forecasting using machine learning classifiers. *Intelligent Automation & Soft Computing, 32*(2).

Nitish, P., Rajeev, K., & Raees, A. K., (2021). An analysis of integrating machine learning in healthcare for ensuring confidentiality of the electronic records. *Computer Modeling in Engineering and Sciences, 130*(3), 1387–1422.

Pathak, N., Sharma, N., Lalitha, K., et al., (2022). Stochastic learning-based artificial neural network model for an automatic tuberculosis detection system using chest x-ray images. *IEEE Access, 10*, 103632–103643.

Prakash, N. C. P., Narasimhaiah, A. P., Nagaraj, J. B., Pareek, P. K., Maruthikumar, N. B., & Manjunath, R. I., (2022). Implementation of NLP based automatic text summarization using spacy. *International Journal of Health Sciences, 6*(S5), 7508–7521. https://doi.org/10.53730/ijhs.v6nS5.10574.

Řehůřek, R., & Petr, S., (2011). *Gensim—Statistical Semantics in Python.* Retrieved from: Genism. org.

Rupali, M., & Patil, A., (2017). A review paper on general concepts of artificial intelligence and machine learning. *International Advanced Research Journal in Science, Engineering and Technology, 4*(4), 79–82.

Shirwandkar, N. S., & Samidha, K., (2018). Extractive text summarization using deep learning. In: *2018 Fourth International Conference on Computing Communication Control and Automation (ICCUBEA).* IEEE.

Singh, P., & Sheetal, S., (2022). *HR 4.0-A Critical Review* (p. 7). The Next Normal: Building Agile, Sustainable, Tech-enabled Organizations (TNN-BASTO-2022).

Swapna, M., Sai Manish, G., & Rachana, B., (2019). Automatic text summarization using NLTK. *Think India Journal, 22*(35), 228–833.

Vasiliev, Y., (2020). *Natural Language Processing with Python and spaCy: A Practical Introduction.* No Starch Press.

Wu, K., Ping, S., & Da, P., (2015). An approach to automatic summarization for Chinese text based on the combination of spectral clustering and LexRank. In: *2015 12th International Conference on Fuzzy Systems and Knowledge Discovery (FSKD)*. IEEE.

Xiao, W., & Giuseppe, C., (2019). *Extractive Summarization of Long Documents by Combining Global and Local Context.* arXiv preprint arXiv:1909.08089.

CHAPTER 10

Amalgamation of AI and Blockchain in Auditing

PAWAN WHIG,[1] SHAMA KOUSER,[2] ASHIMA BHATNAGAR BHATIA,[1] RAHUL REDDY NADIKATTU,[3] and RADHIKA MAHAJAN[1]

[1]*Dean Research, Vivekananda Institute of Professional Studies – TC, New Delhi, India*

[2]*Lecturer, Department of Computer Science Jazan University, Saudi Arabia*

[3]*Senior IEEE Member, University of Cumbersome, USA*

ABSTRACT

This chapter analyzes the literature on the potential effects of blockchain technology on accounting in general and AI-enabled auditing in particular. Using the characteristics of immutability, append-only, shared, verified, and agreed-upon blockchain data, the aim is to examine how blockchain skill container enhance slide and faith in secretarial practice as well as in what way specialists can usage blockchain information to recover choice creation. The blockchain protocols' multi-party validation provides actual period reliable information to the AI schemes used by examiners, increasing pledge then effectiveness. The study advances our understanding of how blockchain technology may be used to reduce information asymmetry and enhance stakeholder cooperation by interpreting the results using agency theory and stakeholder theory. The report also outlines the difficulties and makes corporations' concerns about embracing blockchain more understandable. Finally, the study suggests that future researchers apply the melodies and provide answers to the queries raised inside this appraisal to enhance the

Advanced Digital Technologies in Financial and Business Management: Unleashing the Power of Artificial Intelligence, Machine Learning, Blockchain, and the Internet of Things. Jyoti Batra Arora, Nitish Pathak, and Neelam Sharma (Eds.)

blockchain literature. Additionally, it encourages stakeholders like consultants to collaborate on scheming blockchain ecologies that are appropriate for secretarial and audit as those who alter cloud-based accounting.

10.1 INTRODUCTION

The integration of artificial intelligence (AI) and blockchain technology in auditing represents a significant advancement in the field. By leveraging the strengths of these two technologies, auditors can achieve more accurate, efficient, and secure auditing processes. AI can automate routine tasks, provide data analysis, and detect anomalies that would otherwise go unnoticed. Meanwhile, blockchain can provide a secure, decentralized, and tamper-proof ledger for recording transactions and storing audit evidence. Together, AI and blockchain have the potential to transform auditing into a more efficient and effective discipline.

One major benefit of using AI in auditing is the ability to process vast amounts of data in real-time, providing auditors with quick and accurate insights into a company's financial health. With the ability to analyze large amounts of data, AI can identify patterns and anomalies that would be difficult or time-consuming for human auditors to detect. This can lead to a more thorough and effective auditing process and can help uncover fraudulent activity that may have gone undetected in the past.

In addition to improving the accuracy and efficiency of the auditing process, the use of blockchain in auditing offers numerous security benefits. Blockchain provides a decentralized ledger that is immutable, meaning that once a transaction is recorded, it cannot be altered or deleted. This makes it an ideal platform for storing audit evidence, as auditors can be confident that the data, they are working with is accurate and secure. Furthermore, the decentralized nature of blockchain makes it less vulnerable to cyberattacks and other forms of data tampering, which is a critical factor in maintaining the integrity of the auditing process.

The amalgamation of AI and blockchain in auditing represents a major step forward in the industry, offering numerous benefits in terms of accuracy, efficiency, and security. As these technologies continue to evolve and mature, it is expected to see further improvements in the auditing process, leading to better financial reporting and greater confidence in the financial markets.

Because they can now more easily access powerful computer power and expansive datasets, businesses that have gone digital have been able to streamline business procedures and modify business models to reinvent their operations (Whig, Velu, & Naddikatu, 2022). The most valuable companies in the world today are internet- and platform-based. Blockchain and many new technologies are among the digital forms of technology that receive a lot of attention from academia, social media, businesses, and governments. These developments have a significant impact on both companies and people. Blockchain in particular lays the groundwork for what Hongdan et al. (2023) refer to as a "Internet of value" that will radically alter society and its economy. The 5th support of the IT rebellion, blockchain, is currently seen to be the fundamental technology for the next-generation Internet (Alkali et al., 2022a).

This research assessed how blockchain technology can enhance the trustworthiness and transparency of accounting practice, as well as how its practitioners can enhance decision-making by utilizing the immutable that blockchain can provide (Whig, Velu, & Sharma, 2022). The goal of this inquiry is to ascertain how blockchain will affect accounting, particularly in relation to AI-enabled auditing, as well as to uncover trends that will indicate how blockchain will affect record-keeping and its applicability in accounting. This review was inspired by three observations. First, most of the writing on blockchain technology continues to be centered on the financial elements of Bitcoin, including its pricing and volatility, and how supply-chain management promotes openness and traceability. To find new topics in the discussion around blockchain and its affect the secretarial occupation, there are insufficient scholarly publications in the fields of secretarial and checking compared the expanding corpus of blockchain investigate. Since blockchain began to receive widespread attention in 2017, fewer scholars have looked at how it applies to both accounting and assurance (Whig, Velu, & Ready, 2022).

Second, it is commonly acknowledged in the literature that there are issues with present accounting and auditing procedures. For instance, accounting is currently labor-intensive and far from automated, requiring data to be manually inputted to spreadsheets or accounting software. Accounting divisions are in charge of ensuring that financial reports are accurate since they centrally approve what is entered into Accounting Information system (AIS) databases. The age-old issue of certain managers "cooking the books" to create or alter monetary info to obtain a partial benefit ended savers can particularly affect financial reporting delays (Whig, Velu, & Bhatia, 2022).

Third, accounting scholars and practitioners are encouraged to get familiar with blockchain-based accounting transactions by the emergence of blockchain applications in the financial services, healthcare, supply networks, and government services. Additionally, because it offers superior transparency to other current monetary record custody schemes, blockchain technology has the potential to overcome current accounting difficulties (Whig, Velu, & Nadikattu, 2022).

Blockchain is referred to be a form of distributed ledger technology (DLT), protecting it with cryptography, and operating under a consensus process. According to Xu et al. (2019), a single definition of blockchain is far from being agreed upon given the multitude of definitions that exist today (Madhu & Whig, 2022). The properties of DLT are described in Figure 10.1.

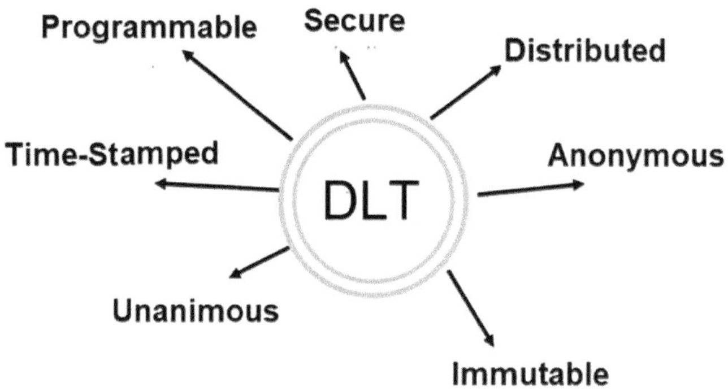

FIGURE 10.1 Properties of DLT.

Blockchain is a protocol—a means of conducting business—rather than a single technology for recording transactions. On contrast to the Internet, where data is shared, ownership may be transferred between parties in a blockchain. The blockchain approach is appealing for a number of reasons. It may eliminate the need to tally up several ledgers, for instance, in a market with many of parties involved in transactions (Jupalle et al., 2022). Being shared among operators also avoids disruptions expense of consuming to wage a dominant expert to keep the book's correctness. All past transactions may be tracked by any user of the ledger, increasing transparency and enabling self-auditing on the blockchain.

10.2 FEATURES AND TYPE OF BLOCKCHAIN

Blockchain technology is a decentralized, distributed ledger that records transactions in a secure, tamper-proof manner. One of the key features of blockchain is its transparency, as all parties have access to the same information and can see the history of all transactions. This makes it ideal for use in financial transactions, as it provides all parties with a clear and accurate record of the transaction history.

Another important feature of blockchain is its immutability, meaning that once a transaction is recorded, it cannot be altered or deleted. This makes it ideal for use in industries where the security and integrity of data are of the utmost importance, such as in the supply chain management and healthcare industries. In addition, there are two main types of blockchain, public and private. Public blockchain, like Bitcoin, allows anyone to join and participate, while private blockchain, often used for enterprise solutions, is permissioned and only allows designated parties to participate. Regardless of the type of blockchain, all transactions are validated by a network of nodes, providing added security to the system.

Transparency, decentralization, immutability, tamper resistance, robust authentication, synchronized networks, and consensus are the main features of blockchains. Features of blockchain is shown in Figure 10.2.

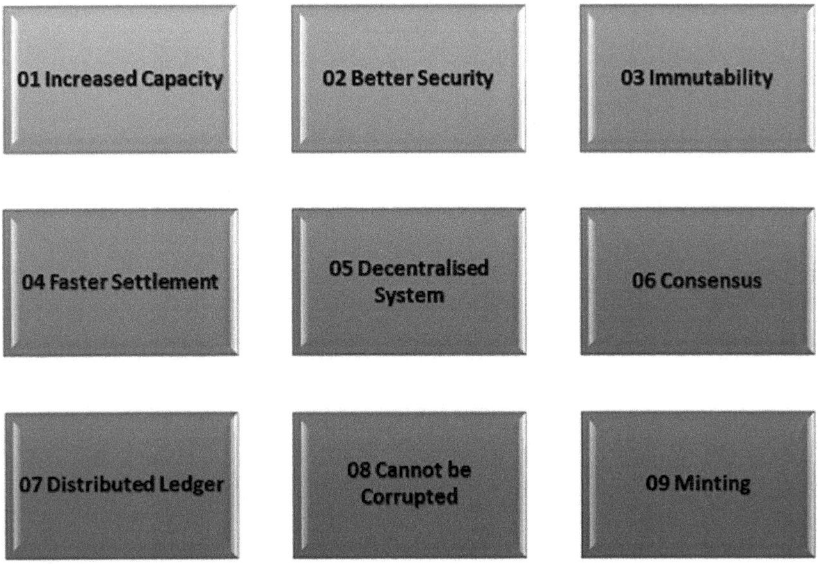

FIGURE 10.2 Features of blockchain.

Different generations of blockchain technology have been distinguished depending on the target audience. Blockchain 1.0 makes it possible to transact using digital currencies. Smart contracts are a feature of Blockchain

2.0. Beyond cryptocurrencies and banking, Blockchain 3.0 expands applications into sectors including supply chains, governance, and healthcare. AI and blockchain will be used together in blockchain 4.0 (Tomar et al., 2021). Characteristics of blockchain is shown in Figure 10.3.

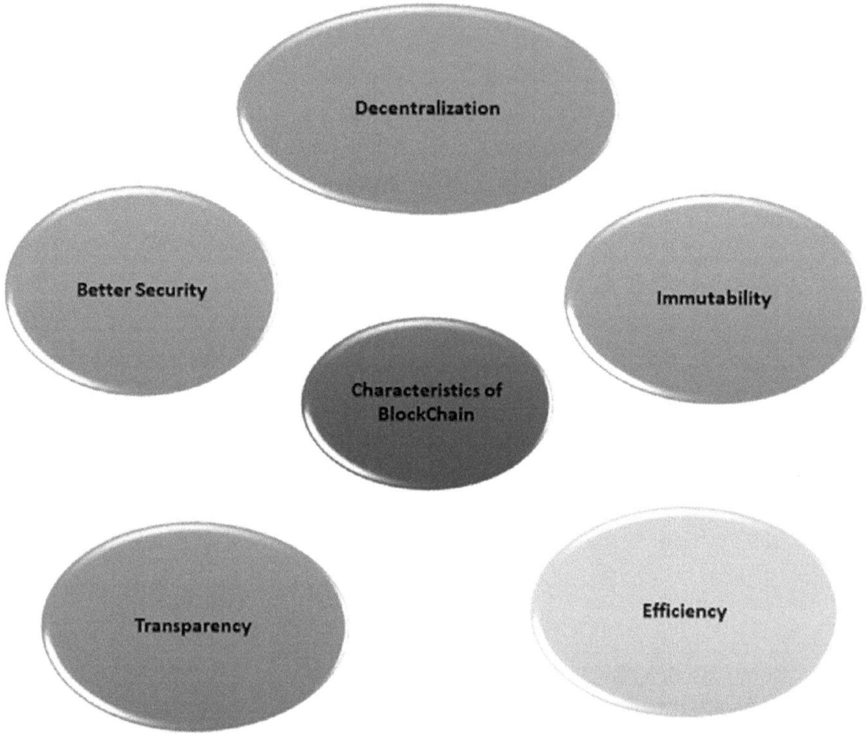

FIGURE 10.3 Characteristics of blockchain.

With a focus on access rights and permission to validate transactions, blockchain technology may be configured in a variety of ways to grant various users varying levels of access rights as well as the ability to record, alter, and validate transaction records. The main differences between public and private blockchains are the network size (i.e., the number of nodes), the requirements to join the network, and the method for verifying transactions. Control, data ownership, privacy, and access are said to be the four main design considerations that assist enterprises in determining which kind of blockchain best suits their objectives. Types of blockchain are shown in Figure 10.4.

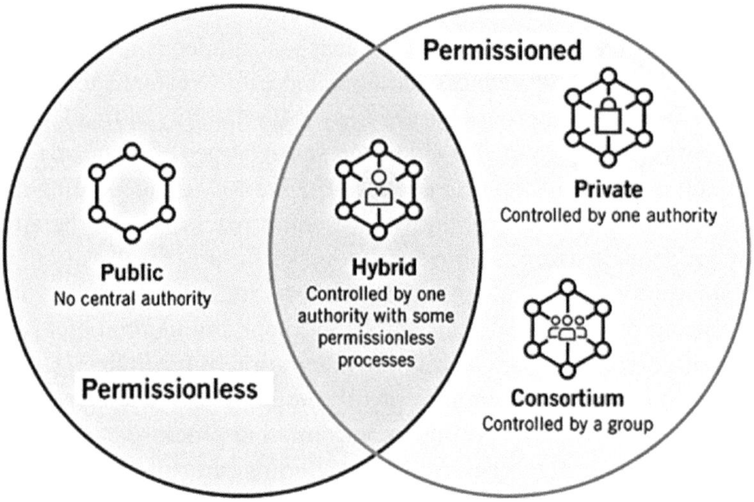

FIGURE 10.4 Types of blockchain.

Like Bitcoin, a public and permissionless blockchain has numerous nodes, anybody may take part as a miner or validator, and everyone can examine the underlying record. However, because to the size of the dispersed network, it is expensive and time-consuming to come to an agreement (Whig, Nadikattu et al., 2022). A private and permissioned blockchain, on the other hand, has a far smaller number of participating nodes and requires authorization from the owner before anyone may access the underlying ledger or participate in mining or verifying transactions on it. Because identities are known, private blockchains require less blind faith and as a result operate more quickly and efficiently (lower risk of ex-post opportunism). The security and privacy of corporate data may be safeguarded by this design.

Additionally, the most revolutionary blockchain use is smart contracts. They are tamperproof and self-enforcing because digital contracts are automatically carried out, and they describe the conditions of a contract between parties using technological codes. Smart contracts reduce the cost of contracting between parties and promote transparency for all network members. Notably, it is still not apparent who is in charge when smart contracts have issues or behave strangely.

10.3 BLOCKCHAIN IN ACCOUNTING

Blockchain technology has the potential to revolutionize the accounting industry by providing a secure, transparent, and tamper-proof ledger for recording financial transactions. With blockchain, financial transactions can be recorded in real-time, allowing for near-instantaneous reconciliation and reporting. This not only reduces the time and effort required for accounting processes, but it also improves the accuracy and reliability of financial reports.

In addition to improving the efficiency and accuracy of financial reporting, blockchain technology can also enhance the security of accounting data. By using a decentralized ledger, the risk of data breaches and cyberattacks is greatly reduced, as there is no central point of failure. Furthermore, the use of cryptographic algorithms in blockchain provides an added layer of security, ensuring that financial transactions are kept confidential and protected from unauthorized access. Overall, the integration of blockchain technology in accounting has the potential to greatly improve the efficiency, accuracy, and security of financial reporting and accounting processes.

Several accounting organizations, including the International Federation of Accountants (IFAC), and the ICAEW, all monitor and report on their websites that are pertinent to blockchain technology. Blockchain in Accounting can be better understood by Figure 10.5.

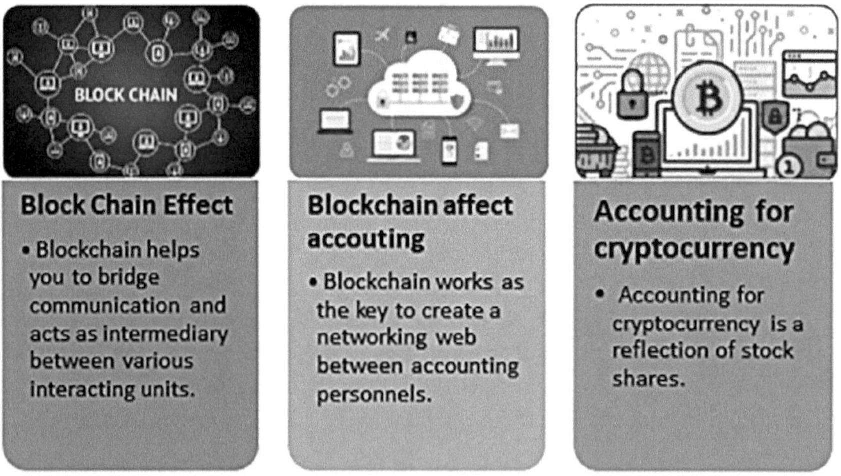

FIGURE 10.5 Blockchain in accounting.

10.4 AI-ENABLED AUDITING GAINS CREDIBILITY THANKS TO BLOCKCHAIN

AI-enabled auditing gains credibility and trust through the use of blockchain technology. By integrating blockchain into the auditing process, auditors can ensure that the data they are using is secure, transparent, and tamper-proof.

This, in turn, provides greater confidence in the accuracy and reliability of financial reports and helps to eliminate the risk of fraud or errors. Furthermore, blockchain provides an immutable ledger for storing audit evidence, ensuring that the audit process is transparent and traceable. With the security and transparency offered by blockchain, AI-enabled auditing is able to achieve greater credibility and earn the trust of stakeholders.

Blockchain's immutability, traceability, and visibility allow participants to witness completely encrypted synchronized transactions, which makes it powerful in current Internet use. This is due to the combination of hash algorithms, private and public keys, and decentralized. Flow chart of AI enabled audit using blockchain is shown in Figure 10.6.

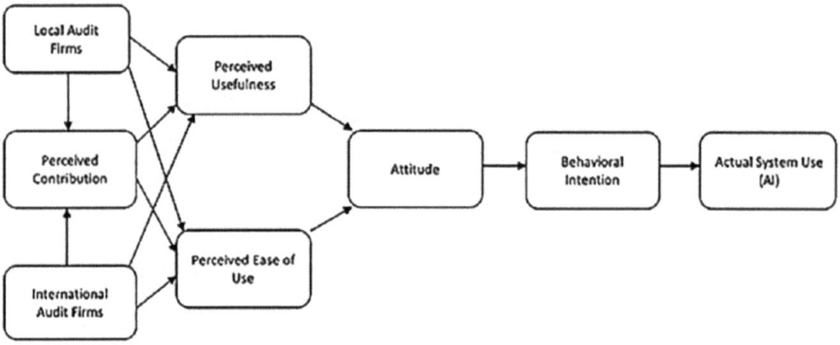

FIGURE 10.6 AI enabled audit using blockchain.

Blockchain is safe and dependable because to the distributed network, digital signature, and consensus validation procedures. The Financial Reporting Council asserts that the immutability and tamper-resistance of records resulting from their distribution and hashing are the basis for the confidence generated from blockchain. Similar to fingerprints, hashes are distinct because any addition of information, no matter how small, results in a change in the hash's unique identity since the block is altered (Anand et al., 2022). Blockchain gaming is challenging due of the consensus method. The distinct blockchain hash properties provide a basis for confidence to foster pliability.

According to a recent IBM artifact, auditing choices and their related data points will be significantly easier if transactions on a blockchain are used to record the decisions and data points. Machine learning may help auditors spot and use trends by creating algorithms based on such patterns and then improving them in response to user input. AI can speed up the document review process for auditors by identifying abnormalities and more accurately assessing risk (Alkali et al., 2022b).

Blockchain allows an additional accurate and agile auditing model that mechanizes pledge, strengthening checking while delivering trust and confidence in AI-based processes' data, models, and analytics. By comparing related accounting records in the blockchains maintained by each trading party, AI technology can help the auditing industry. This process is really simple.

10.5 METHODOLOGY

This study employed the same review methodology as Bakker et al. (2022), which involves physically filtering a slant of pertinent trainings since reputable theoretical publications, shadowed by a thorough search of the pertinent literature using study-related keywords. Additionally, because blockchain technology is still in its infancy, this study also looked through pertinent industry literature including industry publications, blogs, and news on the subject (Velu & Whig, 2022). This method provided thorough treatment of the blockchain literature, paying special attention to how it may be used to create new methods for accounting record-keeping and its auditing component.

These four new trends are also related to how blockchain will affect AI-based accounting and auditing. Using traceable and auditable blockchain data can make auditing more effective:

1. **Increased Transparency:** The use of blockchain in auditing provides a transparent and traceable ledger of all transactions, allowing auditors to quickly and easily access the information they need to complete their audit. This increased transparency helps to eliminate the risk of fraud or errors and provides greater confidence in the accuracy and reliability of financial reports.
2. **Improved Data Security:** Blockchain technology offers a secure, decentralized ledger for storing financial transactions, reducing the risk of data breaches and cyberattacks. This helps to ensure that accounting data is kept confidential and protected from unauthorized access, enhancing the security of the auditing process.
3. **Automated Auditing:** With the integration of AI in auditing, routine tasks can be automated, freeing up auditors to focus on more complex and value-adding tasks. AI can also provide data analysis, identify anomalies, and support decision making, making auditing more efficient and effective.

4. **Increased Collaboration:** The use of blockchain in auditing allows for real-time collaboration between auditors, stakeholders, and clients, enhancing the overall efficiency of the auditing process. By providing a secure and transparent platform for collaboration, blockchain technology can facilitate the exchange of information and improve communication between all parties involved in the audit.

10.6 TYPES OF ACCOUNTING

There are several types of accounting that organizations can use to manage their finances, including:

1. **Financial Accounting:** This type of accounting focuses on providing accurate and complete financial statements that provide a comprehensive overview of a company's financial position. Financial accounting is primarily used for external reporting purposes and is used to meet the needs of stakeholders, such as investors, creditors, and regulators.
2. **Managerial Accounting:** This type of accounting provides internal financial information to help managers make informed decisions about the company's operations and strategy. Managerial accounting provides detailed financial information about the company's operations, such as cost analysis and budgeting, to help managers make informed decisions.
3. **Tax Accounting:** This type of accounting focuses on preparing and filing tax returns, in accordance with tax laws and regulations. Tax accounting helps companies to accurately calculate their tax liability, reduce their tax burden, and avoid costly penalties.
4. **Cost Accounting:** This type of accounting focuses on the analysis and management of the cost of goods and services produced by a company. Cost accounting helps companies to understand the costs associated with producing and selling products, allowing them to make informed decisions about pricing and production strategies.
5. **Auditing:** This type of accounting involves the independent examination of a company's financial statements and records to provide assurance to stakeholders that the financial statements are accurate, complete, and in compliance with relevant accounting standards.

These types of accounting provide organizations with different tools to help them manage their finances and make informed decisions about their operations, strategy, and financial reporting. The type of accounting used will depend on the needs of the organization and the specific goals it aims to achieve.

10.7 EVENT-BASED ACCOUNTING

Event-based accounting is a new trend in financial reporting that leverages the power of blockchain technology to provide a more real-time and accurate picture of a company's financial health. This approach to accounting involves recording transactions as they occur, rather than waiting for a monthly or quarterly close, providing a near real-time view of the company's financial position.

One of the key benefits of event-based accounting is that it provides a more accurate picture of a company's financial health, as transactions are recorded as they occur rather than being subject to delays and errors that can arise during a traditional close process. Furthermore, event-based accounting makes it easier to identify trends and anomalies in financial data, allowing companies to respond quickly to changes in their financial position. Additionally, the use of blockchain technology in event-based accounting enhances the security and transparency of financial reporting, reducing the risk of fraud or errors and providing stakeholders with greater confidence in the accuracy of financial reports.

Because blockchain technology makes it easier to access real-time accounting data, it presents research opportunities for the event approach to accounting. Using blockchain technology to make accounting records more traceable and transparent. By contrasting it with the value approach in accounting, for instance, presents an event approach to accounting theory. Event based accounting flow chart is shown in Figure 10.7.

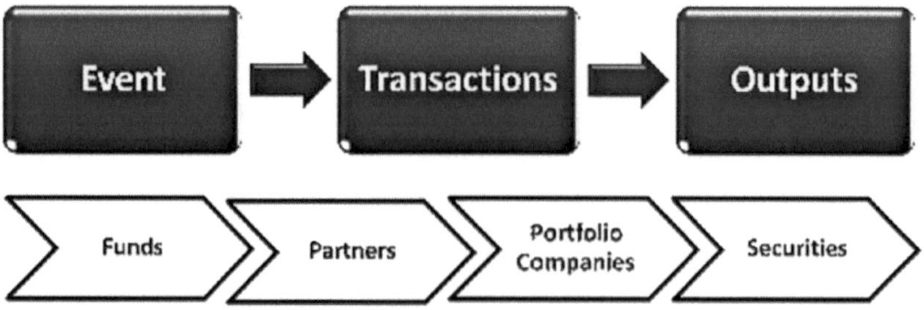

FIGURE 10.7 Event based accounting flow chart.

10.7.1 INSTANTANEOUS ACCOUNTING

Instantaneous accounting refers to a real-time approach to financial reporting, enabled by the use of blockchain technology. With instantaneous accounting, transactions are recorded and processed as they occur, providing a near-real-time view of a company's financial position. This allows companies to respond quickly to changes in their financial situation and make more informed decisions. The use of blockchain technology in instantaneous accounting enhances the security and transparency of financial reporting, reducing the risk of fraud or errors and providing stakeholders with greater confidence in the accuracy of financial reports. Additionally, instantaneous accounting can reduce the time and effort required for accounting processes, improving the efficiency and accuracy of financial reporting.

Blockchain is a cutting-edge technology that has the potential to revolutionize contract management, payment processing, and documentation. Although just-in-time manufacturing inventory, receivables, payables, and cash are already maintained up to year in ERPs (Velu & Whig, 2021).

10.7.2 TRIPLE-ENTRY BOOKKEEPING

Triple-entry bookkeeping is a method of financial reporting that leverages the power of blockchain technology to provide a more secure and transparent ledger of financial transactions. This approach to bookkeeping involves recording a transaction in three separate locations: in the buyer's ledger, the seller's ledger, and in a shared public ledger that is maintained on a blockchain. The use of a shared public ledger provides an additional layer of security and transparency, as all parties involved in a transaction have a record of it and any changes to the transaction can be easily traced and audited. The triple-entry bookkeeping method provides greater confidence in the accuracy and reliability of financial reports and reduces the risk of fraud or errors.

Blockchain-based triple admission secretarial generates a communal book which accessed by corporate networks. By employing multi-party authenticated data, blockchain's shared ledger may fundamentally enhance transparency and trust. An example to show triple entry bookkeeping is shown in Figure 10.8.

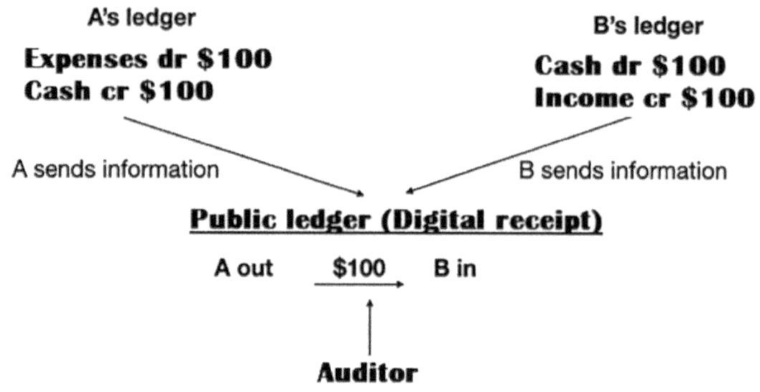

FIGURE 10.8 Triple entry bookkeeping.

There is also an outline for triple entry secretarial, which adds "trebit" to the present debit and credit entries to explain additional income. This ensures confidence and transparency of accounting records by making a digitally signed receipt the third transaction. The digital economy's present and future corporate demands cannot be supported by traditional auditing techniques (Khera et al., 2021).

In order to evaluate controls, analyze risks, find exceptions or anomalies, discover patterns, and examine trends, continuous auditing automates audit operations on a continual basis. It will probably go closer to integrating blockchain and artificial intelligence to create a cohesive ecosystem that will increase assurance.

Along with the four themes, several warnings that businesses should bear in mind before implementing this technology. Blockchains do not offer universally applicable answers since they may be tailored to unique circumstances and are neither the only option nor even the best. However, by switching to multi-party transaction validation, which boosts confidence and is advantageous to digital corporate reporting, blockchain can address the existing accounting issues. No technology is 100% trustworthy, but blockchain can only be changed to add or remove fraudulent information if someone manages to gain 51% of the processing power.

Due to their distribution networks, public blockchains make it difficult to achieve this. Because hackers may breach administrator networks or change the operational principles and contents of private blockchains, the danger of hacking is significantly higher in those blockchains. Furthermore, it is irrational to think that businesses would entirely replace their current IT systems with a blockchain.

10.8 CASE STUDY

The integration of IoT and blockchain technology has the potential to revolutionize the way that supply chain management is approached. By combining the benefits of IoT devices with the security and transparency of blockchain technology, companies can gain real-time visibility into the movement of goods and materials, improve the efficiency and accuracy of supply chain processes, and enhance the overall transparency of the supply chain. In this case study, the benefits of utilizing blockchain-based smart contracts and IoT technology in the supply chain and how these technologies can help companies to achieve greater operational efficiency and transparency. Through real-world examples and analysis, examination, and the impact of these technologies on supply chain processes and explore the potential benefits and challenges of implementing a blockchain-based smart contract and IoT solution in the supply chain.

Blockchain-based smart and the supply chain IoT and blockchain might be linked for supply chain quality assurance. Perishable goods, such as champagne or rare delicacy, are regularly subjected to temperature fluctuations and sun intensity as they transit via the transport and storage facilities. "By integrating IoT and blockchain, one can record the path of perishable commodities from manufacturer to retailer. "At the case or pallet level, location and temperature data may be gathered and put into the blockchain, providing the ability to verify the history of the product as it goes through the supply chain and refuse accepting the goods and transferring it. Flowchart of smart contact is given in Figure 10.9.

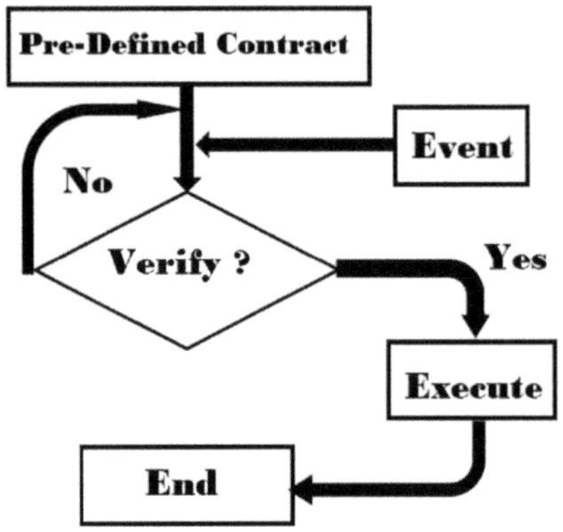

FIGURE 10.9 Flowchart of smart contract.

Source: Adapted from Cheng and Lin (2019).

Aside from storing data, certain blockchain models enable companies to store and operate immutable algorithms in a distributed and decentralized manner, according to Carvahlo. These algorithms, often known as smart contracts, allow businesses to automatically codify business and domain rules (Bhatia & Bhatia, 2013).

IoT devices, such as temperature sensors, can continually check the temperature of shipments and communicate data to a running smart contract, which can notify stakeholders of any temperature decline in real time. Because the smart contract is operating on top of blockchain, the underlying temperature data are saved in an immutable data structure, which aids in data tampering prevention. (Figure 10.10).

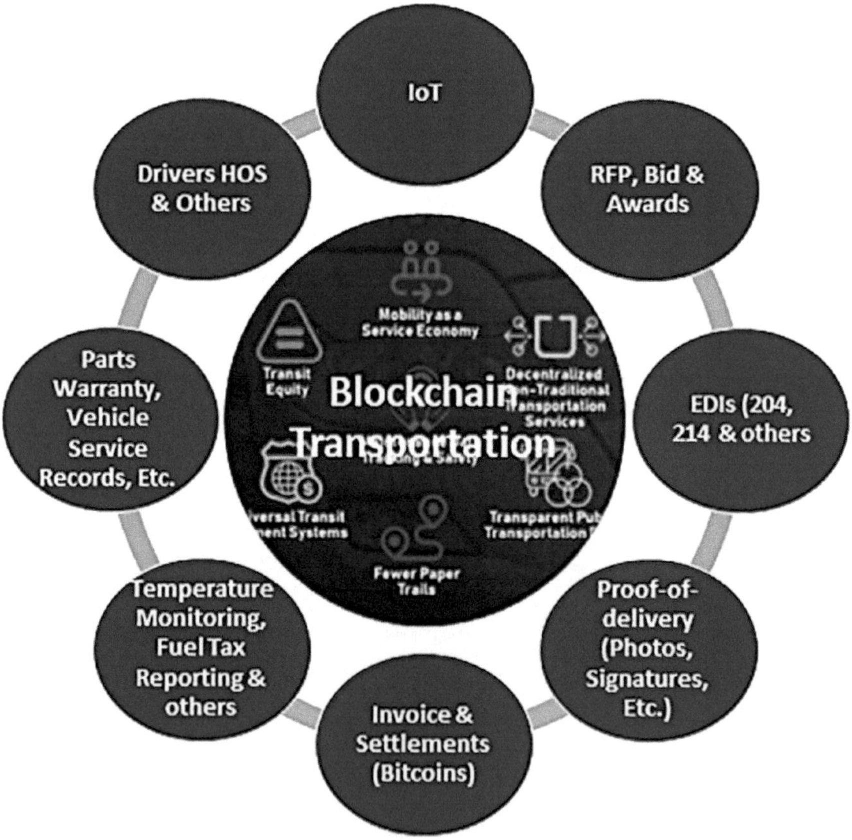

FIGURE 10.10 Blockchain in transportation.

"Integrating Blockchain with IoT Strengthens Trust in Multiparty Processes," Internet sensors installed in leased cars may record crucial events on a blockchain to help track fleet location and return, as well as to allow more relevant billing techniques (Rupani et al., 2017).

"With IoT sensors on board vehicles, truck leasing firms may charge renters' costs based on the torque of the loads rather than distance, as is now the practice,"

"The IoT sensors on the wells assist oil firms in scheduling truck pickups and allowing them to monitor the amount of material picked up and delivered to avoid fraud and false representations," according to the article. "The blockchain distributed ledger technology records critical events in the logistics chain and provides a shared single version of independently verifiable truth throughout the entire logistics chain (Sharma et al., 2015)."

10.9 DISCUSSION

In order to increase openness and confidence in accounting practice, the four topics mentioned above show how accounting and auditing might be transformed with blockchain and AI technology. Real-time accounting on the blockchain may boost productivity, speed up payment settlements, and prevent earnings manipulation. The expense of keeping and reconciling the ledger can be decreased by triple entry accounting. The event method to accounting can make ownership of assets clearer. It may make it possible for auditors to examine the specifics of a transaction's recording and classification. The event method, for instance, would allow auditors to determine if a cash influx is the result of sales, receivables, or new investments. Continuous auditing will be possible thanks to blockchain and AI technologies. Many labor-intensive accounting and auditing activities will be automated thanks to this cutting-edge technology. The effectiveness of the accounting and auditing processes will increase as a result. Additionally, this will simultaneously have a significant impact on how practitioners conduct their business.

10.9.1 CONSEQUENCES OF THEORY

In principle, to a certain extent, organizations may overcome knowledge asymmetry and lessen ethical risks through smart contracts or automation thanks to blockchain technology's unique ability to deliver slide, correct. In addition, the skill can make it easier for managers, accountants, business partners, investors, and auditors to collaborate financially in order to accomplish both collaboration and coordination in blockchain networks or ecosystems. Because it offers smart contracts and precisely records data, blockchain technology will make it harder for managers to alter accounting data, according to the agency hypothesis. Multi-party consensus is used to validate data that is stored on a blockchain. This makes it more difficult to alter the data. Many processes can also be automated. For instance, triple entry accounting automates reconciliation using a shared blockchain ledger. Using blockchain-enabled smart contracts, compliance procedures such as bill payment and expenditure reporting may be automated. Organizations will find it simpler to manage and keep track of accounting data with the help of this technology. Therefore, financial fraud will be more difficult to conceal when combined with AI to spot abnormalities. Theoretically, real-time detection of suspicious financial transactions is also possible.

10.9.2 DECIDING BETWEEN MANY BLOCKCHAIN KINDS

Companies must make sure that blockchain systems are appropriately developed, configured, and used procedures that are backed by their internal controls before using blockchain applications. The affordability, efficiency, and speed of blockchain technology are crucial considerations. Most popular public ones are Bitcoin (BTC), Ethereum (ETH), and Litecoin (LTC). Quorum, Hyperledger, and Corda are the three most popular instances of consortium blockchains. A blockchain's security and throughput are strongly impacted by whether it is permissioned or permissionless.

With known validators, permissioned blockchains often have better throughput whereas permissionless blockchains typically have lower throughput due to increased security demands and the necessity for more stringent consensus procedures. Six factors make it probable that private, permissioned, or consortium blockchains will be the first to enter the commercial world at large:

- to protect the company's sensitive information;
- to provide stakeholders varying access levels based on their need for accounting information to more effectively manage who may view/ update the ledger;

Sharing specific accounting data will reduce the cost of validation since the consensus technique is less costly and requires fewer nodes to reach consensus.

10.10 CONCLUSION

In conclusion, the integration of AI and blockchain technology has the potential to significantly enhance the efficiency, accuracy, and transparency of auditing processes. AI-enabled auditing allows for the automation of routine tasks and provides auditors with powerful tools for data analysis and decision making. Meanwhile, the use of blockchain in auditing provides a transparent and secure ledger of financial transactions, reducing the risk of fraud or errors and enhancing the credibility of financial reports. The combination of AI and blockchain in auditing offers a unique opportunity for companies to improve their financial reporting processes and gain a competitive advantage in today's fast-paced and increasingly complex business environment. As these technologies continue to evolve and mature, it is likely that to see even greater benefits from their integration in the future, making AI and blockchain a powerful tool for the auditing industry. This book chapter examines and condenses four concepts that represent the evolution of accounting recordkeeping with blockchain technology. With the use of this technology, shared, confirmed, and accepted (consensus-driven) auditable data may be made available. Using traceable and auditable blockchain data, audits may be made more successful with AI techniques. Using agency and stakeholder theories to analyzes the findings, Organizations will be challenged by this new, developing technology, though, as they consider the potential hazards of adopting blockchain in accounting.

10.11 FUTURE SCOPE

The future scope for the amalgamation of AI and blockchain in auditing is highly promising, as these technologies continue to evolve and mature. As AI algorithms become more sophisticated, one can expect to see even greater improvements in the efficiency and accuracy of auditing processes, with AI-enabled auditors being able to quickly identify trends, anomalies, and potential risks in financial data. Meanwhile, the use of blockchain in auditing is likely to become more widespread as companies seek to enhance the transparency and security of their financial reporting processes. In addition, as blockchain technology continues to gain wider adoption, one can expect to see the development of new blockchain-based solutions for auditing, such as decentralized auditing platforms, which will provide even greater transparency and security for financial reporting. Furthermore, with the rise of new technologies like quantum computing, it is likely that the use of AI and blockchain in auditing will only continue to grow, allowing companies to stay ahead of the curve and achieve greater efficiency, accuracy, and transparency in their financial reporting processes. In order to investigate further applications of blockchain-enabled accounting, more study is required. Finally, this study raises certain queries that potential future research may attempt to address, expanding the field of blockchain literature through empirical investigation. They might inquire about the costs associated with and the kinds of accounting transactions that can be recorded on a blockchain. How can AI-enabled auditing synchronize blockchain data? What data standards are possible with blockchain and AI? How are blockchain-based accounting information systems managed by businesses? This book chapter is very useful for the researchers working in the same field.

KEYWORDS

- **artificial intelligence**
- **auditing**
- **bitcoin**
- **blockchain**
- **cloud**
- **Ethereum**
- **policymaker**
- **protocol**

REFERENCES

Alkali, Y., Routray, I., & Whig, P., (2022a). Strategy for reliable, efficient, and secure IoT using artificial intelligence. *IUP Journal of Computer Sciences, 16*(2).

Alkali, Y., Routray, I., & Whig, P., (2022b). *Study of Various Methods for Reliable, Efficient, and Secured IoT Using Artificial Intelligence*. Available at SSRN 4020364.

Anand, M., Velu, A., & Whig, P., (2022). Prediction of loan behavior with machine learning models for secure banking. *Journal of Computer Science and Engineering (JCSE), 3*(1), 1–13.

Bhatia, V., & Bhatia, G., (2013). Room temperature-based fan speed control system using pulse width modulation technique. *International Journal of Computer Applications, 81*(5).

Hongdan, H., Radha, K. S., Robin, J., Chima, M., & David, B., (2023). Accounting and auditing with blockchain technology and artificial intelligence: A literature review. *International Journal of Accounting Information Systems, 48,* 100598.

Jupalle, H., Kouser, S., Bhatia, A. B., Alam, N., Nadikattu, R. R., & Whig, P., (2022). Automation of human behaviors and its prediction using machine learning. *Microsystem Technologies*, 1–9.

Khera, Y., Whig, P., & Velu, A., (2021). Efficient effective and secured electronic billing system using AI. *Vivekananda Journal of Research, 10*, 53–60.

Madhu, M., & WHIG, P., (2022). A survey of machine learning and its applications. *International Journal of Machine Learning for Sustainable Development*, *4*(1), 11–20.

Rupani, A., Whig, P., Sujediya, G., & Vyas, P., (2017). A robust technique for image processing based on interfacing of Raspberry-Pi and FPGA using IoT. In: *2017 International Conference on Computer, Communications and Electronics (Comptelix)* (pp. 350–353).

Sharma, A., Kumar, A., & Whig, P., (2015). On the performance of CDTA based novel analog inverse low pass filter using 0.35 μm CMOS parameter. *International Journal of Science, Technology & Management*, *4*(1), 594–601.

Tomar, U., Chakroborty, N., Sharma, H., & Whig, P., (2021). AI based smart agriculture system. *Transactions on Latest Trends in Artificial Intelligence*, *2*(2).

Velu, A., & Whig, P., (2021). Protect personal privacy and wasting time using Nlp: A comparative approach using AI. *Vivekananda Journal of Research, 10*, 42–52.

Velu, A., & Whig, P., (2022). Studying the impact of the COVID vaccination on the world using data analytics. *Vivekananda J Res.*, *10*(1), 147–160.

Whig, P., Nadikattu, R. R., & Velu, A., (2022). COVID-19 pandemic analysis using application of AI. *Healthcare Monitoring and Data Analysis Using IoT: Technologies and Applications, 1.*

Whig, P., Velu, A., & Bhatia, A. B., (2022). Protect nature and reduce the carbon footprint with an application of blockchain for IIoT. In: *Demystifying Federated Learning for Blockchain and Industrial Internet of Things* (pp. 123–142). IGI Global.

Whig, P., Velu, A., & Naddikatu, R. R., (2022). The economic impact of AI-enabled blockchain in 6G-based industry. In: *AI and Blockchain Technology in 6G Wireless Network* (pp. 205–224). Springer, Singapore.

Whig, P., Velu, A., & Nadikattu, R. R., (2022). Blockchain platform to resolve security issues in IoT and smart networks. In: *AI-Enabled Agile Internet of Things for Sustainable FinTech Ecosystems* (pp. 46–65). IGI Global.

Whig, P., Velu, A., & Ready, R., (2022). Demystifying federated learning in artificial intelligence with human-computer interaction. In: *Demystifying Federated Learning for Blockchain and Industrial Internet of Things* (pp. 94–122). IGI Global.

Whig, P., Velu, A., & Sharma, P., (2022). Demystifying federated learning for blockchain: A case study. In: *Demystifying Federated Learning for Blockchain and Industrial Internet of Things* (pp. 143–165). IGI Global.

Xu, C., McDowell, N. G., Fisher, R. A., Wei, L., Sevanto, S., Christoffersen, B. O., Weng, E., & Middleton, R. S., (2019). Increasing impacts of extreme droughts on vegetation productivity under climate change. *Nat. Clim. Change*, *9*(12), 948–953. doi:10.1038/s41558-019-0630-6.

CHAPTER 11

Prominent Portrayal of AI Accompanying Transpiring Technologies in Business and Finance

POOJA SINGH,[1] SEEMA SHOKEEN,[2] SAMIKSHA GARG,[1] and JYOTI BATRA ARORA[3]

[1]*Department of Computer Applications, Maharaja Surajmal Institute, Delhi, India*

[2]*Department of Business Administration, Maharaja Surajmal Institute, Delhi, India*

[3]*Faculty – IT, Institute of Chartered Accountants of India, Noida, India*

ABSTRACT

The transpiring and imminent technologies are transfiguring, the companionship of finance and business in an ameliorating way. In India, 40–45 million grown-ups lay out a considerable portion of their billfold online (over and above 50%). Artificial intelligence is abruptly mutating the global financial services and business look-ins. From the emergence the extension of internet banking and e-commerce portrayed a crucial mantle in the uprising as well as thriving progress along with the comprehensive peril of money laundering. Moreover, we cannot turn a deaf ear to the verity that AI has thoroughly commuted the business fabrication along with financial service. India is recognizing the cardinal significance of fintech by embracing it 87%, substantially towering the global average of 64%. India's fintech fabrication is anticipated to sprout at a CAGR of 20% to outstretch a transaction worth of $138 billion in 2023. Nowadays everybody is diverting towards the thoroughly mechanization structure for any and every work. Even the

Advanced Digital Technologies in Financial and Business Management: Unleashing the Power of Artificial Intelligence, Machine Learning, Blockchain, and the Internet of Things. Jyoti Batra Arora, Nitish Pathak, and Neelam Sharma (Eds.)

banking sector has been converted to a great extant by AI. In this present scenario, the business and financial industry is vigorously looking for the various approaches to leverage the statistical information to yield contemporary and ameliorating assistance. In this chapter there must be culminating of the commercial and monetarily generation using impending technologies and its magnification, actuality, and companionship with the economy. In an approximation India's digital remittance industry is expected to grow 300% higher than its present-day size by 2025. India, which is centralizing the digital economy, has presently outstretch about 70 billion digital payment undertakings in 2022—thriving highest around the globe. Thus, emphasizing the opportunities and requirements through the upcoming AI technologies in the domain of business and finance.

11.1 INTRODUCTION

Artificial intelligence exert as an apparent drift through this ongoing scenario. It is now solicited in numerous streams. Business and finance seek artificial intelligence in profuse innovative approaches. Countless studies and surveys stipulated that by 2035, the providence of more than 20 nations will be duplexed and productivity will be thundering around. AI is imparting the commerce and monetary of industries as a remarkable tempest. Nowadays every single economic sector is wielding AI to liquidize the welfare like, shrinking price, conserving time, and building utility. Not long ago, the 10 topmost and chief intercontinental commercial finance houses and merchant banks have set out the deliberate technological advancement by discovering the AI implementations to serve the frequenters, upgrading performance and maximizing proceeds.

An analysis lately, submerging almost 4,000 business directories beyond 130 countries, declaring that 89% of the contemplated institutions concurred that the automated mechanisms and programed technologies will overwhelmingly mix up their businesses, but 44% credited that they are sufficiently developed for such disarrangement.

Digital Finance is the approaching production for the upcoming business and finance ecosystem that deploy turbulent technology, variation, facts, and figures, and individuals to upraise and metamorphose the proficiency of the monetary function. More than 70% of the purchaser association will be operated by intelligent technologies by 2022 end. Moreover, there is a supposition that over 65% of worldwide GDP (gross domestic product) to be initialized by 2023. This is approximated to propel more than 7 trillion dollars of undeviating automated transformation portion from 2021 to 2023.

Thus, this present chapter, delineates business along with finance must take upper hand of emerging as well as impending technologies to increase mounting around economics, probability threats, and adds value to contributors and associators. Furthermore, description about the commercial and monetary services which got AI opportunities in far-reaching requirements in peril evaluation, and monetary scrutiny.

11.2 COMPONENTS OF AUTOMATED BUSINESS AND FINANCE BY USING TRANSPIRING TECHNOLOGIES

11.2.1 ROBOTIC TASKS AUTOMATION

Software mechanisms having been programed in advance to accomplish monotonous negotiation processes that can automate assignable processes of commerce. These software's are thoroughly capable of alluring the drudgery out of business and finance professionals and to rescue the role for further commercial support as well as monetary analytics. Costing a full-time certified snippet professional, such program results conduct the advancements of value, along with certainty in procedures, while amending the standard of throughput. Globally estimated investment on robotics will be around $58 billion at the end of 2023, forecasting the indications as a probable collision of more than 380 million knowledgeable employees.

11.2.2 COGNITIVE SCANNING

It simulates intuitive and cognitive competency to undergo the tasks that solely humankind has ever operated. IBM has perpetrated $1 billion to commercialize, its evaluation platform according to cognitive standard (Kaya et al., 2019). Applicable in business and finance, emerging cognitive technologies, waged adjoining robotics, can upend financial and commercial function and further outlay unprecedented momentum, flexibility, and lucidity to the processes. For instance, Hong Kong subway carries more than 5 million commuters on a daily basis and gloats a 99.9% on-time track record. Thus, automatically identifying fare passengers for further upliftment, thus constraining estimated efficiency to increase by 450%.

11.2.3 INTERNET OF THINGS

It is the formation of interconnected technological mechanism architectures that safeguards fruitful results by unraveling concealed insights through futuristic analysis (Palepu & Krishna, 2020). IoT-enabled software's can shoot up their revenue, minimalize costs, and reserve time- and business along with finance conclude an exemplary interest in driving the institution plan of action around IoT.

- Enlarging attached gadgets: Several studies have predicted that more than 6.4 billion interconnected things probably be in use till 2020, up to 45% from 2019, and soon that goal would reach 32.9 billion in 2023.
- Worldwide centralized data traffic: Annual universal statistical center IP commerce will reach 17.9 zettabytes by the termination of 2023, up from 5.7 zettabytes every year in 2020.

11.2.4 BLOCKCHAIN

It is a record of all placed undertakings and arrangements that have happened with the instance of an asset, which is further eligible for being swapped for a commercialized build up. More than 95% of the world's humongous finance houses will have taken action on blockchain projects by 2023 (Schueffel, 2016). To further elaborate this, continuous investments of more than $5 billion have been consistently made over the past 7 years (Ron Gill CMA, 2011). And this, has been concluded that $87 billion in project yearly reserves by 2023 for the banking sector solitarily. Blockchain imaginably constitutes the most disruptive potency in business and finance for decades to approach.

11.3 CYBERNATED COMMERCE AND MONETARY SYSTEMS IN FIVE THREADS

1. The mass of commercial and economical processes will be working in a "factory" prototype-allied, interrelated, automated, and foreseeable.
2. All the particulars and details will be obtainable in real-time and will be particularly ubiquitous – with computerized certainty emerging as the not-to-be give and take frontier possibility.
3. Prognostic analysis – from inward and outward resources, based on an incapsulated arrangement and unarranged data – will be the

standard and not the anomaly. The accessibility of cognitive skills to integrate particulars will differentiate the upcoming financial institutions.

4. Economical talent will undergo through non-regimented sources with presently leading generations leadership and narrative merit systems. Millennials in monitorial teams will ask and expect for submerging project models of rewards and effort ethos.
5. The role of top-level management will continue to progress farther and morph into that of an important irreplaceable role. Hard cash, possibility, and economics will be the shepherd strengths.

Figure 11.1 manifests how the commercial, and monetarily systems have divided the whole outgoing structure in 5 broad key themes, which specifies the management as well as utilization of resources along with implied processes.

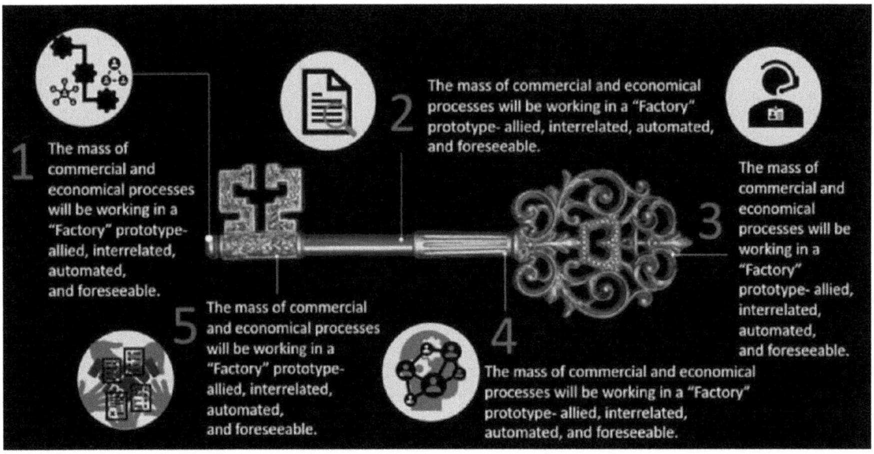

FIGURE 11.1 Top five key components for commercial and monetarily settlement.

11.4 EMANATING APPLIED SCIENCE IN BUSINESS AND FINANCE MANAGEMENT

11.4.1 AI-BASED BUSINESS ANALYTICS AND COMMERCE

If we include analysis, businesses are progressing from unvarying, submissive announcements of artifacts that have heretofore occurred to dynamic analysis with indicator panel that would assist them about the happenings in every frame of time and give vigilantes when something seems to occur without its past persistence (Mhlanga & David, 2020). Suspensions such as AI algorithm are truly based upon the most effective neural crisscrosses which provide up mark perfection in anomaly detection as it absorbs from past situations and statistics. Data-driven industries use intelligence learning policies to master business occurrences in actual problem-solving time, helping slash time to locate as 87% and reduction attentive noises by as much as 98% (Black & Ken, 2019). Global AI-driven apparatus merchandise income is foreseen to stretch up to $256.9 billion in 2025. The assumption for the AI vends compound yearly growth rate from 2020–2027 is 34.7%.

Figure 11.2 stand for the conventional investigation architecture which, incorporates a higher gradation of labor and extended timeframes, which are not applicable for the current, on-growing business topography. Therefore (Ng, 2020), AI acts as a bolster to the operation associated with analytics by coordinating its exigent characteristic, paving the way for the data-directed conclusion building, and authorizing business conductors to carry on the data effortlessly.

FIGURE 11.2 Business analytics through AI implementation.

11.4.2 INFORMATION RELIABILITY

Artificial Intelligence can ascertain prospective ultimatums, even when it approaches towards to the sizeable nugget of information. In a company, there is a regular exchange of information and other particulars both internally and externally (Xavier, 2017). This reliable information needs protection and capable security from malicious people and certain artifice software's. But it's not possible for the cybersecurity workforce to scrutinize all the congestion of feasible unavoidable threats (Kunwar & Manju, 2019). AI is the pre-eminent possible solution for such situation, which can descry any commination hidden in such tailback (Lu et al., 2020). The Cybersecurity which further sequel with data security based upon artificial intelligence sized in value at USD 22.4 billion in 2023, and further foreshadowed to be 60.6 billion by 2028; extending at a CAGR of 21.9% from 2023 to 2028.

Figure 11.3 exhibits worldwide artificial intelligence (AI) commencement proportion was approximately at US$ 119.78 million in 2022, and it is anticipated to cross US$ 1,597.1 million by the year 2030 with an inscribed CAGR of 38.1% from 2022 to 2030, according to the precedence research this much growth has been forecasted.

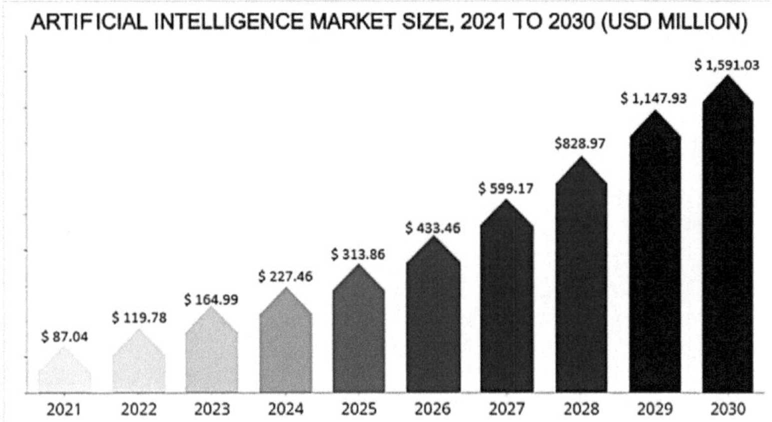

FIGURE 11.3 Precedence research have forecasted growth of artificial intelligence in upcoming years.

11.4.3 INFORMATION AUTOMATION

For the impetus of data analysis automation is implied by over 48% of the companies, and on top of that 20% of businesses apply automation for charging invoice, announcement pinning (up), and further commercial procedures. As the world constructs the terminating shove towards full digitalization, the necessity for AI emulsions keeps on maximizing due to gigantic specifics generation (Burstrom et al., 2021).

Figure 11.4 constitutes mass of the AI solution and implementation associates to the robotic process automation (RPA) (Milana & Ashta, 2021). In comparability, utilizers can compose the particular software robot to imitate humankind deportment and clarify interplays with automated structures (Ranjan et al., 2020). AI can expound the sequence, recognize relatedness, and put forward the finest retaliation. According, to studies more than 69% of habitual and frequent managerial function will be altogether automated by 2024 (Jarrahi, 2018). Also, 51% of automation inventiveness were lay hold of to augment workman regulation. Besides, 31% of the business institutions are surveyed and initiated their high concern about employment that automation may enlarge in upcoming years.

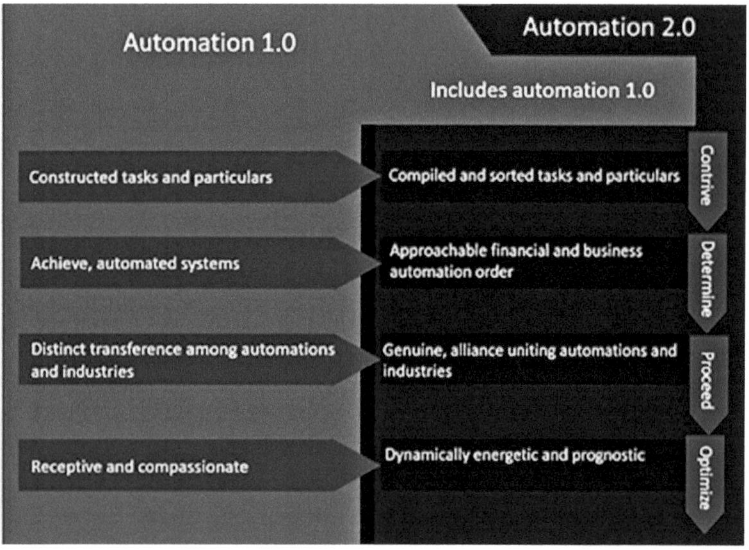

FIGURE 11.4 According to the business progressive automation – in finance and economical domain (change in automation over time) conveys the advancement and growth of automation in industrial and monetarily basis.

11.4.4 DATA LITERACY

Companies that avail AI structures for factual situations get to grips with risk of AI algorithms, i.e., AI mishaps. Breaches of information seclusion, and AI partiality (Younis et al., 2022). One of the techniques is to endanger to engage the technicality and non-automated stakeholders to critically examine the structures and out-turn of the data science complexity. Business associates who are informatively literate portray crucial character in assessing the risks of AI software's and guaranteeing that subsisting AI software's are equitable and ethical. Research has predicted that more than 70% of the business employees are anticipated to work laboriously with AI algorithm-based data by 2025-up from 52% in 2020 (Cao & L, 2022). Big business houses are estimated to squander $641 billion on customer persistency augmenting the data literacy experience. As Figure 11.5 shows the categorization of data literacy according to the obligation's ad contrivances (Table 11.1).

TABLE 11.1 Depicts the Data Literacy Rate among Different Level; Incorporating AI as well as Wellness of Different Technologies

Category	Low	Medium	High
1. Data and privacy awareness	Accepts the terms and conditions without persuading or apprehension.	Attempts to determine credibility of site or app before accepting terms and downloading.	Reads web site and mobile app privacy terms and conditions and validates app and site credibility before engaging.
2. Informed decision-making	Depends upon favorable application, gadgets, or web site to tell you what to think; prone to conspiracy theories.	Researches the issues before making a decision, though still overweighs the opinions of people who "think like me."	Creates model that considers false positives and false negatives before making a decision; practices critical thinking.
3. Al and analytic techniques	Believes that Al is something only applicable to large organizations and three letter government agencies.	Understands how Al is actually a spectrum of analytics, but not sure what each of them are capable of doing.	understands how to collaborate to identify KPls and metrics across a variety of value dimensions that comprise Al utility function.
4. Predictions and statistics	Doesn't seek to understand the probabilities of events happening; blind to unintended consequences of decisions.	Does consider probabilities when making decisions but underweights a thorough assessment of the potential unintended consequences.	Actively seeks out information from credible sources to improve the odds of making an informed decision.
5. Value creation	Doesn't understand the dimensions of "value."	Understands the value dimensions but hasn't identified the KPIs and metrics against which value creation effectiveness is measured.	Understands the value dimensions and has identified the KPIS and metrics against which value creation effectiveness is measured.
6. Ethics	Thinks ethics is something that only applies to "others."	Acknowledges importance of ethics but not sure how best to address.	Actively works to embrace different perspectives and rational when making decisions.

11.4.5 COLLABORATIVE BUSINESS INTELLIGENCE

It surfaces the merging of commerce intelligence software with cooperation implementations, comprising communal as well as networking technologies, to prop up ameliorated information-based settlements (S et al., 2020). Collaborative BI can also be petitioned to endeavor-extensive delineation and analytics, assembling the allocating process uncomplicated and authorizing additional methodical decision making amidst the coordinators who may be authorizing works to conclude the goals on an individual basis (Loureiro et al., 2021). Forecasts assets that over and above 70% of CEOs assume that digital refinement has marshaled towards multiplicative revenue (Boobier & Tony, 2020). Not only this, 89% of all companies have heretofore planned to implement a digital-initialization business collaboration between AI and its requisites.

Figure 11.5 exhibits numerous implementations and ordinance of collaborative business intelligence, and with its various functionalities.

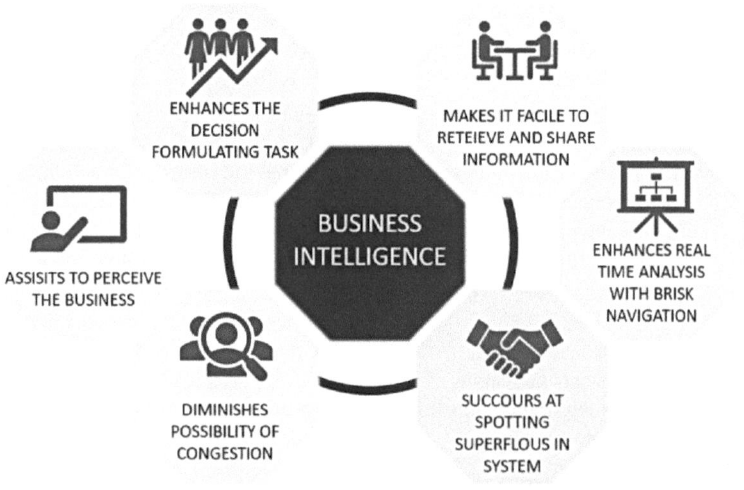

FIGURE 11.5 Components of business intelligence, i.e., amalgamation of business with intelligence.

11.5 APPERTAIN DIFFERING TECHNOLOGIES IN FINANCE CAPITALIZATION AND BUSINESS SUBSIDIZATION

11.5.1 FINTECH

Financial technology refers to fintech which chronicles new and innovative technology which enhances its work nearing and automating the dropship and operation of financial amenity (Fisher et al., 2016). The international market of AI is gigantic, transcending $62 billion in 2021 and prognosticate to augment by over 45% individually in a year. Financial networking is not an anomaly. In 2021, AI in fintech trade was merited at $12 billion and is envisaged to reach $35 billion by 2027. Such cogent outcomes approach from respective origins.

11.5.1.1 EFFICACIES

AI implementations in fintech drop-ship an enormous fecundity amplification. From a pinpoint credit snick tracking proficiency that processes 72% of the debentures immediately, to 87% minimal amount of time depleted on data entry, artificial intelligence put forward colossal merit. This cannot be ignored that it spurs considerable acquisition (D et al., 2022). AI applications in fintech bring up an enormous efficacious boost. By such enactments 66% of the processes work greater than their competence instantly, while 80% less time spent on details listing.

11.5.1.2 PERVASIVE

The quivering conveys in exertion practice created by COVID-19 and the analogous government efforts also elevated the promotion of cutting-fringe tech beyond the plank. The AI-authorized institutions only maximize their fertility throughout the lockdown (EJ et al., 2020). AI based software's ameliorates data extraction and further imply a wide assortment of application and a demonstrated documentation.

11.5.1.3 AMALGAMATION

Fintech is acquiring growingly combination with coupled vocations. Availing AI will elevate the advantage of interweave-punitive software (Go et al., 2020). All-inclusively, 45% of financial assistance corporations are espousing AI. Intelligence has led to an excessive decrease in expenses. Thus, almost $862 billion are invested for the purpose of settlement of covenants (Faboi, 2022).

The artificial intelligence agencies across the globe in fintech market expanse was evaluated as USD 9.45 billion in 2021 and is anticipated to increase at a compound yearly extension appraise (CAGR) of 16.5% from 2022 to 2030.

Figure 11.6 according to the grand view research reports the consistent growth till now as well as the forecasted in the market through its investment and effective utilization has been predicted.

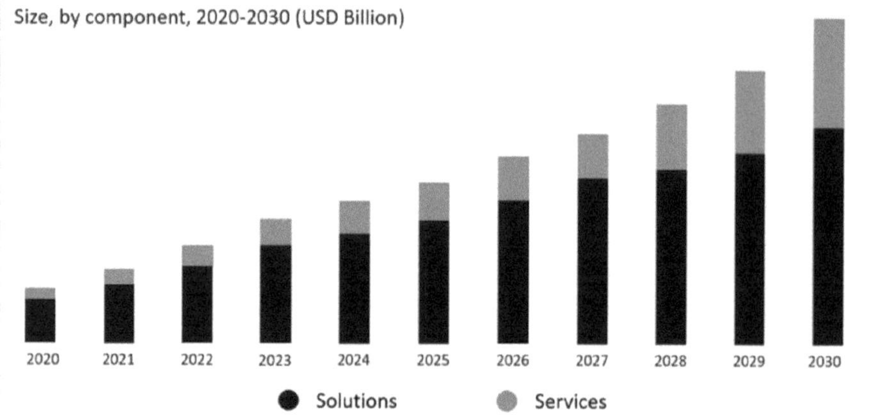

FIGURE 11.6 Content services market platform has exhibited extension of collaboration between facilitation and its technological solutions.

11.6 CLOUD COMPUTING

It is a sort of stipulated service which dispenses access to allocate resources, implementations, or repository over the web. It authorizes financial houses to acquire and operate data in secluded servers instead of confined ones. Cloud computing proffers numerous virtues and assistances for financial institutions such as intensified certainty, speedy rectifying rat, and minimal fetches (Bredt, 2019). Cloud applications present investment worth is over $150 billion worldwide. Across the world more than 200 ZB of data will be stockpiled as an estimation by using cloud till 2025. Still 75% of the corporate world specifics is stow in the cloud (Sebastianelli, 2018). Also, cloud services diligently proven a revenue generation of around $178 billion each and every year or even more than that. In accordance with a survey, around 90% of sizeable corporations have embraced multi-cloud framework. Major implementations of cloud computing in financial institutions, are as in subsections.

11.6.1 CORRESPONDENCE MANAGEMENT

Financial institutions administer cloud-based corresponding systems to superintend customer details and interlinkage. Such deeds authorize financial institutions to keep a regular trajectory of all customers interactions, regardless the verity of whereabouts or time of period (Gao & J., 2022). The correct cloud master plan also enables it in an easier form for monetarily based companies to provide customized service constructed upon consumers preferences (Ahmed et al., 2022). To imply such correspondence, $146 billion is expected to be the market worth by the year 2029, and already around $71 billion is the total value of cloud correspondence market in year 2021.

11.6.2 FRAUD DISCERNMENT

Nowadays, numerous of monetarily based institutions use cloud for fraud spotting and avoidance by analyzing substantial aggregation of data from numerous sources. This assists such institutions to recognize any suspicious activity before it brings out any vandalization (Joveda et al., 2019). To prevent such exploitations cloud data hubs, record more than 5% of the global energy utilization.

11.6.3 DATA SCRUTINY

Cloud has been excessively used for progressive and pioneering inspections in order to procure apprehension into consumer behavior patterns and drifts (Fraisse & Laporte, 2022). By precepting how consumers interrelate with financial outcomes, FIs can generate creative and novel offerings that would rather encounter their requirements better than ever. To scrutinize the data in a secure manner enterprises makes a utilization of 2.6 communal and 2.7 exclusive clouds.

Below specified table manifest, how cloud computing fabricates the accounting work easier for financial institutions, rather than when juxtapose with traditional accounting software's.

11.7 ROBOTIC PROCESS AUTOMATION

Robotic process automation (RPA) is a convenient and handy software which, imbrute and automatize various processes by retrieving user confluence without requiring the fundamental programs (Jung et al., 2018). RPA comes up with a process of acquiring some sort of advantages of systems consolidation without the indistinguishable level of speculation (Anderson et al., 2020; Demirkan et al., 2020). As per the global finance reports, RPA market size is forecasted to be around $7 billion by the year 2030 (evaluated around $ 420 million in 2021). Major applications of RPA are as follows:

1. If adroitly executed, RPA can dispense a great profit as well as dividend on investment, but merchants and stakeholders should tend to imply AI throughout all processes.
2. It would save time, the advancements of RPA also incorporate upgraded correctness, faster procedures, and administration of excessive workloads.
3. RPA is the solo automation alternative and should be differentiated to enterprise resource planning system (ERP) (Younis et al., 2022), remodulations, chop, and changing on ERP prototype and restricted accounting structures.
4. RPA can also be implemented decisively as a fragment of minimal instruction requirement program or diplomatically to supervise-AI software's.
5. Financial institutions should hammer out firmly to make sure the external stakeholders are taking benefits of RPA to minimalize the client tariff and to upgrade assistance.

According to various inspections and explorations growth of RPA, is as in Table 11.2.

TABLE 11.2 RPA Software Market Share by Revenue (Present Scenario along with Forecasted) Worldwide (Millions of Dollars)

2022 Rank (Present Scenario)	2025 Rank (Forecasted)	RPA Extending Businesses	2022 Revenue	2025 Revenue (Forecasted)	2022 Growth (%)	2025 Market Share (%)
5	1	UiPath	20.9	145.8	765.4	13.9
1	2	Automation anywhere	564.2	876.4	56.8	12.5
3	3	Blue prism	45.9	71.0	34.9	8.4
2	4	NICE	62.1	72.8	87.8	7.3
4	5	Pegasystems	34.7	52.0	49.7	4.8
8	6	Kofax	17.5	42.2	225.6	4.4
11	7	NTT-AT	7.8	34.7	488.9	3.4
6	8	Edge verve systems	22.8	27.8	43.3	2.4
7	9	Open connect	23.9	24.9	11.4	1.9
9	10	Help systems	12.7	29.9	39.8	1.6
–	–	Others	321.1	437.9	27.8	39.4
–	–	Total	1336.6	1815.4	1831.4	100.0

11.7.1 PROGRESSIVE CYBER SECURITY

Financial institutions utilize the online banking provisions to enhance their portfolio of assistance along with amenities and to maneuver more methodically. Howbeit, digital banking has propelled proceeds and beneficials, it has further uplift cybersecurity perturbs. Several research have concluded that the financial institutions are among the topmost prioritized industry for cyberattacks (Enholm et al., 2021). For the purpose of futuristic cybersecurity, financial institutions are converting the technologies that has appended enormous worth to their operative-AI. For the enhancement of progressive cyber security $7.86 billion has been investment globally to upgrade AI mechanization (Xue et al., 2020). FIs may utilize AI to elevate cybersecurity fortification; then proportionately it would be unchallenging because AI is a constitutive part of commercial performance; therefore, it enlarges advantages with its applicability as:

1. **Automate Commination Hunting:** Automation can be done with AI, for the motive of hunting threats to ameliorate perception rate over 95% (Valgaeren & Hannah, 2019). This will refine the detection evaluation but also restrain the cybersecurity framework against forecasted upcoming risks.
2. **Equip Upcoming Threats:** New risks or dangers are always on the horizon, but by the implementation of AI, financial institutions got an opportunity of conquering these upcoming challenges by amalgamating automated financial cybersecurity administration into the undertaking (Huang et al., 2022). AI requisition ca also summons additional tools, like observable analytics, to reinforce threat hunting and such techniques could be implied to prosper the development profiles on monetarily applications to rectify vulnerabilities briskly.
3. **Prognosticate Risk Contraventions:** AI can definitely upgrade financial cybersecurity by foreseeing cyber contraventions before they transpire (Yu et al., 2021). AI software's can prognosticate where an attack could be transpired and flag specifically vulnerable petitions for IT persons to manage.

11.7.2 CHATBOTS

Chatbots are moderately obtaining affirmation in the financial and business sector. They are not merely disentangling the procedures for businesses but furthermore authorizing swift ingress to assistance that were previously constricted to mobile applications. Convenience of implying chatbots is s follow:

1. **Intensified User-Experience:** Chatbots can constructively hold business and financial facilitation and beneficially accomplish functioning that were used to handle by externals, thus chatbots are proficient assignments and can customize facilities for frequenters.
2. **Assignment-Automation:** Business and financial houses are deploying this technology to automate the bulk of their labor works like operating users' queries, responding to their complaints, proffering financing counseling, etc., to escalate customer events.
3. **Embarkment:** Bots are habitually being utilized in the financial industry for the purpose of embarkment by authorizing users to elevate a fresh account in a swift way without proceeding towards the quintessential steps at the sectional subdivision.
4. **Depletion in Maintenance Cost:** Financial chatbots can assist businesses to minimalize users' facilities cost up to 45% and because of that the monetarily industry can operate them for the immediate aspiration of risks without any stakeholder's assistance.

Figure 11.7, in accordance with artificial solutions research delineation, shows the appearance of chatbots in business and financial industries along with their eventual activation in the upcoming years.

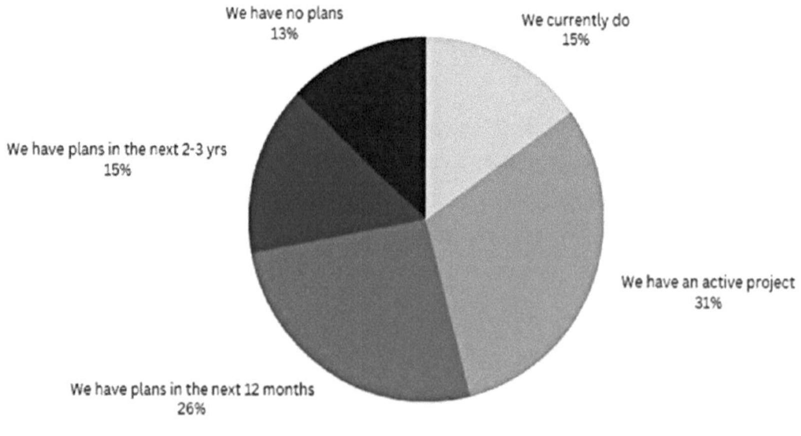

FIGURE 11.7 Current objectives of companies in accordance with upcoming intents.

11.7.3 CHATGPT

ChatGPT (procreative pre-instructed convertor) is a chatbot pioneered by OpenAI recently. ChatGPT has emerged as an artificial intelligence tool, which particularly customized and resized for chatbot prosecutions. It signifies a considerable and substantial impact on finance and business management by confronting its capability to maneuvers monetarily skepticism and to dispense precise, definitive, and well-founded retaliations. By such attributes and hallmarks it is considered as an irreplaceable resource for financial confidants, who can employ it to serve their stakeholders rapidly as well as competently with an extensive scope of interrogation. In supplementation to impart reinforcement to business houses, ChatGPT has also been manipulate a contemporary generation of commercial chatbots (Budzianowski & Vulić, 2019). These chatbots, even can abet the frequenters with assignments such as examining descriptive balances, constructing remittances, and chasing speculations, all through effortless, instinctive consultations (Osterrieder & GPT, 2023).

ChatGPT's impression on finance and business management goes out with just users' facilitation and hold up. Moreover, it has also been implemented to scrutinize financial particulars and construct further enlighten investment resolutions and settlements. By tutelage ChatGPT on enormous aggregation of commercial information, industries have been aped to anchorage its machine learning competencies to recognize inclination and motif that can't be visibly factualized to personage analysts. Comprehensively, ChatGPT has demonstrated itself as a cogent and compelling contrivance for the commercial and economical based companies, portioning the aerodynamic procedures, ameliorated customer facilitation, and to implement more illuminated determinations. It can also be concluded that the elemental component is to impersonate a human confab or consultation, it could be multifaceted in its retaliations and even extemporize (Phillips et al., 2022). ChatGPT and its prospective implementation:

1. **What is ChatGPT?** A chatbot that maneuvers GPT technology to initiate retaliations to consumer input.
2. **Ascendancies and Superiority of ChatGPT:** It can dispense personalized as well as personage interlinkage, can acknowledge and counter to an extensive assortment of inputs, can be amalgamated into enormous number of diversification and platforms.
3. **Prospective Solicitation:** Crypto mining, sequential accumulation of data, facilitation feedback, new-fangled solutions, and an astonishing frame of reference.

4. **Future Interpretation:** ChatGPT is anticipated to subsists its growth in approvability and admiration as well as to dilate into new realms as GPT technology ameliorates and becomes extensively accessible.

11.8 DIVERGENT METHODS HOW INTELLIGENCE TRANSMUTING THE MONETARY INDUSTRY

Contemplate various tactics they can abet financial institution efficiently control its own menace profile, detect changes to intramural key benchmark, improve collateral comportment and sustain compliance.

11.8.1 DESCRY FRAUD PRIOR TO MONEY DEPART FROM ACCOUNT

Financial institutions must cease fraudsters prior to their negotiation because it fends off financial mislaying and retains a commend client connection. Institutions soak up the rental for deprivations, but in few occurrences, banks are not accountable (Mbizvo et al., 2021). By contriving AI, principally products being applicable for monetizing, financial institutions can sum up the distance in recognizing and terminating contraventions prior to their occurrence. AI frames a touchstone of proceedings patterns and can recognize incongruity a proactive correspondence. In 2021, Javelin Strategy and Research picked out the swindling scam forfeiture of around $28 billion, which resultant hoodwinked more than 27 million U.S. frequenters.

11.8.2 MINIMALIZE ERRONEOUS POSITIVES

Due to the rigorous implantation of technology and the risks of cyberattacks pursue in an everlasting nip and tuck competitiveness, enter additional candidate: erroneous positives (Wen & Chunhui., 2021). By dwindling erroneous positives with the assistance of AI, it gradually turns out to be less dependent on staff then those priceless human resources can emphasis on scrutinizing real and compound commination (Al-Satwari et al., 2022). The prevalence and magnitude of such things are endangering continuously, but by implementing emerging cybersecurity automated software's can serve in lessening the bombardment of alerts.

11.8.3 PRODUCTIVELY IN SCRIPT REGULATORY SWAP MANAGEMENT

Financial institutions are cannonaded by frequently substituting directives, thus the laboring or physical system for evaluation has become incapable. There are institutions who would spend abundance of their time for not only going through and comprehending the current regulations (Pallathadka et al., 2021), but also implying further necessary conversions. Intelligent process automation (IPA) is casted-off to appraise abundance aggregation of particulars swiftly, precisely, and in real time so that financial institutions can stay in amenability (Abbasi et al., 2019; Dietzmann et al., 2020). Coalescing such techniques with the capability and eligibility of human resource who can understand the intricate dictates of the financial industry can govern superior upshots.

11.8.4 AMPLIFY ANOMALY DISCERNMENT

Frequently assessing undertakings for peculiar deportment is an enervating and time-consuming assignment. AI can appraise the copious aggregation of data to initiate customary transactional structures and then further in encouraging in detecting anomalies that might instigate the risk of cyberattack (Kunnathuvalappil Hariharan, 2019). AI is efficient enough of scanning through different sorts of statistics and particulars in gregarious volumes to recognize a breach in the applied algorithms. Moreover, AI is capable at discovering anomalies that are overlooked by a single size fit of utter rules-based approach to fraud unearthing. With AI, accounts are supervised and examined frequently, continuously, and impetuously, authorizing the FIs to dispense a higher level of security while tailoring reliability and dependability to clients customized needs, sooner or later preventing such exasperating red ensigns.

11.8.5 DECREASE HUMAN FALLACY

Each and every financial institution has to encounter obstacles effectuate by human inaccuracy. Studies have concluded that more than 95% of all breaches are caused by human delusion grant, whether the fallacy is caused within the data analysis or an unintentional clicking on a phishing electronic mail, every infringement leads an institution to vulnerable breach situation

(Easton et al., 2018). AI system in co-occurrence with a SOC team can be emphasized by the financial institutions, which can obverse and further can detect the alerts and then analyze for upcoming threats which can be a conduction for fraud, peril, and even a compliance to substitute the workload and justification can be done more effectively (Giudici, 2018). For the first line of security automated apparatus must be opted which permits abilities out with the restrictions of human resource capability, thus subtracting the occurrence of delusion.

11.8.6 EXTENSION OF AMBITIOUS SUPERIORITY

Finance houses are consistently in contesting among each other to dispense the most coherent services inside their industry (Kruse et al., 2019). Fintech's are consistently framing new calibers with the effective assistance of technology to come up with a higher-caliber client encounter. To linger the competitiveness, FIs obliged to persuade their frequenters that they will secure their particular and monetary fundings by applying a superior magnitude of security (Vasista & Kola., 2021). AI cybersecurity consequences that mitigate menace, fraud, and the compliance which are being produces specifically for the purpose of banking to come up with streamlined and industry-determined preservation, catering the FI' distinctive necessitates.

11.9 E-COMMERCE APPLICABILITY BY APPERTAINING AI

For a business it is decisive along with climacteric to have an ecommerce platform to be capable to engage with other distributive businesses. If an e-commerce trading isn't able to vend online, revenue can't be accelerated further in a progressive way (Hansraj & Kugi, 2021). Above all that, e-commerce businesses have perceived a mounting surge following the pandemic era (McBride et al., 2022). The throughgoing and transformative utilization of technology has conducted the route towards an era where the business is and will be immersed in social networking platforms, contrivances, and the internet as it was never have been selfsame previously (Kunnathuvalappil Hariharan, 2020). Because of all such state of affairs, lot of victorious businesses have districted to clasp the online market and are endeavoring the opportunities to meliorate sales.

E-commerce availing AI: A survey stated that 63% of clients or frequenters aren't even enlightened by the fact that they wield AI technologies (Malali et al., 2020). This concluded that the businesses could deploy AI for their ecommerce website secondarily or without even undeniably premeditated it. How AI is pinnacling e-commerce, is as in subsections.

11.9.1 VOICE NEGOTIATIONS AND VIRTUAL SUBORDINATION

E-commerce virtual assistants (VAs) are chatbots which make successive use of vernacular filtering and machine learning technologies to acknowledge customer skepticism and proffer the demanded support accordingly. This is not an unrevealed or unspecified deed in preset scenario. Voice assistants are prioritized in e-commerce businesses because they are operative on 24/7 basis and can manipulate queries in a straightforward manner (Harmon & Psaltis, 2021). Chiefly, this ameliorates a business's accendibility, too. Virtual subordination can also be cast-off for several assignments ranging from outcome research to registering to operational inventory. More than 80% of consumers (Sanz et al., 2021), who are regular purchasers with voice subordination are pleases as well as contended with such acquaintance. Also, voice commerce is anticipated to surpass $30 billion by 2024.

Voice technology is not a modernist. Businesses have been consistently implementing it since the 1960s (Goncharenko & Andrea, 2019). Until today, voice commerce has had astounding extension. It's a technology which authorize its users to purchase or do exploring using their own voices. Voice commerce is tendered by numerous for its momentum and expediency because by implying that users don't have to type their search, or anything correlated to that.

11.9.2 SMART SEARCH

Generally, customers make use of search box to perceive or discover their desired products on an ecommerce website. But for such situations smart search is there as it referred to as the combination of merchandising and search. It mingles a combination of merchandising methodology with the online search technology (Pallathadka et al., 2021). It necessitates newfangled constituents, like, for instance, faceted exploration, navigation, auto-completion, advocated upshot listings, contemporary searches, and numerous attributes that has consolidated with demonstrated forage approaches. E-commerce objectives implies them to appertain image annotation to volunteer personalized, untroublesome yet straightforward and functional search occurrences etiquette data.

11.9.3 PERSONALIZATION

In the E-commerce business personalization cites upon the alteration of experience according to a solitary patron's proposal points, requirements, predilection, and impression. It can also be interpreted as the approach of personalizing online surfing experience by synchronously or rigorously exhibiting content, whether it be crusades, brands, or spin-off, to users. This hang on their click-through, window-shop deportment, obstinance past, etc.

Personalization was one of the important character e-commerce industries before the execution and application of AI (Jędrzejka, 2019). However, now systems can crunch substantial data sizes that enables them for escalation as well as actual-time analytics. Software's and even an algorithm can swiftly analyze the particulars immediately and summon the tendency in customer comportment. E-commerce stores can take welfare from customer's predisposition for personalized products recommendation for instinctive purchase.

11.9.4 AUTOMATION

Online businesses are now accessible on numerous passages with 24/7 availableness. Some sort of automation is often required (Wang, 2021). By automating users buttress, merchants can liberate time, vitality, and functioning monetary resources. AI can be a substantial assistance when it led to automation for e-commerce business possessors.

With the application of automation, an e-commerce business can be controlled and implemented all monotonous jobs and simplify the internal and external-end workflow (Olan et al., 2022). Because of AI, e-commerce businesses can automate each and every thing from promoting and spotlighting upcoming products on multiple platforms to synchronizing sales, recognizing hazardous transactions, benefacting discounts to frequenters, etc.

11.10 FUTURE PROSPECTS

Artificial intelligence is feasibly the most substantial trifecta in the financial and business world presently. Espousing discerning determinations can permit financial and business institutions a keen supremacy over other contenders by assisting them in amending their benefactions in their ever-changing, unforeseeable world. In this present scenario, AI has been enormously incorporated with other emanating technologies to operate groundbreaking transformations in both business and financial institutions. Today, AI has progressed afar its probing juncture and is being effectuated in real-world instances. Several businesses and financial institutions are implying AI bots to onboard clientele and accomplish automated instability analysis of borrowers. They are utilizing computer inventiveness, corresponding pattern, and cavernous learning to recognize procedure inefficiencies. Intelligence based anti-ethical money concealment results are assisting them to prevent deceit, amid additional use cases.

In the upcoming future, AI could be operated to bestow personalized monetarily counseling or guidance, assists commercial institutions to recognize contemporary revenue succession, and moreover to make contributive settlements. Furthermore, AI could be helpful to minimize the revenue by automating procedures and activities such as frequenters facilities and bank-workplace duties. Starting with chatbots to prognostic analysis, AI is speedily as well as swiftly transforming into a centerpiece in the industry. In accordance with forecasted reports, the global AI fintech markets is on an uproot extension from 2019 with 7.78 billion and is extrapolated to strike a shrieking USD 27.8 billion by 2027. However, this is fair-mindedly just the starting of this peripheral growth, as it actually stimuluses the potential of artificial intelligence it will continue to evolve, it will probably influence the financial and businesses. And those who clasp this turn of technology will surely be competently stationed to reap the trump card of this transformative mechanization.

Subsequently AI assures disentangle encounter and the termination of grappling with trivial endeavors. With AI, there is no hesitancy related to modification of several industries, with new technologies making an appearance and determining jobs and a consequential transference of valuable human resource towards analytical and empirical businesses. Over 97% of supreme business houses use AI simulations by 2027 for real-time analysis their business accomplishment. The construction of commercialism and facilitation in business and financial institutions will upgrade, but new applications will also make their impactful presence. The future of business and financial industries is already glancing brilliant with the growth of AI and automation. Such technologies will permit for additional systematic and precise transactions, emancipating personnels to emphasize more on esteemed and upscaled works. FIs encapsulating these mechanizations will surely be pleasantly positioned to fulfill it in future. By implanting all such technologies AI market will boom and expand its size to around $21 trillion from $97.6 billion in present scenario.

In business and finance management AI surely will be bestriding bright. AI optimizes the procedures across the emplane and convey monotonous assignments proficiently, pledging compound works with valuable perceptions. As an outcome, it amplifies experience, conserve time, and authorizes businesses to assemble consequential conclusions. The AI revolution in regard to business and finance management are proficient at lessening pertinent business possibilities by corroborating full lucidity and belief. The collaboration of AI with respect to finance and business intelligence will notice the analysis of enormous quantities of interpretative particulars in real-time. So, such mechanism will rapidly apprehend the needs and priorities according to the circumstances and will do what is necessitates. Also, such automations will refer hyper-personalized exhortation, such future of AI may impetuously decipher the instincts of an individual.

Both artificial intelligences along with other emerging technologies will be prevailing to consolidate with futuristic technological implications, finance, and economics authorizing companies to initialize data beyond the uninterrupted estimation and to analyze comprehensive economic and commercial tendencies for the profound perception of reliable growth. With the escalating supposition for business and financial sector have a secure establishment in technical and data-based analytics, there are already couple of introduced software's which has the selfsame province like fintech, thus implicating them using disruptive technologies for shareholders, collaborators, and colleagues in the upcoming economical domain. There should be an acceptance of certitude that intelligence's subsistence might subsequently change business and finance management.

11.11 CONCLUSION

As evidenced by the present scenario, the role of AI in financial and business managerial services is gigantic and impossible to disregard. According to an economic survey on management aspects, 78% of senior financial managers anticipate constructive outcomes from the utilization of AI in financial services. This further concludes that in 2022, 80% of companies have incorporated artificial intelligence into their managerial processes. The advent of certain technologies allowed businesses and financial institutions to rationalize and systematize their financial justifications. Around 72% of the ecommerce companies still implement AI tools to dispense the flawless and error free practice and professionalism. Moreover, AI can operate additional nexus scenarios, including the concluded automation of humdrum, hand-operated procedures. With the increase of automation, it also meant ameliorated precision across the business structures. Copious research reports that the worldwide market size of business and finance management by the termination of 2023 would be around $138.97 billion, with the identical progression extension. Furthermore, the forecasted market size with selfsame growth is expected to be over $1632.4 billion by 2030 along with a lodged CAGR of 43.2% from 2023 to 2030. Hus, the estimated yearly extension of AI betwixt 2023 to 2028 is 39.4%. AI unblocks access to actual time accounting particulars and monetarily intuitions, business figureheads can swiftly identify salient business staging barometers and make necessary executions as they emerged. Implementation of AI along with other emerging technologies in business finance management can substitute the techniques businesses are sprinted. Furthermore, intelligence plays a crucial role in associative finance as it can forecast and assess possibilities in a superior manner. AI market share with emergence of new technologies is expected to be around $560.78 billion by 2025, inclusive other models and igneous mechanizations, additionally some evaluations have concluded that AI software market size solitarily would be around $321.4 billion in 2025. For industries who are constantly forethought to secure their management, AI mechanisms aids them by loan financing and to minimalize financial endangers. Some estimations have concluded that the tools associated with AI could initiate $18.9 trillion of proceeds and earnings by 2030, thus magnifying the GDP (gross domestic product) of confined providences by a supplementation of 29%. AI can allay the financial misdemeanor through newfangled fraud perception and speck anomalous activity as industrial actuary. Also, 88% of customer facilitation interactivity would be responded by AI, supporting that 64% of business houses have reported that the customer facilitation would be their topmost prioritization for the usage of emending technological tools. Thus, this chapter amalgamates the productive relation between AI and other emanating technologies with respect to business and finance management. As, due to increasing growth of technologies in these sectors will definitely be proven as a virtuous implementation.

KEYWORDS

- **artificial intelligence**
- **business management**
- **commerce**
- **emanating technologies**
- **financial institutions**
- **monetarily**

REFERENCES

Abbasi, W. A., Wang, Z., Zhou, Y., & Hassan, S., (2019). Research on measurement of supply chain finance credit risk based on internet of things. *International Journal of Distributed Sensor Networks, 15*(9).

Ahmed, S., Muneer, M. A., Anis El, A., & Helmi, H., (2022). Artificial intelligence and machine learning in finance: A bibliometric review. *Research in International Business and Finance 61*, 101646.

Al-Sartawi, M., Abdalmuttaleb, M. A., Khaled, H., & Anjum, R., (2022). The role of artificial intelligence in sustainable finance. *Journal of Sustainable Finance & Investment,* 1–6.

Anderson, D. R., Sweeney, D. J., Williams, T. A., Camm, J. D., & Cochran, J. J., (2020). *Modern Business Statistics with Microsoft Excel*. Cengage Learning.

Aweke, D., Genale, A. S., Bedada, M. L., Pandey, A., Janga, V., & Sundaram, B. B., (2022). Big data statistics analysis of computer intelligence and machine learning technology. In: *2022 6th International Conference on Intelligent Computing and Control Systems (ICICCS)* (pp. 1220–1225). IEEE.

Bertoni, F., et al., (2022). Digitization in the market for entrepreneurial finance: Innovative business models and new financing channels. *Entrepreneurship Theory and Practice, 46*(5), 1120–1135.

Black, K., (2019). *Business Statistics: For Contemporary Decision Making*. John Wiley & Sons.

Boobier, T., (2020). *AI and the Future of Banking*. John Wiley & Sons.

Bredt, S., (2019). Artificial intelligence (AI) in the financial sector—Potential and public strategies. *Frontiers in Artificial Intelligence, 2*, 26.

Budzianowski, P., & Vulić, I., (2019). *Hello, it's GPT-2--How Can I Help You? Towards the Use of Pretrained Language Models for Task-Oriented Dialogue Systems*. arXiv preprint arXiv:1907.05774.

Burström, T., et al., (2021). AI-enabled business-model innovation and transformation in industrial ecosystems: A framework, model, and outline for further research. *Journal of Business Research, 127*, 85–95.

Cao, L., (2022). AI in finance: Challenges, techniques, and opportunities. *ACM Computing Surveys (CSUR)*, *55*(3), 1–38.

Demirkan, S., Demirkan, I., & McKee, A., (2020). Blockchain technology in the future of business cyber security and accounting. *Journal of Management Analytics*, *7*(2), 189–208.

Dietzmann, C., Heines, R., & Alt, R., (2020). The convergence of distributed ledger technology and artificial intelligence: An end-to-end reference lending process for financial services. In: *Proceedings: 28th European Conference on Information Systems (ECIS2020).* Association for Information Systems.

Easton, P. D., McAnally, M. L., Gregory, A. S., & Xiao-Jun, Z., (2018). *Financial Statement Analysis & Valuation*. Boston, MA: Cambridge Business Publishers.

Enholm, I. M., Emmanouil, P., Patrick, M., & John, K., (2021). Artificial intelligence and business value: A literature review. *Information Systems Frontiers*, 1–26.

Fisher, I. E., Garnsey, M. R., & Hughes, M. E., (2016). Natural language processing in accounting, auditing, and finance: A synthesis of the literature with a roadmap for future research. *Intelligent Systems in Accounting, Finance and Management*, *23*(3), 157–214.

Fraisse, H., & Laporte, M., (2022). Return on investment on artificial intelligence: The case of bank capital requirement. *Journal of Banking & Finance, 138*, 106401.

Gao, J., (2022). Research on financial management informatization mode of SME under cloud computing. *International Journal of Science and Research (IJSR), 11*, 793–796.
Giudici, P., (2018). Fintech risk management: A research challenge for artificial intelligence in finance. *Frontiers in Artificial Intelligence, 1*, 1.
Go, E. J., Junhwan, M., & Jinhwa, K., (2020). Analysis of the current and future of the artificial intelligence in financial industry with big data techniques. *Global Business & Finance Review (GBFR), 25*(1), 102–117.
Goncharenko, I. A., & Andrea, M., (2019). Artificial intelligence and automation in financial services: The case of Russian banking sector. *Law and Economics Yearly Review, 8*(1), 125–147.
Harmon, R. L., & Psaltis, A., (2021). The future of cloud computing in financial services: A machine learning and artificial intelligence perspective. In: *The Essentials of Machine Learning in Finance and Accounting* (pp. 123–138). Routledge.
Hasanaj, P., & Kuqi, B., (2019). Analysis of financial statements. *Humanities and Social Science Research, 2*(2), 17–27.
Huang, T., Yuxuan, Y., & Fred, S., (2022). Based on the intelligent statistical software stata15. 0 to study the impact of executive compensation incentives and managerial capabilities on business performance in artificial intelligence companies. *Signal and Information Processing, Networking and Computers: Proceedings of the 9th International Conference on Signal and Information Processing, Networking and Computers (ICSINC)*. Singapore: Springer Nature Singapore.
Jarrahi, M. H., (2018). Artificial intelligence and the future of work: Human-AI symbiosis in organizational decision making. *Business Horizons, 61*(4), 577–586.
Jędrzejka, D., (2019). *Robotic Process Automation and its Impact on Accounting* (Vol. 105, pp. 137–166). Zeszyty Teoretyczne Rachunkowości.
Joveda, N., Md Tarek, K., & Abhijit, P., (2019). Cyber laundering: A threat to banking industries in Bangladesh: In quest of effective legal framework and cyber security of financial information. *International Journal of Economics and Finance, 11*(10), 54–65.
Jung, D., Dorner, V., Glaser, F., & Morana, S., (2018). Robo-advisory: Digitalization and automation of financial advisory. *Business & Information Systems Engineering, 60*, 81–86.
Kaya, O., Schildbach, J., AG, D. B., & Schneider, S., (2019). Artificial intelligence in banking. *Artificial Intelligence.*
Kruse, L., Wunderlich, N., & Beck, R., (2019). Artificial Intelligence for the Financial Services Industry: What Challenges Organizations to Succeed Proceedings of *the 52th Hawaii International Conference on System Sciences (HICSS 2019),* Maui, Hawaii, USA.
Kunnathuvalappil, H. N. (2021). *Artificial Intelligence and Human Collaboration in Financial Planning.*
Kunwar, M., (2019). *Artificial Intelligence in Finance: Understanding how Automation and Machine Learning is Transforming the Financial Industry, 2019.*
Loureiro, S. M. C., Guerreiro, J., & Tussyadiah, I., (2021). Artificial intelligence in business: State of the art and future research agenda. *Journal of Business Research, 129*, 911–926.
Lu, H., Qing, W., & Jing, Y., (2020). *Fintech and the Future of Financial Service: A Literature Review and Research Agenda. 22*(3), 107–136.
Malali, A. B., & Gopalakrishnan, S., (2020). Application of artificial intelligence and its powered technologies in the Indian banking and financial industry: An overview. *IOSR Journal of Humanities and Social Science, 25*(4), 55–60.

Mbizvo, G. K., & Andrew, J. L., (2021). Receiver operating characteristic plot and area under the curve with binary classifiers: Pragmatic analysis of cognitive screening instruments. *Neurodegenerative Disease Management, 11*(5), 353–360.

McBride, R., Dastan, A., & Mehrabinia, P., (2022). How AI affects the future relationship between corporate governance and financial markets: A note on impact capitalism. *Managerial Finance*.

Mhlanga, D., (2020). Industry 4.0 in finance: The impact of artificial intelligence (ai) on digital financial inclusion. *International Journal of Financial Studies, 8*(3), 45.

Milana, C., & Ashta, A., (2021). Artificial intelligence techniques in finance and financial markets: A survey of the literature. *Strategic Change, 30*(3), 189–209.

Ng, C. W., (2020). The future of AI in finance. *The AI Book: The Artificial Intelligence Handbook for Investors, Entrepreneurs and FinTech Visionaries*, 6–8.

Olan, F., Shaofeng, L., Jana, S., Uchitha, J., & Emmanuel, O. A., (2022). The role of artificial intelligence networks in sustainable supply chain finance for food and drink industry. *International Journal of Production Research, 60*(14), 4418–4433.

Osterrieder, J., & GPT, C., (2023). *A Primer on Deep Reinforcement Learning for Finance.* Available at SSRN 4316650.

Palepu, K. G., et al., (2020). *Business Analysis and Valuation: Using Financial Statements.* Cengage AU.

Pallathadka, H., Ramirez-Asis, E. H., Loli-Poma, T. P., Kaliyaperumal, K., Ventayen, R. J. M., & Naved, M., (2021). Applications of artificial intelligence in business management, e-commerce, and finance. *Materials Today: Proceedings.*

Phillips, T., Saleh, A., Glazewski, K. D., Hmelo-Silver, C. E., Mott, B., & Lester, J. C., (2022). Exploring the use of GPT-3 as a tool for evaluating text-based collaborative discourse. *Companion Proceedings of the 12*th (p. 54).

Ranjan, S., Gupta, D. R., & Gupta, D. A., (2020). Artificial intelligence in financial acumen: Challenges and opportunities. *Cosmos Journal of Engineering & Technology, 10*(1), 1–5.

Ron, G., (2011). Why cloud computing matters to finance. *Strategic Finance, 92*(7), 43.

Sanz, J. L. C., & Yada, Z., (2021). Toward scalable artificial intelligence in finance. In: *2021 IEEE International Conference on Services Computing (SCC)*. IEEE.

Sanz, J. L., & Zhu, Y., (2021). Toward scalable artificial intelligence in finance. In: *2021 IEEE International Conference on Services Computing (SCC)* (pp. 460–469). IEEE.

Schueffel, P., (2016). Taming the beast: A scientific definition of fintech. *Journal of Innovation Management, 4*(4), 32–54.

Sebastianelli, R., (2018). Multiple student learning objectives in basic business statistics: Strategies, assessment, and recommendations. *Journal of Education for Business, 93*(7), 341–352.

Valgaeren, H., (2019). *Robotic Process Automation in Financial and Accounting Processes in the Banking Sector*. PhD diss., MSc Thesis, Ku Leuven Faculty of Economics and Business.

Vasista, K., (2021). Regulatory compliance and supervision of artificial intelligence, machine learning and also possible effects on financial institutions. Machine learning and also possible effects on financial institutions. *International Journal of Innovative Research in Computer and Communication Engineering*| e-ISSN, 2320-9801.

Vives, X., (2017). The impact of FinTech on banking. *European Economy, 2*, 97–105.

Wang, Y., (2022). Financial crisis prediction model of listed companies based on statistics and AI. *Scientific Programming, 2022.*

Wen, C., et al., (2021). Big data driven internet of things for credit evaluation and early warning in finance. *Future Generation Computer Systems, 124*, 295–307.

Xue, M., Xiu, G., Saravanan, V., & Montenegro-Marin, C. E., (2020). Cloud computing with AI for banking and e-commerce applications. *The Electronic Library*, *39*(4), 539–552.

Younis, H., Balan, S., & Malek, A., (2022). Applications of artificial intelligence and machine learning within supply chains: Systematic review and future research directions. *Journal of Modelling in Management, 17*(3), 916–940.

Yu, T. R., & Song, X., (2021). Big data and artificial intelligence in the banking industry. In: *Handbook of Financial Econometrics, Mathematics, Statistics, and Machine Learning* (pp. 4025–4041).

CHAPTER 12

The Collaboration Between Humans and Machines

RICHA VIJAY[1] and ARVIND KUMAR[2]

[1]*Assistant Professor, Faculty of Computer Applications, MRIIRS, Aravalli Hills, Faridabad, Haryana, India*

[2]*Associate Professor, Faculty of Computer Applications, MRIIRS, Aravalli Hills, Faridabad, Haryana, India*

ABSTRACT

Human-machine collaboration research encompasses a wide range of topics, including the design of interfaces and interactions that enable effective collaboration between humans and intelligent systems, the study of how humans and machines can complement each other's strengths, and the development of algorithms and systems that can adapt to the needs and preferences of individual users. This research's applications include manufacturing, transportation, healthcare, and education. Some key challenges in this field include understanding how to design systems that can effectively support human decision-making, ensuring that humans trust and accept the recommendations of machines, and ensuring the safety and security of human-machine interactions.

All facets of the economy are being changed by artificial intelligence, but there is no cause for concern that machines will completely replace humans. According to the research, businesses that automate their processes primarily to reduce workforce would only experience short-term productivity benefits. Collaboration between intelligent technology and people results in the greatest performance gains.

Advanced Digital Technologies in Financial and Business Management: Unleashing the Power of Artificial Intelligence, Machine Learning, Blockchain, and the Internet of Things. Jyoti Batra Arora, Nitish Pathak, and Neelam Sharma (Eds.)

AI agents must be trained, their outputs must be explained, and their responsible use must be ensured. AI bots can help people with data processing, routine customer service, physical labor, and information collecting, freeing them up to work on higher-level activities that call for leadership, creative thinking, judgment, and other human abilities.

12.1 INTRODUCTION

Together, people and robots will work on one another's working capacities, expand on one another's assets, and cover each other's limitations. Collaboration would reduce the chance of human blunders while additionally alleviating the staff. Machines would ensure that individuals could execute things they couldn't do independently. The Worth of Cooperation streamlining the association between people and artificial consciousness is profitable to organizations (Ajvazi, 2022).

Streamlining the association between people and artificial consciousness is profitable to organizations. They can do this by keeping these five guidelines: Upgrade work to integrate computer-based intelligence and foster related staff capacities. Reconsider business processes. Embrace trial and error. Representative contribution. Effectively immediate artificial intelligence methodology. Dependable information assortment. The greater amount of these standards organizations executed, the better their simulated intelligence projects fared regarding speed, cost reserve funds, incomes, or other functional measures, as indicated by a study of 1,075 organizations across 12 industries (Ajvazi, 2022).

12.2 TYPES OF HUMAN-MACHINE COLLABORATION

- **Augmented Cognition:** Where technology enhances human cognitive abilities.
- **Human-in-the-Loop Systems:** Where machines assist humans in decision-making.
- **Human-Robot Collaboration:** Where humans work alongside robots to complete tasks.
- **Cooperative Control:** Where humans and machines work together to control systems or processes.
- **Human-Agent Collaboration:** Where humans work with autonomous agents to accomplish tasks.

- **Collaborative Robotics:** Where multiple robots work together with humans to accomplish tasks.
- **Teleoperation:** Where a human remotely controls a machine or robot to complete tasks.
- **Human-Computer Interaction (HCI):** Where humans interact with computers through various input and output devices, such as a keyboard or touch screen.
- **Collaborative Artificial Intelligence (AI):** Where AI systems work with humans to make decisions and perform tasks.
- **Human-Machine Learning (HML):** Where machines learn from human feedback and input to improve performance.
- **Human-Machine Teaming (HMT):** Where humans and machines work together to accomplish tasks and achieve goals.
- **Human-Machine Hybrid Systems:** Where humans and machines are integrated to work seamlessly and efficiently.

Some of these types of human-machine collaboration may overlap or be used in combination with each other in different applications (Figure 12.1).

Future industrial settings will require various forms of collaboration, but all will require human and robot employees to share a workplace and make physical touch, according to Michalos et al. (2015). HRC entails more than only operating in the same location and at the same time. HRC in Industry 4.0 needs to be seen as a complex sociotechnical system in which agency is distributed among humans and nonhuman agents, such as machines, robots, sensors, algorithms, and similar devices, rather than being exclusively attributed to humans. We contend that using cobots in an Industry 4.0 setting generates new constellations of shared control and distributed agency, building on the work of Latour (Ajvazi, 2022; Suchman, 2009; Rammert, n.d.).

12.3 HUMAN-MACHINE INTERACTION DESIGN

Human-machine interaction design refers to the process of designing how people interact with technology. It involves understanding the needs, goals, and abilities of users, as well as the capabilities and limitations of the technology itself, in order to create interfaces that are easy to use, efficient,

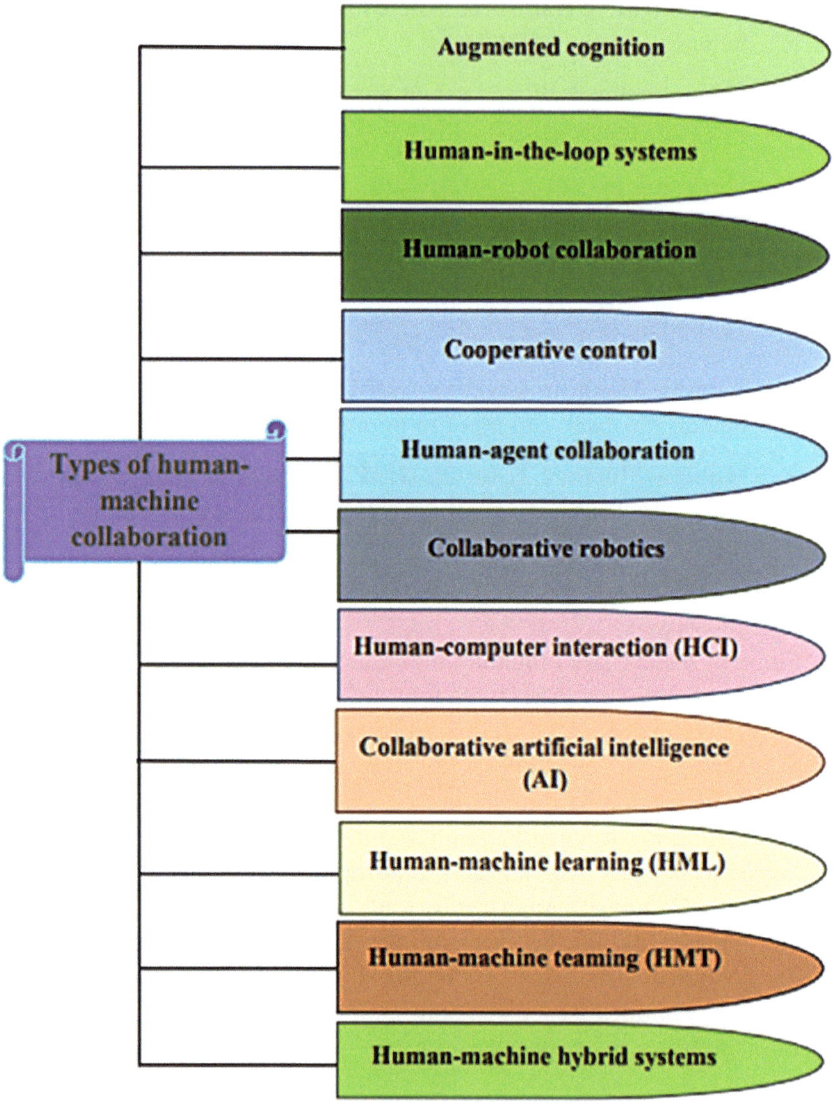

FIGURE 12.1 Types of human-machine collaboration.

and effective. This can include designing the layout and functionality of a website or app or creating user-friendly controls for a machine or piece of equipment. The goal of human-machine interaction design creates a seamless and intuitive experience for users to accomplish their tasks with minimal effort and frustration.

Human-machine interaction design is a multidisciplinary field that draws on principles from psychology, sociology, computer science, and design. It involves various activities such as user research, prototyping, usability testing, and evaluation.

One of the key principles of human-machine interaction design is that it should be user-centered, meaning that the design should be based on the needs, goals, and abilities of the people using the technology. This often involves conducting user research to understand the target users, their tasks and objectives, and the context in which they will use the technology.

Another important aspect of human-machine interaction design is creating interfaces that are easy to use and understand. This often involves simplifying complex information and tasks, providing clear feedback, and using consistent design patterns and conventions.

In addition to designing the interface, human-machine interaction design also involves evaluating the design to ensure that it is effective and efficient. This can be done through usability testing, where users are observed and asked to complete tasks while using the technology, or through other evaluation forms such as user surveys or metrics analysis (Figure 12.2).

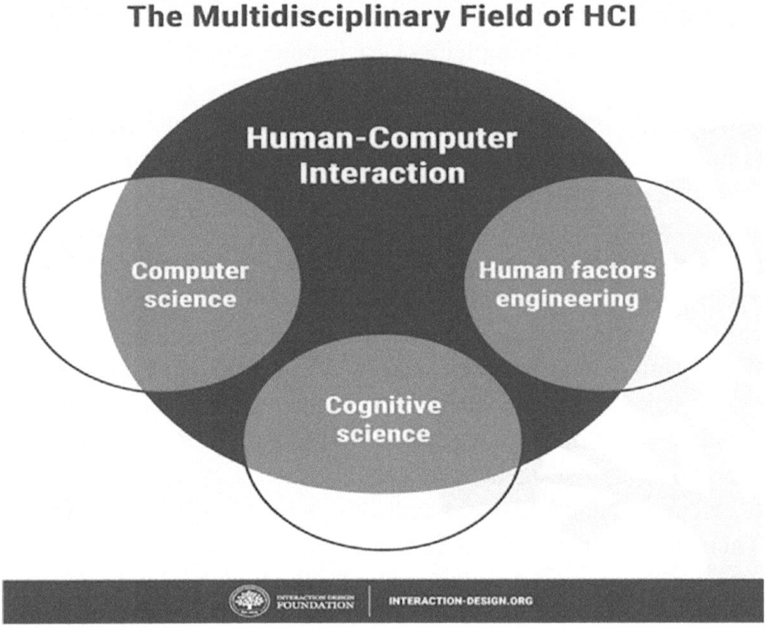

FIGURE 12.2 Human-computer interactions.

Source: Interaction Design Foundation. https://www.interaction-design.org/literature/topics/human-computer-interaction.

Overall, human-machine interaction design is an ongoing process that requires iterative design, testing, and refinement to create effective, efficient, and satisfying interfaces.

12.4 COLLABORATIVE DECISION-MAKING

Collaborative decision-making in Human-computer interaction refers to the process by which humans and computers work together to make decisions. This can involve using computational tools and algorithms to assist in the decision-making process, as well as integrating human expertise and judgment to ensure that the decisions made are accurate and appropriate. Collaborative decision-making can be used in various applications, such as in healthcare, finance, and transportation, to make more accurate and efficient decisions than those made by humans or computers alone.

In collaborative decision-making, human and computer agents have strengths and weaknesses. For example, computers can process large amounts of data quickly and accurately, while humans can make complex judgments and decisions based on experience and intuition. By working together, the two can complement each other's abilities and make better decisions.

There are different ways in which human and computer agents can collaborate in decision-making. One common approach is to use the computer to analyze data and present the results to the human, who then makes the final decision. Another approach is using the computer to make a recommendation or proposal, which the human can accept or reject. Some systems use a more interactive approach, where the human and computer agents work together in real-time to explore different options and reach a decision.

Collaborative decision-making can be implemented using various technologies, such as natural language processing, machine learning, and artificial intelligence. One important aspect of designing such systems is ensuring that human and computer agents can communicate effectively and that human users can understand and trust the decisions made by the computer.

There are many potential benefits of collaborative decision-making, such as improved decision quality, increased efficiency, and reduced errors. However, it is important to consider such systems' ethical and social implications, such as the potential for bias and the impact on jobs and employment.

12.5 HUMAN-MACHINE TEAMING

Human-machine teaming (HMT) is a concept in which human and machine intelligence are combined to achieve a common goal. It involves the collaboration and coordination of humans and machines to perform tasks that would be difficult or impossible to accomplish. The goal of HMT is to leverage the strengths of both human and machine intelligence to improve performance, efficiency, and decision-making.

Examples of HMT include:

- A human operator working alongside a robot to complete a manufacturing task.
- A doctor and a diagnostic AI work together to make a diagnosis.
- A human pilot is flying an aircraft with the assistance of an autopilot system.

HMT is becoming increasingly important as technology advances, and machines become more integrated into our daily lives. It is designed to improve the system's overall productivity, efficiency, and safety.

Successful interactions between human and machine agents and between these agents and their surroundings are necessary for HMT to work (Stowers, 2017). However, it is challenging to design artificial intelligence (AI) agents with the sophisticated competencies (i.e., knowledge, skills, and abilities) required to enable these intricate interactions (Suchman, 2009). As a result, not all HMT leads to improved performance at the individual, team, or organization level. Teams' researchers and computer scientists have identified competencies crucial for successful teaming in their respective (Kumar, 2020); Tellex, 2020; Sukthankar, 2023), but efforts to identify promising new technologies in this area have yet to be made.

12.6 ETHICAL CONSIDERATIONS IN HUMAN-MACHINE COLLABORATION

There are several ethical considerations in human-machine collaboration, including (Figure 12.3):

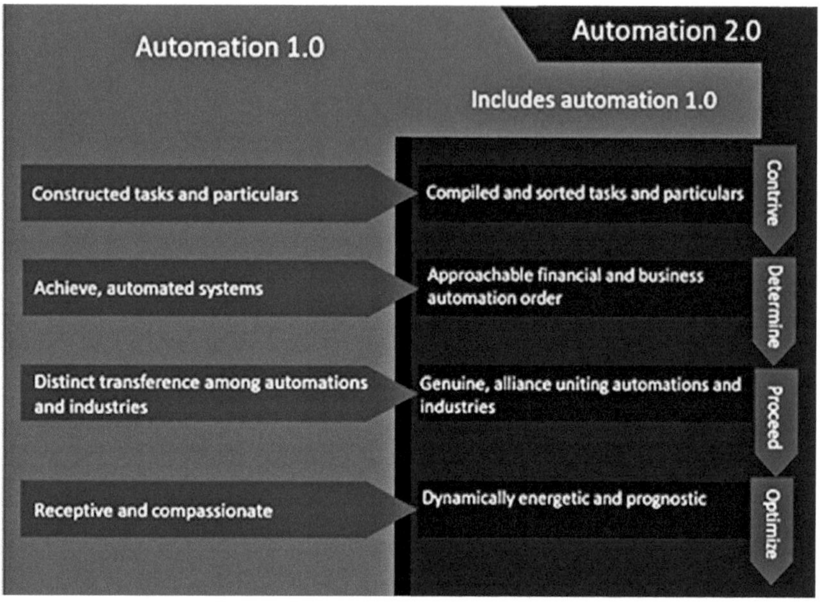

FIGURE 12.3 Ethical considerations in human-machine collaboration.

1. **Transparency:** The machine's decision-making process should be transparent and explainable to human users so that they can understand and trust the machine's actions.
2. **Bias:** Machine learning algorithms can inadvertently perpetuate societal biases if trained on partial data. It is important to ensure that the algorithms are free from bias and that any issues are addressed.
3. **Autonomy:** As machines become more autonomous, there is a risk that they could make decisions that are harmful to humans. It is important to establish clear guidelines and protocols for human intervention.
4. **Privacy:** Human-machine collaboration often involves the collection and processing of personal data. It is important to ensure that personal data is collected, stored, and used in a way that complies with privacy laws and regulations and respects individuals' rights to their data.
5. **Security:** As machines become more integrated into critical systems, there is an increased risk of cyber-attacks. It is important to ensure that machines are secure and that security measures are in place to protect against potential threats.

12.7 APPLICATIONS OF HUMAN-MACHINE COLLABORATION IN VARIOUS INDUSTRIES

Human-machine collaboration, also known as human-robot collaboration (HRC), has a wide range of applications in various industries, including (Figure 12.4):

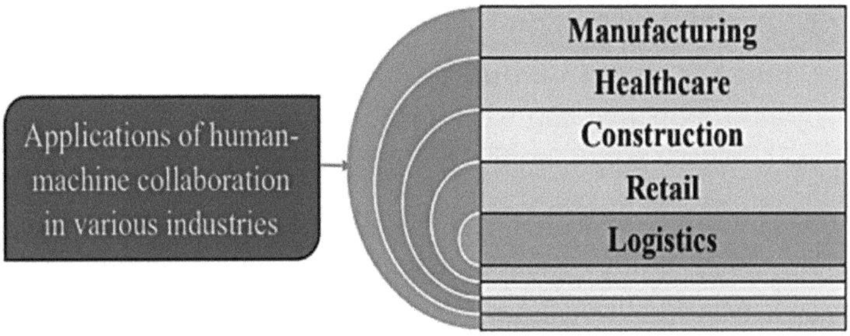

FIGURE 12.4 Applications of human-machine collaboration.

1. **Manufacturing:** HRC is widely used in manufacturing to enhance productivity and efficiency, reduce labor costs, and improve the safety of workers. For example, human workers and robots can work together on assembly lines to perform tasks that would be dangerous or difficult for humans to do alone.
2. **Healthcare:** HRC assists medical professionals with surgical procedures and patient care. For example, robots can be used to assist with surgeries or to help patients with mobility issues.
3. **Construction:** HRC is used to improve job site efficiency and safety. For example, robots can work digging trenches, laying pipes, and welding.
4. **Retail:** HRC is used to enhance the customer experience and improve productivity. For example, robots can assist with stocking shelves, customer service, and inventory management.
5. **Logistics:** HRC is used to improve efficiency in warehouses and distribution centers. For example, robots can pick up and pack orders, load and unload trucks, and sort packages.

Human-Machine collaboration is a way to enhance productivity, improve efficiency, and increase the safety of different industrial processes.

12.8 FUTURE DEVELOPMENTS AND RESEARCH IN HUMAN-MACHINE COLLABORATION

There are several areas of research and development in human-machine collaboration, including (Figure 12.5):

1. **Intelligent Agents and Virtual Assistants:** These technologies are being developed to assist humans in various tasks, such as scheduling, data entry, and customer service.
2. **Human-Robot Collaboration:** This research focuses on developing robots that can work safely and efficiently alongside humans in industrial and manufacturing settings.
3. **Augmented and Virtual Reality:** These technologies enhance human-machine collaboration in fields such as medicine, education, and manufacturing.
4. **Machine Learning and AI-Driven Decision-Making:** With the development of AI, there is much research on improving the machine's decision-making process and making it more aligned with human decision-making.
5. **Explainable AI:** As AI systems become more complex, research is focused on developing methods for making the inner workings of AI systems more transparent and interpretable to humans.
6. **Human-AI Teams:** There is research on how to improve the collaboration and coordination between humans and AI in a team setting, to make the team more effective and efficient.
7. **Human-AI Co-Creation:** With the development of AI, research is focusing on how to use AI as a tool to enhance human creativity and to co-create new things with humans.
8. **Multi-Modal Interaction:** Developing methods for natural, intuitive interaction between humans and machines, such as speech, gesture, and facial expression recognition.
9. **Personalization and Customization:** Research is being conducted on how to personalize and customize the interaction between humans and machines, to improve the user experience and make the collaboration more effective.

10. **Human-AI Trust and Accountability:** As AI systems become more prevalent in society, research is being conducted on how to establish trust and accountability in human-AI collaborations. This includes issues such as bias, transparency, and ethical decision-making.
11. **Human-AI Cognitive Augmentation:** Research is being conducted on how to use AI to enhance human cognitive abilities, such as memory, attention, and problem-solving.
12. **Human-AI Emotional Intelligence:** Developing AI systems that can understand, interpret, and respond to human emotions to improve collaboration and communication.
13. **Human-AI Creativity:** With AI's development, research focuses on how to use AI to enhance human creativity and co-create new things with human-AI collaboration.
14. **Human-AI Ethics:** As AI systems become more prevalent in society, research is being conducted on the ethical implications of human-AI collaboration, including issues such as bias, transparency, and autonomy.

12.9 CHALLENGES AND LIMITATIONS OF HUMAN-MACHINE COLLABORATION

Challenges of human-machine collaboration include:

1. **Mismatch in Communication Styles:** Machines may not understand natural language as well as humans, leading to confusion and miscommunication.
2. **Lack of Trust:** Humans may hesitate to rely on machines to make decisions, particularly in critical situations.
3. **Task Allocation:** Determining which tasks are best suited for human or machine execution can be difficult.
4. **Safety Concerns:** There may be concerns about the safety of humans working alongside machines, particularly in industries such as manufacturing or construction.
5. **Privacy Concerns:** The collection and sharing of data between humans and machines raises questions about privacy and data security.

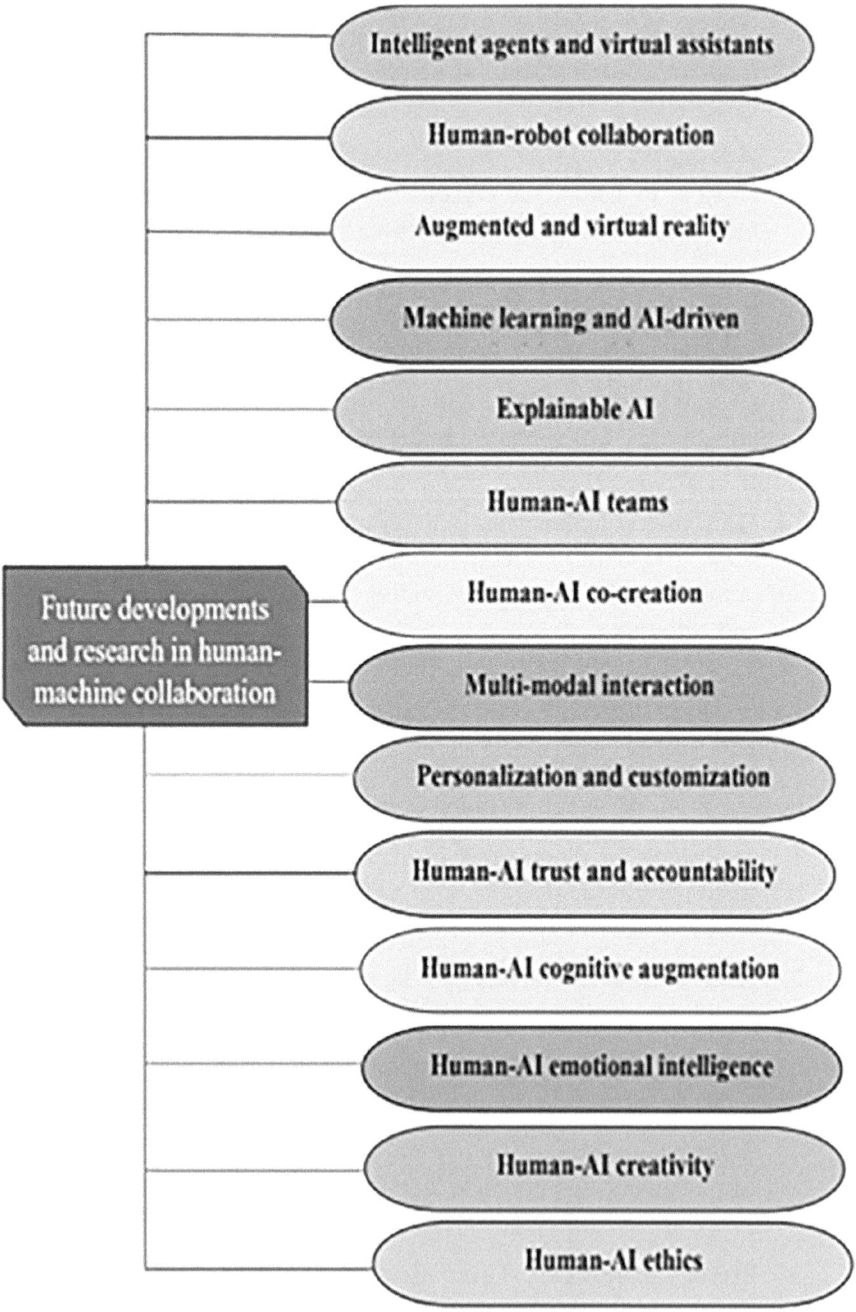

FIGURE 12.5 Future development and research.

6. **Lack of Transparency:** It can be difficult for humans to understand how machines make decisions, leading to mistrust (Figure 12.6).

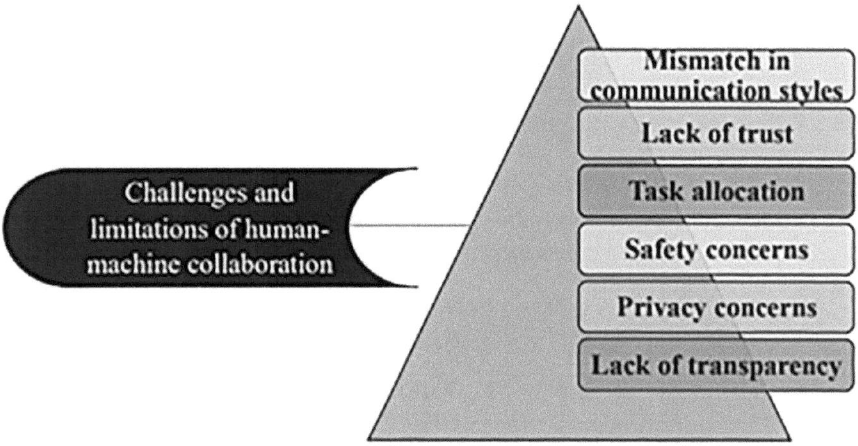

FIGURE 12.6 Challenges and limitations of human-machine collaboration.

Limitations of human-machine collaboration include (Figure 12.7):

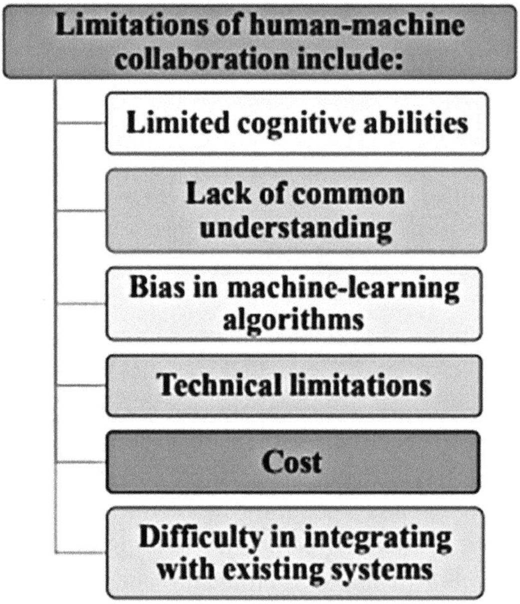

FIGURE 12.7 Limitation of human-machine collaboration.

1. **Limited Cognitive Abilities:** Machines may not be able to replicate the flexibility and creativity of human thought.
2. **Lack of Common Understanding:** Humans and machines may have different understandings of a situation, leading to errors or inefficiencies.
3. **Bias in Machine-Learning Algorithms:** If the data used to train a machine-learning algorithm is biased, the algorithm will also be biased.
4. **Technical Limitations:** The technology used for human-machine collaboration may have limitations regarding processing power, storage capacity, and connectivity.
5. **Cost:** Implementing human-machine collaboration systems can be costly, particularly for small and medium-sized businesses.
6. **Difficulty in Integrating with Existing Systems:** Human-machine collaboration systems may be difficult to integrate with existing systems and processes, leading to inefficiencies.

12.10 CONCLUSION AND FUTURE OUTLOOK

The development of artificial intelligence is at a crucial point. Early adopters are investing in cutting-edge, autonomous sensing systems that can communicate, decipher, and learn independently. Businesses are developing optimum company plans based on alternate human-machine communication solutions. It will improve human capacities and open up previously unimaginable business opportunities. Some experts predict that organizations' revenues will increase by an astounding 38% on average if they continue to invest in human and artificial intelligence collaboration. Although it is currently unknown whether or not humans can handle machine intelligence, the future will certainly provide business executives with incredible opportunities and change the foundations of our working environment.

Human-machine collaboration concludes that it can greatly improve efficiency, accuracy, and productivity in various industries and tasks. However, it raises ethical and societal concerns, such as job displacement and privacy.

The future outlook for human-machine collaboration is positive, with technology advancing and becoming more integrated into everyday life. The increasing use of automation and artificial intelligence (AI) in various industries is expected to improve efficiency and productivity. However, it is important to address the ethical and societal concerns that come with the increased use of technology. Additionally, there is a need for more research and development on how to effectively integrate human and machine capabilities to achieve the best results.

In the future, we expect to see more sophisticated forms of human-machine collaboration, such as machine learning systems that can adapt to and learn from human input. This will allow for more personalized and efficient collaboration, as the machine will better understand the human user and their needs.

Another important aspect of human-machine collaboration is the user interface. As technology becomes more advanced, the user interface will need to be designed to be intuitive, user-friendly, and accessible for all users. This will become increasingly important as technology becomes more integrated into everyday life.

One of the key challenges for human-machine collaboration is ensuring that the technology is trustworthy and reliable. With the increasing use of automation and AI, there is a need for robust and transparent algorithms that can be trusted to make important decisions. Additionally, there is a need for regulations and standards to ensure technology's safe and ethical use.

Overall, human-machine collaboration has the potential to greatly improve efficiency and productivity in various industries. However, it is important to address the ethical and societal concerns that come with the increased use of technology. The future of human-machine collaboration will be shaped by the ability to effectively integrate human and machine capabilities and by ensuring that the technology is trustworthy, reliable, and accessible to all users.

KEYWORDS

- **artificial intelligence**
- **cobot**
- **collaborations**
- **healthcare**
- **human-machine collaboration**
- **interaction**
- **machines**
- **trustworthy**

REFERENCES

Ajvazi, I., (2022). *Reading Bruno Latour's Reassembling the Social: An Introduction to Actor-Network-Theory.* https://doi.org/10.31219/osf.io/jemhx

Benanav, A., (2020). *Automation and the Future of Work.* Verso.

Carroll, J. M., (n.d.). *What is Human-Computer Interaction (HCI)?* The Interaction Design Foundation. Retrieved from: https://www.interaction-design.org/literature/topics/human-computer-interaction (accessed on 03 October 2023).

Kumar, A., (2020). Disruptive technologies and impact on the industry: An exploration. *Journal of Business Management and Information Systems*, *7*(1), 1–10. https://doi.org/10.48001/jbmis-2020-v07-i01-001.

Michalos, G., Makris, S., Tsarouchi, P., Guasch, T., Kontovrakis, D., & Chryssolouris, G., (2015). Design considerations for safe human-robot collaborative workplaces. *Procedia CIRP.* Retrieved from: https://www.sciencedirect.com/science/article/pii/S2212827115008550 (accessed on 03 October 2023).

Rammert, W., (n.d.). *Distributed Agency and Advanced Technology: Or How to Analyze.* Retrieved from: https://www.researchgate.net/publication/298214159_Distributed_agency_and_advanced_technology_Or_how_to_analyze_constellations_of_collective_inter-agency (accessed on 03 October 2023).

Stowers, K., Oglesby, J., Sonesh, S., Leyva, K., Iwig, C., & Salas, E., (2017). A framework to guide the assessment of human–machine systems. *Human Factors: The Journal of the Human Factors and Ergonomics Society*, *59*(2), 172–188. https://doi.org/10.1177/0018720817695077.

Suchman, L., (2009). *Human-Machine Reconfigurations: Plans and Situated Actions.* Cambridge Univ. Press.

Sukthankar, G., Shumaker, R., & Lewis, M., (n.d.). *(PDF) Intelligent Agents as Teammates.* ResearchGate. Retrieved from: https://www.researchgate.net/publication/265227488_Intelligent_Agents_as_Teammates (accessed on 03 October 2023).

Tellex, S., Gopalan, N., Kress-Gazit, H., & Matuszek, C. (n.d.). Robots that use language. *Annual Review of Control, Robotics, and Autonomous Systems Volume 3*, 2020 https://www.annualreviews.org/doi/full/10.1146/annurev-control-101119-071628 (accessed on 03 October 2023).

CHAPTER 13

Application of Data Science and Artificial Intelligence in Retail Sector

KIRAN MENGHANI[1] and NITISH PATHAK[2]

[1]*Assistant Professor, School of Business, Woxsen University, Hyderabad, India*

[2]*Bhagwan Parshuram Institute of Technology (BPIT), GGSIPU, New Delhi, India*

ABSTRACT

Data science applications in the retail sector have increased as a result of the advantages being fully utilized by internet behemoths like Netflix and Amazon. Deep analytics are used by these companies, and their supply chains are improved. Marketing strategies are also tailored. Customers enjoy their experiences more as a result, and businesses profit more. Behavioral analytics and consumer intelligence are also used by AI in retail to enhance a number of customer service touchpoints and gain insightful knowledge about various market demographics. The chapter is based on the configuration of data science applications and implications of AI on the retail sector.

In this chapter, the proposed method is based on empirical data drawn from various research papers and journals, as well as domain sites and online shopping apps of retail giants running business online, brick and mortar, or even omnichannel way. It presents the importance of Data science and AI technology used in the retail sector with complete technology solutions given and illustrations attached herewith. The secondary data is collected keeping in view the technology introduced and on cards in relation to AI and data science application in the retail sector post year 2020.

Results and findings in this chapter show that data science applications in the retail industry like CRM, behavior analytics, Fraud detection,

Advanced Digital Technologies in Financial and Business Management: Unleashing the Power of Artificial Intelligence, Machine Learning, Blockchain, and the Internet of Things. Jyoti Batra Arora, Nitish Pathak, and Neelam Sharma (Eds.)

merchandise management, etc., are being explained. AI applications like AI-based self-checkout technology, Chatbots, point of sale automation, AR, computer vision, etc., are elucidated in the chapter.

New technologies are being adopted by retailers. Consumer behavior, society, and retail are all constantly evolving. The retail industry has done a good job of adapting to the times. Retailers are making changes to their business plans, store designs, methods of interacting with customers, and operational procedures. For marketing, retail operations, and commercial transactions, modern merchants use new technologies. Social networking is a tool that modern businesses utilize to connect with their customers. Artificial intelligence (AI) is transforming the retail sector. Retailers can utilize artificial intelligence (AI) to interact with customers and operate more efficiently. Techniques include using computer vision to tailor promotions in real time and machine learning for inventory management. Digital transformation in retail is made feasible by data science. It entails transforming data into insights that inform choices and boost corporate performance. AI in retail, more specifically machine learning and deep learning, is responsible for a major portion of these discoveries. Amazing customer experiences, opportunities to enhance revenue, rapid innovation, and savvy operations are the results for retailers, all of which aid them in achieving operational and financial efficiency. High consumer expectations and a new covenant of data-driven retail experiences define the current retail sector. To develop a meaningful and relevant personalized shopping experience at scale, however, is not an easy task for retailers. When digital and physical purchase channels mix, the retailers who can grow their retail channels will stand out as the market leaders.

13.1 INTRODUCTION

The retail sector includes all companies that provide goods and services to customers. There are many different sorts of retail sales and stores, including grocery, convenience, discount, independent, department, DIY, electrical, and specialized stores, all around the world. The English word "retail" comes from the French verb "retailer," which means "to cut a piece" or "to break bulk." Products and services are covered throughout the whole sales cycle. The world's second-largest industry, retail, is extremely competitive. What makes it popular is its ability to give clients more freedom of choice, accessibility to a wide range of items, and access to numerous services. The typical retail store size varies significantly between countries, in part depending on how developed an economy a country possess.

"Retail is a pretty simple business, but what adds complexity is the size and scale. We couldn't do it without technology." ***—Bob Nardelli (American Businessman)***

Cities of today are congested, their infrastructure has changed, there are more ways to get around, and information is shared at a breakneck pace. New technologies are being adopted by retailers. The consumer, the society, and the stores are all evolving. The retail industry has been able to adapt to the times. Retailers are altering their business models, store designs, customer communication channels, and methods for managing business transactions. For marketing, retail operations, and commercial transactions, modern merchants are implementing new technology. Automation of store operations and lower operating expenses are both possible with artificial intelligence. Retailers and suppliers can profit from automation in their retail intelligence tools and processes, however this largely applies to retail areas that directly affect customers' shopping experiences. The job of the store manager can be made easier by artificial intelligence in retail by automating back-office duties and enhancing quality assurance using robotics. Retailers benefit from automation in terms of retail intelligence since it frees up staff to complete more work. Automation can handle efficiency, free up time for creative thought on the part of retail staff and deliver a fantastic online and in-store experience.

13.2 RELEVANCE AND JUSTIFICATION OF TECHNOLOGY IN RETAIL SECTOR

Technology is like a catalyst. Any action or process where it is correctly applied becomes more efficient. Technology has long played a significant role in business. Different locations have experienced different levels of development. Telephone and television were once regarded as the technological boundaries. Long distance calling is still a technological marvel in remote Indian villages. The main results of technical efficiency are the smoothness of business interactions.

The local grocer used to address his family members and clients by their first names back in the day. The interactions were regular and deeply intimate. Thus, the retailer acted as a close family friend. In addition, there weren't many alternatives offered for each product. Selection therefore wasn't an issue. Most significantly, because there were so few brands and items available, customers were never motivated to manually look for a superior option or a better deal.

The situation is different today since there are many products available to meet specific needs, and there are several brands in each category. To top it off, both the number of customers and the number of retailers has multiplied. Sales promotion plans and purchasing schemes have so taken the role of the interpersonal connections and interactions that once drove store loyalty. In this context, both business procedures and retail management have grown more difficult and complex. It is crucial to implement a mechanism because of the complexity and lack of time involved.

Any such technique ought to be accurate as well as timesaving. Technology plays a critical role in this regard.

Different retailing divisions can benefit from technology, or rather are already benefiting from it. It will be beneficial if we examine each department individually before looking at how technology is used.

13.2.1 MERCHANDISING

1. **Sourcing:** This category can be used to group together a variety of tasks. We start with the product sourcing process. Determining the number of categories to be maintained as well as the depth to be maintained in each category is part of the sourcing process. It also covers planning orders, vendor shortlisting, and selection.
2. **Consumer Behavior:** A shop needs to learn about the many market-trending categories. In this setting, he must stay current on trends. Retailers now gather their own shop purchase information to research consumer patterns. He is similarly gathering information online from vendors who can be shortlisted. Finding acceptable product suppliers can be done using a variety of vendor databases. Through the internet, it is possible to check for product availability and place orders.
3. **Stocking/Warehousing:** In this case, technology is used to keep track of received stock information. Regular adjustments are made in accordance with store use. The reorder level is decided by a retailer depending on usage and delivery lead time. Therefore, the procurement department receives notice as soon as the stock reaches that level. The level of technological advancement in this area has reached the point where, if the retailer has a long-standing relationship with the vendor, an automatic order can also be issued to him once the stock level reaches the reordering level. The ERP program

makes this possible. Retailers can easily integrate and manage all key activities with the help of ERP, which is a collection of adaptable programs. This includes managing several locations for stores, often shifting inventory, price adjustments, product discount offers, and much more. Manually performing these tasks could be time-consuming and difficult, but ERP software offers the quick, easy, and dependable management solutions needed to run organizations more successfully. Despite being more recent than more established sales techniques, point of sale has grown in importance within the retail sector. A system that monitors the transactions taking place in any retail establishment is the point-of-sale system. The POS machine has the important advantage of automatically entering transaction details into the system, removing the need for additional work and the possibility of human error. Real-time data is largely due to the integration of ERP systems with POS devices (both hardware and software). Simply put, ERP expands on the benefits of POS systems by ensuring that all transactional data is instantaneously reflected in retail locations and the main ERP tool.

4. **Customer Relationship Management and Marketing:** Every business wants to advertise itself. To assure increased foot traffic into the store, they have been using all cutting-edge strategies. The goal of every retailer is to have a significant number of devoted customers. Such customers tend to influence their friends' shopping decisions in favor of the particular store in addition to remaining loyal to it. To store information about clients and their purchases, all of the large retail establishments today employ the available software. This is then categorized to identify the most valuable clients, clients who visit regularly, and the most popular categories, colors, and variants. In the past, this was accomplished using bin cards or store purchase cards.

Retailers are increasingly providing loyalty cards, which have been popular in the airline industry for quite some time. Scores are accrued in accordance with purchases made, which eventually results in appealing prizes. Here, a specific account is activated with merely a card swipe. In this scenario, there is a single data center where all the data is kept. The retail outlet has access to the central database's classified information at any time. The term "CRM technologies" refers to the group of technologies that fall under this general heading. Using CRM software, we can pinpoint niche markets that were previously statistically determined through cluster analysis.

Data mining is the most recent method being employed in this because of advances in technology. The accuracy of processed data is the biggest advantage of technology from the perspective of marketing. When a retailer has precise knowledge of customer preferences and clusters of similar interests, he can arrange his marketing promotion approach appropriately. Promotional plans may also be created using the information now accessible.

13.3 HOW AI AND DATA SCIENCE TECHNOLOGY IS BENEFICIAL IN RETAIL SECTOR?

1. **Increased Customer Satisfaction:** Retailers can provide each client a customized purchasing experience based on their interests and behavior when they employ AI-powered solutions like Autonomous shopping carts, self-checkouts to enhance the customer experience. The amount of complaints or returns can be decreased, and customer satisfaction can be raised with the aid of this form of customization. Retailers can focus relevant promotions at the proper time by evaluating footfall data.
2. **Accurate Analysis of Footfall:** AI is able to combine information from several sources, including CCTV cameras, door counters, sensors, and mobile phone apps, to build a more accurate picture of how customers move through a mall or business. By identifying trouble areas where there are either too many or too few individuals walking through, businesses will be able to enhance their footfall analyzes.
3. **Enhanced Operational Effectiveness:** Predictive analytics systems that can forecast future occurrences based on historical data can help you increase productivity and improve efficiency by minimizing manual activities in your retail operations. By enabling you to make better personnel level, stock availability, and inventory allocation decisions right away rather than having to wait for reports from suppliers or vendors or waste time manually gathering data, this will help you save time.
4. **Analytics for Automated People Counting Using Machine Learning:** Retailers study foot traffic and understand how customers navigate their stores using people counting devices. Understanding how customers use their establishments allows companies to modify

their layout in order to enhance sales and boost customer happiness. In order to identify persons in photos captured by cameras positioned in store doors or other locations with heavy pedestrian traffic, this system uses computer vision algorithms. In contrast to analytics software that leverages aggregated historical data from other merchants who have already embraced this technology, this sort of analytics enables firms to alter workforce levels in accordance with actual demands rather than merely projections from surveys.

5. **Increased Security:** Data is a major component of our contemporary economy. This is especially accurate for the retail sector, where understanding consumer behavior and sales patterns is invaluable. The issue is that data leaks could cost businesses a lot of money. However, the introduction of AI-powered systems has enabled businesses to monitor data in real-time, identify anomalies, and quickly notify authorities of potential dangers. The same precautions can protect the cash, clientele, and human resources of your company. Stores can also stop theft by using computer vision to monitor the area. This technology alerts workers, security, or the police if any suspicious conduct is detected.
6. **Better Choice of Site:** Retailers can employ AI algorithms to analyze mobile phone data to identify which areas of their businesses are the most popular with customers and which ones aren't receiving enough attention from them. They can use this information to determine whether they should stock up on certain items or place them in these areas in order to draw more clients who might not otherwise stop by.
7. **Improved Competitive Advantage:** One of the most important benefits of employing AI to monitor retail foot traffic is its ability to give your organization a competitive edge over other businesses in your market. This is so that you may learn things about the behavior, preferences, and purchasing habits of your clients that are hard to learn through routine data analysis.
8. **Increased Consumer Awareness of Brands:** The use of artificial intelligence in retail footfall analytics has the additional benefit of raising brand recognition among customers who are more inclined to return to your store after experiencing its distinctive products. Over time, when customers develop a sense of loyalty and improve their

profitability, this can result in higher sales. Example AI marketing can help you reach out to clients with tailored messaging at key points in the customer lifecycle. Additionally, it can help digital marketers locate at-risk customers so they can send them communications intended to reacquaint them with the business.

13.4 BIG DATA

When computers first entered the workplace in the 1960s, data were unstructuredly stored, and it was labor-intensive to extract any value from them (O'Regan, 2008). Relational databases were subsequently created in order to offer data structure, enable organizations to better manage them, and derive value from them. As the amount of structured data grew faster than the capacity of computers, data warehouses and data marts were created to split the data into subsets and acquire better insights (Marwala & Hurwitz, 2017).

The amount of unstructured data, however, has started to rise quickly as the Internet has developed because it is no longer solely limited to data tables. In addition to web content, sensor, and device-generated data, like that from cameras or GPS transceivers, has also become more accessible (Davenport).

In addition to web content, it is also become simpler to access data produced by devices and sensors, such as data from cameras or GPS transceivers. There has been a considerable amount of data collected and kept, but research on how to analyze it and make inferences from it is still in progress (McAfee & Brynjolfsson, 2012; Balfour, 2013). Despite the fact that 23% of the data are considered to be valuable beyond their original purpose, just 1% of the data are supposedly assessed (Chen et al. 2012). Due to the development of computer technologies like distributed computing and cloud computing, these data may be promptly analyzed (Jacob, 2009). As the cost of storage, processing, and gathering decreased, more data were being included in analyzes (Purcell, 2013).

13.4.1 APPLICATIONS OF BIG DATA IN RETAILING

With knowledge of end-user demand, retailers are now operating more actively in the supply chain than they previously did when distributing items (Fernie & Sparks, 2014). The four key activities that comprise the retail supply chain are product assortment, product breakdown into smaller packaging, client-proximity inventory storage, and value-added services like gift-wrapping and warranties (Levy & Weitz, 2013). Agrawal and Smith mapped the supply chains of two major US retailers of home furnishings and offered a wide range of planning recommendations, including product design (private label products) and assortment planning, sourcing, and vendor selection, logistics planning, distribution planning, and inventory management, as well as clearance and markdown optimization and cross-channel optimization.

Choosing what to carry, how to sell it to clients (promotion, including price), and how to properly carry out these tasks (supporting functions, like logistic planning) are the three core activities of retailing. OOS issues and insufficient shelf availability lead to customer dissatisfaction and a subsequent loss of market share (OSA) (Sparks, Fernie, & McKinnon, 2010). Big data analysis is expected to be useful for challenging retail operations activities like assortment, pricing, and store design. When it comes to assortment and price, there are many minute decisions to be made, which can be influenced by a number of factors such customer choices, store vicinity, and demand elasticity. Without a solid quantitative analysis, making these judgments can be time- and resource-consuming.

13.4.2 DATA SCIENCE AND RETAILING

In a commercial setting, data is the starting point from which knowledge is forged. Data is the catalyst factor behind every business these days. The potential advantages of the data are being tapped into by numerous significant organizations from various industries. Thanks to the solutions offered by data scientists, several economic sectors are undergoing a radical transition. Information has increased greatly in this way for businesspeople looking to make wise decisions. In-depth analysis of enormous volumes of data can also be used to sway or even manipulate customer decisions. For this purpose, a variety of information and communication techniques are used.

The retail sector is expanding rapidly. Retailers can use data analysis to build a personalized psychological profile of a customer and pinpoint their pain points:

1. **Personalized Marketing:** Retailers may gain from putting a marketing strategy into action because it is the best way to draw customers. It functions by gathering data regarding customer financial transactions. This technique may be able to predict preferences

and decisions for the future on an enormous scale. Insider knowledge of consumer preferences and product previews is more advantageous for marketing scenarios.

Retailers use this approach to offer customers personalized suggestions based on their interests and past behavior. Additionally, it enables retailers to create highly targeted marketing tactics that increase ROI. If retailers have data to use and can draw applicable conclusions from it, they can accomplish all of this.

This is one situation where data science can be helpful. Future consumer behavior predictions could be made by amalgamating information from various sources.

2. **Augmented Reality:** It can help customers experience a product in real time. The use of augmented reality by merchants has quickly become essential. ASOS has increased its use of "See My Fit," an augmented reality program that allows clothes to be "digitally fitted" on models. This change happened after the 2020 pandemic made it necessary for many artists to work from home.

   It is not unusual to see Augmented Reality used in retail, driven by data science. Up until a certain point, the Ikea Place app allowed you to virtually decorate a space. Utilizing the iPhone's integrated LiDAR sensor, the brand-new Ikea Studio app enables users to take images of entire rooms and then digitally transform them with furnishings, paint colors, and carpeting.

   To try out cutting-edge retail technologies, Amazon Salon, first hair salon of E Commerce opened its doors. By pointing to a product on a display shelf, users of Amazon's "Point and Learn" function can access brand videos and educational materials. Customers can view the product page on the e-commerce website by scanning the QR code on the shelf. Adidas has made it simpler for iOS app users to decide to make a purchase without ever stepping foot in a store by including this feature in November 2019. The augmented reality app mimics how sneakers would seem on bare feet by tracking the user's movements using the computer vision platform Viking.

3. **Inventory Management:** Retailers attempt to foresee how much of a particular good or service customers will purchase over a certain period of time in order to stock up appropriately. With the aid of

this demand forecasting, they can stockpile necessities in case of emergency.

Delivering the appropriate goods to the appropriate consumer at the appropriate time, in the appropriate manner, and at the appropriate location is the core objective of every prosperous retail operation. Retailers use a range of data analysis platforms and machine learning techniques to discover and identify trends and correlations within supply chains. It helps in determining the best stock and inventory management strategies. Plans are created to maximize the effectiveness of product delivery and inventory management after trends in sales are studied in relation to patterns discovered.

Advanced data analysis tools and machine learning algorithms find patterns, correlations, and supply chain connections. An algorithm that is always changing and tweaking its parameters and values determines the optimum stock and inventory management techniques. As a result of the analysts' usage of incoming data, supply chain management and inventories are optimized while high demand patterns are detected, and Future sales patterns are planned for.

4. **Merchandising:** The practice of merchandising has grown to be a significant facet of the retail sector. The vast majority of activities and strategies aimed at boosting sales and promotion of the product are included in this idea.

   Through visual channels, the use of merchandising methods helps to facilitate an impact on the consumer's decision-making process. The range appears to be fresh and fascinating because of the frequently switched-out products. Visually appealing packaging and branding can increase visual appeal and increase customer retention. Great amount of data science analysis is required in this specific case.

   The merchandising mechanisms sift through the data, extracting insights from it, and use them to construct priority sets for consumers while taking into account elements like seasonality, relevance, and trends.

5. **Behavior Analytics-CRM:** Companies more than anything else need to understand their customers to be successful in retail. Using this information, businesses may raise conversion rates, target specific consumers with their marketing, boost revenue and client retention, and cut the cost of customer acquisition.

Data on customer activity may be obtained through a variety of channels, such as mobile devices, social media, physical storefronts, and e-commerce websites. They will be able to gather and analyze the data due to their data science training. Additionally, the data enables companies to determine which clients are the most valuable, as well as what drives them to purchase particular goods. This helps businesses draw in new customers and keep their current ones.

6. **Location of New Store:** The Utility of data science in retail to acknowledge the location of the new shop proves to be an incredibly effective approach. Prior to making a decision of this nature, extensive data analysis is typically necessary.

   The approach is straightforward but highly efficient. The analysts examine the client data from the internet, paying close attention to the data's demographics. Understanding the market's potential is based on the coincidental pairing of geographic location and ZIP code.

   Additionally, special arrangements for the closeness of other retail locations are taken into account. An analysis of location network of the retail establishment is additionally performed. The algorithms link each of these sites together to find the solution. The store's platform can easily be updated to incorporate this data, giving it more possibilities for analysis across all of its operational areas.

7. **Optimization of Prices:** Around 70% of consumers responded that when making a final choice, price is very important. True, the retail price depends on the type of customer who purchases the product and the quantity of resources used in manufacturing, as per the reasoning of the producer price. We can solve this problem more effectively than ever before thanks to data analysis technologies.

   Finding a pricing level that is agreeable to both the customer and the retailer is a significant advantage provided by the optimization techniques. The process of setting prices depends not only on the costs associated with manufacturing an item but also on the purchasing power of a typical customer and the discounts other businesses provide. The data analysis technologies on hand offer a new technique to solving this problem.

8. **Detecting Fraud:** Frauds arising out of financial losses are a problem that affects everyone in the world. Customers and businesses alike

are impacted by credit risks, money losses, and delivery fraud. Fraud risks have increased recently as a result of digitization and internet transactions. These activities cause customers to lose faith in the stores. Here is where applying data science to the retail industry may be advantageous.

Due to the fact that they pit the fraudster against the seller's system, rule-based fraud detection strategies are useless. We can make precise predictions about fraudulent ones using the vast volumes of data currently collected from online transactions. The conventional approach, on the other hand, is rigid and unable to adjust to changing conditions. The company's reputation can be preserved by using data science in retail. For retailers, it is getting harder to spot fraudulent transactions. Modern digital technologies like deep learning are being used by businesses for support as a result of recent financial losses. They are able to keep an eye on everything at all times and identify any fraudulent activity as soon as it takes place.

Additionally, a number of outlier detection techniques are utilized to spot fraudulent behavior. The only way outlier identification systems approach the problem is through Techniques include transaction monitoring in real-time, time series analysis, cluster analysis, and others. Information on customers and retailers is gathered and examined using data science. After that, it uses a variety of data visualization techniques to determine the underlying patterns in data.

9. **Social Media Trend Analysis:** The most effective channel for utilities to communicate with one another is social media in the present day. New technologies in worldwide marketing and communication are being used by many retail companies to grow their operations. Retailers may gain a lot from the abundance of consumer data supplied by social media in terms of recognizing trends, patterns, and consumer behavior.

   On the vast platform of social media, anyone can express anything. As a retailer, social media offers crucial information that could help you spot trends.

   Unstructured data, which includes a sizable amount of text, photographs, and videos, makes up the majority of social media. Techniques for Natural Language Processing (NLP) take information from social media. The information is utilized to spot trends and predict consumer demand. When data scientists and researchers at social media companies have unrestricted access to the code base, they are free to make any modifications and advancements they deem necessary. Instead of being limited to hooking onto extant procedures and putting instrumentation together to impart meaning, users may create the code to do so if they require a certain amount of data to be collected on a regular basis.

Data scientists first group together various social media marketing strategies, and then they utilize sophisticated modeling to assess the results in carefully monitored advertising campaigns. Data scientists and media teams work together to create micro-campaigns, which enable the controlled testing of specific data combinations.

13.5 ARTIFICIAL INTELLIGENCE – DEFINITION AND CONCEPT

In the 1950s, the phrase "artificial intelligence" was first used. The US Department of Defense's Advanced Research Projects Agency (DARPA), which is interested in this kind of technology, prompted this. Since then, they have created robots that are capable of carrying out more complex activities. Initially, they started to teach computers to emulate simple human thinking and problem-solving.

An artificial intelligence system must exhibit human behaviors like planning, learning, and thinking in order to be called such solving issues Knowledge, Motion, perception, representation, and manipulation. The two categories of this are specific AI and broad AI. A machine with narrow AI can only handle one task at once. General AI describes a machine's capacity to mimic human thought and behaviors. Narrow artificial intelligence is goal-oriented, built to perform a single task, like driving a car or doing an online search, and is incredibly intelligent at doing the specific task it is taught to accomplish. The concept of a machine with general intelligence that mimics human intelligence and/or behaviors, with the ability to learn and apply its intelligence to solve any problem, is known as artificial general intelligence (AGI), also known as broad artificial intelligence (AI), or deep artificial intelligence (AI). Examples include autonomous vehicles, fraud detection, and consumer behavior forecasting, among others. Artificial intelligence is currently in high demand across a variety of job sectors, including healthcare, retail, manufacturing, and sports, despite the fact that it is mostly used in robotics.

13.5.1 ARTIFICIAL INTELLIGENCE AND RETAILING

The incremental sale of goods and services by a business to the end user is known as retailing. Because it combines a wide range of consumer needs with manufacturer special offers, retail functions as the economic engine (Reinartz & Imschloss, 2019). As a link in the value chain, retailing entails all the individuals and activities required to deliver a finished good or service to the consumer. Maintaining direct touch with the consumer, as well as ensuring product diversity and the physical flow of goods for sale, are some of retailing's fundamental responsibilities. These actions ensure that information is consistently flowing and that consumer desires and needs for goods and services are accurately assessed.

The value chain continues to benefit from physical retailing, but new digital technologies have transformed markets into multi-channel structures by eliminating physical merchandising, shattering the conventional retail business model, and radically changing the customer purchasing process (Oosthuizen et al., 2020, p. 2). Retailers are working harder to give their customers a smooth experience when buying both online and offline, in addition to harnessing personal social currency to market and promote their brands and products (Koumbis, 2021). Digital technologies have changed how we study, make decisions, and interact, and no industry is exempt from the upheaval this causes (Day & Schoemaker, 2019).

13.5.2 APPLICATION OF ARTIFICIAL INTELLIGENCE AND OTHER RELATED TECHNOLOGIES IN RETAIL SECTOR

Understanding and discussing artificial intelligence requires an understanding of massive data sets and analytical methods. It is hard to talk about intelligence without understanding the Internet of Things (IoT), Blockchain, 5G networks, and machine learning, which serves as the basis for artificial intelligence.

Machine learning is the concept that a computer program can learn new knowledge on its own and adapt to different environments. Machine learning uses algorithms that extract rules or patterns from the data to reduce prediction error (Jansen, 2020, p. 1). Machine learning keeps a computer's internal algorithms current despite broad changes. Machine learning algorithms can also analyze vast amounts of historical data to determine which adverts are most effective for which demographics and at when phases of the buying cycle (Pearson, 2019). On the flip side, machine learning needs to figure out how to create systems that progressively get better on their own. Can it grant computers the flexibility to decide for themselves which computational architectures and techniques are appropriate for altering data to yield a particular result? (Sterne, 2017).

Deep learning enabled many of the most recent advancements in artificial intelligence, such as the ability of computers to identify what or whose skill is displayed in an image or video (Ward & Bernard, 2019). When we use chatbots to make purchases on websites, we now have the ability to understand and recreate textual or verbal content thanks to a technique called natural language processing.

The Internet of Things is a dynamic network of physical and digital objects that have software built into them the communication, reasoning, and interaction with their surroundings. The following are the technologies used in retail sector:

1. **Chatbot:** While chatbots have been around since 1966, machine learning and big data technology have made them considerably smarter and better in terms of processing speeds and responding to contextual awareness. This makes it possible to interact with people only in dire circumstances. The robot speaks less formally and more like a buddy than like a person working in field. To discover any information, the navigation experience relies less on text and more on communication. Chatbots powered by AI improve search, deliver a better customer experience, alert users to new products, and suggest items based on their preferences. It represents a new approach for brands, companies, and publications to communicate with customers without requiring them to download additional custom apps or learn how to use them. Alternatively, it can be set up and updated as a pre-installed messaging app.

   As a result, it offers lower development costs for communication channels in electronic shopping. The fact that chatbots assist in direct customer communication is what matters most in this situation. Chatbots help businesses reach their goals of providing accurate information to customers while preventing mistakes brought on by employees repeatedly gathering information.

2. **Robot Assistant:** By utilizing robots in the logistics and supply chain, merchants can make significant savings from shrinkage brought on by human error and stock-out shortages. Additionally, it gives businesses the freedom to transfer their salespeople to jobs that will result in increased sales. Human labor functions can occasionally

be deceptive. The specialized and trained robots, however, cannot manage that. These robots not only carry out retail-related tasks, but they also provide information to customers about product locations, prices, and quick discount coupons, among other things. Robotic sales associates in a store offer a tangible shopping experience that boosts the retailer's customer-centricity and growth.

3. **Assistants with Voice:** It is a voice-activated, practical, and effective IoT-based technology (Internet of Things). It is able to complete operations like purchases, searches, help, etc., by responding to voice requests from the users. To conserve energy, it can completely switch off the light while carrying out the commands. The Internet of Things (IoT) can be controlled verbally thanks to voice technologies (devices). These consist of computers, cellphones, smart speakers, and other devices. Prior to the development of Conversational AI and related technology, speech technology could only be utilized for dictation. IoT devices will be able to comprehend the context and purpose of vocal requests after AI.

4. **Delivery via AI-based Drone and Droid:** Although drones have been around for a while, no one ever expected that they would be used to carry goods to residential homes. Yes, it is one of the most cutting-edge technologies that will influence the retail industries of the future. Drone neural networks are utilized for object identification, categorization, and tracking while the drone is flying in the air thanks to AI drone machines, which also enable high-performance onboard image processing.

   Drones' neural networks assist in the detection of a wide range of objects, including automobiles, foothills, buildings, trees, items on or near the surface of the sea, and many types of terrain.

   Flirtey, a new startup company based in the United States that delivers medical supplies, has already made successful commercial deliveries of the packages to the addresses of the intended recipients. Additionally, the United States and Europe are constructing airports particularly for parking drones, or "droneports." The drones have a maximum speed of 60 miles per hour and can fly up to 400 feet in the air. They can move objects weighing up to two pounds.

   Drone navigation and movement control can be automated with the help of AI. Numerous techniques, such as GPS tracking, computer vision, and machine learning algorithms, can be used to accomplish this. A Droid is a little robotic device of various sizes and shapes that carries out activities as instructed. These move across the pavement in the pedestrian lane and may lift weights of 20 to 30 pounds in 30 minutes or less. They are able to ascend and descend the stairs, have nine cameras to see everything around them, and feed live footage. Additionally, these have a microphone for consumer interaction and GPS tracking between the source and destination. Their sensors are able to detect disturbances like pedestrian activity on sidewalks.

5. **Augmented Reality and Virtual Reality:** In order for real and computer-generated digital information to appear as one environment in the user's vision of the physical world, augmented reality (AR) is a technique. Through a virtual layer that can add images, text, movies, or other virtual elements to the user's real-time observation of the physical environment, augmented reality (AR) merges the virtual and physical worlds. Real-world data is frequently captured using AR, typically using a digital camera in a webcam or smartphone. AR allows users to engage with virtual goods via gadgets like smartphones, tablets, wearables (headsets), projectors, or fixed interactive screens. This is a unique and innovative technique to draw customers' attention. Product simulation, media richness, sound, GPS data, and films all add experiential value. The AR shopping experience enables customers to easily interact with virtual goods, boosting their ability to visualize objects and, presumably, their subsequent perception of the brand, which in turn increases customers' buying intentions.

   In contrast, VR uses a wearable device (usually a headset) that shuts out sensory sensations from the "real world" to deliver a shopping environment that is arguably more inventive and engaging by submerging consumers in virtual, amusing 3-D worlds. Here, people can engage in real time and move around the virtual environment physically, usually by moving their heads, but possibly also by tracking the motion of their limbs. The headgear must be cozy and provide believable immersive virtual effects for VR to thrive. Therefore, VR can be described as a media made up of interactive computer simulations that that replace or augment the feedback to the user's actions through one or more senses, conferring the feeling of being psychologically immersed in the simulation – in other words, a virtual world.

6. **AI Technology for Self-Checkout:** In self-checkout technology, artificial intelligence has emerged as a crucial part of loss prevention. Retailers can get insights on the self-checkout process by integrating AI into their video and scanning systems to discover friction points in the checkout process, predict patterns, and gain a better understanding of how theft occurs. Self-checkout machines equipped with AI algorithms can spot irregularities during consumer checkouts, flag suspicious transactions, and notify personnel of possible shoplifting in progress. Self-checkout systems can make use of computer vision and machine learning technology to help prevent lost incidences. Additionally, AI can be included into a larger retail technology platform, enabling it to draw conclusions and make predictions from a different data source. Using information gathered from sources such as traffic measurement, inventory intelligence, self-checkouts, and other points of sale, creates a holistic view of shopper behavior and thus greater shrink visibility.
7. **Offering Customized Experience:** One of the most reliable strategies to increase and sustain the customer loyalty count is to respond to the specific needs of the customers. Something that is conveniently made achievable by combining customer experience with artificial intelligence Retail brands can easily track and then analyze prior purchases, consumer behavior, and loyalty cards with the help of transactional data, AI, and machine learning to provide more specialized services. Sephora's Color IQ is a prime example of customer-focused AI in retail. The brand's AI-powered in-store service analyzes the skin's surface and makes makeup product recommendations based on the customer's skin tone.
8. **Computer Vision for Crowd Analysis:** Computer vision, a specific use of deep learning in artificial intelligence utilized in retail, is being embraced by physical stores. You get eyes in the appropriate places because of computer vision, which "sees" and decodes visual data. This opens up new retail use cases for customer experience, demand forecasting, inventory management, and other areas.

   A limitless amount of personalization is possible thanks to computer vision, which can do everything from recognize objects of interest in selfies to monitor real-world interactions and develop recommendation engines for anything.

Virtual checkouts cut costs and rush hour waits, while virtual mirrors for fitness and fashion bring the best instructors and icons into your home. CrowdAI automates image- and video-based analysis to assist shops in reducing operating costs.

9. **ChatGPT:** The retail sector is continually changing and catching up with emerging trends and technologies. One of the most recent developments in this field is the use of ChatGPT and other artificial intelligence (AI) technologies to provide omnichannel shopping experiences.

   ChatGPT is a powerful AI system that uses natural language processing (NLP) to understand human language and respond to customer requests and enquiries. This technology will make it easier and easier for customers to find and purchase the products they want, potentially revolutionizing the way we shop online. ChatGPT and other AI technologies can be utilized in the retail sector to evaluate consumer data and provide customers with seamless and personalized shopping experiences.

10. **The Mobile Shift:** E-commerce has moved to mobile platforms in an effort to gain more importance. Businesses today have technology that are mobile-friendly. Some of the technologies specifically used in mobile commerce include location-based marketing, Internet of Things, VR/AR guidance, and mobile apps. These innovations make the entire industry simple to operate.

13.6 CONCLUSION

Technology is advancing rapidly. The retail sector is being drastically changed by many of these technologies. New technologies like drones, robotics, 5G, VR, AR, MR, IoT, and micro-cloud computing are fundamentally altering the retail industry. By utilizing data science and artificial intelligence, the retail industry, and more specifically store management and the shopping experience, will undergo a dramatic transformation. The retail industry has experienced significant changes that have been accelerated by recent technological advancements. Personalized suggestions, smart speakers, one-click ordering, anticipatory shipping, etc., are a few examples of technology breakthroughs. By assisting consumers and shoppers in making decisions, artificial intelligence is transforming partnerships with retailers. First off, AI technology gives retailers more precise information about their consumers' wants, which helps with tailored service, search results that are more relevant, and suggestions. We can already have a peek of the future thanks to chatbots, autonomous vehicles, and networked devices in retail stores and warehouses. Businesses can benefit from the application of artificial intelligence in numerous ways, including increased productivity, less repetition, and improved customer service.

KEYWORDS

- **artificial intelligence technology**
- **business interactions**
- **data science**
- **retail sector**
- **sourcing**
- **warehousing**

REFERENCES

Agrawal, N., & Smith, S. A., (2008). Supply chain planning processes for two major retailers. In: Agrawal, N., & Smith, S. A., (eds.), *Retail Supply Chain Management* (1st edn., pp. 11–23). Springer: Berlin, Germany. ISBN 978-1-4899-7562-1.

Balfour, B., (2013). How AI is making big data smarter. *Forbes*. Retrieved from https://www.forbes.com.

Balfour, G., (2013). Big data's big promise. *Backbone*, *4*, 12–15.

Bernard, M., & Ward, M., (2019). *Artificial Intelligence in Practice: How 50 Successful Companies Used ai and Machine Learning to Solve Problems*. Chichester, WS: Wiley.

Chen, H., Chiang, R. H. L., & Storey, V. C. (2012). Business intelligence and analytics: From big data to big impact. *MIS Quarterly, 36*(4), 1165–1188.

Chen, H., Chiang, R. H. L., Lindner, C. H., Storey, V. C., & Robinson, J. M., (2012). Business intelligence and analytics: From big data to big impact. *MIS Q.*, *36*, 1165–1188.

Clouds, Big Data, and Smart Assets: 10 Tech-Enabled Business Trends to Watch. Available online: http://www.mckinsey.com/industries/high-tech/our-insights/clouds-big-data-and-smart-assets-ten-tech-enabled-business-trends-to-watch (accessed on 03 October 2023).

Davenport, T. H. (2013). Analytics 3.0. *Harvard Business Review*, *91*(12), 64–72.

Day, G. S., & Schoemaker, P. J. H., (2019). *See Sooner Act Faster: How Vigilant Leaders Thrive in an Era of Digital Turbulence.* Cambridge, MA: The MIT Press.

Fernie, J., & Sparks, L., (2014). *Logistics and Retail Management: Emerging Issues and New Challenges in the Retail Supply Chain* (4th edn., pp. 1–28). Kogan Page: London, UK. ISBN 9780749468231.

Fernie, J., Sparks, L., & McKinnon, A. C., (2010). Retail logistics in the UK: Past, present, and future. *Int. J. Retail Distrib. Manag.*, *38*, 894–914.

Hurwitz, J., Nugent, A., Halper, F., & Kaufman, M., (2013). *Big Data for Dummies* (1st edn., pp. 9–24). John Wiley & Sons: Hoboken, NJ, USA. ISBN 978-1-118-50422-2.

Jacob, F. (2009). Artificial intelligence in marketing: Emerging trends and ethical considerations. *Journal of Marketing Research, 46*(2), 220–228.

Jacobs, A., (2009). The pathologies of big data. *Commun. ACM, 52*, 36–44.

Jansen, S., (2020). *Machine Learning for Algorithmic Trading: Predictive Models to Extract Signals from Market and Alternative Data for Systematic Trading Strategies with Python* (2nd edn.), Birmingham, UK: Packt.

Koumbis, D., (2021). *An Introduction to Fashion Retailing: From Managing to Merchandising (Basics Fashion Management).* (2nd edn.). New York, NY: Bloomsbury.

Levy, M., & Weitz, B. A., (2013). *Retailing Management* (9th edn., pp. 514–539). McGraw-Hill Irwin: New York, NY, USA. ISBN 978-1259060663.

Marwala, T., & Hurwitz, E. (2017). *Artificial Intelligence and Economic Theory: Skynet in the Market* (Vol. 1). Cham: Springer International Publishing.

McAfee, A., & Brynjolfsson, E., (2012). Big data: The management revolution. *Harv. Bus. Rev.*, *90*, 60–68.

O'Regan, G., (2008). *A Brief History of Computing* (1st edn., pp. 53–62). Springer: Berlin, Germany. ISBN 978-1-4471-2359-0.

Oosthuizen, K., Botha, E., Robertson, J., & Montecchi, M., (2020). Artificial intelligence in retail: The AI-enabled value chain. *Australasian Marketing Journal (AMJ)*, 1–10. https://doi.org/10.1016/j.ausmj.2020.07.007.

Pathak, N., Sharma, N., Larguech, S. R., et al., (2022). "Performance enhancement of adaptive neural networks based on learning rate. *Computers, Materials & Continua, 74*(1), 2005–2019 ISSN:1546-2226. https://doi.org/10.32604/cmc.2023.031481.

Pearson, A., (2020). Personalization the artificial intelligence way. *Journal of Digital & Social Media Marketing, 7*(3), 245–269.

Purcell, B., (2013). The emergence of "big data" technology and analytics. *J. Technol. Res.*, *4*, 1–7.

Reinartz, W., Wiegand, N., &Imschloss, M., (2019). The impact of digital transformation on the retailing value chain. *International Journal of Research in Marketing, 36*(3), 350–366. https://doi.org/10.1016/j.ijresmar.2018.12.002.

Sterne, J., (2017). *Artificial Intelligence for Marketing: Practical Applications* (1st edn.). Habokan, NJ: Wiley.

TDWI Best Practices Report. *Big Data Analytics.* Available online: https://tdwi.org/research/2011/09/best-practices-report-q4-big-data-analytics.aspx (accessed on 03 October 2023).

The Internet of Things. Available online: http://www.mckinsey.com/industries/high-tech/our-insights/the-internet-of-things (accessed on 03 October 2023).

CHAPTER 14

AI and Data Science in Business Services: Enhancing Efficiency and Driving Innovation

ABDO H. GUROOB[1] and D. H. MANJAIAH[2]

[1]*Department of Business Information Technology, Zanzibar University, Zanzibar, Tanzania*

[2]*Department of Post Graduate Studies and Research in Computer Science, Mangalore, Karnataka, India*

ABSTRACT

The integration of Artificial Intelligence (AI) and Data Science into the business services sector is transforming the way companies operate and is driving efficiency and innovation. These technologies are providing businesses with new opportunities to automate repetitive tasks, improve decision-making processes, and gain valuable insights from large amounts of data. The integration of AI and Data Science is changing the business services industry by increasing productivity, streamlining processes, and improving customer engagement.

This chapter provides a comprehensive overview of AI and Data Science in business services, examining the various applications of these technologies and their impact on the industry. We explore how AI is being used to automate tasks such as customer service inquiries and data entry, while data science is providing businesses with insights into customer behavior, market trends, and overall business performance. Predictive analytics, customer sentiment analysis, and advanced data visualization techniques are just a few of the ways that data science is enhancing the business services sector.

Advanced Digital Technologies in Financial and Business Management: Unleashing the Power of Artificial Intelligence, Machine Learning, Blockchain, and the Internet of Things. Jyoti Batra Arora, Nitish Pathak, and Neelam Sharma (Eds.)

Our novel contribution to this field of research is the emphasis on the importance of combining AI and Data Science to maximize their benefits. By using AI to automate tasks and data science to gain insights, businesses can improve their operations and gain a competitive edge. Additionally, we highlight the benefits of using AI and data science to better understand customers, leading to improved customer engagement and increased customer satisfaction.

14.1 INTRODUCTION

The incorporation of Artificial Intelligence (AI) and Data Science into the business services industry is revolutionizing the manner in which companies' function and compete in the rapidly evolving business landscape. With the exponential growth in data volume and complexity and advancements in machine learning and natural language processing, AI and data science have become essential tools for organizations looking to stay ahead of the curve (Gad-Elrab, 2021).

14.1.1 AI IN BUSINESS SERVICES

The incorporation of AI technologies in business services has the potential to revolutionize the way organizations operate. AI-powered systems can automate a range of routine tasks, reducing human error and providing real-time insights into complex data, resulting in faster and more informed decision-making. In customer service, AI-powered chatbots can handle a high volume of inquiries, providing quick and accurate responses to customers (Vishnoi et al., 2018). In finance and accounting, AI can be used to automate financial reports, invoicing, and budgeting processes, improving efficiency, and reducing the risk of errors. Additionally, AI can also be used to optimize supply chain management, predict market trends, and provide predictive maintenance, resulting in significant cost savings and improved operational efficiency.

14.1.2 DATA SCIENCE IN BUSINESS SERVICES

Data Science provides organizations with the ability to extract valuable insights from large datasets, enabling companies to make informed decisions based on data-driven evidence. Predictive analytics can be used to analyze customer behavior, predict future market trends, and improve product development. Customer sentiment analysis can also be used to determine customer preferences and expectations, enabling businesses to provide more personalized services. Data visualization techniques can be used to present complex data in an intuitive and actionable manner, providing organizations with a better understanding of their operations and customers (Sun et al., 2018).

14.1.3 IMPACT OF AI AND DATA SCIENCE ON BUSINESS SERVICES

The integration of AI and Data Science into the business services sector has the potential to greatly enhance the efficiency and competitiveness of organizations. By automating routine tasks, businesses can reduce operational costs, improve speed and accuracy, and allow employees to focus on more strategic tasks. Data-driven insights can provide businesses with a better understanding of their customers, market trends, and overall performance, leading to improved customer engagement, increased sales, and reduced risk (Ram et al., 2016). However, the adoption of AI and Data Science in the business services sector also brings with it several challenges. Ensuring data privacy, security, and ethical use of these technologies is crucial, as is ensuring their accessibility and affordability to small and medium-sized enterprises. Addressing these challenges is essential to ensure the long-term success and sustainability of AI and Data Science in the business services sector.

In this chapter, we aim to provide a comprehensive overview of AI and Data Science in the business services sector, exploring their applications, benefits, and impact on the industry. We will examine the challenges faced by organizations in incorporating these technologies and provide recommendations for overcoming these challenges. Through this exploration, we hope to provide a better understanding of the role of AI and Data Science in the business services sector and their potential to drive efficiency and innovation. Ultimately, this chapter will provide a detailed analysis of the future of AI and Data Science in the business services sector and their potential to shape the way organizations operate and compete in the years to come. Our goal is to provide valuable insights and recommendations for organizations looking to harness the full potential of these technologies to stay ahead in today's rapidly changing business environment.

14.2 INNOVATION IN BUSINESS SERVICES

Artificial Intelligence (AI) and Data Science have brought about a new era of innovation in the business services industry. Companies are now able to leverage these cutting-edge technologies to streamline operations, improve decision-making, and uncover hidden insights in their data. This article will explore the many ways in which AI and Data Science are transforming the business services sector, and how they are being used to boost efficiency, drive growth, and enhance performance (Figure 14.1).

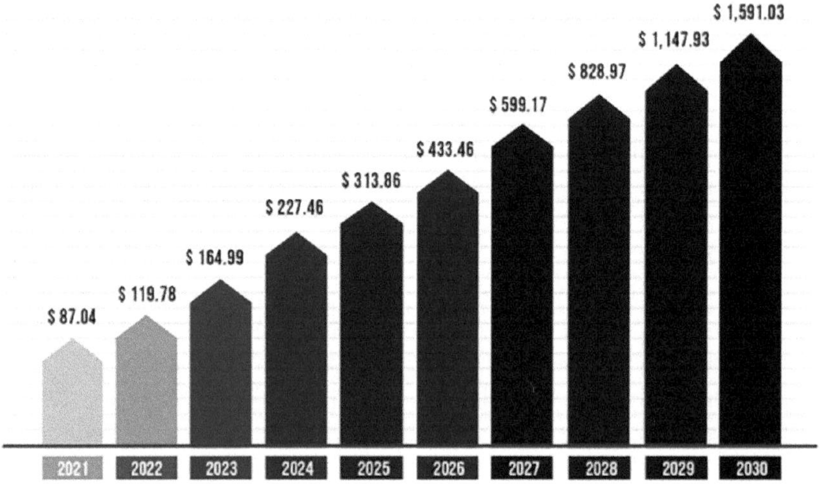

FIGURE 14.1 The global AI market is projected to reach $1,597.1 billion by 2030, with an estimated CAGR of 38.1% from 2022 to 2030. The market was valued at $119.78 billion in 2022. North America's AI market was estimated at $147.58 billion in 2021.

Source: Shakuro. https://shakuro.com/blog/breaking-barriers-how-ai-makes-app-development-accessible-for-startups

14.2.1 ROUTINE TASK AUTOMATION

One of the most powerful applications of AI in the business services sector is the automation of routine tasks. The implementation of AI-powered tools has made it possible for organizations to automate tedious jobs such as data entry, invoicing, and customer service, freeing up time and resources for more valuable and complex tasks. The automation of these tasks has led to improved accuracy, speed, and reliability, resulting in increased efficiency and productivity across the organization (Fountaine et al., 2019). Moreover, the implementation of AI-powered decision-making processes such as credit scoring and fraud detection can also be automated. AI algorithms can quickly process vast amounts of data, detecting patterns and correlations that are difficult or impossible for human analysts to uncover. This leads to faster and more precise decision-making, reducing the risk of fraud and improving risk management (Table 14.1).

TABLE 14.1 Advantages of Automating Routine Tasks with AI

Task	Advantages
Data entry	Improved accuracy and speed, reduced risk of errors.
Invoicing	Streamlined process, reduced time and resources required.
Customer service	Improved response time, increased efficiency.

14.2.2 BIG DATA ANALYSIS

Another area where AI and Data Science are having a profound impact in the business services sector is data analysis. With the ability to analyze large datasets at lightning speed, AI and data science have the potential to reveal insights that would otherwise be missed by human analysts. These insights can inform decision-making, target new markets, and drive the creation of new products and services. For example (Lee et al., 2021), AI algorithms can be used to analyze customer data to find trends and preferences. This information can then be utilized to guide marketing strategies and product development. AI can also be used to analyze sales data, giving organizations a deeper understanding of their customer's buying behaviors and preferences.

14.2.3 IMPROVED CUSTOMER EXPERIENCE

AI and Data Science are also revolutionizing the customer experience. The use of AI-powered chatbots, voice assistants, and other tools has made it possible for organizations to provide customers with fast and convenient access to information and support, at any time and from any location. This has led to improved customer satisfaction and a more positive overall customer experience (Khan & Iqbal, 2020). AI can also be used to create customized customer experiences, such as making recommendations based on previous purchases or behavior. By analyzing customer data, AI algorithms can identify patterns and preferences, enabling organizations to tailor their products and services to meet the unique needs of each customer, resulting in a more personalized and satisfying experience.

14.2.4 DATA-DRIVEN DECISION-MAKING

The impact of AI and Data Science on decision-making has been significant in the business services sector. Using advanced machine learning algorithms, organizations can analyze large datasets to uncover patterns and correlations, informing decision-making. This leads to improved accuracy and speed in decision-making, resulting in a more efficient and effective problem-solving approach (Bag et al., 2021). For instance, AI can be used to analyze customer data to find trends and preferences, guiding the development of new products and services. AI algorithms can also be used to analyze financial data, giving organizations valuable insights into their financial performance, and informing decision-making.

14.3 THE GROWING IMPORTANCE OF DATA SCIENCE IN BUSINESS SERVICES

As the business services sector continues to evolve and become increasingly data-driven, the role of Data Science has become increasingly important. This has led to a growing demand for professionals with expertise in Data Science and the ability to leverage its potential for organizational growth. From predictive analytics to real-time insights, the applications of Data Science in the business services sector are vast and diverse.

14.3.1 THE IMPACT OF DATA SCIENCE ON BUSINESS SERVICES INNOVATION

One of the primary ways in which Data Science is driving innovation in the business services sector is by enabling organizations to uncover new patterns and trends in their data. This information can be used to inform decision-making and drive the development of new and innovative products and services. For example, Data Science can be used to analyze customer data to understand their needs and preferences, helping organizations to tailor their offerings and meet the evolving needs of their customers (Popescu, 2018) (Table 14.2).

14.3.2 IMPROVING OPERATIONAL EFFICIENCY WITH DATA SCIENCE

In addition to driving innovation, Data Science also has a significant impact on operational efficiency in the business services sector. By analyzing data from various sources, organizations can identify opportunities to streamline processes, automate routine tasks, and reduce costs. This results in increased efficiency, improved resource allocation, and enhanced productivity

TABLE 14.2 Data Science Tools and Techniques Used in Business Services

Tool/Technique	Description	Application
Predictive analytics	The use of statistical algorithms and machine learning to make predictions about future events.	Customer behavior analysis, market trend analysis, resource utilization analysis.
Data mining	The process of discovering patterns and relationships in large data sets.	Customer segmentation, process optimization, market research.
Machine learning	A subfield of artificial intelligence that allows systems to learn and make decisions based on data.	Customer behavior analysis, market trend analysis, process optimization.
Statistical analysis	The use of statistical methods to analyze data and draw conclusions.	Customer behavior analysis, market trend analysis, process optimization.
Natural language processing (NLP)	The use of machine learning algorithms to analyze and understand human language.	Customer sentiment analysis, text-based data analysis.
Data visualization	The use of visual representations, such as charts and graphs, to communicate data insights.	Data presentation, data communication, decision-making support.

(Popescu, 2018). The use of Data Science in the business services sector can also help organizations to identify potential issues and implement corrective actions before they become major problems.

14.3.3 PREDICTIVE ANALYTICS AND ITS ROLE IN BUSINESS SERVICES

Predictive Analytics is a key area of focus for many organizations in the business services sector, as it provides valuable insights into future trends and events. By leveraging Data Science techniques such as machine learning and statistical analysis, organizations can predict future customer behavior, market trends, and other key indicators of business performance. This information, when combined with effective decision-making strategies, can help organizations to anticipate changes in the market and adjust their strategies accordingly (Alharthi, 2018).

14.3.4 THE IMPORTANCE OF DATA-DRIVEN DECISIONS IN BUSINESS SERVICES

Data-driven decision-making is becoming increasingly important in the business services sector, as organizations strive to stay ahead of the competition and meet the evolving needs of their customers. By leveraging the power of

Data Science, organizations can gain a deeper understanding of their operations and performance and make informed decisions that drive growth and improve overall outcomes (Schoenherr & Speier-Pero, 2015). For example, Data Science can be used to analyze sales data, customer behavior, and financial information, providing organizations with the insights they need to make informed decisions and stay ahead of the curve.

14.4 THE ADVANTAGES OF INTEGRATING AI AND DATA SCIENCE

The integration of AI and data science has revolutionized the way organizations operate, making it possible to tackle complex problems and gain valuable insights in ways that were previously impossible. AI and data science are two of the most rapidly evolving fields of our time, and their combination has led to numerous advancements and benefits in a wide range of industries.

The growth of data has been explosive, and it is estimated that 90% of all the data in the world has been created in the last two years alone. This growth in data has put enormous pressure on organizations to find ways to process, store, and analyze it in a meaningful way. AI and data science have come to the rescue, enabling organizations to extract valuable insights from large amounts of data and make informed decisions (Willcocks, 2020).

14.4.1 FRAUD DETECTION

One of the key advantages of integrating AI and data science is the ability to detect fraudulent activity more effectively. Fraud is a growing problem for organizations of all sizes, and traditional methods of detecting fraud are often time-consuming and resource intensive. AI algorithms, on the other hand, can quickly analyze large amounts of data to identify patterns and anomalies that might indicate fraudulent behavior. This enables organizations to stay ahead of potential fraudsters and protect their assets and customers.

One example of how AI and data science are being used to detect fraud is in the financial sector. AI algorithms are trained on vast amounts of data to identify transactions that are potentially fraudulent. The algorithms can then flag these transactions for further investigation, reducing the time and resources required to detect fraud. This not only saves organizations money, but it also helps to reduce the risk of fraudulent transactions going unnoticed (Ariga et al., 2020).

14.4.2 ENHANCED DECISION-MAKING

AI and Data Science have also had a profound impact on decision-making processes. AI algorithms are capable of processing massive amounts of data in real time, delivering real-time insights that inform decision-making and drive innovation. According to a study by Forrester Research, investment in AI and advanced analytics will grow at a compound annual growth rate (CAGR) of 17.0% from 2018 to 2023. Predictive analytics, for example, enables organizations to forecast future market trends, customer behavior, and sales, equipping them with the information necessary to make informed decisions and target new markets. By providing actionable insights, predictive analytics can help businesses make better decisions, reduce risks, and improve their chances of success (Awan et al., 2021).

14.4.3 DRIVING INNOVATION

Innovation has always been at the forefront of progress and growth, and AI and Data Science are playing a significant role in this. According to a report by Accenture, AI has the potential to increase productivity by up to 40% and create economic value of up to $14 trillion by 2035 (Morabito, 2021) (Figure 14.2).

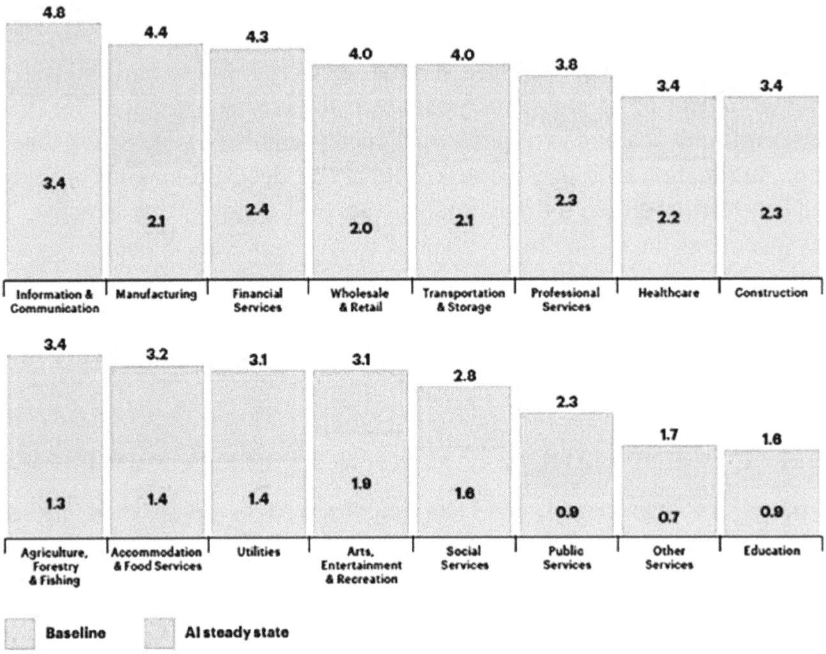

FIGURE 14.2 Artificial intelligence has the potential to boost economic growth rates by an average of 1.7% points, based on a weighted average, across 16 industries by 2035, leading to an increase in real annual gross value-added growth.

By analyzing large amounts of data, organizations can identify new market opportunities, develop new products and services, and stay ahead of the competition. Predictive analytics play a crucial role in this process, providing organizations with accurate predictions about future events such as customer behavior and market trends, which inform the development of innovative strategies. Predictive analytics can assist companies in making more informed decisions, uncover new possibilities, and maintain a competitive advantage.

14.4.4 ADVANCEMENTS IN TECHNOLOGY

Advancements in technologies such as robotics and autonomous vehicles are being powered by AI and Data Science and have the potential to revolutionize business operations in the services sector. The global Artificial Intelligence Robots market is projected to reach a revenue of USD 28.5 billion by 2028, growing at a compound annual growth rate (CAGR) of 27.2%, according to Verified Market Research. These technologies can automate complex processes, improve efficiency, reduce costs, and create new opportunities for growth and innovation. For example, the use of autonomous vehicles in delivery and logistics can not only improve efficiency but also reduce the costs associated with human error. The use of robotics in manufacturing can also lead to improved efficiency, increased production, and reduced costs (Javaid et al., 2021).

The impact of AI and Data Science on the business services sector has been profound, leading to improved efficiency, competitiveness, and innovation. Automation of repetitive tasks, enhanced decision-making processes, and innovation driven by data analysis are just a few of the benefits. The advancements in technology powered by AI and Data Science have the potential to revolutionize business operations, creating new opportunities for growth and efficiency. As these technologies continue to evolve and mature, they will play an increasingly important role in shaping the future of the business services sector.

14.5 COMBINING AI AND DATA SCIENCE FOR MAXIMUM IMPACT

Artificial Intelligence (AI) and Data Science are two rapidly evolving technologies that are transforming the business services sector. The integration of these two technologies has the potential to deliver significant improvements in efficiency and competitiveness, making it a topic of great interest for businesses seeking to stay ahead in a rapidly evolving market. In this section, we will delve into the benefits of integrating AI and Data Science and how it contributes to optimal results (Verma et al., 2021).

14.5.1 COMPLEMENTARY STRENGTHS

The most significant advantage of integrating AI and Data Science is the complementarity of their strengths. Data Science provides a robust foundation of analysis and insights by processing vast amounts of data and uncovering patterns (Benzidia et al., 2021). It involves the use of statistical and mathematical algorithms to extract meaningful information from data, providing a solid foundation for decision-making. Meanwhile, AI automates complex tasks and offers real-time processing capabilities, enabling businesses to quickly respond to changes in the market. The integration of these technologies results in a comprehensive understanding of customer behavior, market trends, and sales patterns, empowering businesses to make informed decisions and drive innovation.

14.5.2 AGILE RESPONSIVENESS TO MARKET CHANGES

Another key benefit of integrating AI and Data Science is the ability to quickly respond to changes in the market. With real-time processing capabilities, businesses can quickly adapt to new trends and capitalize on new opportunities (Munirathinam, 2020) (Table 14.3).

TABLE 14.3 The Growth and Impact of the AI Industry

Statistic	Value	Source
Projected AI contribution to the global economy by 2030.	$15.7 trillion	World Economic Forum (2020)
AI industry market size (expected)	$266.92 billion	Fortune Business Insights (2020)
CAGR (2020–2027)	33.2%	Fortune Business Insights (2020)
Largest AI market (expected)	North America	Fortune Business Insights (2020)
AI adoption in retail industry (expected)	80% of business executives	Fortune Business Insights (2020)
Global AI-driven hardware market revenue (expected)	$234.6 billion	Statista (2020)
Major obstacle to AI market growth	Limited number of AI experts	Allied Market Research (2018)

Source: Word Economic Forum.

For example, predictive analytics enables businesses to forecast future market trends, customer behavior, and sales, providing a competitive edge and promoting innovation. By integrating AI and Data Science, businesses can gain a real-time, holistic view of the market, allowing them to quickly identify new opportunities and respond to changes. This agility is a critical factor in today's fast-paced business environment and is essential for maintaining a competitive advantage.

14.5.3 TRANSFORMATION OF INNOVATION STRATEGIES

The integration of AI and Data Science also has the potential to transform innovation strategies. By analyzing large amounts of data, businesses can identify new market opportunities, develop new products and services, and stay ahead of the competition. The combination of AI and Data Science allows businesses to make accurate predictions about future events, such as customer behavior and market trends, informing the development of innovative strategies. This ability to analyze vast amounts of data and identify patterns enables businesses to stay ahead of the competition and respond to market changes in a timely and effective manner (Uzialko, 2022).

The integration of AI and Data Science delivers numerous benefits, including a comprehensive understanding of customer behavior and market trends, agile responsiveness to market changes, and the potential to transform innovation strategies. This combination contributes to optimal results and provides businesses with a competitive advantage in the business services sector. Businesses that embrace the integration of AI and Data Science are likely to experience improved efficiency, competitiveness, and innovation, positioning them well for success in the future.

14.6 USE CASES OF AI AND DATA SCIENCE IN BUSINESS SERVICES

Artificial Intelligence (AI) and data science are playing a vital role in transforming business services and driving efficiency and innovation. In this section, we will explore some of the most impactful use cases of AI and data science in business services and discuss their impact on various industries.

14.6.1 CUSTOMER SERVICE

One of the most impactful use cases of AI in business services is customer service. AI-powered chatbots and virtual assistants are becoming increasingly popular in customer service, allowing organizations to handle customer queries and resolve issues more efficiently (Table 14.4).

TABLE 14.4 Comparison of Traditional Customer Service Methods and AI-Powered Chatbots/Virtual Assistants

Feature	Traditional Customer Service	AI-Powered Chatbots/Virtual Assistants
Efficiency	Limited availability during business hours.	24/7 availability, fast response time.
Cost savings	High labor costs for live support.	Lower operational costs, automated support.
Personalization	Limited personalization capabilities.	Ability to personalize interactions and recommendations.
Error resolution	Dependent on live support availability.	Immediate resolution through pre-programed solutions.
Customer data analysis	Limited data analysis capabilities.	Ability to analyze customer data and improve customer experience.

For example, chatbots can be trained to understand customer inquiries and provide relevant answers or direct them to the appropriate department for further assistance.

Moreover, AI can be used to analyze customer data and improve the customer experience by personalizing interactions and recommendations. By leveraging AI in customer service, organizations can improve customer satisfaction and reduce the workload of customer service teams.

14.6.2 MARKETING

AI and data science are transforming the way organizations approach marketing. AI can be used to analyze customer data and provide insights into customer behavior and preferences, allowing organizations to target their marketing efforts more effectively (Varadarajan, 2020). For example, AI can be used to analyze customer interactions on social media and suggest the most effective marketing strategies (Table 14.5).

AI can also be used to automate routine marketing tasks, such as email marketing and lead generation, freeing up time for marketing teams to focus on more strategic initiatives. By leveraging AI in marketing, organizations can improve the effectiveness of their marketing efforts and achieve better results.

14.6.3 OPERATIONS

AI and data science can be used to optimize operations in a variety of ways. For example, AI can be used to automate routine tasks, such as inventory management, freeing up time for operations teams to focus on more strategic initiatives. AI can also be used to analyze operations data, providing insights into areas for improvement and identifying bottlenecks in the supply chain.

TABLE 14.5 Cumulative Global AI Revenue Forecast 2016–2025/Ranked by Use Case (in Millions of Dollars)

Application	Cumulative Revenue (2016–2025)
Machine/vehicular object direction/identification/avoidance.	$8,986.57 million
Static image recognition, classification, and tagging.	$7,642.83 million
Patient data processing.	$7,259.35 million
Algorithmic trading strategy performance improvement.	$6,394.41 million
Localization and mapping.	$5,950.55 million
Predictive maintenance.	$5,713.60 million
Prevention against cybersecurity threats.	$5,385.10 million
Converting paperwork into digital data.	$5,370.85 million
Intelligent recruitment and HR systems.	$5,295.03 million
Medical image analysis.	$5,111.31 million

Source: Adapted from Tractica.

Additionally, AI can be used to improve the accuracy of forecasting and demand planning, reducing the risk of stockouts and overstocking. By leveraging AI in operations, organizations can improve the efficiency and effectiveness of their operations and reduce costs (Riesenegger & Hübner, 2022).

14.6.4 FINANCE

AI and data science are transforming the way organizations approach finance. For example, AI can be used to automate routine tasks, such as accounts payable and receivable, freeing up time for finance teams to focus on more strategic initiatives (Polak, 2020). AI can also be used to analyze financial data, providing insights into areas for improvement and identifying fraud.

Additionally, AI can be used to improve the accuracy of financial forecasting, reducing the risk of errors, and improving financial planning. By leveraging AI in finance, organizations can improve the efficiency and accuracy of their financial operations and reduce costs (Figure 14.3).

14.6.5 HUMAN RESOURCES

AI and data science are transforming the way organizations approach human resources. For example, AI can be used to automate routine tasks, such as

FIGURE 14.3 Framework to incorporate AI into finance.

Source: Adapted from Klein, 2020

resume screening and candidate matching, freeing up time for HR teams to focus on more strategic initiatives. AI can also be used to analyze HR data, providing insights into areas for improvement and identifying potential diversity and inclusion issues. Additionally, AI can be used to improve the accuracy of performance evaluation and talent management, reducing the risk of mismanaging talent (Tambe et al., 2019).

AI and data science are playing a significant role in transforming business services and driving efficiency and innovation. By leveraging these technologies, organizations can improve customer experience, optimize operations, and improve financial and human resource management. As technology continues to advance, we can expect to see even more innovative uses of AI and data science in business services, transforming the way organizations operate and compete.

14.7 CHALLENGES IN ADOPTING AI AND DATA SCIENCE IN BUSINESS SERVICES

The implementation of Artificial Intelligence (AI) presents numerous opportunities for organizations to enhance their operations and drive growth. Despite this, some companies may exhibit reluctance towards embracing AI due to their apprehension towards altering existing workflows and processes. Furthermore, concerns regarding job displacement and the possibility of biases within AI systems may also contribute to their hesitancy. Nevertheless, it is crucial for organizations to recognize that AI has the potential to augment human work rather than replace it (Jarrahi, 2018) (Table 14.6).

TABLE 14.6 The Challenges and Obstacles that Businesses Face when Adopting AI Technology

Challenge	Percentage of Businesses Affected	Source
Reluctance to migrate to cloud-based services	16% (CX leaders) 15% (large organizations) 14% (SMBs)	Adobe (2020)
Legal concerns, risks, or compliance issues with AI adoption.	4%	O'Reilly (2020)
Inadequate budget as an obstacle to digitization.	47% (SMBs and large organizations) 30% (CX leaders)	Adobe (2020)
Fear of AI causing disruption to business operations.	46%	PwC (2020)
Lack of recognition of the need for AI.	23%	O'Reilly (2020)
Lack of skilled individuals as a barrier to AI adoption.	18%	O'Reilly (2020)
Technical infrastructure challenges with AI adoption.	8%	O'Reilly (2020)

Source: PwC 2021 AI Predictions.

Table 14.6 provides an overview of the challenges and obstacles that businesses face when adopting AI technology, along with the percentage of businesses affected and the source of the information. The information highlights the need for businesses to carefully consider the potential risks and obstacles associated with AI adoption, as well as the need for organizations to develop the necessary skills and capabilities to effectively implement AI solutions.

14.7.1 DATA PRIVACY

Data privacy is one of the biggest challenges organizations face when adopting AI and data science. AI and data science rely on large amounts of data to provide insights and make predictions. However, this data can be sensitive and subject to privacy regulations (Campion et al., 2020). Organizations must have protocols in place to protect customer and employee data and comply with privacy regulations such as the General Data Protection Regulation (GDPR) and the California Consumer Privacy Act (CCPA).

To mitigate this challenge, organizations must adopt a privacy-by-design approach and ensure that data privacy and security are considered at every stage of the AI and data science project. This may involve implementing robust data management processes, secure storage and transmission of data, and regular audits to ensure compliance with data privacy regulations.

14.7.2 *ETHICAL CONSIDERATIONS*

AI and data science can have unintended ethical consequences, particularly when it comes to decision-making and bias. AI algorithms that are trained on biased data can perpetuate these biases in their predictions and decisions. As a result, organizations must ensure that they have a clear ethical framework in place to guide the development and deployment of AI and data science and regularly evaluate their systems for bias and unintended consequences (Eitel-Porter, 2021) (Table 14.7).

Organizations can implement ethical considerations by incorporating diversity and fairness into their data sets, performing regular audits of their AI systems to identify and correct biases, and involving stakeholders such as ethics committees and external experts in the development and deployment of AI and data science.

14.7.3 *LACK OF TECHNICAL EXPERTISE*

Another challenge organizations face when adopting AI and data science is a lack of technical expertise. AI and data science require specialized skills and knowledge, and organizations may struggle to find the talent they need to effectively implement these technologies. Organizations must invest in talent development and attract top talent in the field of AI and data science to ensure the success of their initiatives (Grover et al., 2018).

Organizations can address this challenge by partnering with AI and data science specialists, offering training and upskilling programs for employees, and promoting a culture of continuous learning and development.

14.7.4 *RESISTANCE TO CHANGE*

Change can be difficult for organizations, and the adoption of AI and data science may be met with resistance from employees who are concerned about job loss or the impact of automation on their work. Organizations must have a clear strategy for communicating the benefits of AI and data science and how they will be used to support and enhance employees' work rather than replace them (Benbya et al., 2020).

To mitigate this challenge, organizations must involve employees in the implementation of AI and data science and provide opportunities for collaboration and engagement. This may include regular updates on the progress of AI and data science projects, training and upskilling programs, and opportunities for employee feedback and input.

TABLE 14.7 Ethical Principles for AI and Data Science Deployment

Ethical Principle	Explanation
Transparency	The algorithms and decision-making processes of AI systems should be transparent, allowing stakeholders to understand how decisions are being made and why.
Responsibility	Organizations should be accountable for the outcomes of their AI systems and ensure that the systems are not causing harm to individuals or society.
Fairness	AI systems should not perpetuate or amplify existing biases in society and should ensure that all individuals are treated fairly and equitably.
Privacy	Organizations should protect the privacy of individuals and ensure that data is collected, stored, and used in a manner that is consistent with privacy laws and regulations.
Non-discrimination	AI systems should not discriminate against individuals based on factors such as race, gender, sexual orientation, or any other characteristic that is protected by law.

14.7.5 INTEGRATION WITH LEGACY SYSTEMS

Many organizations have legacy systems in place that are not designed to integrate with AI and data science. Integrating these technologies with legacy systems can be a significant challenge, requiring significant time and resources. Organizations must plan for this integration and allocate the necessary resources to ensure the success of their initiatives (Grover et al., 2018).

Organizations can address this challenge by adopting a phased approach to integration, working with experienced IT professionals and vendors, and ensuring that their legacy systems are updated and maintained to support the integration of AI and data science.

14.8 BEST PRACTICES FOR IMPLEMENTING AI AND DATA SCIENCE IN BUSINESS SERVICES

Artificial intelligence (AI) and data science are increasingly being used in business services to drive innovation, improve efficiency, and create new opportunities for growth. However, implementing these technologies can be a complex process and organizations must be strategic in their approach to ensure success. In this section, we will explore some of the best practices organizations can follow when implementing AI and data science in their business services.

1. **Start with a Clear Business Problem:** One of the first steps in implementing AI and data science in business services is to have a clear understanding of the problem that the organization is trying to solve. This will help guide the development and deployment of AI and data science and ensure that the technology is aligned with the organization's goals and objectives.

   Having a clear understanding of the problem will also help to prioritize the initiatives that need to be undertaken and determine the scope of the project. It is essential to involve key stakeholders, including business leaders and technical experts, in defining the problem and identifying the objectives. This will ensure that everyone is on the same page and that the implementation of AI and data science is aligned with the organization's overall strategy.

2. **Invest in Data Management:** Data is the foundation of AI and data science, and it is critical that organizations have a robust data management infrastructure in place to ensure the success of their initiatives. This includes data storage, data processing, and data governance. Organizations must also ensure that their data is accurate, up-to-date, and properly categorized.

   Data management is not just about storage and processing; it also involves ensuring data quality and integrity, establishing data security protocols, and managing data privacy and compliance. Organizations must invest in the right tools, systems, and processes to manage their data and ensure that it is reliable and accessible to support their AI and data science initiatives.

3. **Focus on Talent Development:** AI and data science require specialized skills and knowledge, and organizations must invest in talent development to ensure they have the technical expertise they need to effectively implement these technologies. This includes providing training and development opportunities for employees and attracting top talent in the field of AI and data science.

   Organizations must have a well-defined talent strategy that aligns with their overall goals and objectives for AI and data science. This should include a focus on developing internal talent and attracting external talent, as well as creating opportunities for cross-functional collaboration and continuous learning. Organizations must also be prepared to invest in the necessary resources, including tools, systems, and training, to support the development of their talent.

4. **Foster a Culture of Innovation:** To successfully implement AI and data science, organizations must foster a culture of innovation. This includes encouraging experimentation, promoting creativity, and embracing failure as a learning opportunity. Organizations must also be open to new ideas and approaches and be willing to pivot when necessary.

   A culture of innovation starts with leadership and must be embraced throughout the organization. This includes encouraging employees to share their ideas, experimenting with new technologies, and promoting collaboration and teamwork. Organizations must also create an environment that supports learning and experimentation and provides opportunities for employees to develop new skills and knowledge.

5. **Establish an Ethical Framework:** AI and data science can have unintended ethical consequences, and organizations must have a clear ethical framework in place to guide the development and deployment of these technologies. This framework should include guidelines for data privacy, bias, and unintended consequences, and be regularly reviewed and updated as needed.

   Organizations must consider the ethical implications of AI and data science, including issues such as data privacy, bias, and unintended consequences. They must have a clear and well-defined ethical framework in place that guides their development and deployment of these technologies and must regularly review and update this framework as needed. Organizations must also ensure that their employees understand the ethical implications of AI and data science and that they are trained and equipped to implement these technologies in an ethical and responsible manner.

6. **Plan for Integration with Legacy Systems:** Many organizations have legacy systems that are not designed to integrate with AI and data science. To ensure the success of their initiatives, organizations must plan for the integration of AI and data science with their legacy systems and allocate the necessary resources to ensure a smooth transition. This can include identifying areas where legacy systems need to be updated, investing in technology to enable integration, and developing a plan for data migration and system integration.

7. **Measure and Evaluate:** To effectively measure and evaluate success, organizations must first set clear goals and objectives for their AI and data science initiatives. This can include goals related to increased

efficiency, improved customer experience, and increased revenue. Next, organizations must establish metrics to measure progress against these goals, and regularly track progress over time. This can include metrics such as time saved, customer satisfaction scores, and revenue generated.

The implementation of AI and data science in business services can be a complex process, but organizations can increase their chances of success by following best practices. This includes starting with a clear business problem, investing in data management, focusing on talent development, fostering a culture of innovation, establishing an ethical framework, planning for integration with legacy systems, and measuring and evaluating progress. By following these best practices, organizations can ensure the success of their AI and data science initiatives and drive innovation in their business services.

14.9 FUTURE OF AI AND DATA SCIENCE IN BUSINESS SERVICES

Artificial Intelligence (AI) and data science are rapidly changing the way organizations operate and deliver services. As these technologies continue to evolve, it is important to consider the potential future developments and advancements in AI and data science, and how they are likely to impact business services. In this section, we will explore some of the key trends and developments that are likely to shape the future of AI and data science in business services.

1. **Increased Automation:** Automation is one of the key trends shaping the future of AI and data science in business services. As AI algorithms and technologies continue to evolve, we can expect to see increased automation of routine and repetitive tasks, freeing up employees to focus on more value-added activities (Grønsund & Aanestad, 2020).
2. **Improved Customer Experience:** AI and data science can be used to provide a more personalized and engaging customer experience, using data to drive insights and recommendations. For example, organizations can use AI to analyze customer data to better understand their needs and preferences, and to develop personalized marketing and sales strategies (Campbell et al., 2020).
3. **Advanced Predictive Analytics:** Predictive analytics is a key application of AI and data science, and it will continue to advance as these technologies evolve. Predictive analytics can be used to forecast future trends, identify potential risks, and make informed

business decisions, providing organizations with a competitive advantage (Ehwerhemuepha et al., 2020).

4. **Expansion of Machine Learning:** Machine learning is a subset of AI that allows algorithms to learn from data, and it is likely to continue to expand as AI technologies evolve. Machine learning can be used to automate complex decision-making processes, and it is already being used in areas such as fraud detection, natural language processing, and computer vision.
5. **Development of Natural Language Processing:** Natural language processing (NLP) is a key area of AI that is likely to continue to develop, allowing organizations to interact with customers and employees using natural language. NLP can be used to automate customer service, conduct sentiment analysis, and generate insights from text data.
6. **Rise of AI-Powered Business Intelligence:** AI-powered business intelligence (BI) is likely to become increasingly important, allowing organizations to make data-driven decisions in real-time. AI-powered BI can be used to provide real-time insights and recommendations, and it can be integrated with other AI technologies such as predictive analytics and machine learning (Yeo et al., 2022).
7. **Growth of Edge Computing:** Edge computing is the process of processing data at the edge of a network, rather than in the cloud. Edge computing is likely to become increasingly important as organizations look to process large amounts of data in real-time, and it is already being used in areas such as autonomous vehicles, internet of things (IoT) devices, and smart cities (Al-Ansi et al., 2021).
8. **Development of Ethical AI:** As AI continues to evolve, there is growing concern around the ethical implications of these technologies. As a result, there is likely to be a continued focus on developing ethical AI, with organizations looking to ensure that their AI algorithms are transparent, fair, and accountable.

In conclusion, the future of AI and data science in business services is likely to be shaped by trends such as increased automation, improved customer experience, advanced predictive analytics, the expansion of machine learning, the development of natural language processing, the rise of AI-powered business intelligence.

14.10 CONCLUSION

The integration of Artificial Intelligence (AI) and Data Science has brought about a tremendous shift in the business services sector, resulting in significant improvements in efficiency and driving innovation forward. The use of AI has enabled businesses to automate tasks and improve decision-making processes, providing a competitive edge in a fast-paced market. On the other hand, data science has played a crucial role in providing valuable insights and improving overall performance by analyzing large amounts of data. This has led to a transformation of innovation strategies and the creation of new business opportunities.

The applications of AI in business services are diverse and cover a wide range of functions. From customer service to human resources, AI is being used to automate routine tasks, freeing up resources and improving accuracy. The implementation of AI-driven chatbots, for example, has greatly improved the customer experience, providing instant answers to common queries, and freeing up human representatives to focus on more complex issues. Furthermore, AI is being utilized to analyze large amounts of data and provide insights that help businesses make informed decisions. For instance, predictive analytics, a subfield of AI, can be used to analyze customer behavior and predict future trends, leading to improved marketing strategies and increased sales.

Data science, on the other hand, has become an indispensable tool for businesses in the services sector. With the ever-increasing volume of data generated in the digital age, businesses need sophisticated techniques to process and make sense of this information. Data Science provides organizations with the necessary tools to extract meaningful insights from this data, helping to improve decision-making processes and drive innovation. The use of data science in business services has led to the creation of new business models, such as data-driven marketing and customer relationship management, which have brought about significant improvements in efficiency and cost savings.

The combination of AI and data science has unlocked new levels of potential for businesses in the services sector. This integration provides a comprehensive solution that not only automates tasks but also provides insights and decision-making capabilities, leading to even greater outcomes. For instance, AI-powered customer relationship management systems can use predictive analytics to identify customer trends and provide tailored solutions, resulting in improved customer satisfaction and increased sales.

In conclusion, the future of AI and data science in business services is promising, with continued advancements in technology driving growth and improvement. Organizations that embrace these technologies will be well-positioned to remain competitive in a rapidly changing market. As AI and Data Science continue to evolve, they will play an increasingly critical role in business services, leading to even greater outcomes and results. It is evident that the integration of AI and Data Science has already had a profound impact on the business services sector and holds immense potential for continued growth and development. Organizations that adopt these technologies will be poised for success in the competitive landscape of the future.

KEYWORDS

- **artificial intelligence**
- **automation**
- **business services**
- **chatbots**
- **data science**
- **decision-making**

REFERENCES

Akter, S., Michael, K., Uddin, M. R., McCarthy, G., & Rahman, M., (2022). Transforming business using digital innovations: The application of AI, blockchain, cloud and data analytics. *Annals of Operations Research, 1*, 2–33.

Al-Ansi, A., Al-Ansi, A. M., Muthanna, A., Elgendy, I. A., & Koucheryavy, A., (2021). Survey on intelligence edge computing in 6G: Characteristics, challenges, potential use cases, and market drivers. *Future Internet, 13*(5), 118.

Alharthi, H., (2018). Healthcare predictive analytics: An overview with a focus on Saudi Arabia. *Journal of Infection and Public Health, 11*(6), 749–756.

Ali, Q., Salman, A., Yaacob, H., Zaini, Z., & Abdullah, R., (2020). Does big data analytics enhance sustainability and financial performance? The case of ASEAN banks. *The Journal of Asian Finance, Economics and Business, 7*(7), 1–3.

Ariga, T., Ayers, J., Gillich, T., Weeks, N., Hiromoto, S., & Skorczynski, M., (2020). Artificial intelligence creates new opportunities to combat fraud. *International Journal of Government Auditing, 47*(3), 42–44.

Awan, U., Kanwal, N., Alawi, S., Huiskonen, J., & Dahanayake, A., (2021). Artificial intelligence for supply chain success in the era of data analytics. *The Fourth Industrial Revolution: Implementation of Artificial Intelligence for Growing Business Success*, 3–21.

Bag, S., Gupta, S., Kumar, A., & Sivarajah, U., (2021). An integrated artificial intelligence framework for knowledge creation and B2B marketing rational decision making for improving firm performance. *Industrial Marketing Management, 92*, 278–289.

Benbya, H., Davenport, T. H., & Pachidi, S., (2020). Artificial intelligence in organizations: Current state and future opportunities. *MIS Quarterly Executive, 19*(4).

Benzidia, S., Makaoui, N., & Bentahar, O., (2021). The impact of big data analytics and artificial intelligence on green supply chain process integration and hospital environmental performance. *Technological Forecasting and Social Change, 165*, 220557.

Campbell, C., Sands, S., Ferraro, C., Tsao, H. Y., & Mavrommatis, A., (2020). From data to action: How marketers can leverage AI. *Business Horizons, 63*(2), 227–243.

Campion, A., Hernandez, M. G., Jankin, S. M., & Esteve, M., (2020). Managing artificial intelligence deployment in the public sector. *Computer, 53*(10), 28–37.

Dimeas, F., Fotiadis, F., Papageorgiou, D., Sidiropoulos, A., & Doulgeri, Z., (2019). Towards progressive automation of repetitive tasks through physical human-robot interaction. In: *Human Friendly Robotics: 10th International Workshop* (pp. 151–163). Springer International Publishing.

Ehwerhemuepha, L., Gasperino, G., Bischoff, N., Taraman, S., Chang, A., & Feaster, W., (2020). HealtheDataLab–a cloud computing solution for data science and advanced analytics in healthcare with application to predicting multi-center pediatric readmissions. *BMC Medical Informatics and Decision Making, 20*, 1–12.

Eitel-Porter, R., (2021). Beyond the promise: Implementing ethical AI. *AI and Ethics, 1*, 23–80.

Fountaine, T., McCarthy, B., & Saleh, T., (2019). Building the AI-powered organization. *Harvard Business Review, 97*(4), 62–73.

Gad-Elrab, A. A., (2021). Modern business intelligence: Big data analytics and artificial intelligence for creating the data-driven value. *E-Business-Higher Education and Intelligence Applications*. 135.

Grønsund, T., & Aanestad, M., (2020). Augmenting the algorithm: Emerging human-in-the-loop work configurations. *The Journal of Strategic Information Systems, 29*(2), 101614.

Grover, V., Chiang, R. H., Liang, T. P., & Zhang, D., (2018). Creating strategic business value from big data analytics: A research framework. *Journal of Management Information Systems, 35*(2), 388–423.

Jarrahi, M. H., (2018). Artificial intelligence and the future of work: Human-AI symbiosis in organizational decision making. *Business Horizons, 61*(4), 577–586.

Javaid, M., Haleem, A., Singh, R. P., & Suman, R., (2021). Substantial capabilities of robotics in enhancing industry 4.0 implementation. *Cognitive Robotics, 1*, 28–75.

Khan, S., & Iqbal, M., (2020). AI-powered customer service: Does it optimize customer experience? In: *2020 8th International Conference on Reliability, Infocom Technologies and Optimization (Trends and Future Directions) (ICRITO)* (pp. 590–594). IEEE.

Lee, M., Kwon, W., & Back, K. J., (2021). Artificial intelligence for hospitality big data analytics: Developing a prediction model of restaurant review helpfulness for customer decision-making. *International Journal of Contemporary Hospitality Management, 33*(6), 2117–2136.

Morabito, F. C. (2018). *Artificial Intelligence and Economic Growth* (pp. 177–186). Las nuevas áreas del poder económico mundial.

Munirathinam, S., (2020). Industry 4.0: Industrial internet of things (IIoT). In: *Advances in Computers* (Vol. 117, No. 1, pp. 129–164). Elsevier.

Polak, P., Nelischer, C., Guo, H., & Robertson, D. C., (2020). "Intelligent" finance and treasury management: What we can expect. *AI & Society, 35*, 215–226.

Popescu, C. C., (2018). Improvements in business operations and customer experience through data science and artificial intelligence. In: *Proceedings of the International Conference on Business Excellence* (Vol. 12, No. 1, pp. 804–815).
Ram, J., Zhang, C., & Koronios, A., (2016). The implications of big data analytics on business intelligence: A qualitative study in China. *Procedia Computer Science, 87*, 221–226.
Riesenegger, L., & Hübner, A., (2022). Reducing food waste at retail stores—An explorative study. *Sustainability, 14*(5), 2494.
Schoenherr, T., & Speier-Pero, C., (2015). Data science, predictive analytics, and big data in supply chain management: Current state and future potential. *Journal of Business Logistics, 36*(1), 120–132.
Sun, Z., Sun, L., & Strang, K., (2018). Big data analytics services for enhancing business intelligence. *Journal of Computer Information Systems, 58*(2), 162–169.
Tambe, P., Cappelli, P., & Yakubovich, V., (2019). Artificial intelligence in human resources management: Challenges and a path forward. *California Management Review, 61*(4), 15–42.
Uzialko, A. C., (2019). *How Artificial Intelligence Will Transform Business* (p. 22). Business News Daily.
Varadarajan, R., (2020). Customer information resources advantage, marketing strategy and business performance: A market resources-based view. *Industrial Marketing Management, 89*, 29–97.
Verma, S., Sharma, R., Deb, S., & Maitra, D., (2021). Artificial intelligence in marketing: Systematic review and future research direction. *International Journal of Information Management Data Insights, 1*(1), 100002.
Vishnoi, S. K., Bagga, T. E., Sharma, A. A., & Wani, S. N., (2018). Artificial intelligence enabled marketing solutions: A review. *Indian Journal of Economics & Business, 17*(4), 167–177.
Willcocks, L., (2020). Robo-Apocalypse cancelled? Reframing the automation and future of work debate. *Journal of Information Technology, 35*(4), 286–302.
Yeo, S. F., Tan, C. L., Kumar, A., Tan, K. H., & Wong, J. K., (2022). Investigating the impact of AI-powered technologies on Instagrammers' purchase decisions in digitalization era–A study of the fashion and apparel industry. *Technological Forecasting and Social Change, 177*, 221551.

Index

C

E

F

G

H

I

J

K

L

M

Q

R